AF478054

The New Frontier

A Contemporary History of Fort Worth & Tarrant County

by Ty Cashion

Commissioned by
the Tarrant County Historical Society and the Fort Worth Stockyards Business Association

Historical Publishing Network
A division of Lammert Incorporated
San Antonio, Texas

✧

On the cusp of the modern age. Fort Worth, c. 1910.

COURTESY OF THE FORT WORTH PUBLIC LIBRARY.

First Edition

Historical Publishing Network, 11555 Galm Road, Suite 100, San Antonio, Texas, 78254. Phone (800) 749-0464.

ISBN: 9781893619562

Library of Congress Card Catalog Number: 2006923128

The New Frontier: A Contemporary History of Fort Worth and Tarrant County

author:	Ty Cashion
cover artist:	Samuel P. Ziegler
contributing writers for "Sharing the Heritage":	Scott Williams

Historical Publishing Network

president:	Ron Lammert
vice president:	Barry Black
project managers:	Curtis Courtney
	Sydney McNew
director of operations:	Charles A. Newton III
administration:	Angela Lake
	Donna M. Mata
	Judi Free
book sales:	Dee Steidle
production:	Colin Hart
	Michael Reaves
	Charles A. Newton III
	Craig Mitchell
	John Barr
	Evelyn Hart

PRINTED IN SINGAPORE

Contents

4 Acknowledgments

6 Foreword

8 Introduction — *The Old Frontier*

24 Chapter 1 — *Dressed Up and Ready to Go, 1900-1909*

38 Chapter 2 — *The Great War and Other Crusades, 1910-1919*

54 Chapter 3 — *The Front Porch of West Texas, 1920-1929*

68 Chapter 4 — *Depression Pains, New Deal Gains, 1930-1939*

82 Chapter 5 — *"Look—Up in the Sky!" 1940-1949*

96 Chapter 6 — *Greater Fort Worth, 1950-1959*

112 Chapter 7 — *A New Modernity, 1960-1969*

126 Chapter 8 — *The "Metroplex," 1970-1979*

140 Chapter 9 — *Renaissance, 1980-1989*

152 Chapter 10 — *Cowboys & Culture, 1990-2005*

166 Endnotes

174 Index

178 Sharing the Heritage

271 Sponsors

ACKNOWLEDGMENTS

A work of this nature, without fail, depends largely on the selfless assistance of many individuals whose areas of expertise or knowledge about particular subjects ultimately set the parameters for what the author is able to produce. Just as surely, they do it out of a love for "place," and most often without compensation, and in near anonymity. In this respect, ***The New Frontier*** is true to form. This project has indebted me to a host of newfound friends and acquaintances who have shared with me their love for Fort Worth and a passion for historical detection and preservation. Collectively, they have read the manuscript critically, lent photographs and paintings, pointed the way to archival sources, and offered advice and encouragement unstintingly. They have also extended kindnesses along the way for which I will be forever grateful. I could never express adequately the debt I owe these good women and men, and only hope that this book will reflect well on their gracious generosity. Among them include: Susie Pritchett and Dee Barker of the Tarrant County Historical Commission; at the Fort Worth Public Library, Max Hill, Kimberley Wells, Ken Hopkins, and Ken Jackson, retired, along with Amy Bearden of the library's Foundation office; Carol Roark, who manages the Texas-Dallas History & Archives Division at the Dallas Public Library; attorney Jenkins Garrett, whose philanthropy has made the Special Collections Library at the University of Texas at Arlington one of the state's premier research institutions, and members of the staff, Sally Groves, Ann Hodges, Shirley Rodnitzky, Blanca Smith, Kit Goodwin, Brenda McClurklin, and Colin Toenjes; Mike Strom and Susan Swain of the Special Collections at the Mary Couts Burnett Library, Texas Christian University; Douglas Harman, president and CEO of the Fort Worth Convention & Visitors Bureau; Jon McConal and Cissy Stewart Lale, both retired, of the *Fort Worth Star-Telegram*, and Mrs. Lale's husband, longtime journalist Max Lale as well as Jen Fennel, formerly of the *Star-Telegram*; Pat Pate of the Pate Museum of Transportation; and private collectors Scott Barker, Ace Cook, Gretchen Denny, Dalton Hoffman, Quentin McGown, Morris Matson, and Jack White; authors Mark Beasley and Carlos Cuellar; Mary Lenn Dixon of Texas A&M Press, and at TCU Press Judy Alter and Susan Petty; Jessica Beard of the Texas Rangers' baseball organization; Margaret Kramer at the North Fort Worth Historical Society; the members of the Tarrant County Historical Society, particularly Steve Murrin; Ron Lammert, founder and president of Historical Publishing Network, and his staff, particularly Production Director Colin Hart, Sydney McNew; and a host of individuals who lent documents and photographs: Marsha Anderson, Mark Angle, Michael Bates, Paul Camfield, Joel Carranza, Jeffrey King Coffey, Sandra Daniels, Ron Jackson, Chris Lane, Greg Last, Debra McStay, Emil Moffatt, Carol Murray, Buddy Myers, St. Clair Newburn III; Charles Newton, Kim Novak, John T. Roberts, Tom Russell, Eric Salisbury, Janet Schmelzer, Lyndon Simpson, Robert B. Sturns, Renee Tucker, Paul Valentine, and Tom Wayne.

As a university professor, the indulgences and well wishes of colleagues provides another essential ingredient for success. Certainly no one could ask for a more supportive department, or a more responsive administration than resides at Sam Houston State University. Chair Jim Olson, and Terry Bilhartz who recently succeeded him, have both been charitable with scheduling classes, providing travel expenses, and otherwise encouraging my efforts. Dean of Humanities & Social Sciences Terry Thibidoueax, and Brian Chapman, former Dean of Arts & Sciences, have been particularly solicitous of my progress, and I appreciate their cheerful stewardship. They, along with Provost David Payne and President James Gaertner have truly established a climate that encourages and rewards scholarship.

Special thanks are also due my family and some friends: Buddy Hamm, who helped me recall the Fort Worth of our youth; my sister, Michelle Redwine, who has never been far away with a kind word and exhortation; my parents, Bob and Joann, always looked forward to my research visits and helped me by taking care of many little things that I could not do from Huntsville and The Woodlands (they also read everything as it took shape, even if their only constructive criticism was: "It's looks perfect to us, dear."). My wife, Peggy, and son, Sam, as always, have provided loving support.

Ty Cashion
January 2006

For Sam, native son of the Panther City.

The publisher, Ron Lammert, also wishes to express heartfelt appreciation
to the businesses and foundations that made this book possible

✧ *Fort Worth was among the first U.S. cities to operate electric trolleys. The first drivers, like this one, stood outside in the elements, just as they did when the cars were powered by mules.*

COURTESY OF SPECIAL COLLECTIONS, UNIVERSITY OF TEXAS AT ARLINGTON LIBRARIES, ARLINGTON, TEXAS, AR 407 1-9-54.

✧ *A jitney operator, registered and licensed, picks up a nickel fare in the early twentieth century.*

COURTESY OF THE FORT WORTH, TEXAS, PHOTOGRAPH COLLECTION, SPECIAL COLLECTIONS, UNIVERSITY OF TEXAS AT ARLINGTON LIBRARIES, ARLINGTON, TEXAS, FWPC 2000-19.

✧ *Toll booths on the Dallas-Fort Worth Turnpike await the opening day's traffic, August 26, 1957.*

COURTESY OF SPECIAL COLLECTIONS, UNIVERSITY OF TEXAS AT ARLINGTON LIBRARIES, ARLINGTON, TEXAS, AR 406 1-37-39.

FOREWORD

Fort Worth's history and development is interesting as well as complicated, and can be viewed from many different perspectives. It was a frontier fort, but only briefly. At the conclusion of the Civil War, Fort Worth was a small town struggling to find a reason to grow. Within a few years, cattle and the railroad became major factors that led to significant growth by the turn of the century. After the development of the Stockyards north of the business district, Fort Worth became widely known as "Cowtown." It was a rugged village with a rowdy red-light district, Hell's Half Acre, but it also possessed significant refinement, which its leading citizens built upon consistently over the next decades.

While Fort Worth's cattle, agricultural and railroad traditions remained strong in the twentieth century, aviation became another major factor in its continued evolution. Amon Carter, Sr., newspaperman and promoter of Fort Worth as the city "Where the West Begins," became one of the chief advocates to make Fort Worth a major aviation center through civilian and military developments, including Convair—the "Bomber Plant"—American Airlines, and Bell Helicopter. He was also a leading supporter in the city's cultural development, pushing the creation of an arts district and establishing a foundation for one of the city's great museums. Mr. Carter was only one, if perhaps the most vocal, of many key persons to guide Fort Worth along several progressive paths simultaneously.

Ty Cashion has done a masterful job of presenting a chronological story of contemporary Fort Worth and Tarrant County. The New Frontier includes many new insights and perspectives. Professor Cashion has also provided a wonderful book illustrated with many rare photographs. Over the decades, Fort Worth has evolved in some surprising ways and has been involved in some controversial issues. The very identity of the city as "Cowtown" has not always been embraced by all community leaders. However, today Fort Worth has become more comfortable with a dual identity that embraces both "cowboys and culture," an asset that has paid tremendous dividends in attracting both tourism and business growth. Ty Cashion has made a significant contribution by identifying the many factors that have worked in concert to make contemporary Fort Worth a city with a distinctive past and a future with unlimited possibilities.

Douglas Harman , Ph.D., President & CEO
Fort Worth Convention & Visitors Bureau
2005

✧

Fort Worth High School, located at 610 West Dagget Street. The Justin Boot Company factory presently occupies the site.

COURTESY OF THE FORT WORTH PUBLIC LIBRARY.

✧

City Hall as it appeared at the beginning of the new century.

COURTESY OF THE QUENTIN MCGOWN COLLECTION, FORT WORTH.

✧

The Stock Yards Hotel and Exchange in Fort Worth's North Side at the end of the old century.

COURTESY OF W. D. SMITH PHOTOGRAPH COLLECTION, SPECIAL COLLECTIONS, UNIVERSITY OF TEXAS AT ARLINGTON LIBRARIES, ARLINGTON, TEXAS, AR 430, 67-1-45.

✧

The first "skyline," so to speak, was captured in this oil on canvas, "First Settlement of Fort Worth," by Caroline Usher, date unknown. Commissioned by descendants of Fort Worth's first doctor, Carroll M. Peak and his wife Florence, the work came into the possession of local automobile dealer Frank Kent (a Peak relation) who had it reproduced as a gift to his customers on the occasion of the city's centennial in 1949. Usher most likely based her painting on a work by Christina MacLean, a Scottish immigrant, who in 1907 produced a detailed sketch of the fort that drew on the recollections of surviving pioneers as well as local lore and drawings left by the U.S. Army. One thing is certain. A scene of nature all but unspoiled by the works of men surely greeted the Peaks, who arrived at the edge of the prairie overlooking the Trinity River in 1853. Today the original painting hangs in the offices of Frank Kent Cadillac.

COURTESY OF THE W. D. SMITH PHOTOGRAPH COLLECTION, SPECIAL COLLECTIONS, UNIVERSITY OF TEXAS AT ARLINGTON LIBRARIES, ARLINGTON, TEXAS, AR 430 47-1-24.

INTRODUCTION

THE OLD FRONTIER

Fort Worth! By itself, the name evokes images of the Old West. A frontier history of cowboys and cattle drives, railroad building, and Hell's Half Acre tells a rousing story, one often repeated and readily familiar to those who claim "Cowtown" as their home. Even as we begin a new century, this formative experience echoes from every corner of the city: in the wistful ambiance of Sundance Square; in the gritty, but welcoming Stockyards; in the arts district, where Goya and Cézanne find harmony with Remington and Russell. That same connection with the past resonates in many other, more ordinary places throughout Tarrant County as well. It can be as simple as gaining a sense of continuity by driving west on I-20 over the open, rolling hills and through the Walsh Ranch that cowman V. O. Hildreth founded in the nineteenth century. On the other side of the county that connection with the past might come unexpectedly in a chance encounter with "Puffy," a nineteenth-century steam train, as it chugs and whishes its way along the route between North Side and the restored Cotton Belt Depot in Grapevine. Certainly such reminders lend weight to the claim that Fort Worth remains today, as always, the city "Where the West Begins."

Just as surely as the frontier story of the pioneers left a deep and lasting impression on the popular imagination, those who succeeded the city's founders often merited weighty sequels of their own. In fact, the twentieth century represents a history much broader in scope, one whose treasure writers have mined in parts, resulting in a wealth of biographies and thematic accounts of organizations, places, and episodes from the city's past. There exists, however, no broad treatment of Fort Worth that gives contemporary times a voice in proportion to the city's early-day heritage. Typically, these kinds of historical surveys rely on works already published; and, while the city's twentieth-century canon is indeed ample, there have remained too many gaps to compose a well-rounded narrative without consulting the archival records. The remedy—an examination of such basic resources as newspapers and magazines, and special collections at local public and university libraries—has proven more tedious than daunting. I hope the product of this endeavor will bring some long-forgotten experiences back into the public consciousness and keep alive some well-known tales worth repeating.

The goal of *The New Frontier* is to introduce general readers to the Fort Worth that emerged out of its earthy, but mostly glorious beginnings. Each chapter attempts to convey, decade-by-decade, what an astute observer might have seen and heard, or even experienced. It does not dodge the controversial issues that confronted Fort Worthians; to do so would diminish the good fights of those who fought them. Surely, the men and women who helped advance such causes as social justice or historical preservation, and even those who violated the public trust through criminal acts and pursuits of vanity, deserve some attention. At the same time, the parade of events that comprises the historical record recalled here marches at a pace that allows only brief glimpses, rather than exacting stares.

Along the way, three identifying characteristics of twentieth-century Fort Worth should come clearly into focus. First, the banner slogan "Where the West Begins" is no hollow euphemism. From its very beginning as a U.S. military post, Fort Worth fixed its sights on the western horizon, and the village that emerged there grew into a city by appending itself to the region economically, politically, and culturally to the mutual benefit of both. West Texans, until well after World War II, regarded Fort Worth as a kind of "nature's metropolis," a place where they marketed their goods, brokered their resources, and obtained the supplies and material services that kept the region's economic engine purring. They also looked to the big city as a source for financing their land-intensive businesses, a place that gave them relevant news and information, and a cultural beacon under whose lights members of every social class could indulge their varied tastes. By the time Fort Worth began to realize there were other, equally profitable markets to tap, the western legacy itself became an asset that distinguished the city from so many other competitors.

✧

Third and Main, near the heart of Sundance Square.

COURTESY OF JOHN ROBERTS, FORT WORTH, WWW.FORTWORTHARCHITECTURE.COM

The other two identifying characteristics of the twentieth century are closely related. The second is a sense of ambivalence over the city's self-identity. Fort Worthians alternately embraced and discounted a popularly told heritage that was, at once, both grandly heroic and coarsely unrefined. Situated so close to Dallas—the confident and urbane financial giant that always seemed to stay a step ahead—Fort Worth endured a "second city" inferiority cultivated in cow-country commerce. Only lately, in relative terms, have Fort Worthians shed completely any lingering self-doubts. That slow reckoning heralds the century's third

✧

The Fort Worth Stockyards today.

COURTESY OF THE FORT WORTH CONVENTIONS & VISITORS BUREAU.

✧

"Puffy," formerly the Tarantula Train, pulls out of the Cotton Belt Depot at Grapevine, bound for the Stockyards on an autumn run in 2003 (the line is now the Grapevine Vintage Railroad).

COURTESY OF PAUL A. VALENTINE, WWW.VALENTINE.PRO.

✧

Amon Carter Museum. An endowment from the estate of publisher Amon Carter, which included his personal collection of western paintings and sculptures by such acclaimed artists as Frederic Remington and Charles Russell, gave his namesake a measure of élan from the beginning. That did not stop Time *magazine from characterizing the institution as the "Museum of 'Yippi-Yo-Ti-Yay'" when it opened as the Amon Carter Museum of Western Art in 1961. What hung from the walls and rested on pedestals inside the gallery, however, quickly silenced any insinuations that it lacked sophistication. Before long, officials from museums in such places as New York City and Washington, D.C. were coming to Fort Worth, hat in hand, to borrow works of art for their own exhibitions. When the United States and the Soviet Union initiated a cultural exchange in 1973, the Amon Carter's paintings and sculptures eloquently conveyed to our Cold War adversaries the raw spirit that is America.*

COURTESY OF THE FORT WORTH CONVENTION & VISITORS BUREAU.

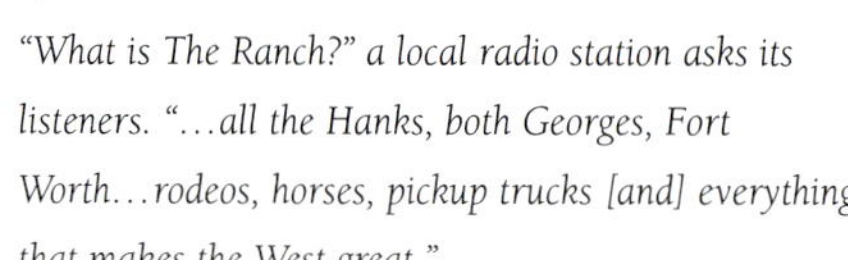

✧

"What is The Ranch?" a local radio station asks its listeners. "…all the Hanks, both Georges, Fort Worth…rodeos, horses, pickup trucks [and] everything that makes the West great."

COURTESY OF KIM NOVAK, WWW.SSMROCKS.COM/KIMNOVAK/

distinguishing trait: a persistence and continuity of the pioneer spirit. The never-say-die attitude that buoyed the city's founding fathers through times of civil war, social chaos, and ruinous economic depressions set a course for later generations of civic leaders, who likewise met each new obstacle with the same grit and determination. By the time Fort Worth commemorated its 150th anniversary in 1999, its citizens had come to appreciate fully the seminal link that bound each new present with the past. That distant past, in turn, became an integral part of the self-identity that has transformed twenty-first-century Fort Worth into one of the country's most livable cities.

The people of Cowtown, or, the Panther City, as many of them lovingly refer to their home, have surely come to appreciate the powerful mystique of what a recent generation of "new" western historians have derisively called our national creation myth—the idea that this great country was born of the westering experience, and that each new frontier reaffirmed the American character. These triumphal stories, even if whitewashed and routinely exaggerated, nevertheless provide the purest expression of such time-honored virtues as individual enterprise, initiative, and self-reliance. The way Fort Worth's tourist industry today promotes the seemingly ill-matched theme of "Cowboys & Culture" is, in one respect, merely another way of declaring: "We've arrived, and we got here on our own terms."

As Fort Worth expanded, it gradually charted the destiny of other Tarrant County communities, some to a greater extent than others. As part of this volume, these cities and towns enter the story as they relate to the development of Fort Worth. Naturally, each possesses a distinct history and identity. Old-time residents of places such as Grapevine and Arlington are quick to point

✧

The Fort Worth Star-Telegram's "home delivery" service once offered an airdrop to subscribers on isolated ranches in West Texas.

COURTESY OF THE *FORT WORTH STAR-TELEGRAM* PHOTOGRAPH COLLECTION, COURTESY, SPECIAL COLLECTIONS, UNIVERSITY OF TEXAS AT ARLINGTON LIBRARIES, ARLINGTON, TEXAS, AR 406 1-26-53A.

The sculpture *High Desert Princess*, by artist Mehl Lawson, greets visitors to Fort Worth's National Cowgirl Museum and Hall of Fame, representing the comfortable expression of both refinement and traditional western culture that the city has cultivated.

COURTESY OF THE NATIONAL COWGIRL MUSEUM AND HALL OF FAME, WWW.COWGIRL.NET, WWW.RHONDAHOLEPHOTOGRAPHY.COM.

Anthropologists believe the earliest inhabitants of this area practiced trepanning—a kind of "surgery" that released evil spirits responsible for causing such maladies as headaches and dizziness. Remarkably, they became rather proficient at it. This lifelike diorama portraying the scene was for many years a popular attraction with children and grownups alike at the Fort Worth Museum of Science & History.

COURTESY OF THE FORT WORTH MUSEUM OF SCIENCE & HISTORY.

out that pioneer settlements within their present corporate limits actually predate the arrival of the soldiers who founded the military post Fort Worth.

The first inhabitants, of course, are lost to history, but occasionally some ancient reminder bestirs mute testimony to an occupancy that can date back thousands of years. When the Texas Department of Transportation released its environmental study of the proposed Southwest Parkway late in 2004, the report noted that archaeologists working along the Clear Fork of the Trinity River had peeled back a three-to-four-foot strip of earth, exposing artifacts scattered around rock-lined hearths where prehistoric hunters and gatherers camped between 500 and 2,000 years ago. These people would have been relative newcomers if the historical marker located on the seventh tee at Lake Arlington Golf Course is accurate. Artifacts found there are said to date back almost nine millennia.

Other native groups attracted the attention of explorer-diplomats who traversed the future Tarrant County long before people calling themselves Americans arrived. During the last quarter of the eighteenth century, Frenchmen Athanase de Mézières and Pierre Vial, working in the service of the Spanish king, became familiar with the land while visiting bands of Wichita and Tonkawa Indians, whose semi-sedentary lifestyle suited a place where the well-watered eastern woodlands gave way to the arid plains. De Mézières, in fact, glowed about this lush, riverine country characterized by fertile prairies and wooded valleys abounding in fish and game. Any plans that the Spanish had for the upper Trinity country soon fell apart, and, as one century gave way to another, American filibusters such as Philip Nolan swept through the area rounding up wild mustangs and gathering intelligence for men with even loftier visions.

It was an ignominious beginning for the next group of European-Americans who entered the all-but-forgotten land in 1837, this time as citizens of the Texas Republic. That November, eight footsore survivors of an eighteen-man ranging company from near the Little River, between Austin and Waco, limped into present Tarrant County from the west. They were lucky that a much larger force of Wichita and Caddo warriors they had engaged on the Rolling Plains did not kill them all, and luckier still that the Caddo village they happened upon extended them guarded hospitality.

White men returned in greater numbers the following spring, 1838, and this time they were not on foot. A militia expedition, ninety men strong, assembled at Fort Inglish, in present Bonham, to pursue an Indian raiding party that had lit out for the western prairies. Somewhere between the modern-day cities of Euless and Arlington, the Texans attacked a small Indian village, killing several of the inhabitants and recovering a few horses.

These years of the old Republic were times of mortal calamity for native peoples with hereditary claims to the future Tarrant County. Bands of Wichitas, Tonkawas, Caddos, and Comanches had long resided in the area, or at least hunted on its prairies and along the watercourses. Members of several non-Texas tribes like the Cherokees, the Choctaws, the Delawares, the Shawnees, and

About the time Anglo Texans began exploring the future Tarrant County in 1838, Maribeau B. Lamar succeeded Sam Houston as president of the Republic of Texas, replacing the old general's enlightened Indian policy with one that offered only expulsion or extermination.

COURTESY OF THE TEXAS STATE ARCHIVES AND LIBRARY, AUSTIN.

Bird's Fort, on the Trinity River, the 29th day of September, 1843.

Whereas, for sometime past, hostilities have existed and war been carried on between the white and red men of Texas, to the great injury of both parties; and whereas, a longer continuance of the same would lead to no beneficial result, but increase the evils which have so long unhappily rested upon both races; and whereas, the parties are now willing to open the path of lasting peace and friendship, and are desirous to establish certain solemn rules for the regulation of their mutual intercourse:

Therefore, the Commissioners of the Republic of Texas, and the chiefs and Headmen of the before mentioned Tribes of Indians being met in Council at Bird's Fort, on the Trinity River, the 29th day of September, 1843, have concluded, accepted, agreed to and signed the following articles of treaty:

Article I. Both parties agree and declare, that they

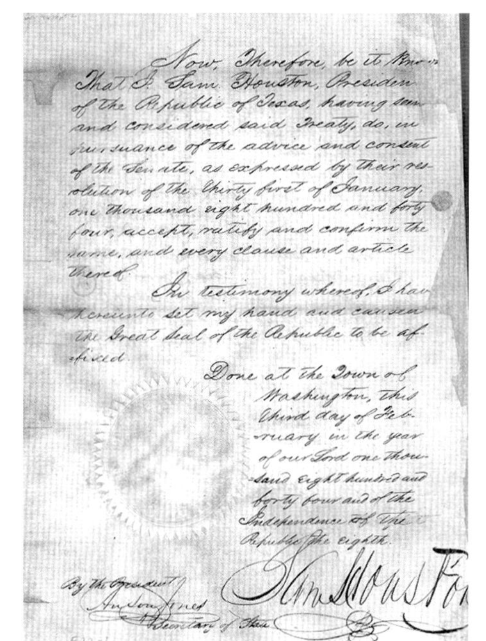

Now, Therefore, be it Known That I, Sam Houston, President of the Republic of Texas, having seen and considered said Treaty, do, in pursuance of the advice and consent of the Senate, as expressed by their resolution of the thirty first of January, one thousand eight hundred and forty four, accept, ratify and confirm the same, and every clause and article thereof.

In testimony whereof, I have hereunto set my hand and caused the Great Seal of the Republic to be affixed.

Done at the Town of Washington, this third day of February in the year of our Lord one thousand eight hundred and forty four and of the Independence of the Republic the eighth.

Sam Houston

By the President, Anson Jones, Secretary of State

✧

President Sam Houston visited the abandoned Bird's Fort in 1843 to initiate a treaty signed by the Republic of Texas and nine Indian tribes on September 29 of that year. Unfortunately, the Comanches and Wichitas were not among the signatories. Designed to repair some of the damage of the Lamar years by setting a boundary line between the two peoples, the treaty soon failed as the pressure of Anglo settlement forced the Indians farther west. By 1854 most of the tribes had accepted reservation life along the Brazos River in present-day Young County. Continued harassment ultimately compelled them to flee to Indian Territory in 1859.

COURTESY OF THE TEXAS STATE ARCHIVES AND LIBRARY, AUSTIN.

the Kickapoos were also attracted to this geographic borderland where no Anglos at present had settled. That, however, was about to change. Added to the mix were the alternating Indian policies of presidents Sam Houston and Maribeau B. Lamar—the former offering an enlightened coexistence, the latter promising only expulsion or extermination.

Another foray in September 1838 penetrated as far as the Clear Fork of the Trinity and netted about the same deadly results as the first. It was followed two months later by a more imposing campaign. At Clarksville, near the Red River, a force of five-hundred volunteer militiamen marched to the southwest and through the Eastern Cross Timbers, before stopping to make camp on the Clear Fork, in, or certainly near, present-day Fort Worth. There, General Thomas Rusk took command. The advancing Texans overawed the residents of a nearby Caddo village who immediately fled, leaving behind "Buffalo Skins, a few blankets, some guns &c." After militiamen gathered trophies and set the Indians' dwellings afire, the expedition was declared a success—and none too soon. The officer in charge of bringing up some cattle to feed the troops, then-captain Edward H. Tarrant, failed to appear. By then it was December. Cold, hungry, and tired, the men unhitched the oxen that had pulled their five wagons into the upper Trinity country and enjoyed a tremendous barbecue. Unburdened by the conveyances, they afterward returned to Northeast Texas. Despite their privation, Adjutant General Hugh McLeod extolled the agricultural potential of the surrounding prairies and bottomlands, a place that others, he sneered, had called a "sterile waste." In his opinion, it represented "the finest portion of Texas."

Such reports excited the imaginations of men who had taken part in the expedition as well as others who had not yet seen the land themselves, but dreamed of owning a piece of it. In 1841, under the terms of the Republic's Military Road Act, Major Jonathan Bird applied for a grant of land just inside the future Tarrant County, south of where Euless would one day emerge. Confident that Congress would confirm his application, he put volunteer militiamen to work constructing a bulwark for a group of pioneers on their way from Fannin County, in Northeast Texas.

Arriving in a wild land unbroken by plows, and expecting a contest from the native inhabitants, the settlers no doubt gained a sense of security jacketed as they were inside the palisade of Bird's Fort, the name they gave to the citizens' post. They need not have worried, however. The Indians were already gone. Earlier that year the militia had prosecuted the only significant engagement the future Tarrant County would ever experience. A few miles south of where Bird soon erected his post, several bands of various Indian groups had accumulated in a series of concealed encampments along the thickly wooded Village Creek, near the boundary where Arlington and Fort Worth meet today. Upon discovering their location, General Tarrant and Captain John B. Denton distinguished themselves in the aborted Battle of Village Creek; the former for wisely ordering his troops to withdraw as Indian resistance grew stronger, the latter for becoming the Anglos' only fatal casualty. It was for these men that Tarrant and Denton Counties were named.

The auspicious circumstance as it affected the prospects for the Bird's Fort settlement soon mattered little. In January 1842 an agent of the Texan Immigration & Land Company, or colloquially, the Peters Colony, arrived and informed the pioneers they were "squatters," and ordered them off the land. After the disbelieving leaders of the little band verified that Bird's conflicting claim was indeed invalid, most, if not all of them, retreated eastward in the direction of the recently founded log village of Dallas.

As these unlucky émigrés from Fannin County learned, the Republic of Texas in 1841 had awarded the colonization company an immense grant of land. Upon its annexation to the U.S., the state legislature sustained the act. Even though the venture frustrated the Bird's Fort settlers, it nevertheless gave impetus to a larger and more significant pioneer movement that introduced many hundreds of immigrants from states primarily of the Upper South and lower Midwest. In that way, the Peters colonists distinguished the demographic character of North Texas and diluted the influence of the plantation economy that made East Texas an extension of Dixieland.

First-comers from these sections, later joined by families and individuals arriving from the Lower South, laid out the future county's earliest settlements. Peters colonists from states such as Missouri, Tennessee, and Illinois began plowing fields and erecting log homes in the middle 1840s in what would become northeast Tarrant County. By 1846 a community began emerging that went through a succession of names before folks there agreed to call it Grapevine. About fifteen miles to the south a trading house had been established in 1845 at Marrow Bone Springs in present Arlington. By the time war broke out the following year between the United States and Mexico, it became a ranger station. It was also the place where former Republic legislator Middleton Tate Johnson was assigned frontier duty after returning from fighting below the Rio Grande. Sometime after the war ended and the Peters Colony contract expired, he took possession of the surrounding land. He also introduced large-scale cotton farming to the area—along with the attendant institution of slavery. The community that grew up around his fiefdom became Johnson Station.

As these developments unfolded, settlers in North Texas were anticipating the U.S. government making good on its promise to establish a fort for their defense. The annexation of Texas in December 1845, of course, precipitated war with Mexico, forestalling any plans to erect a strategic line of military posts bordering the state's western frontier. With the return of peace in 1848, Major General William Jenkins Worth took charge of an undermanned Eighth Military Department headquartered at San Antonio. Oddly enough, the individual for whom the fort and town would be named expressed no enthusiasm for making it all happen. Despite the overweening demands of settlers in North Texas, he agreed only to "study the matter," and sent General W. S. Harney to gather information and make a recommendation.

Hardly had the inspection party returned when Worth died of cholera. It was May 9, 1849. The very next day, Harney, who had assumed temporary command, ordered Major Ripley A. Arnold to lead Company F of the Second Dragoons back into the upper Trinity country to select the site for a federal post. Stopping at Marrow Bone Springs, the major secured the help of some guides, led by M. T. Johnson, who had come to know the land intimately as a frontier ranger. The men could not have found a more suitable location than the commanding bluff overlooking the confluence of the West and Clear forks of the Trinity River. After reaching the stream's south bank, the men watched the sun set from a peninsular prominence, where a grove of live oaks provided cover. Samuels Avenue would one day bisect this ridge, and the early wealth that the future city generated would produce its first exclusive neighborhood there. That evening, however, Company F and its guides feasted on a deer in the rough camp they made beside a cold spring that spilled onto an ancient *metate*, a bowl-shaped rock that generation-upon-generation of native women had used for grinding their corn and grain. The next morning, the party made its way south and west for about a mile, just below the cusp of the ridge to a spot where the major determined to erect the fort. Much later, one of the men in M. T. Johnson's company, Simon B. Farrar, recalled: "I thought it the most beautiful and grand country that the sun ever shown on." Like both Arnold and Johnson, Farrar had served under General Worth in Mexico. It was right then, he insisted, that they decided to name the post in honor of the "Hero of Monterrey and Chapultepec Castle." Almost a century later, another federal project, the Ripley Arnold Housing Center, would arise on the property bordering the western edge of the one-time military reservation where the post and city were birthed. Today the campus of RadioShack occupies that site; the Tarrant County Courthouse stands at the other end, where the soldiers drilled and paraded.

✧

Johnson Station log home as it looked in 1861.

COURTESY OF THE J. W. DUNLOP PHOTOGRAPH COLLECTION, SPECIAL COLLECTIONS, UNIVERSITY OF TEXAS AT ARLINGTON LIBRARIES, ARLINGTON, TEXAS, AR 446, D499.

✧

Middleton Tate Johnson.

COURTESY OF THE FORT WORTH PUBLIC LIBRARY.

✧

Major General William Jenkins Worth.

COURTESY OF THE FORT WORTH MUSEUM OF SCIENCE & HISTORY.

Anticipating the boon to civilian settlement, the Texas state legislature at that time adopted a motion to carve a new county out of Navarro. Governor George T. Wood on December 20, 1849, signed into law the act that created Tarrant County, named for its primary booster, Indian fighter Edward H. Tarrant. Over the ensuing months a horseman canvassed the area and recorded for the 1850 U.S. Census the names of 664 inhabitants within its boundaries.

For troops stationed at Fort Worth during the four-and-half years the post stood sentinel atop the bluff, life produced few idyllic memories. Even the fort's commanding vista came at the cost of being "exposed all winter to the northers and sleets of the country and in summer the scorching heats," as a War Department inspector candidly reported in 1851. The soldiers' existence, in fact, could be quite bleak, as the record of thirty-one desertions attests. Only an occasional opportunity to go fishing at the river or hunting along its banks broke the monotonous routine of drilling and maintaining military order. Yet, for the officers at least, there were happier occasions, the most notable being their first Christmas season at the post, when several barefooted farmers' daughters living in the surrounding area accepted invitations to attend a party. No doubt the irregular visits by Lieutenant Colonels Robert E. Lee, Albert Sidney Johnston, John Bell Hood, and a handful of other future Civil War generals grew more pleasant in the minds of both the officers and enlisted men as time wore on.

About the only native peoples the troops encountered were the traders, the curious, and the alms seekers who came to the post, and others whom they met while on patrol, and these were normally respectful if not always friendly. Nevertheless, the popular canon includes tales of two hostile encounters, one invented by yarn spinners, the other a fragmentary account rooted at least partly in fact. The first involved a preemptive strike—a massacre really—in which the soldiers took the fight to two bands of Comanches led by Chiefs Jim Ned and Feathertail, who had determined to erase Fort Worth from the landscape and reclaim their lost hunting ground. The mythical contest did not end until the dragoons cornered the harried warriors in a Palo Pinto canyon, killing Jim Ned and setting the survivors to flight. While there really was a Jim Ned, the singular fact in this episode, he was in reality a Delaware Indian, who occasionally scouted for soldiers of both the old Republic and the U. S. Army. As for Feathertail, he does not appear to have existed at all. In the other confrontation, made popular as the vignette in which Oliver Knight began his classic history of Fort Worth, the garrison faced down a war party of Comanches and their Caddo allies with a blast from the fort's cannon. While many historians later declared that the account was entirely apocryphal, Clay Perkins, in *The Fort in Fort Worth*, dutifully revealed two additional sources that suggest Knight's recounting of an old soldier's tale—while largely insignificant and probably exaggerated—at least possessed credibility at its core.

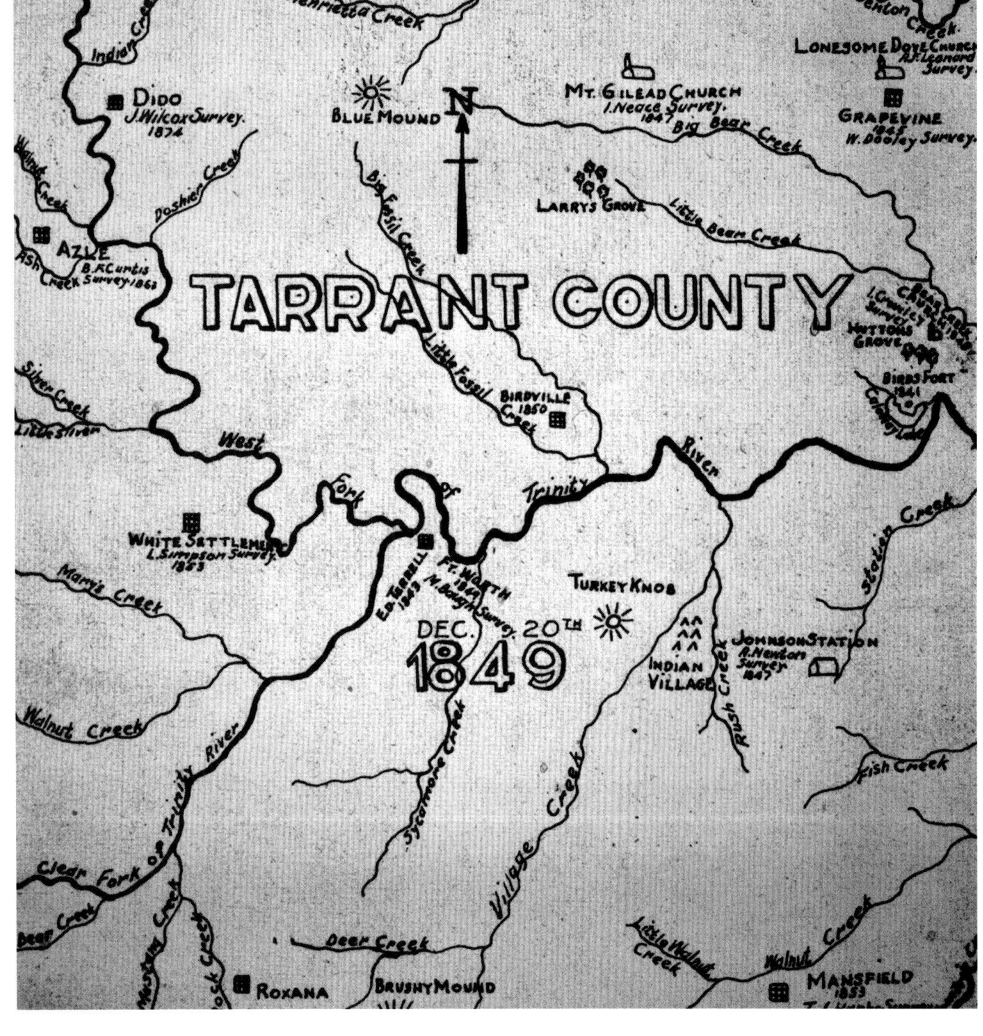

A hand-drawn map of Tarrant County showing early settlements and landmarks.

COURTESY OF THE *FORT WORTH STAR-TELEGRAM* COLLECTION, SPECIAL COLLECTIONS, UNIVERSITY OF TEXAS AT ARLINGTON LIBRARIES, ARLINGTON, TEXAS, AR 406, H-187.

Even if the troops never engaged hostile warriors in battle, mortal peril was nevertheless omnipresent. Luckily, the garrison was never struck with such deadly epidemics as cholera and influenza, yet outbreaks in other places made the possibility seem real enough. Malaria, on the other hand, was endemic. The post surgeons who served at Fort Worth reported about a thousand more cases of the malady than there were soldiers. During the post's occupation, enlisted men died of such diseases as typhoid fever, scurvy, dysentery, and diarrhea, over which post surgeons might poison them with "cures" of mercury or calomel; almost without fail the ill were subjected to bleedings. Even Major Ripley Arnold, whose career ended suddenly on the losing end of a shootout with the post surgeon at Fort Graham, was preceded in death by two of his children, after they had fallen ill at their post home.

Other than seeding a sparse and scattered civilian settlement and providing a living for those who filled army contracts, the fort's greatest impetus to growth arguably came with its abandonment on September 17, 1853. A restriction that forbade civilians from establishing shops within a mile of the post stanched the emergence of anything resembling a business district. Then, suddenly, the removal of the troops farther west left the raw material for a readymade village, and the fort's namesake town took off. The army stable became a combination

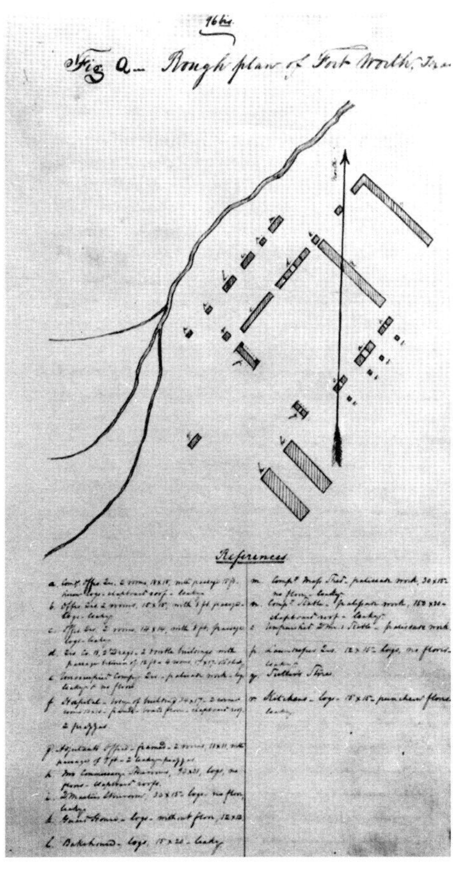

✧

"Rough plan of Fort Worth, Texas," in the report of U.S. Army inspector Colonel William G. Freeman, September 7, 1853. In his notes below the sketch, the visiting officer wrote that almost every building leaked, several had no floors, and the entire fort sat on a disputed tract of land.

COURTESY OF THE *FORT WORTH STAR-TELEGRAM* COLLECTION, SPECIAL COLLECTIONS, UNIVERSITY OF TEXAS AT ARLINGTON LIBRARIES, ARLINGTON, TEXAS, AR 406, H240.

hotel-tavern; the soldiers' barracks a general store. While the officers' quarters provided a home and workplace for the village's first physician, Carroll M. Peak, the post hospital housed the first school, run by Kentuckian John Peter Smith, who would soon turn to business and city politics, becoming one of the guiding forces in the new town's development. Nearby, the parade ground left a convenient public square, where travelers rested, farmers sold produce, and men and women bartered, while others idled and planned their futures.

The military roads leading from Fort Worth into West Texas had already established the post as a jumping off point for the vast, sparsely settled rolling plains at a time when settlers were beginning to test the unfamiliar land. Westering pioneers continued to trickle through this welcoming gateway, turning the trails into arteries of trade between Fort Worth and villages such as Jacksboro, Weatherford, and Palo Pinto. Contractors, who had supplied the garrison atop the bluff, afterward staged their deliveries at Fort Worth before sending them off to Forts Belknap and Phantom Hill and Camp Cooper that guarded the emerging frontier of Northwest Texas.

Then, in November 1856, the forward-looking little community on the Trinity improved its prospects considerably by jerking the county seat from under neighboring Birdville. Arguably, it was a stolen election. Fort Worthians first siphoned off their rivals' get-out-the-vote keg of whiskey sometime during the previous evening, doubling their own quantity of free spirits. No doubt the mean prank helped swing the tight contest. Padding the count were fifteen cowboys from what would soon become Wise County. The men possessed an abiding interest in moving their neighboring seat closer to the developing range and determined to do their part to make it happen. Yet, despite the belief that they were voting ineligibly, any man residing in unrepresented territory adjoining Tarrant County could legitimately cast a ballot. Nevertheless, their leader, Sam Woody, warned that if the polling judges exposed their scheme it would mean the penitentiary for them all. The thirsty cowboys, then, watched their kindred partisans raise glass after glass to victory, passing up the grand hootenanny of which they were rightly a part. The coup, however ill-gotten the intention, provided the highlight in a year that also marked the opening of a U.S. Post Office and a regular stagecoach route between Fort Worth and Jacksboro. Both made connections with the Southern Overland Mail—the Butterfield—further inserting the upstart village into the growing stream of frontier commerce and communication.

Among the procession of pioneers who passed through Fort Worth during these years was Jonathan Hamilton Baker of Virginia, who stopped long enough to teach public school for a session in 1858 before settling at Palo Pinto. A diary he kept left the impression of a bustling frontier center struggling to emerge from the pack of so many small places with big visions. "Some good buildings and the town seems to be improving rapidly," he noted upon first laying eyes on Fort Worth. After accepting a position as schoolmaster, he found a place where "room, board, and washing cost $8 a month." Predictably, he made note of the ever-changing springtime weather: late-season northers that rendered the mornings cool and the afternoons sunny and warm; evening thunderstorms that illuminated a vast panorama, dumping "tremendous rain," but leaving only muddy roads to betray a cloudless morning sky. Then, there was the heat, "hot enough," in fact, to "cook eggs in the sand"—and it was yet only the first week of July.

Certainly, the Fort Worth he described was a product of the frontier. Scattered willy-nilly over the immediate landscape, small farms surrounded log and clapboard homes where skyscrapers would one day arise. Yet at this early date the smell of barnyard animals saturated the air, and the "chattering" of prairie chickens and crowing of roosters heralded the beginning of each new day. Amused by the proceedings in a temporary, makeshift wooden hall of justice, this man from the land of the House of Burgesses charitably described "court day" as "novel," its members of the bar "presenting quite a disparity of talent and physical appearance." Baker spared no measure of disgust, however, over the way merchants conducted business on the Sabbath. Each week, at the ringing of a bell—located, ironically, at Steele's Tavern—those accustomed to honoring the day of the Lord gathered inside the homes of fellow townsmen, where they read and discussed the Bible, and, when opportunity presented, worshipped at services led by circuit riders. Once the crops were laid by in August, it was the season for revivals, and Baker mounted his "young and foolish" mule on which he crossed the Clear Fork to camp beside a brush arbor six miles west of the village. At the end of the term, the county treasurer remitted him precisely $21.25, and Baker shortly afterward departed for Palo Pinto.

✧

Jonathan Hamilton Baker in his later years.

REPRODUCED FROM *THE PALO PINTO STORY*, BY MARY WHATLEY CLARK; PUBLISHED IN FORT WORTH BY THE MANNEY CO., 1956, FOLLOWING P. VIII.

Beneath the veneer of those serene observations, a brief feud between Fort Worth and Birdville over the so-called stolen election portended even graver events. An argument that began at a picnic resulted in Fort Worth's only documented showdown in the middle of the street. Just outside the courthouse Sheriff John B. York happened upon disgruntled Birdville supporter, Hiram Calloway. Locking eyes, they paused momentarily, then drew their guns and fired, each killing the other. Following another slaying, the editors of two Birdville newspapers similarly shot it out there, this time leaving only the Fort Worth sympathizer dead.

Added to the editors' enmity was their larger war of words over the impending crisis of secession. As the people of Tarrant County chose sides, the "Texas Troubles" unfolded during the torpid summer of 1860, attended by a series of mysterious fires and rumors of slave insurrections that plagued communities largely in the northern part of the state. A mood of hysteria swept away all reason, along with the middle ground on which a tenuous coexistence between Unionists and secessionists rested. Mobs executed as many as a hundred suspected arsonists and abolitionists in North and East Texas, including at least two in Fort Worth. One of the men was a Methodist minister, Anthony Bewley, whom activists "extradited" from his Missouri home. Both victims of the mob dangled in the same hanging tree until birds picked them clean; later, someone cut them down and casually discarded their bones atop a downtown building.

By then, war was imminent. Once it was declared, legions of North Texas men marched off to fight, and the brisk momentum Fort Worth had enjoyed lost all forward progress. Soon, in fact, the conflict brought a retrograde movement that rolled back the population, all but isolating the two-hundred-and-fifty-odd citizens who remained. Beyond the village, on the rolling plains of Northwest Texas, Comanche and Kiowa war parties contested for the land with an itinerant cavalry and a home guard conscripted mostly from "cow hunters," who forted up their families for protection. In Tarrant County, Indian warriors raided near Johnson Station and got as close to Fort Worth as Marine Creek, where the Stockyards district would later emerge. If profiteering in scarce commodities cheapened pretensions of Confederate patriotism, then surely the failure of Tarrant County's 850-plus slaves to rise up and throw off their shackles laid bare the Texas Troubles as nothing but empty

✧

Khleber M. Van Zandt. A native Tennessean, Van Zandt was practicing law in Marshall when the North and South became embroiled in war. There, in East Texas, he helped organize a Confederate infantry company. Captured at Fort Donelson, Van Zandt, by then a major, gained his freedom in a prisoner exchange. After the war he moved to Fort Worth and became a driving force in developing the economy, particularly the infrastructure of railroads and streetcars. As principal in the K. M. Van Zandt Land Company and founder of a bank that grew into the Fort Worth National, he sold and financed the farms, ranches, homes, and businesses that seeded the area's rapid growth. He became a steward of wise development as well, by serving on the boards of businesses, schools, and civic groups, and presided over the directors of the First Christian Church from 1877 until his death in 1930. Van Zandt's legacy also included fourteen children, many who became prominent local citizens by continuing to build upon his work.

COURTESY OF THE FORT WORTH PUBLIC LIBRARY.

vituperation. As if providing a metaphor for these dark times, a half-finished courthouse presented an omnipresent reminder of a larger job abandoned. Arising from a stone façade covering the first floor, the frame of a second story cut the sky like a skeleton of another kind, existing only to mock the self-ennobling cause that left it in such condition.

When the war ended, Fort Worth lay prostrate. Behind the locked doors and shuttered windows of business houses, empty shelves lined the walls. There was neither post office nor saloon. Hogs that roamed freely through streets overgrown with weeds found a suitable home in the unfinished courthouse. Elsewhere "there were many more houses than people to occupy them," wrote newcomer Khleber Van Zandt, who arrived in 1865, about four months after the South's surrender at Appomattox. This once-vibrant village, he concluded, had become in the space of four exhaustive years, the very "picture of desolation."

During the period of Reconstruction, Fort Worth like the rest of North Texas was overrun with Confederate veterans seeking a new start. And although Southern sympathies ran deep, there would be little time to wallow in the Lost Cause. Where Dallas grew into the financial center for the postwar cotton economy of slaveless plantations and tenant farmers, Fort Worth reasserted its claim to the Great West. Out there, cattle had multiplied on ranges where bison ran in seemingly infinite numbers. Ranchers and frontiersmen with the mettle to challenge the native claimants found an exploitable land that the antebellum society composed mostly of farmers had written off as worthless. In these years Fort Worth reemerged as a true western boomtown, enjoying a resurrected commerce in east-west traffic as well as new trails that led cattle drovers to railheads in Kansas and distant ranges as far away as Montana.

It did not happen all at once, of course. In the spring of 1866, Fort Worth presented a disheartening scene to cowman J. J. Myers of Lockhart, Texas, who rode into town ahead of about a thousand cattle. Entering the courthouse, he encountered old pioneer Charles Biggers Daggett, who quickly gathered some willing men, and together with Myers' crew, they guided the herd through the desultory village and then down the bluff, where they forded the Trinity. The sight of all those bawling cattle, their horns bobbing through a cloud of dust, caused quite a sensation. Such processions soon became a routine sight, but they still quickened the pulse of men who recognized the opportunities at hand. Directly, Fort Worth became the last stop of any consequence on the northbound trail into Indian Territory, and the business of outfitting each crew was rivaled only by the lucrative rewards of entertaining them.

That first year drovers trailed their herds to the railhead at Sedalia, Missouri, but ran into problems that threatened to strangle the infant industry in the cradle. There, they ran into the fierce opposition of farmers whose cattle contracted a tick fever from the hearty longhorns, and when Missouri passed laws barring the importation of Texas cattle, other states followed suit. By the next year, however, cowmen and railroad officials had effected a compromise with their opponents, and Abilene became the first in a succession of Kansas cattle towns that provided a final destination for the Chisholm Trail. From there, drovers sent their animals by rail to the packing plants at Chicago.

Then, in 1867 and 1868, respectively, federal troops established Forts Griffin and Richardson in Northwest Texas. Citizens in the settled eastern third of the state resented the soldiers for meddling in local affairs, but on the frontier, men and women were begging to be occupied. Soon, old roads that had fallen into disuse once again came alive as soldiers worked with ranchers and settlers to clear the emerging range country of Indians and outlaws. From Fort Worth, contractors filled their orders, sending freight wagons with goods and supplies westward; others who raised horses and mules and grew the provender that fed them also found a brisk trade. With each passing year the stream of westbound immigrants grew, and those who made Fort Worth their final destination found opportunities aplenty.

By 1868 the meager population doubled, which was no great feat, but soon it doubled again, and Fort Worth began taking on a more substantial appearance. The courthouse on the county square, at last completed, dominated the scene below. From a narrow veranda circling the cupola, observers could survey stone and masonry buildings gradually replacing the log business houses that had been recently boarded shut. Beyond the modest commercial district, new homes sided with finished lumber similarly emerged among the old pioneer homes.

Serving the prosperous community by 1873 were hotels and restaurants as well as saloons and gaming houses that enjoyed a vigorous trade with the floating population of cowboys and frontierspeople. Shop owners peddled such merchandise as dry goods, hardware, and water-well supplies, many of them from false-fronted buildings in which they lived on a second floor. Manufacturers of ice, leather goods, and tin products also found a steady market, as did blacksmiths, printers, and a photographer. While a professional class of doctors and attorneys established comfortable practices, bankers operated out of three separate institutions. There were also clergymen enough to minister to the spiritual needs of Fort Worth's mainstream Protestants, and although irregularly, Catholics and Episcopalians enjoyed mass as well. Education, too, thrived in upwards of twenty schools that instructed the children of Fort Worthians, black as well as white, most of them one-room buildings that operated under public supervision. After a succession of weekly newspapers came and went during these years, Confederate veteran B. B. Paddock arrived in 1872 and took over the *Fort Worth Democrat*, which he soon turned into a bully pulpit for boostering the city in much the same way as Amon Carter would later do with the *Fort Worth Star-Telegram*.

Eighteen seventy-three also marked another important milestone. To gain better control over their affairs, community leaders applied to the state of Texas for a city charter, and effective March 1, Fort Worth won the right to incorporate roughly four square miles of land that extended over the bluff from the Trinity River. Voters soon established a mayor-alderman form of government that promised to regulate vice, restrict the carrying of firearms, and even to build sidewalks and plant ornamental trees.

Certainly, by 1873 Fort Worth possessed all the features that would assure it a prominent place among the state's leading cities, save for one key feature, a railroad. That seemed like a sure bet, however, because officials of the Texas & Pacific, then building across the state from east-to-west, were as anxious as Fort Worthians to establish a railhead at this gateway to a western market that had scarcely been tapped. Already, the line extended about six miles past Dallas, to Eagle Ford. In anticipation of its impending arrival, Fort Worth's leading businessmen set aside a 320-acre donation for a railroad reservation, around which hopeful entrepreneurs and job seekers were already clustered in a subdevelopment of tents. Then, just at the moment when T&P President Thomas Scott was in London entertaining investors at a congratulatory banquet, a cable from New York arrived—Jay Cooke and Company, one of America's most substantial business houses, had failed.

The ensuing Panic of 1873 set off the most severe depression the country had known up to that time. The prospective investors in the T&P were among the first to withdraw their support, sending ripples through the economy that dashed the plans of men in Fort Worth who had wagered their futures on the railroad's arrival. The bottom collapsed under the market for cattle as well, and a killing blizzard that winter only added to the industry's woes. B. B. Paddock later reflected: "The population dwindled as rapidly as it had grown." Perhaps a thousand people remained, but business

✧

Cowboys on the range outside of Fort Worth.

COURTESY OF *FORT WORTH STAR-TELEGRAM* COLLECTION, SPECIAL COLLECTIONS, UNIVERSITY OF TEXAS AT ARLINGTON LIBRARIES, ARLINGTON, TEXAS, AR 406 H019.

✧

The economic pall that followed the Panic of 1873 still hung heavy over Fort Worth when Dallas attorney Robert E. Cowart visited in 1875. According to local lore, Cowart returned home and, tongue-in-cheek, reported that business was so poor in the neighboring village he spotted a panther sleeping undisturbed in the middle of a desolate downtown street. Rather than express indignity, Fort Worthians embraced the lethargic cat. Its name and image would become ubiquitous, inspiring everything from the Fort Worth Cats minor league professional baseball team to countless businesses and civic organizations. The Panther Division, whose program is pictured here, trained at Fort Worth's Camp Bowie during World War I and found the mascot to be a fitting symbol of its fierce pride.

SOUVENIR PROGRAM OF THE *MILITARY REVIEW*, COURTESY OF SPECIAL COLLECTIONS, UNIVERSITY OF TEXAS AT ARLINGTON LIBRARIES, ARLINGTON, TEXAS, UA 473 1918, 2.

came to a standstill, and despondency replaced the giddy sense of optimism that had prevailed in the preceding months. "The grass literally grew in the streets," insisted the editor. "This was not a metaphor to indicate stagnation but a doleful fact."

Yet, while the country in general continued to flounder for the remainder of the decade, West Texas, and, in turn, Fort Worth, soon rebounded. Following the winter "die-up" of 1873-1874, prices for cattle quickly recovered. At the same time, the U.S. Army pressed its Red River Campaign against the Comanches and Kiowas. The conquest complete, settlers fleeing the economic depression found Northwest Texas a welcoming safety valve. Then, during the winter of 1874-1875, buffalo hunters tested the range beyond Fort Griffin, and by the next season the great slaughter began in earnest. Even without its railroad, Fort Worth enjoyed an enviable position as the provisioning point for all those westering endeavors.

In the meantime, community leaders had not given up on the idea of becoming a railhead. The Texas legislature postponed the deadline for completing the road to Fort Worth until the date of adjournment, extending to the T&P its promise of granting sixteen sections of land for each mile of track laid. With the fortunes of so many hanging in the balance, construction on the twenty-six mile leg to Fort Worth continued at a feverish pace. Businessmen did their part by releasing employees to work on the line, while women shuttled food and water to harried crews. In Austin, Tarrant County Representative N. H. Darnell, although gravely ill, was carried into the House chamber on a cot, where, each day for fifteen days, his vote helped block the move to adjourn. Meanwhile, workers laid the last few miles of track over dirt roads and heaved a makeshift crib over Sycamore Creek that allowed the locomotive to pass. Finally, as chronicler Oliver Knight so eloquently described the scene, "old No. 20…its diamond stack sending streams of pungent wood smoke into the shimmery summer air, rolled into town at 11:23 a.m. on July 19, 1876." At last Fort Worth had its railroad. There followed a celebration, the likes of which the city had never seen.

The new era began immediately. A count of businesses a few weeks after the railroad arrived numbered fifty-nine; four years later the city directory listed 460. For the better part of those four years Fort Worth represented the end of the T&P line, yet the westbound traffic continued. Lines of wagons pulling freight embarked each day for destinations as far away as the Caprock and the Pecos River country. On their return, it was not unusual to see the skins of such animals as bears and panthers, but mostly the wagons brought mountains of buffalo hides. In November 1876 alone, teamsters from Fort Griffin delivered ten thousand of the reeking specimens to the T&P reservation, where at times the stacks covered as much as fifteen acres and topped ten feet in places. And even though the Western Trail through Fort Griffin diverted some of the cattle traffic, drovers continued to push their herds northward through the streets of Fort Worth, a few blocks east of Main.

Otherwise a welter of activity emanated from the saloons and brothels that inevitably attended the boom in frontier commerce. During the trailing season, cowboys regularly "took the town," as they called the routine of riding wildly up the street, whooping and firing their six-shooters at anything that made a good target. On the sidewalks, men gambled openly, while others, only a bit more discreetly, laid their money down on fights in the back rooms of such dives as Henry Burns' saloon where pairs of cocks, dogs, and men squared off. At variety houses like the Adelphi

✧

The arrival of the railroad heralded a period of spectacular growth. Men who controlled enough land to open businesses such as this one, run by E. B. Daggett, were among the first to benefit.

COURTESY OF THE *FORT WORTH STAR-TELEGRAM* COLLECTION, SPECIAL COLLECTIONS, UNIVERSITY OF TEXAS AT ARLINGTON LIBRARIES, ARLINGTON, TEXAS, AR 406, FWST 2494, 3.

✧

Mule-drawn streetcars provided a convenient means for transporting riders from the railroad reservation to the courthouse at either end of Main Street—convenient, that is, to the degree that the animals cooperated and the vehicles remained on the tracks.

COURTESY OF THE *FORT WORTH STAR-TELEGRAM*, SPECIAL COLLECTIONS, UNIVERSITY OF TEXAS AT ARLINGTON LIBRARIES, ARLINGTON, TEXAS, AR 446, D601.

and Theater Comique, patrons took pleasure in the company of chorus girls, with whom they drank and danced and fornicated.

The blocks centered on Twelfth Street and Rusk (now Commerce) were wild, to be sure, but it was not nearly as violent as the creation myth would have it. In fact, the number of prostitute suicides far outnumbered the incidents of violence that found their way into the public record. As businessmen knew, wildness attracted money, and plenty of it; violence chased it away. There was always a pious element in Fort Worth that abhorred Hell's Half Acre, as the district came to be called, but as long as the business of sin paid in cash, the voices of reform could never maintain their occasional ascendancy. During one of those brief periods, just as the cattle trailing season of 1879 was beginning to heat up, businessmen paid for an advertisement, pleading with their fellow citizens for more leniency: "...everyone is aware of the amount of money spent in this city by the cattlemen and cowboys, thus making every trade and business prosper." Yet, on account of the cleanup movement, they lamented, "almost all of them remain in their camps a few miles from the city." The petition must have worked, for directly, the paper proclaimed: "The voice of the cowboy is once again heard in the land."

Soon enough, however, the sight of bawling cattle trampling through the streets once again became a novel experience. The long drive through Fort Worth ended when the final Kansas-bound herd passed over the bluff during the middle Eighties; the great buffalo hunt was all but over as the decade began, the last freight wagons topped off with the hides of varmints. In 1880 the Texas & Pacific continued building westward, and before the calendar turned again, Fort Worth became an important stop on a new transcontinental line, supplying stores with all the accouterments of living that could be loaded aboard a railcar. The decade of the Eighties that began with 6,663, finished with 23,076 in 1890. By the end of the century, 26,668 people resided in Fort Worth, numbers that no doubt seemed astonishing to old-timers who had weathered the years of the Civil War and Reconstruction.

The railroad, just as its original boosters had promised, transformed the frontier village into a prosperous city. In 1873, even before the first locomotive belched a curl of smoke into the sky above Tarrant County, an overenthusiastic B. B. Paddock had published a few scribbled lines emanating from Fort Worth that editors in nearby communities ridiculed as the "Tarantula Map." During the 1880s, the many-legged spider started taking shape, and by the end of the decade it had become a reality.

As a key transportation center that employed legions of railroad workers—many who were members of the Knights of Labor—it came as no surprise that when the Great Southwest Strike of 1886 began tying up the region's traffic, Fort Worth found itself at the center of the controversy. Railroad titan Jay Gould determined to break the deadlock by hiring scabs to replace the striking workers and sending Pinkerton detectives to intimidate them. The situation reached critical mass when the Knights stopped a train attempting to run its blockade at Buttermilk Switch, about where the 2200 block of South Main is today. A short, sharp fight ensued, in which a man on either side later died of gunshot wounds. At the behest of Fort Worth Mayor John Peter Smith, Governor John Ireland called out Texas Rangers and three-hundred militiamen, who joined federal marshals already on hand. Ultimately the strike failed, leaving many working class Fort Worthians bitter over the way their government at every level had aligned with big business to frustrate their efforts.

Much of the acrimony centered on former City Marshal Timothy "Longhair Jim"

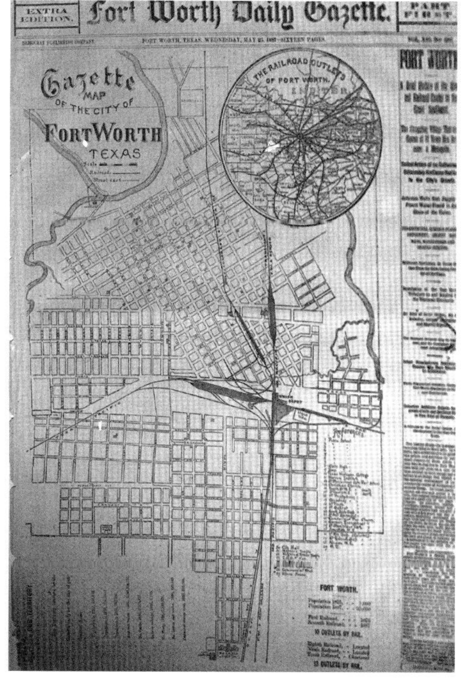

✧

In 1887 the Fort Worth Daily Gazette *published this map of the city, emphasizing a network of railroads that echoed the Tarantula Map that B. B. Paddock had drawn by hand in 1873—a scribbling, really, with nine lines emanating from it that were likened to a spider's legs. At the time, the only roads leading into town were carved out of the earth.*

COURTESY OF THE *FORT WORTH STAR-TELEGRAM*, SPECIAL COLLECTIONS, UNIVERSITY OF TEXAS AT ARLINGTON LIBRARIES, ARLINGTON, TEXAS, AR 406, FWST 2502.

Timothy "Longhair Jim" Courtright (right) and friend

COURTESY OF THE FORT WORTH PUBLIC LIBRARY.

Courtright, who had fallen on the side of management. At the time he was operating a detective agency that was allegedly little more than a thinly disguised protection racket for shaking down the owners of gambling houses and brothels. When the strike erupted, he accepted a U.S. deputy marshal commission and took charge of the railroad guards. It was he, in fact, who took credit for mortally wounding the picketer. Tall and ruggedly handsome, Courtright's quiet, but sure manner and the way he carried a brace of pistols butts-forward on his hips had at one time projected the very picture of a fearless frontier peacekeeper. After the strike, however, most citizens came to view him for what he was—a venal opportunist who operated on the edges of the law he was earlier bound to enforce.

Then, on the evening of February 8, 1887, Courtright's checkered career came to an end when Luke Short, owner of the White Elephant Saloon at 308 and 310 Main Street, gunned him down. Presumably, the two were arguing over the terms of protection, and words escalated into a one-sided contest of arms. In contrast to fanciful depictions pitting the two experienced gunmen facing each other in the middle of the street, the fight erupted at near point-blank range in the doorway of Ella Blackwell's shooting gallery, a half block from the White Elephant. According to friends of Short, Courtright reached for his gun first, but only because his adversary had indicated he was unarmed. Magician-like, Short produced a concealed Colt .45 and fired five rapid shots, three that found their mark. The second one, which passed through Courtright's heart, knocked him backwards and onto the floor, just inside Blackwell's gallery. He never even managed to clear his holster. There the former lawman lay almost still, while a crowd gathered and watched him die.

The widely reported "shootout" instantly became part of Fort Worth's frontier lore, but more accurately it represented an exceptional event in a city whose wildest days were already in the past. Although Hell's Half Acre itself would survive into the twentieth century, even by 1887 the district seemed something of an anachronism as the city reached out to embrace a new age of civic improvements, industry, and refinement. The *Fort Worth Gazette* declared that even four years earlier it was evident "the roughness of frontier life was passing away." To the extent that the Acre's red light continued to glow, beginning in 1885 it was charged by electricity. By then, telephone service had already been available for eight years. A local board of trade, which business leaders during the previous decade could not sustain, was revived during the 1880s and worked to attract desirable growth from the offices of its six-story building on the northwest corner of Seventh and Houston. The same year of the so-called shootout, developers laid out the Fairmount Addition south of the rail yards, where the neat homes of an expanding middle class began springing up along streets that were graveled, curbed, and guttered. One of the country's first electric streetcar services soon provided its residents access to other lines in various parts of the city, signaling the end for the old mule-drawn cars. The last years of the century also counted among its civic improvements a municipal water system and sanitary sewers, up-to-date fire and police departments, a city hall and new county courthouse, tax-supported public schools, and home delivery of mail.

Full of pride and confidence in the way the city was flourishing, civic leaders in 1888 had put B. B. Paddock in charge of amassing a $50,000 fund to cover the costs of an event aimed at focusing the nation's attention on the

The state's cornucopia yawned widely for the Texas Spring Palace, covering its wooden frame with a magnificently colorful blanket fashioned from such products as cotton, oats, wheat, nuts, straw, and corn of every hue, as well as a wide assortment of fruit and vegetables, and even cactus, moss, and Johnson grass.

COURTESY OF THE FORT WORTH PUBLIC LIBRARY.

The exhibition's officials issued formal invitations such as this one to far-flung dignitaries, calculating that their presence would add prestige to the event.

COURTESY OF RUBY SCHMIDT, GRANBURY.

✧

The Texas Spring Palace, its striped domes at either end recently completed for the 1890 season, rises like a fairytale castle from among the prosaic structures surrounding it. This view, looking south from the Board of Trade Building at Houston and West Seventh Streets, reveals the first floor of St. Patrick's Catholic Church under construction at 1206 Throckmorton. Closer to the foreground, the Flatiron Building would arise in 1907 on the site occupied by the two-story brick structure. Immediately north and across the street (Jennings Avenue) the fenced lot on which the tiny white home sits provided the location for the 1901 Carnegie Library.

COURTESY OF RUBY SCHMIDT, GRANBURY.

Panther City. Inspired by such material tributes to nature's bounty as the "Corn Palace" in Sioux City, Iowa, during this age when Populism was on the ascendancy, the ambitious result was The Texas Spring Palace—an exhibition building covered entirely, inside and out, with virtually every kind of agricultural product grown in the state. When completed, the raw materials alone doubled the budget, but workers brought the project in on time. The aptly named hall opened in May with enough exhibition space to showcase the products of each Texas county. Among the attractions were historical artifacts, hundreds of brightly colored native birds, a miniature lake stocked with fish, and, of course, the products that represented the labor of men and women who extracted their livelihoods from the land. Daily entertainment featured the Watch Factory Band of Elgin, Illinois, and a man billed as "Mr. Leroy," who parachuted from the basket of a balloon that rose a thousand feet above the city.

Despite its popularity the exhibition lost over $20,000. Yet far from discouraged, its promoters planned a second season for the following year that would eclipse their initial effort. Stage shows, dress balls, and excursion trains engaged the swelling multitudes that arrived from every corner of the state and throughout the nation.

As the ending date approached, officials decided to add a grand finale to cap their success. That evening, May 30, 1890, a crowd estimated at seven thousand packed the hall. After the Elgin band completed its last concert and exhibition-goers prepared for the farewell ball, fire suddenly broke out, greedily devouring inestimable acres of dried and brittle decorations. Outside, horrified witnesses watched as people and smoke boiled from every door and window, propelled by the intense heat. In fifteen minutes the Spring Palace had fallen in, taking on the appearance of a sprawling bonfire. Miraculously, the only fatality was Englishman Alfred. S. Hayne. Several times he could have escaped unharmed, yet every time he emerged from the inferno with a rescued patron, the desperate pleas from those still trapped inside induced him to return until at last—with clothes aflame and an unconscious woman cradled in his arms—he leaped from a second-story window. Three hours later, doctors pulled a sheet over his burned and broken body.

Although Fort Worthians vowed to rebuild a fireproof Palace, the reluctance of insurers delayed their plans, and the Panic of 1893 dashed whatever hopes remained. That year, however, the city raised a fitting tribute to Al Hayne by erecting a monument at the conjunction of Houston, Main, and Lancaster Streets. Later, in 1922, vandals

✧

Members of the Watch Factory Band of Elgin, Illinois, pause long enough during a concert at the Spring Palace to preserve the moment.

COURTESY OF RUBY SCHMIDT, GRANBURY.

William Fife Somerville of Scotland, director general of the Spring Palace exhibition, came to Fort Worth early in the 1880s as assistant manager of the Matador Land & Cattle Company's office in the city.

COURTESY OF, RUBY SCHMIDT, GRANBURY.

William Fife Somerville built a comfortable home on Penn Street, between Jackson and Thirteenth, where he took this photograph of his wife, Mary (left), Mrs. H. H. Campbell, whose husband co-founded the Matador Ranch, and his sons, Harold (next to the wagon) and Alfred. Landmarks fix the date of this early panorama between 1884 and 1885. Using the Second Empire courthouse as a point of reference, they include the Second Ward School at West Belknap and Lamar (left), and the home of John Peter Smith (right) mostly blocking the view of the Opera House. A few months after the great fire, the Scotsman climbed a windmill situated on this property to free the blades, which had become stuck. The tail ended up swinging into Somerville, throwing him onto an iron fence on which he was mortally impaled. Afterward, his widow buried him at Oakwood Cemetery and returned to Scotland.

COURTESY OF THE JACK WHITE PHOTOGRAPH COLLECTION, SPECIAL COLLECTIONS, UNIVERSITY OF TEXAS AT ARLINGTON LIBRARIES, ARLINGTON, TEXAS, AR 407, 1-8-44.

carried it away, but the city reaffirmed its veneration for the "Hero of the Texas Spring Palace" by building a new memorial in 1934, one that has survived all the construction, demolitions, and regeneration that changed the landscape surrounding it.

Fort Worth, at the century's end, was beginning to show signs of maturing into a first-class city. While critical eyes need not have strained to catch sight of shacks and litter-strewn lots on almost every block, such blemishes were steadily giving way to pretensions of refinement.

As the old century waned, the boom in home-market industries continued almost unabated, even as businessmen rode out two economic downturns. The Texas Brewing Company, the city's first large-scale plant, began operation in 1891 and was soon loading three thousand freight cars a year with its popular suds. The brewery joined a local economy that already boasted mills, foundries, machine shops, brick and lumber yards, and a marble works. A number of factories also contributed to the city's growth, turning out such items as mattresses, carriages, windmills, boilers, tin roofing, and clothing. While the brief, but severe nationwide Panic of 1893 scarcely registered in Fort Worth—not a single one of its eight banks failed—it nevertheless slowed the momentum of capitalists who hoped to turn the city into a major packing center. Soon, however, another group of operators settled north of the river and built a stockyards district that would bridge the economy of the nineteenth century with the new age just around the corner.

There remained a final chapter, however, one that just crossed the century mark, before the Old West gave way completely to the new. It was at that time when two seemingly cultivated, well-dressed visitors to the city arrived, one Jim Lowe and a Harry Longbaugh. Although they walked the streets in anonymity, almost everyone they passed would have known them by their aliases—Butch Cassidy and the Sundance Kid, two key members of the legendary Wild Bunch. The gang represented the last gasp of an era of "social bandits," outlaws condemned by lawmen and business executives as thieves and murderers, but praised by common folk for striking a blow against the cold powers of bankers, railroad men, and big ranchers who connived to rob them legally. With the gregarious and detail-minded Butch Cassidy at the head of the Wild Bunch, they deserved as much misplaced

This view of Main Street in 1889 betrays what was normally a scene of vibrant commerce.

COURTESY OF SPECIAL COLLECTIONS, UNIVERSITY OF TEXAS AT ARLINGTON LIBRARIES, ARLINGTON, TEXAS, AR 407 1-9-32.

adoration as any gang. In Cassidy's career as an outlaw he never killed a man and discouraged the kind of unnecessary gunplay that generated panic among bystanders. He and the others would not hesitate, however, to pull out a stick of dynamite to gain access to express cars and locked safes. Those equal measures of mercy and élan matched their efficiency for planning every phase of a robbery, from their lightening quick strikes to their wraith-like getaways, after which they would regroup at faraway places, including, at least once, Fort Worth.

After the Wild Bunch hit a bank at Winnemucca, Nevada, in August 1900, local posses, U.S. marshals, and detectives of the Pinkerton Agency and Wells Fargo scoured the Northwest, while Butch and Sundance casually steamed into the Panther City aboard a Fort Worth & Denver City train. Inside Hell's Half Acre the pair rendezvoused with their compatriots in the job, Harvey Logan, otherwise known as Kid Curry, and Will Carver. A fifth member of the gang who had not taken part in the robbery, Ben Kilpatrick, also joined them.

So far, the Wild Bunch had escaped the law once more. Safe in Fort Worth, the gang melted into the transient population, where, according to Kid Curry, "we rented an apartment and were living in style." From their base at 1014 ½ Main Street, a boarding house known as Maddox Flats, the outlaws unbuckled their gun belts and lightened their pockets, going on shopping sprees and seeking entertainment in the Acre's saloons and gambling halls. They also began forging signatures on some of the Winnemucca bank notes, all which bore registered serial numbers. Compounding their carelessness, the five men walked into the Swartz View Company at 705 Main Street and sat for a portrait that would soon be reproduced on about fifteen thousand wanted posters. Even today, it remains one of the most recognizable images in the illustrated history of the Wild West. At last Cassidy came to his senses and advised the gang to clear out. The Sundance Kid, who had taken up with a lovely, but enigmatic young woman, Etta Place, joined him, and the threesome fled for New York City with plans for South America. By the time the Pinkerton men were able to locate and search the Maddox Flats apartment, the only trace of the gang the detectives found were some of the bank notes the fugitives had dropped in their getaway. The rest, as it's said, is legend. It was the last hurrah for the old frontier, and the time for a new era was at hand.

✧

Fort Worth Opera House (1883), located at Third and Commerce Streets.

COURTESY OF SPECIAL COLLECTIONS, UNIVERSITY OF TEXAS AT ARLINGTON LIBRARIES, ARLINGTON, TEXAS, AR 407 1-3-8.

✧

Tarrant County Courthouse, completed 1895.

COURTESY OF QUENTIN MCGOWN COLLECTION, FORT WORTH.

✧

Easily one of the most recognizable images in the illustrated history of the Wild West, this photograph identified its subjects as members of the "Wild Bunch." The Pinkerton Detective Agency made sure it became popular by reproducing it on fifteen thousand wanted posters. Left-to-right (sitting), Harry Longbaugh ("The Sundance Kid"), Ben Kilpatrick, and Jim Lowe ("Butch" Cassidy); (standing) William Carver and Harvey Logan ("Kid Curry).

COURTESY OF THE LIBRARY OF CONGRESS, WASHINGTON, D.C.

✧

Fort Worth at the turn of the century, looking north from the vantage of the T&P terminal on Front Street (now Lancaster Avenue). Neat rows of new masonry buildings clearly signaled that the days were numbered for the few hovels clearly visible in the photograph. While the five-year-old courthouse dominates the scene, other structures are tall enough to peek over their neighbors as well. The Wheat Building at Main and Eighth, its rooftop garden popular in the 1890s but then converted to another floor of offices, is the large structure close to the courthouse. To its left, the Board of Trade can be seen on Houston Street (parallel to Main on the next block).

COURTESY OF W. D. SMITH PHOTOGRAPH COLLECTION, SPECIAL COLLECTIONS, UNIVERSITY OF TEXAS AT ARLINGTON LIBRARIES, ARLINGTON, TEXAS, AR 430 48-1-22.

CHAPTER 1

DRESSED UP AND READY TO GO

1900-1909

The people of Fort Worth counted down the last days of 1899, self-possessed with satisfaction that they had turned the corner of fortune. Among a crowd gathered at the foot of Main Street in the waning days of the old century were men and women who had come of age with the town and shared in its growing pains during much of the fifty years since the U.S. Army first planted its guidon on the nearby prominence overlooking the Trinity River. This December day the assembly convened, not to commemorate a half-century of history, but to mark another milestone, the dedication of the new Texas & Pacific passenger station. Nevertheless, former mayor John Peter Smith and other civic leaders, whose efforts helped bring the T&P to town in 1876, recounted the city's ups and downs. Surveying the crowd, Smith estimated that "the sons and daughters of Fort Worth have built their commonwealth upon a solid foundation." The Romanesque monolith that towered behind him surely added weight to his words. As the old pioneer continued his reminiscence, he likened the city's struggle to one that mirrored the checkered growth of the state itself. Concluding his remarks, Smith said: "From this day we can look back fifty years and determine the development of Texas." It was a proud day for the Panther City.

Four years later the grand terminal would burst into flames, leaving a stark and hollowed out hulk straddling its own ashes. It would be a bitter loss, but the city had survived even graver precedents. In the years to come it would bear even greater tragedies. Each time citizens set their jaws, rolled up their sleeves, and met the challenges at hand. As for the T&P, it was soon rebuilt, only to be razed by a later generation for an even grander station. Such are the ways of big cities. Fort Worth had indeed turned the corner of fortune.

With a new century upon them, the leading citizens of Fort Worth felt they had done everything they could do to transcend their frontier image and assure the city a stable and prosperous future. Certainly, there was the popular perception of Fort Worth as a wide-open community that had earned another, less desirable, nickname—"Cowtown." That impression had taken root in Hell's Half Acre, the earthy periphery of saloons and brothels that attended the cattle and railroad booms on which earlier town fathers had pinned their dreams for affluence. But there was another Fort Worth, one that by 1900 had grown into the fifth largest city in Texas. It enjoyed an infrastructure that anticipated a much greater population than the 26,668 souls who made their homes and livings there.

Everywhere signs pointed to a greater destiny. Anchoring the north end of Main Street, the Tarrant County Courthouse commanded a presence that would make many state capitols pale by comparison. Five years earlier voters had threatened to punish the commissioners responsible for approving the $500,000 building by turning them out of office at the next election. Now it was a gemstone that begged company. At the other end of Main Street, the railroad yards provided arteries that connected Fort Worth with the world beyond the bluff. There, at the T&P Station and the rival Union Station of the Santa Fe—a beaux arts masterpiece itself—as many as fifty passenger trains arrived and departed daily at the turn of the century aboard the two host lines as well as others that shared their facilities. Over the network of lines that converged on the city, steam engines pulled an annual load of a million and a half freight cars.

A story of the twentieth century. Firemen and volunteers work frantically to save the four-year-old Texas & Pacific Passenger Station, while a crowd of stunned onlookers gathers. The station was soon restored to its original splendor, but by 1930 rail traffic had outgrown the once-imposing structure, and it was razed for a new warehouse and terminal. Eventually, the times caught up with the new facilities as well, yet fortunately they have survived. The terminal is once again a busy passenger station, this time serving the Trinity Railway Express. No doubt the warehouse will also see a second life, most likely as offices and condominiums for businesspeople and the growing class of city dwellers. As for the sleek commuter train, it connects the downtowns of Fort Worth and Dallas, just like the old interurban that the Northern Texas Traction Company put into service in 1902, more than a century earlier. Unlike its predecessor, however, the TRE makes numerous daily stops to accommodate passengers using D/FW Airport.

TOP, LEFT IMAGE COURTESY OF THE *FORT WORTH STAR-TELEGRAM* PHOTOGRAPH COLLECTION, SPECIAL COLLECTIONS, UNIVERSITY OF TEXAS AT ARLINGTON LIBRARIES, ARLINGTON, TEXAS. TOP, RIGHT IMAGE COURTESY OF THE *FORT WORTH STAR-TELEGRAM* PHOTOGRAPH COLLECTION, SPECIAL COLLECTIONS, UNIVERSITY OF TEXAS AT ARLINGTON LIBRARIES, ARLINGTON, TEXAS, AR 406 1-62-46. BOTTOM, LEFT IMAGE COURTESY OF THE *FORT WORTH STAR-TELEGRAM* PHOTOGRAPH COLLECTION, SPECIAL COLLECTIONS, UNIVERSITY OF TEXAS AT ARLINGTON LIBRARIES, ARLINGTON, TEXAS, 6-3, AR 406 1-62-46. BOTTOM, RIGHT IMAGE COURTESY OF MICHAEL BATES, MCALESTER, OKLAHOMA, MBATES@MARTINAIRE.COM.

Fort Worth also possessed the kinds of services and amenities that befitted its cosmopolitan pretensions. It enjoyed a full range of municipal services as well as a system of streetcars that fanned out to islands of commerce and residential neighborhoods that lay beyond the city's core. Religion was well represented in the numerous houses of worship whose congregations entreated a God who listened to the prayers of Jews and Catholics and African Methodist Episcopals as readily as those of the Baptists and Methodists who dominated religious affairs in the Southwest. A free public school system was augmented by Fort Worth University, chartered in 1881 as Texas Wesleyan University, and Polytechnic College, founded ten years later. Oddly, it was the latter school that eventually evolved into the present TWU.

The 1900s would also begin with Fort Worth in America's spotlight as host of the National Livestock Association's annual meeting. "The livestock men of Fort Worth are known all over the country," trumpeted the association's president, John H. Springer of Denver. "By reason of their well-known hospitality, this great convention was brought to Fort Worth rather than a number of Northern cities, who made a fight for it."

Over four thousand stockmen from every state and territory in the West as well as many Midwestern and Northeastern states arrived in Fort Worth on special trains for meetings and festivities. A grand parade attracted a crowd of about twenty thousand people. Leading the procession were two hundred members of the Mystic Knights of Bovinia—a group of enthusiastic local cowmen and prominent citizens who "sprang as naturally from the circumstances in which it originated as the grass that grows in the great pastures beyond Fort Worth." Behind them, waves of other fraternal organizations and groups of horsemen followed, along with a burlesque company from whose "uncouth instruments" emanated a sound that reporters likened to the "bellowing of a bunch of bulls, making an effect that was grotesquely pleasing."

✧

This iron bridge over the Trinity River replaced a ferry and proved sufficient to handle traffic between downtown and the North Side at the turn-of-the-century. That quickly changed when Swift and Armour came to town. By 1913 the Paddock Viaduct was completed, and workers unceremoniously scrapped the old crossing.

COURTESY OF THE AMON CARTER MUSEUM COLLECTION, FORT WORTH PUBLIC LIBRARY.

That evening the Knights staged a ball at the Elks Hall, where the city's elite entertained the most distinguished of their guests in a more sublime manner. For the four hundred prominent wives who accompanied their husbands, the Women's Federation Clubs of Fort Worth created a Japanese tearoom that served as their headquarters during the meeting. Led by Mrs. John B. Slaughter, wife of the legendary West Texas cattleman, the women arranged all manner of events, from informal receptions and organ recitals, to speeches and carriage tours of the city.

No less than the governor of Texas, Joseph D. Sayers, formally opened the convention, while his counterparts from Oklahoma, South Dakota, and Colorado looked on from the dais. The most important guest, though, was Phillip D. Armour of Chicago. At Fort Worth the millionaire meatpacker did something he had never done before, deliver a paper: "The Relation of the Packer to the Cattle Industry." At the stock barns, expert judges from all over the country had to look at so many entries that their work was not over until the evening after the convention ended.

Awash in success, President Springer predicted that great things would result from the annual meeting. "There is no telling how many hundreds of thousands of dollars of Northern capital will be advanced in Texas as a direct result of showing those northerners what we have in Texas." His words proved prophetic.

Clearly, Fort Worth was enjoying the progress that its leaders had hoped for, one that would complete the transformation from a frontier town into a first-class city. Notwithstanding the celebrated visit by Butch Cassidy and the Sundance Kid, a more visible metaphor for the closing of the frontier came during that same autumn of 1900, when Buffalo Bill brought the Wild West to Fort Worth. Eleven thousand people witnessed the troupe's "feats of fearless skill and hazardous pastimes." Upstaging the normal fare of cowboys and Indians was a re-creation of Teddy Roosevelt's charge up San Juan Hill. The popular politician and recent events of the country's war with Spain struck a chord with worshipful Americans eager to glorify the modern age.

Buffalo Bill Cody himself, who had last visited Fort Worth in 1870, marveled at all the changes, but commented that they were part of a pattern he was observing throughout his travels. "Her pioneers have fast passed away," he lauded, "their places have been taken by those who now enjoy the homes, farms, and ranches located by the early settlers."

If the Fort Worth of 1900 had impressed Cody, a visit to the Panther City a decade later would have left him awestruck. Almost imperceptibly during the century's first ten years a new downtown emerged from a city that was one part cosmopolitan, the other a bloated frontier village. On the threshold of the new century, dilapidated wooden buildings among the brick and stone business houses blighted every block. From the seemingly ubiquitous wagon yards and livery stables the pungent odor of urine-soaked hay wafted through streets dappled with the equally noisome excrement of horses and mules. Only cold weather brought relief from the swarms of flies thus attracted. Plodding over the rock-and-gravel-graded streets, the animals churned up mud after every rain; during the long dry spells they wracked their loads over a corrugated surface, whipping up a choking dust. Protruding trolley rails presented another menace that threatened to pull askew the wheels of wagons and buggies alike. Crisscrossing over this scene was an

✧

Central Fire Hall, erected 1899; razed 1938 for the widening of Throckmorton Street.

COURTESY OF THE JACK WHITE PHOTOGRAPH COLLECTION, SPECIAL COLLECTIONS, UNIVERSITY OF TEXAS AT ARLINGTON LIBRARIES, ARLINGTON, TEXAS, AR 407 1-2-19.

✧

A lonely trolley heads to a distant suburb. Soon, the city would absorb such empty spaces.

COURTESY OF THE W. D. SMITH PHOTOGRAPH COLLECTION, SPECIAL COLLECTIONS, UNIVERSITY OF TEXAS AT ARLINGTON LIBRARIES, ARLINGTON, TEXAS, AR 430 49-1-33.

unsightly web of telephone and electric lines projecting from constellations of glass insulators mounted on power poles, many of them standing at odd angles.

When the century began, a single block of cobblestone paving spanned Sixth Street between Main and Houston. But within a month, twelve carloads of vitrified Thurber brick arrived from West Texas and soon covered the macadam surface between the T&P and Santa Fe passenger stations. Slowly, too slowly to suit complaining citizens, work crews laid brick on the downtown streets, while on the outskirts of the city, convicts labored to grade and gravel the roads that linked Fort Worth to its rural markets.

The pressure for contractors to rush their jobs provoked the *Fort Worth Record* in 1903 to grouse about the shoddy workmanship that left Houston Street in poor condition. "Ruts, holes, and low places can be found along its length at almost any point, and vehicles risk damage wherever they are drawn." Nevertheless, the paving campaign continued successfully, extending to the residential streets beyond downtown. A street commissioner predicted in 1907 that at the rate they were going, Fort Worth would have a hundred miles of paved streets within five years.

Increasingly, horses and wagons yielded to automobiles, and false-fronted firetraps surrendered to rows of graceful masonry buildings. Beginning as early as 1902 the first flivvers sputtered across city streets, drawing crowds of onlookers. The novelty of be-goggled drivers sporting white dusters and special gloves and hats soon wore thin as the cacophonous clattering and sharp backfiring caused men to jump and sent horses reeling.

In 1904 a municipal code began regulating automobile traffic. H. R. Cromer—bicycle salesman-turned auto dealer—enjoyed the honor of being the first to register his car, a topless, chain-driven Model E Rambler. Among the restrictions he was compelled to observe was a ten-mile-per-hour speed limit and the sounding of a "gong" or horn that was to begin at a

✧

Looking north on Main Street, c. 1900. This picture was taken from roughly the same vantage where TCU art professor Sam Ziegler in 1936 would compose the painting that provides the cover art for this book.

COURTESY OF THE DALTON HOFFMAN COLLECTION, FORT WORTH.

✧

The Federal Building and post office at Eleventh and Jennings. Note the Weather Bureau and National Weather Service facilities located on the roof.

COURTESY OF JACK WHITE PHOTOGRAPH COLLECTION, SPECIAL COLLECTIONS, UNIVERSITY OF TEXAS AT ARLINGTON LIBRARIES, ARLINGTON, TEXAS, AR 407 1-3-43.

✧

By the end of the decade, automobiles were becoming commonplace on downtown streets. Within the next decade, it would be the once-ubiquitous wagons that seemed out of place.

TOP IMAGE COURTESY OF THE SOUTHWESTERN MECHANICAL COMPANY PHOTOGRAPH COLLECTION, SPECIAL COLLECTIONS, UNIVERSITY OF TEXAS AT ARLINGTON LIBRARIES, ARLINGTON, TEXAS, 1-1, 98-97-11. BOTTOM IMAGE COURTESY OF THE DALTON HOFFMAN COLLECTION, FORT WORTH.

✧

A local automobile enthusiast readies his Franklin for a test of speed and endurance along the dirt and gravel roads between Fort Worth and Waco.

COURTESY OF THE *FORT WORTH STAR-TELEGRAM* PHOTOGRAPH COLLECTION, SPECIAL COLLECTIONS, UNIVERSITY OF TEXAS AT ARLINGTON LIBRARIES, ARLINGTON, TEXAS, AR 406 H029.

distance of a hundred feet prior to an intersection and continue until the car passed through. By 1909 the police were willing to give the gong a rest, but they still insisted that drivers maintain a safe speed. In fact, nineteen-year-old Henry Lewis, the city's first motorcycle cop, set up a speedtrap at the 1100 block of West Seventh. There he handed out two dozen citations to motorists for exceeding the ten-mile-an-hour limit before running out of tickets. That kind of initiative eventually earned him the position of police chief, a job that he held from 1933-1937.

Once outside of town, the road conditions normally conspired to limit such speed demons. A pick, shovel, and wire cutters were standard equipment on Cromer's Rambler. Some do-it-yourself roadwork came with the territory for early drivers, especially when they left the city limits. Cromer admitted to cutting fences and crossing fields and pastures in order to avoid having to use the heavier tools. Certainly, he had plenty of opportunities. Shortly after buying the one-cylinder, seven-horse-power car, he set out for San Angelo; another time he boasted of touching six counties in just three days. A trip to the St. Louis World's Fair in 1903, however, had to be aborted because of long stretches of mud.

Despite its limitations, the automobile was here to stay. In the same paper in which the Wood & Wood Carriage Repository ran a full-page ad offering substantial discounts on its $30,000 inventory of buggies, local car dealers peppered the classifieds with announcements. The arrival of a sixty-horsepower Pierce Arrow, for example, was peddled as news. An alluring photograph of the stylish vehicle and the dealer's address accompanied the piece.

Throughout the decade promoters came up with all kinds of imaginative ways to generate enthusiasm for this new wonder of the twentieth century. In January 1909 a garden show came to town that featured 301 automobiles, a number that equaled fully one-third of all the cars then registered in Fort Worth. Regular features such as "Automobile News of Local and General Interest" appeared in newspapers as well. Typical of most columns was some kind of eyebrow-raising accomplishment, such as making a trip to Dallas in a little under an hour-and-a-half. Speed also grabbed readers' attention. There was the White Steamer whose two cylinders managed to boil up enough pressure to propel the car sixty-three miles per hour. A fifty horse power American roadster reportedly topped seventy.

One of the major routes between Fort Worth and Dallas led through the country town of Arlington. The mineral well at Center and Main was already a favorite gathering spot when this picture was taken around 1908.

COURTESY OF THE *ARLINGTON CITIZEN-JOURNAL* PHOTOGRAPH COLLECTION, SPECIAL COLLECTIONS, UNIVERSITY OF TEXAS AT ARLINGTON LIBRARIES, ARLINGTON, TEXAS, 1-2, ACJ 96-10.

In every part of the city, new businesses and residences provided destinations for the increasing traffic. An emerging downtown cultural district began to rival the coarse fare of the Acre. At its center stood the Carnegie Library, built in 1901, capping an eight-year effort by women's clubs. Fort Worthians were already accustomed to enjoying dramatic performances. The imposing Greenwall's Opera House attracted some of the most popular actors of the day, including Lilly Langtry, Sarah Bernhardt, Douglas Fairbanks, and the Barrymores, John, Ethel, and Lionel. Down the street, the Vendome Theater hosted repertoire companies, while venues such as the Majestic Theater and the Lyric offered vaudeville. Film made its Panther City debut in 1903 with The Great Train Robbery, but using bed sheets for a screen did not exactly elevate the new medium as an art form. "In the cheaper class of amusements such as the moving picture theaters and 10-cent houses," deigned the *Fort Worth Record* in 1907, "the town has an untold supply."

All manner of commercial and institutional structures as well as homes and churches date their existence to the building boom around the turn of the century. The three-story Texas Lodge of the Knights of Pythias at 315 Main Street typified both the average commercial building and the innovative spirit of downtown businessmen. In 1901 the fraternal organization began holding its meetings on the third floor of the medieval-inspired castle hall and leased out the other two floors to offset the costs. Shortly after the building was completed, the Renfro Drug Company opened its first store there. As it grew into a significant chain, the anchor nevertheless remained a Knights' tenant until just before World War II.

Building permits reflected Fort Worth's growth at a $24-million-a-year clip by the end of the first decade. Later in the century, investors could sink that much and more into a single office tower, but at the turn of the century a dollar went much farther. In 1907

In 1904, a farmer from Decatur, just northwest of Fort Worth, became the proud owner of a brand-new two-cylinder Schacht automobile, manufactured in Cincinnati, Ohio. Traveling through Fort Worth on his way to Mansfield, the car broke down. Returning with a wagon, the disillusioned farmer took apart the unreliable contraption and then tucked it under his house. There it remained, all but forgotten, for several decades. A subsequent owner of the home discovered the Schacht—save for two wheels that the now elderly farmer was using on a trailer. After striking a deal, the farmer got new tires, and the new owner of the Schacht was able to claim the original wheels. The car, on loan from the James Cogdell family, is part of the collection at the Pate Museum of Transportation.

VEHICLE ON DISPLAY AT THE PATE MUSEUM OF TRANSPORTATION, CRESSON, TEXAS. PHOTOGRAPH BY THE AUTHOR.

A horse and mule team on the median of Camp Bowie Boulevard helps a steam-powered shovel grade the roadbed for a new streetcar line.

COURTESY OF THE JACK WHITE PHOTOGRAPH COLLECTION, SPECIAL COLLECTIONS, UNIVERSITY OF TEXAS AT ARLINGTON LIBRARIES, ARLINGTON, TEXAS, AR 407 1-9-53A.

✧

Buggies and wagons command the traffic at Tenth and Throckmorton, c. 1906. St. Patrick's Catholic Church stands in the foreground, left; city hall is on the next block.

COURTESY OF THE FORT WORTH, TEXAS PHOTOGRAPH COLLECTION, SPECIAL COLLECTIONS, UNIVERSITY OF TEXAS AT ARLINGTON LIBRARIES, ARLINGTON, TEXAS, FWPC 2000-12-3.

Dr. Bacon Saunders, dean of the Fort Worth University's medical school, produced the seven-story Flatiron Building on a triangle bordered by Houston and Ninth Streets and Jennings Avenue for a mere $70,893. Although the masonry Wheat Building remained the city's tallest, the steel-framed Flatiron was recognized as Fort Worth's first modern skyscraper. Based on New York City's Flatiron Building, this prairie cousin distinguished itself with such features as a ring of carved panther heads outlining the top of the two-story base. A couple of blocks up the street, workers broke ground on the ten-story First National Bank building in 1909. When completed, its Bedford, Indiana, limestone base and French gray brick cut an imposing, but graceful figure on the emerging skyline.

✧

Workers install brick paving near the T&P terminal.

COURTESY OF THE JACK WHITE PHOTOGRAPH COLLECTION, SPECIAL COLLECTIONS, UNIVERSITY OF TEXAS AT ARLINGTON LIBRARIES, ARLINGTON, TEXAS, AR 407 1-4-26.

The building boom that had the greatest effect on the economy of Fort Worth, however, did not take root in downtown; it did not even emerge within the city limits. Rather, it was across the Trinity River at bucolic little Marine where Fort Worth was transformed into nature's metropolis. Along the creek from which the village took its name, local investors had founded a tenuous meatpacking operation in the 1890s that attracted some Eastern capital. In turn, those interests induced Chicago packinghouse giants Armour and Swift to build plants in the infant Stockyards. On March 4, 1903 the packers officially opened amid the festivities of the eighth annual Fat Stock Show.

After the National Livestock Association meeting in 1900 there was no question that Fort Worth possessed the potential for meeting the mammoth demands of the meat packing industry. Its rail network and proximity to the great herds of Texas, New Mexico, and Indian Territory made it a logical choice. By this time, too, Boston businessmen Greenlief W. Simpson and Louville V. Niles had gained control of the nascent Stockyards facilities and much of the land along the creek. The next year they began negotiating with the Chicago meatpackers. Simpson and Niles pledged almost twenty-one acres of prime Stockyards real estate to both Armour and Swift along with half their shares in the Fort Worth Stock Yards Company in return for the promise of opening plants in Fort Worth. It was not until local investors raised an additional $50,000 inducement, however, that the amicable competitors finally agreed to come to Texas.

The transformation was total. In 1903, Marine incorporated and expanded as North Fort Worth. Plant buildings, livestock pens, railroad spurs and trolley lines, a burgeoning business district, and all manner of dwellings from tents to mansions sprang up like mushrooms in the ensuing years. At the heart of it all was the Livestock Exchange Building—home to the Fort Worth Stock Yards Company, the commission offices, and other related businesses. Next door was its Mission Revival companion, the Coliseum. The magnificent twelve-thousand-seat arena dominated its neighbor, serving as the focal point for such civic functions as the National Breeders and Feeders Show, created expressly to showcase the district. Each year new pens, new tracks, and new buildings added to the

✧

Looking northeast from the Federal Building. The Carnegie Library commands the "Y" intersection, while the Flatiron Building looks over the scene just to the right. In the foreground, left, is City Hall; beyond it in the distance is the courthouse.

COURTESY OF THE JACK WHITE PHOTOGRAPH COLLECTION, SPECIAL COLLECTIONS, UNIVERSITY OF TEXAS AT ARLINGTON LIBRARIES, ARLINGTON, TEXAS, AR 407 1-9-38

✧

The Flatiron Building, completed in 1907 at a cost of $70,893, was hailed as the city's first modern skyscraper.

COURTESY OF QUENTIN MCGOWN COLLECTION, FORT WORTH.

operation. By the end of the decade only Chicago and Kansas City enjoyed larger livestock markets.

Soon, North Side, composed of Rosen Heights, Diamond Hill, and Washington Heights, became the city's fastest growing suburban district. Packinghouse workers and other laborers naturally gravitated to the affordable and well situated developments, but so, too, did doctors, lawyers, and professional men. Residents could enjoy all the luxuries of municipal services, public schools, and a popular amusement park, White City, yet still live a somewhat rural lifestyle, planting gardens and small orchards and keeping cows and chickens.

If the professional men of North Side comprised what the *Fort Worth Star-Telegram* called "the better class of people," then the "best" resided on Quality Hill. The development of lavish homes on the city's western bluff emerged as Fort Worth's most exclusive neighborhood. The elevation afforded a breathtaking view of the Trinity River and distant prairies and caught the inviting breezes that helped its occupants better tolerate the oppressive summer heat. Old money took root there in ornate Victorian homes, broad-slung Prairie Styles, and other architectural forms that showcased the success of the city's leading citizens. Joining bankers, doctors, attorneys, and businessmen were several prominent West Texas cattlemen. Burk Burnett of the Four-Sixes, W. T. Waggoner, whose ranch occupied much of adjoining Wise County, and George Reynolds of Lambshead, northeast of Abilene, all kept baronial homes on Quality Hill so that their families could enjoy the advantages of city life.

In other parts of town, the social drums beat different rhythms. Down the bluff and across the river from Quality Hill lay the manufacturing district of Brooklyn Heights, where workers turned out glass, windmills, coffins, and light machinery. On the east end of downtown another manufacturing center emerged at unincorporated Glenwood, "home to the working man." There, hourly wage earners assembled furniture, stuffed mattresses, and rolled cigars, while others worked for the International and Great Northern Railroad, whose roundhouse and terminal anchored the district.

The Garden of Eden, a small African-American community on the Trinity River, south of Birdville, cultivated a truck farming industry that supplied most of the city's

✧

New homes and businesses surrounding the Armour and Swift companies quickly arose on the North Side prairie not long after the meatpackers opened.

COURTESY OF THE SOUTHWESTERN MECHANICAL COMPANY PHOTOGRAPH COLLECTION, SPECIAL COLLECTIONS, UNIVERSITY OF TEXAS AT ARLINGTON LIBRARIES, ARLINGTON, TEXAS.

✧

While the Coliseum (left) showcased the great events of the day, the Fort Worth Livestock Exchange (right) housed the Stockyards management, commission offices, and other related businesses.

COURTESY OF THE DALTON HOFFMAN COLLECTION, FORT WORTH.

vegetables and fruit. South of downtown, neighborhoods such as the Fairmount addition had already taken shape on either side of Hemphill Street, and new residential building extended so far into the countryside that the formerly sleepy hamlet of Prairie Chapel—about where the Travis Avenue Baptist Church is today—applied for annexation during the decade and became the tenth ward. Other pockets of homes accumulated around Fort Worth University, which occupied the present site of Trimble Tech High School, and Polytechnic Heights.

Similarly, African-American neighborhoods developed in small clusters at the edges of commercial districts and, like the Garden of Eden, on other bottomlands that hugged the Trinity. Black Fort Worth provided an army of domestic workers, porters, and laborers who kept the engine of society running smoothly. Yet slowly, they developed a viable and distinct engine of their own, adding new schools, churches, and black-owned businesses.

One African American in particular, Bill McDonald, enjoyed the kind of success that was normally reserved for only the elite of white society. A skillful East Texas politician, he tied his wagon to the star of Texas Midland Railroad scion H. R. Green as his chief advisor. Spotted together in 1896 at the Democrats' national convention in St. Louis, a local newspaper identified him as a "goosenecked sort of Negro," and, no doubt to his chagrin, the name "Gooseneck" Bill McDonald stuck. Settling in Fort Worth at the turn of the century, he founded the Fraternal Bank & Trust Co. at Ninth and Jones and built a two-story mansion, where he lived for the next half-century.

As the people of Fort Worth worked, so, too, did they play. At amusement parks such as Lake Erie, Hurst Lake, White City, and Lake Como, people set out in rowboats and rode roller coasters, strolled along shaded walks and danced at pavilions, and enjoyed calliope music and fireworks displays. Many ethnic European citizens created their own diversions. Hermann Park grew out of a *biergarten* near the confluence of the West and Clear forks of the Trinity. There, the German Society, or *Deutscher Verein*, held its May festival each year. Heralding the event, their band strolled dreamily down residential streets, coaxing people from their homes with Viennese melodies, finally leading a lazy parade back to their open-air pavilion.

America's favorite pastime was also Fort Worth's. Quite naturally the baseball team that first took the field in 1877 adopted the Panther as their mascot, but fans always referred to them affectionately as "The Cats." Occasionally, they got to see their boys match up with the best in the business, as when the Saint Louis Browns, the Detroit Tigers, and the New York Giants passed through the city during exhibition season in 1909. More often

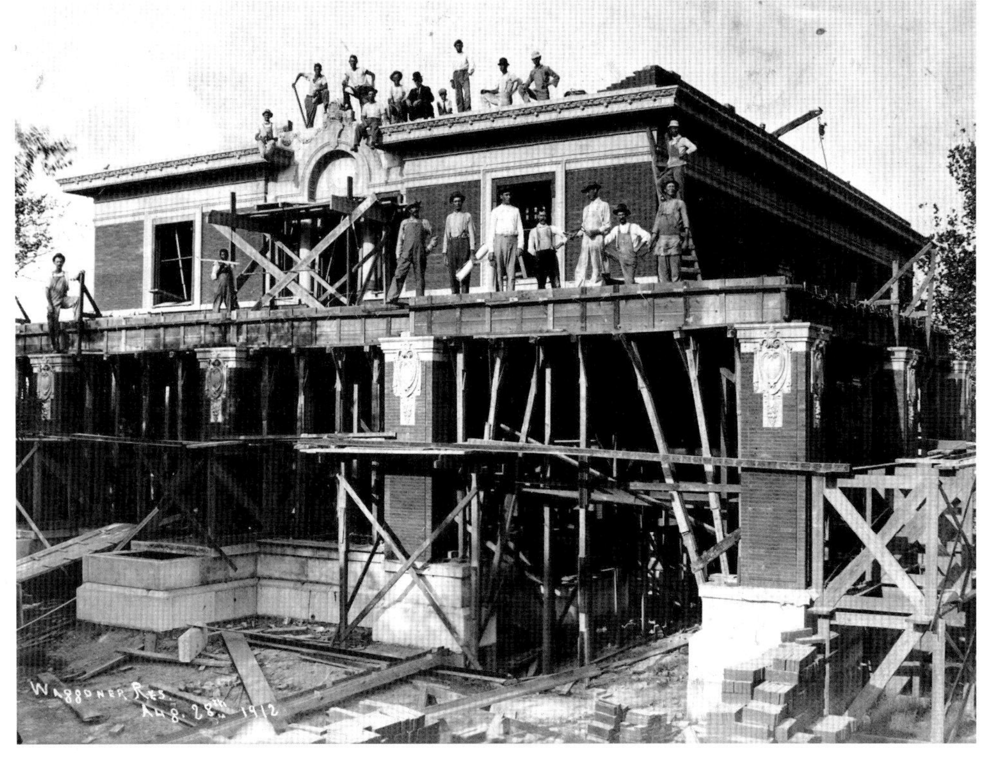

✧

A proud construction crew pauses for a picture while working on the Quality Hill home of cattle baron W. T. "Pappy" Waggoner. Although it was completed in 1912, it was typical of the palatial homes built in the new century's first decade.

COURTESY OF THE *FORT WORTH STAR-TELEGRAM* PHOTOGRAPH COLLECTION, SPECIAL COLLECTIONS, UNIVERSITY OF TEXAS AT ARLINGTON LIBRARIES, ARLINGTON, TEXAS, AR 406 5-20-13.

✧
William Madison McDonald became the first African American in Texas to open a financial institution, the Fraternal Bank & Trust Company. Here, he sits behind a partition in the bank's lobby (far right).

COURTESY OF THE FORT WORTH BLACK HISTORICAL & GENEALOGY SOCIETY COLLECTION, FORT WORTH PUBLIC LIBRARY.

they would find themselves paired up with lesser-known talent. "Claws proved more effective than Tomahawks," declared the *Star-Telegram*, when the Cats defeated a feisty Oklahoma team composed of Chickasha and Pottawatomie Indians. Football's heady days were still well in future, but on the same day that Buffalo Bill came to town in 1900, the Fort Worth Heavyweights issued a call for prospective gridders to meet at the parlor of the Y.M.C.A.

Academic events, too, commanded a place in the hearts of Fort Worthians. As the decade drew to a close, almost the entire student body of Fort Worth University gathered at the Union Station to greet R. P. Lightfoot, who returned home victorious from the state oratorical contest at Waco. According to the *Star-Telegram*, "As he left the train he was seized by the strong arms of fellow students and perched on the shoulders of athletic Coach Cavanaugh and hurried to the head of the throng of students who rushed cheering through the station." From there they marched to the school, where students and alumni held a bonfire and enjoyed refreshments.

Families also looked forward each year to such local traditions as the Fat Stock Show that got its start in 1896, the Fort Worth Fair, and the Flower Parade and Festival. Just as often some spectacular event like Buffalo Bill's Wild West Show would hit town for a brief run. In 1907, Pawnee Bill brought his version of the "Grand Congress" to Fort Worth, kicking off the show with a spectacular parade in which Cossacks, Hottentots, cannibals, and Hindu magicians marched beside western sharpshooters and Indians in war paint. No doubt the greatest crowd-pleaser of the decade was a visit by President Teddy Roosevelt in 1905; a close second was "The Big Train Crash" of 1907.

On a clear, crisp April morning, the president arrived in Fort Worth on his way to an Oklahoma wolf hunt with West Texas ranchers Burk Burnett and Tom Waggoner. The parade route stretched from the depot to the courthouse, along which row after row

✧
McDonald's home at 1201 Terrell Avenue was a fitting mansion for a bank president.

FROM WILLIAM O. BUNDY, *BIOGRAPHY OF HONORABLE WILLIAM MADISON MCDONALD* [FORT WORTH, 1925].

✧

White City was the creation of North Side developer Sam Rosen. Opened in 1905 as the terminus on Rosen's streetcar line, it featured a small lake on which couples could go through a "Tunnel of Love" before hitting the dance floor at the spacious pavilion or playing games of chance along the midway. Other attractions included a mini-steam train that puffed around the park's perimeter, a Ferris wheel, theater, baseball diamond and grandstand, and a massive calliope that lent a carnival-like ambiance to the amusement park.

COURTESY OF QUENTIN MCGOWN COLLECTION, FORT WORTH, TEXAS.

of streamers, flags, and bunting hung on ropes stretched over the street. The procession electrified a crowd that the *Fort Worth Record* estimated at eighty thousand—larger than the entire population of Fort Worth. Most of the multitude started cheering even before laying eyes on the Rough Rider, the din becoming almost deafening.

As TR stopped to plant an elm tree at the Carnegie Library, twenty-five or more men and boys were positioning themselves for a better look atop a small frame real estate office across the street. "The boys believed in the saying, 'There's always room for one more,' and finally the roof became so heavily loaded that it gave way." The crashing beams and the shrieks of nearby women added a comedic touch to the sight of those grappling at the pants legs of others clinging to the ledge, who were just as eager to keep their drawers up.

As the president passed city hall on his loop back to the depot, a choir of six hundred African-American schoolchildren strained to sing the "Star-Spangled Banner" over the multitude of cheering well-wishers. Onlookers packed the sidewalks and seemingly hung out of every window along the route; others climbed up telephone poles and stood on their toes atop barrels and balanced themselves on stepladders. The envy of the packed masses, though, was a resourceful young man who climbed the Hayne Fountain across from a stage constructed for the occasion. There, nestled high upon the monument, he sat grinning and waving a little American flag. Behind the stage a red, white, and blue curtain blocked the view of thousands of disappointed attendees, until TR bellowed: "Remove that bunting, the boys and girls have a misguided idea that they want to see me!"

At last the crowd grew quiet. After praising Fort Worth and Texas, Roosevelt imparted a patriotic message. Then, in a few minutes it was all over. An hour and twenty minutes after arriving, "the presidential special pulled out of the train shed for the land of the big wolves."

Finished in another instant, two years later, was a spectacular train crash—the grand finale of the second annual Fort Worth Fair. The veteran promoters of this unique form of

✧

Lake Como, west of the city, also attracted crowds of pleasure seekers.

COURTESY OF QUENTIN MCGOWN COLLECTION, FORT WORTH, TEXAS.

✧

The procession carrying President Theodore Roosevelt (waving his top hat) makes its way through the crowded downtown streets.

COURTESY OF THE *FORT WORTH STAR-TELEGRAM* PHOTOGRAPH COLLECTION, SPECIAL COLLECTIONS, UNIVERSITY OF TEXAS AT ARLINGTON LIBRARIES, ARLINGTON, TEXAS, AR 407 1-7-57.

entertainment drew a crowd of over twenty thousand paying customers, teasing the public for a week with newspaper articles and handbills. "No man who has not actually seen a collision," read one tract, "can have any conception of what a thrill it gives one to see two big monsters steaming and snorting and tearing at one another as they race to the mighty clash."

When the momentous day arrived, the promoters eased the heaving Baldwin locomotives up and down the half-mile makeshift track for over four hours, the crowd growing restless with anticipation. At last the eighty-ton titans backed off and stopped, puffing and whishing great clouds of smoke and steam. A band that had been entertaining the crowd fell silent. As the trains highballed toward each other "at a clip that was calculated to make the hair of the cab inmates stand on end," the signal to "jump" came right before the moment of impact.

Then…BOOM! In the space of a heartbeat came the body-jarring concussion, a resounding crash, a gigantic cloud of smoke, and debris exploding through a blinding vapor. All at once the crowd swarmed the crash site, only to surge back when the mangled boilers loosened one last gasp of steam. In another moment, however, men were all over the wreck, checking out the damage and collecting souvenirs.

In Fort Worth, as in the rest of the country, men and women with leisure time split their energies between having fun and promoting progressive causes. Men's clubs leaned toward the former, while women comprised the movement's foot soldiers. At the Commercial Club a veritable "Who's Who" of the city's movers and shakers gathered in a cavern-like, dark-paneled room atop the red sandstone C. W. Connery Drug Store on Sixth Street. There, the coterie relaxed in the kind of environment that men enjoyed. "There was no dining room…no bedrooms," remembered a woman who was a rare visitor to the all-male club, "Just a big room where men could congregate to talk, smoke, play poker and billiards." As a routine, members dispensed political favors, cut deals, and bankrolled the dreams of men with vision. In 1906 they settled on a new name, The Fort Worth Club, a fitting designation for their proprietary mission of shaping the city.

While the men cultivated business, the business of women was changing the world in which they lived. Empowered as the "City Federation of Women's Clubs of Fort Worth," their various organizations directed the building of outdoor gyms, tennis courts, playgrounds, and picnic facilities. They held clean-up days and gained control of

✧

Indistinguishable on the tiny platform, President Theodore Roosevelt addresses the multitude before departing for a West Texas wolf hunt.

COURTESY OF THE *FORT WORTH STAR-TELEGRAM* PHOTOGRAPH COLLECTION, SPECIAL COLLECTIONS, UNIVERSITY OF TEXAS AT ARLINGTON LIBRARIES, ARLINGTON, TEXAS, AR 406 5-22-2.

✧

A train wreck, such as this one outside of the city, would always draw a crowd of curiosity seekers. In 1907, over 20,000 Fort Worthians paid for the opportunity to see one staged for their amusement. The "Big Train Crash" provided the grand finale for that year's Fort Worth Fair.

COURTESY OF THE KENNETH STEWART PAPERS, SPECIAL COLLECTIONS, UNIVERSITY OF TEXAS AT ARLINGTON LIBRARIES, ARLINGTON, TEXAS, GA 193.

Forest Park, transforming the natural advantages of woods and meadows that hugged a particularly scenic bend of the river. It also provided a natural setting for a zoo that opened in 1909 with one lion, two bear cubs, an alligator, and a small collection of other animals native to the area.

The Federation also embraced the consummately progressive slogan: "An ounce of prevention is worth a pound of cure." Women helped probation officers look after troubled juveniles and worked to ease suffering in the city's slums. They rescued orphans and abandoned children, including several living out of boxes at the railroad yards. From the courthouse basement, volunteers performed settlement work.

Then, there was always the bothersome Hell's Half Acre. Early in 1901 the *Fort Worth Register* reported that the last gambling house in the district had been put out of business, predicting "the closing will be permanent." It was not. Five years later an irate saloonkeeper shot and killed County Attorney Jefferson McLean, who was leading the city's latest anti-vice campaign.

While the popular crusader was mourned, the community seldom expressed compassion over the loss of an Acre patron. Many unfortunates ended up at FWU's medical college, perched on the edge of the district. From the second floor, a few hard-hearted students were said to have amused themselves by flipping body parts onto pedestrians—particularly delighting in scaring African Americans.

The new century began with great hope for the city's black population. On New Year's Day, 1900, a national emancipation celebration convened at city hall, where Mayor B. B. Paddock welcomed the assembly. Professor I. M. Terrell presided over the meeting, and a program opened with the spiritual, "All Hail the Power of Jesus' Name." Local minister F. P. Gibson provided the headliner, reading his paper, "The Negro and the Present Hour."

In the Old South, with which Fort Worth shared great affinity, the hour was nearing midnight. Every Sunday the *Fort Worth Record* featured a comic strip, "'S'cuse Me, Missah Johnson." Its buffoonish characters and exaggerated likenesses reinforced all the negative stereotypes of African Americans—laziness, overweening sexual proclivities, and an inclination toward dishonesty and criminality.

The attitude that engendered racism certainly carried over into the administration of justice. During the spring of 1909 a great fire erased over a score of city blocks in the vicinity of the rail yards. In the aftermath, police and militiamen patrolled the South Side, protecting property that the conflagration had spared. Among thirty-four arrested was one Bob Brooker, "an aged negro," who was carrying away a tow sack containing two "sad irons" and some broken pieces of a brass lamp. With a cold slap of the gavel, Judge John L. Terrell levied a $100 fine on Brooker for looting and sentenced him to six months in jail.

On the other hand, the rapacious fire did not discriminate, and many African Americans who lost their homes benefited from the relief effort that followed. The smoldering ashes of dozens of homes and businesses, three churches, the

Firefighters extinguish the last gasps of the blaze that devastated the south end of downtown, 1909.

COURTESY OF THE DALTON HOFFMAN COLLECTION, FORT WORTH.

The remains of the Texas & Pacific shops and roundhouse.

COURTESY OF THE DALTON HOFFMAN COLLECTION, FORT WORTH.

A stark view of the damage. The building in the distant is the old Fort Worth High School, which itself would fall victim to another fire.

(COURTESY OF THE DALTON HOFFMAN COLLECTION, FORT WORTH)

Walker Sanitarium and the T&P roundhouse—where thirty-five locomotives were parked—brought another odd response. City spokesmen praised the disaster as a partner in urban renewal. The T&P announced that it needed a new roundhouse anyway, and the unsightly district composed of nineteenth-century leftovers was due a makeover. Work got started even before the second decade began.

The rebuilding effort augmented the breathtaking growth spurt that marked the new century's first decade. In those ten years the city limits expanded to 16.83 square miles, embracing new neighborhoods and commercial centers, including all of North Fort Worth, save for the half-square mile that surrounded the packinghouses. The city's population more than tripled; its business receipts grew at an even greater clip. Truly, Fort Worth more resembled the cosmopolitan city that it aspired to be, rather than the seedy frontier village, from whose past it was trying to flee.

Progress could also be measured in the way the decade ended—as it began—with the city playing host to yet another gathering of cattle raisers. Only this one would attract two-and-a-half times the number who attended in 1900. Many of the ten thousand cattlemen preferred to travel by automobile, rather than cram aboard special railroad cars chartered for the event. In fact, the Reid Auto Company, owner of a parking garage, doubled its facilities, while its competitor, the Lewis Garage, rented a Summit Avenue skating rink to make room for all the cars that clattered into town.

The welcoming speech for the event, delivered by the old frontier editor and former mayor B. B. Paddock, drew a response that provided an appropriate metaphor for dreams fulfilled. W. W. Turney of El Paso, ex-president of the Texas Cattle Raisers' Association, told the crowd: "I remember how Captain Paddock stood upon a dry goods box when the first train rolled into Fort Worth and told the first passengers that Horace Greeley meant the Panther City when he said 'Go west and grow up with the country.'" Indeed, many stayed and did just that. Fort Worth was growing up. During the new century's first decade the city recommitted itself as the front porch for the great grasslands and rolling plains beyond the Trinity River, the masthead of its leading newspaper, the *Fort Worth Star-Telegram*, always reminding—"Where the West Begins."

Fort Worth had taken great strides during the new century's first decade, but its downtown silhouette in 1910 had yet to cut the sky in a way that bespoke its rising prominence. Nevertheless, several buildings reached upward, as this view looking north from the base of Houston Street attests. In the distance to the right is the Wheat Building; the tall, white structure to its left is the First National Bank, located at Houston and West Seventh. The Tarrant County Courthouse peeks through the gap between them. Across Houston Street from the bank is the Board of Trade Building that had enjoyed an unobstructed vista when it was completed in 1889. Farther down the street, what appears to be a rather plain structure is actually the back side of the ornate Flatiron Building. Continuing to its left, across Jennings Avenue, the top of the Carnegie Library is barely visible; beyond it, the spires of the Cumberland Presbyterian Church point heavenward. The expanse of low rooftops between City Hall and the Federal Building (its view partially blocked by St. Patrick's Catholic Church) by then had developed into a residential area that stretched all the way to the bluff overlooking the Trinity River.

COURTESY OF THE LIBRARY OF CONGRESS, WASHINGTON, D.C.

CHAPTER 2

THE GREAT WAR AND OTHER CRUSADES

1910-1919

Fort Worth, as a popular phrase of the times put it, was "going some." It could be seen on the crowded sidewalks downtown and on the busy streets, where the drivers of automobiles grew impatient with the sluggish wagon traffic. It was registered in the books of thriving businesses that flocked to join the Chamber of Commerce, which replaced the old Board of Trade. It was manifest in row upon row of neat new homes on the fringes of the city, their yards dotted with spindly saplings and infant shrubs. When Majestic Theater manager Mr. Mullaney interrupted a show to read the results of the 1910 census, everybody expected some big numbers. As he called out, "seventy-three thousand, three-hundred and twelve," a spontaneous chorus of cheers broke out. The tremendous growth that had marked the century's first decade would continue almost unabated during the 1910s.

Few vestiges of the old frontier survived these years. The White Elephant Saloon, made famous in the 1880s for its part in the Short-Courtright "shootout," became a chili parlor. It was noted that on market square, just northwest of the courthouse, "a cluster of four old gnarled live oak trees...have bowed their lofty tops...to the path of progress." With them went memories of picnics and community gatherings. Ignoble recollections of Hell's Half Acre prompted merchants on Rusk Street to pressure the city into changing the name to Commerce. By the end of the decade the vice district itself at last passed from the scene.

A grisly reminder of bygone days came when workers on Samuels Avenue uncovered a man's skeleton. Judging from the bullets and buckshot that lay beside it, they presumed he had been a hunter. A reporter speculated that at the time of his death the man had been stalking a "stretch of boundless prairie." Now, marveled an old-timer who had come to town for a reunion of trail drivers, there were "skyscrapers where the corn grew and limousines running where the oxen were drawing carts."

Yet some people feared the world would come to an end before the decade could even get started. Halley's Comet—hailed as "the pride of astronomers and the nemesis of the superstitious"—was making one of its regular visits in 1910. Scientists were not too worried, nor was the *Star-Telegram*, which ran a cartoon spoof, "Our Daily Comet." One depicted the streaking comet as a baseball labeled "Panthers"; another, a grinning Teddy Roosevelt. Yet another showed the progressive former Governor Tom Campbell plummeting toward a grave marked "political oblivion."

When the "mortal threat" was finally over, the *Star-Telegram* reported that Earth had passed through the twenty-five-million-mile-long tail—"and the world still revolves." Those who attended the many comet parties in Fort Worth were disappointed by a thick cover of clouds. Perhaps no one was more forlorn than the young swain who had planned to pop the big question to his girlfriend by Halley's light.

The very next day reformer Carrie Nation paid a brief visit to Fort Worth, and, like Halley's Comet, "was just about as effective." A reporter chided that "cocktails are still concocted and fizzes are still fizzing." While her notorious hatchet "remained unhatched," she nevertheless "bawled out" some smokers, declaring Fort Worth "the worst cigarette smoking city in the country."

✧

"Downtown Fort Worth," 1915. Murray P. Bewley, a Fort Worth artist who studied in Paris from 1907 until the Great War compelled his return, produced this impressionist-inspired art on canvas at his studio in the Continental Bank building at Houston and West Seventh Streets.

COURTESY OF THE FAMILY OF SAMUEL A. DENNY, FORT WORTH, TEXAS.

✧

Pennsylvania Avenue. A residential street in one of the city's most exclusive neighborhoods when it opened, the close proximity to the business district assured that all but a few of the grand old homes would eventually give way as the central city expanded.

COURTESY OF W. D. SMITH PHOTOGRAPH COLLECTION, SPECIAL COLLECTIONS, UNIVERSITY OF TEXAS AT ARLINGTON LIBRARIES, ARLINGTON, TEXAS, AR 430 48-1-20.

✧

As modernity gained ground with every passing year, eyes that had seen cattle drives and arteries of commerce lined with false-fronted business houses became fewer and dim. Even if fleetingly, Fort Worthians by the 1910s were beginning to appreciate their history. Here, the Fort Worth & Denver Railway places one of its original locomotives on display…right before retiring it to the scrapyard.

COURTESY OF THE COLORADO RAILROAD MUSEUM, GOLDEN, COLORADO.

Even though Nation got the cold shoulder, Fort Worth continued to turn out for other visiting celebrities and notable events. In 1915 it was the inanimate Liberty Bell that drew a crowd of seventy thousand. Weeks of preparation resulted in more than thirty historically themed floats to accompany the "the nation's most treasured relic." A holiday was declared, and most businesses closed long enough for their employees to see the parade and a pageant depicting events from the country's founding era. As usual, out-of-town officials declared the people of Fort Worth to be among the most enthusiastic on the tour.

Several times aerial shows commanded crowds of curious spectators. The first one came to town on a train in 1911. Business leaders raised $5,000 to lure a group of touring European aviators to Fort Worth, where a crowd of fifteen thousand assembled across the Trinity, just northwest of downtown. There, they waited four hours for the wind to die down before marveling at a diminutive yellow *Demoiselle* that skipped across the field and made a few jerky hops before landing. Soon, however, the crowd again grew restless, which provoked Frenchman Roland Garros to challenge the capricious breeze in his *Statue of Liberty*. The "birdlike contour of the aeroplane became a blur against the sky," wrote a reporter, and when his ride was over, Garros "alighted gracefully in almost the exact spot where the rubber-tired wheels of his machine had left the earth." With that, the crowd went wild and rushed the infield to congratulate the daring pilot.

Teddy Roosevelt also returned, his visit coinciding with the fifteenth annual Southwestern Exposition and Fat Stock Show of 1911. At a breakfast at the Westbrook Hotel, a jovial TR led a hundred Fort Worth notables in singing "Ain't Got No Style." Making his way into the Coliseum, the former Rough Rider was hailed by a fellow veteran of the Cuban campaign, one-legged Charley Buckholtz. The old soldier—his wife and six children standing off to one side—touched the sensitive Roosevelt with his story about the government holding up his pension. While five thousand people inside were beginning to wonder what was going on, TR was calmly dictating a note to his secretary. Buckholtz got his pension.

By the time of Roosevelt's second visit, the Fat Stock Show had put a distinct "Cowtown" stamp on Fort Worth. Befitting its southern-cum-western roots, the festivities regularly opened with the Stock Show Band marching into the Coliseum arena playing "Dixie" to a crowd that always "threatened to raise the roof," as one observer remarked. Typical of the venue's horse show, the *Fort Worth Record* noted of one performance: "Every seat was filled and hundreds lined the walks on either side." During the decade an indoor rodeo—billed as the world's first—was added to the program and quickly became a key feature of the extravaganza.

Elsewhere, citizens enjoyed the amenities of a growing and prosperous city. The River Crest Country Club opened in 1911, east of Arlington Heights. Its developers, headed by D. T. Bomar, bought 640 acres and laid out a handsome eighteen-hole golf course financed by selling home lots in the exclusive addition. Like its precursor at Arlington Heights, this one, too, had sand greens, but at least it had a fence around it to keep out

Aviation began attracting an enthusiastic following during the 1910s. Here, a crew readies the Demoiselle for Fort Worth's first flight, January 12, 1911.

COURTESY OF THE *FORT WORTH STAR-TELEGRAM* PHOTOGRAPH COLLECTION, SPECIAL COLLECTIONS, UNIVERSITY OF TEXAS AT ARLINGTON LIBRARIES, ARLINGTON, TEXAS, AR 406 6-56-3.

livestock. A social event and tournament to promote the course and neighborhood drew five-hundred men and women, many who bid on lots that averaged over two thousand dollars apiece. The *Star-Telegram*'s Bert Honea walked away with a silver loving cup for winning the inaugural round. When the affair was over, lot sales covered the cost of building a clubhouse with eight thousand dollars to spare. The next year Glen Garden opened, boasting an even grander clubhouse and Scotsman Wilbur Larimer as course pro.

Shortly after the completion of Lake Worth in 1914, a million-dollar casino arose at the center of a three-thousand-acre park. Surpassing the amusements of the century's first decade, the beachside facility offered any number of rides, boat races, carnival attractions, and a pavilion built over the water's edge, where hundreds of couples did the fox trot and other popular steps to the music of featured bands that often played until the wee hours of the morning. On the lake itself, a double-decker boat cut a lazy wake through the water, impressing sight-seers with breathtaking views of the wooded hills beyond the shoreline.

On the baseball diamond Fort Worth enjoyed an intense rivalry with Dallas, but it would be the next decade before the Cats, or minor league baseball for that matter, gained a true measure of professionalism. The volatile John King, for example, was always the crowd pleaser, but not particularly for his prowess on the field. Once, he fell victim to the "hidden ball trick." As King took a lead off of first base, the opposing player stood on the bag and chided: "John, take a look at what I've got!" Seeing that he had been suckered, King turned on him, threatening: "You son of a bitch, don't touch me with that ball!" Suddenly, the angry Cat was on the first baseman's heels, chasing him around the field and finally beneath the bleachers, the entire time screaming, "I'm going to kill you, boy!"

Free weekend concerts that rotated among outdoor locales provided a milder diversion during the summer months. From the balconies at the Westbrook and Metropolitan Hotels, and on bandstands at Trinity and Triangle Parks, symphony orchestras began limbering up their instruments just before dusk, while concert goers bought peanuts and sodas at concessions opened for the occasions. When the band played at Forest Park, families spread out blankets and picnic baskets under the massive oaks.

Most of the crowd arrived by special streetcars, but each year the line of automobiles grew longer. Men were willing to put up with a few inconveniences for the privilege of mobility. The autos had to be hand-cranked, and drivers were compelled to get out at dusk to light the kerosene headlamps of older models. They measured their fuel supply with a stick, pinned up side curtains against storms, and did tire and mechanical repairs on the spot.

Even so, women, too, began showing an interest in driving. Five of them, in fact, caused a stir when they were seen alighting from an auto on Main Street—"and there was no man at the wheel." But not all of them were as sophisticated. Tom Leahy, who worked at the Allen-Vernon dealership, remembered a couple of women who came in to look at his Packards. "Like I always did, I started it up, and they took out screaming...thought it was going to explode."

Airplanes assembled from a kit, such as this one built by two brothers who lived on the prairie just northwest of the city, became popular during the 1910s. Another determined pair, starting from scratch, so alarmed their father that he compromised by buying them a kit from a New York factory. Upon completing the project, the brothers were left with a bronze shaft that did not seem to fit anywhere. An inquiry to the company resulted in an apologetic letter that said it belonged to a motorboat and found its way into the box by mistake.

COURTESY OF THE *FORT WORTH STAR-TELEGRAM* PHOTOGRAPH COLLECTION, SPECIAL COLLECTIONS, UNIVERSITY OF TEXAS AT ARLINGTON LIBRARIES, ARLINGTON, TEXAS, AR 406 4-1-9.

A special feature of the annual Stock Show was a pageant, held inside the Coliseum. In 1916 the theme was the "Persian Garden." Note the band, tucked just under the platform, right.

COURTESY OF THE AMON CARTER MUSEUM COLLECTION, FORT WORTH PUBLIC LIBRARY.

The North Texas Traction Company had opened the first interurban line between Fort Worth and Dallas in 1902. By the 1910s, customers were demanding better facilities, so the Fort Worth Traction Company teamed up with Dallas's Stone & Webster to build an improved interurban line. Here, a construction crew lays parallel rails next to an existing streetcar track. Long after this form of public transportation became a quaint memory, the Amon Carter Museum would occupy the empty lot to the right.

COURTESY OF THE JACK WHITE PHOTOGRAPH COLLECTION, SPECIAL COLLECTIONS, UNIVERSITY OF TEXAS AT ARLINGTON LIBRARIES, ARLINGTON, TEXAS, AR 407 1-9-53B.

Increasingly, the automobile was becoming the preferred choice of transportation. In 1910 the "Buick Texas Special"-a forty-one-car freight train loaded with the largest single consignment of autos ever shipped-made its way through the Panther City, where it dropped off 127 cars. Shortly afterward, a Chevy plant went into production in Fort Worth, and by 1917 workers were turning out forty cars a day.

The growing traffic put pressure on the city to begin regulating the movements of drivers, who had not quite mastered the law. The chief of police distributed twenty-five thousand copies of a new handbook and gave the public fair warning. "These people who take the wrong side of the street," he advised, "will be arrested and fined." Shortly afterward, he gave copies of the city traffic laws to his force with instructions to "learn it by heart." He then stationed men at the four busiest crossings on Main Street where they were expected to "enforce it to the letter."

City departments themselves became motorized early in the decade. "Jealous of the new automobile fire wagon," read a 1910 newspaper article, "the police department is to have an automobile patrol" to "replace the rickety old wagon that is now in use." Envy no doubt turned to smug satisfaction, when just five days later the new fire truck hit a telephone pole after failing to extinguish a fire that destroyed two houses and a grocery store on West Bluff Street.

✧

The Fort Worth Men's Advertising Club, 1915. Formed in 1909, the club gained importance in the 1910s, attracting every major business in town. At a time when the public was unguarded by watchdog groups and government oversight, advertisers could make virtually any claim and be free from the consequences of their exaggerations. Under the leadership of Ed R. Henry, the homegrown club pointed the way for a national organization whose aim was to provide truth in advertising. Pearson's, *a leading magazine of the day, gave the city a national stage, calling the reform the "Fort Worth Movement."*

COURTESY OF THE *FORT WORTH STAR-TELEGRAM* PHOTOGRAPH COLLECTION, SPECIAL COLLECTIONS, UNIVERSITY OF TEXAS AT ARLINGTON LIBRARIES, ARLINGTON, TEXAS, AR 406 4-3-19.

Despite the network of all-weather roads that was beginning to emerge by the end of the decade, trolley and interurban lines continued to provide regional transportation for the masses. The *Fort Worth Record*, pointing to lines that fanned out to Dallas, Cleburne, Denton, and Mineral Wells, trumpeted Fort Worth as the "interurban center of Texas." A car left for Dallas every thirty minutes for a trip that lasted about an hour. After passing through the outskirts of places like Handley, where pleasure seekers might get off at Lake Erie, passengers rode through open country on the electric line without the bother of smoke or cinders, or the worry of having to stop and fix a flat tire.

Passengers arriving in Fort Worth could get around on streetcars or take a jitney to places where the lines did not go. These taxies opened up a new occupation, attracting a host of moonlighters who competed with men who made the service their livelihood. In the space of a few months in 1915, the number of "nickel fare cars" jumped from sixty nine to over a hundred, and then to about three hundred, putting a tremendous strain on the sixty five who bothered to file for licenses and join the jitneurs union. Freelancers flouted regulations, such as the one that forbid them from allowing fares to ride on the running boards, and otherwise operated as they pleased. Soon, however, a spate of tickets put the illegal operators out of business.

Likewise, the 1910s saw motion pictures eclipse the variety theaters. "Show Row"

✧

One of the city's great entrepreneurial success stories, "Mrs. Baird's" became a household name in Fort Worth during the 1910s. Widowed in 1908 and left with eight children, Ninnie L. Baird provided for her family by turning to what she did best. The bakery soon outgrew her home at 512 Hemphill, and by the end of the decade she owned a fleet of Ford panel trucks that lined up each day before dawn at her first plant at Sixth and Terrell Streets to deliver baked goods to Fort Worth homes and businesses.

COURTESY OF THE DALTON HOFFMAN COLLECTION, FORT WORTH.

✧

Flivvers wait in line for repairs at Radcliffe & Sons garage.

COURTESY OF THE AMON CARTER MUSEUM COLLECTION, FORT WORTH PUBLIC LIBRARY.

✧

The Allen-Vernon automobile dealership.

COURTESY OF THE *FORT WORTH STAR-TELEGRAM* PHOTOGRAPH COLLECTION, SPECIAL COLLECTIONS, UNIVERSITY OF TEXAS AT ARLINGTON LIBRARIES, ARLINGTON, TEXAS, AR 406 1-30-13.

✧

During the 1910s, most businesses, such as this creamery company, fully modernized their rolling stock with the latest equipment.

COURTESY OF THE W. D. SMITH PHOTOGRAPH COLLECTION, SPECIAL COLLECTIONS, UNIVERSITY OF TEXAS AT ARLINGTON LIBRARIES, ARLINGTON, TEXAS, AR 430 65-221-1.

developed along a South End strip that included such movie houses as the refashioned Majestic, the Gem, the Hippodrome, the Bijou, the Rialto, the Gayety, and the Princess. There was also the Egypt that played mostly to a female audience as well as the first suburban theater, the Isis, which opened at North Side in 1914.

The last of the holdouts was the Standard Theater at Commerce and Twelfth, whose owners decided to go legitimate, rather than throw up another movie screen. With the variety shows went a form of entertainment that for decades had characterized downtown nightlife. The band that played outside to attract customers fell silent. No longer would patrons enter the auditorium through the bar, where they could sit in the balcony and drink beer and throw bottles and vegetables at the rube acts that performed behind a net curtain.

The passing of Fort Worth University heralded another change. The school retreated to Oklahoma City after Texas Christian University and the Southwestern Baptist Theological Seminary abandoned Waco for Fort Worth in 1910. The latter had outgrown its facilities; TCU was left homeless after a fire destroyed its main building.

Even as TCU trustees were arranging temporary quarters for their four hundred students, a committee from Fort Worth was formulating a plan of action. Organized as the Fairmount Land Company, a group of businessmen offered the school $300,000 in cash and donated fifty-six acres on a hill southwest of Forest Park, promising also to provide city services and a streetcar line. After rejecting bids from Dallas and some other hopeful cities, the Texas Convention of the Christian Church announced that the institution was coming home.

TCU actually traced its origins to Fort Worth, where in 1869 brothers Addison and Randolph Clark opened a one-room private school for children. Unfortunately, it sat on the fringes of the district that developed into Hell's Half Acre. Disgusted, but not disillusioned, the brothers determined to find a place where the moral climate was more salubrious, and in 1873 they relocated to Thorp Spring, near Granbury. The next year they chartered the Add-Ran Male and Female College. After another move, this time to Waco in 1895, the school attracted the support of the Disciples of Christ Church, which gave the growing institution of higher learning its present name.

During the 1910-1911 school year, TCU convened in a group of two-story brick buildings called Ingram Flats at the corner of Weatherford and Commerce. The next fall students made their way out to a barren and lonely prairie, where their new campus awaited. An administration building and two dormitories—all four-storied, classical-styled halls—provided a stark, but impressive sight. If nothing else, there was plenty of room to grow, and soon a new section of town was springing up around the busy campus.

The Christian enlightenment represented in TCU and the Baptist seminary certainly elevated the city's reputation, but at ground level, religious forces cultivated in a rural Southern tradition seemed to eclipse some of the gains. Pulpit-pounding preachers regularly condemned Sunday baseball, and churchgoers drew up resolutions condemning as wicked the excursions that competed with Sabbath worship. Congregations also cast out pastors whom they felt had fallen out of step with their doctrinal beliefs. The Reverend N. T. Bell, for example—"given to speaking in tongues"—refused to budge while members of his Baptist church "waited upon him" to recant. Aligning himself with the Apostolic Faith, he took with him a large following of working class families from Glenwood and the North Side.

Nobody, however, could galvanize a congregation—or divide a city—like combative crusader J. Frank Norris of the First Baptist Church. The recent divinity school graduate got his first taste of power when he breathed life into the Baptist Standard, the denomination's leading Texas newspaper. His muckraking style attracted a wide circulation. The success he enjoyed in haranguing the state legislature into outlawing racetrack gambling put Norris in the public eye. Along the way, he accepted a $25 fee to speak at the First Baptist Church of Fort Worth, known popularly as the "Church of the Cattle Kings" for the thirteen millionaire ranchers who were members there. Norris was soon at the head of the congregation, where he became the highest paid minister in the South. "Anytime they heard of a pastor making more money than me I got a raise," he crowed.

Norris could have settled into the comfortable life of ministering to the large and prosperous congregation, but the fiery preacher was determined to shake things up. "The whole city," he later reflected, was "given over to idolatry and wickedness. And I was not causing a ripple." Norris's first holy war targeted Hell's Half Acre. His refusal to take down a revival tent that violated city regulations provoked Mayor Bill Davis to order the fire department to disassemble it. Before long the confrontation escalated into a feud that pitted Norris against many of the city's most prominent politicians and businessmen. It also provoked an exodus of the millionaire cattlemen and others.

Then, in the early hours of February 4, 1912, fire raced through the church at Fourth and Taylor. At the very same time Norris and his wife said they were awakened by the smell of smoke at their home on Fifth Street. The results of an investigation sent a

✧

During the decade the Majestic Theater would close briefly, then reopen as a showcase for the silent film era.

COURTESY OF THE JACK WHITE PHOTOGRAPH COLLECTION, SPECIAL COLLECTIONS, UNIVERSITY OF TEXAS AT ARLINGTON LIBRARIES, ARLINGTON, TEXAS, AR 406 1-32-5A.

✧

The inside the opulent Majestic Theater, just before workers added a projection room and big screen.

COURTESY OF JACK WHITE PHOTOGRAPH COLLECTION, SPECIAL COLLECTIONS, UNIVERSITY OF TEXAS AT ARLINGTON LIBRARIES, ARLINGTON, TEXAS, AR 407 1-3-341.

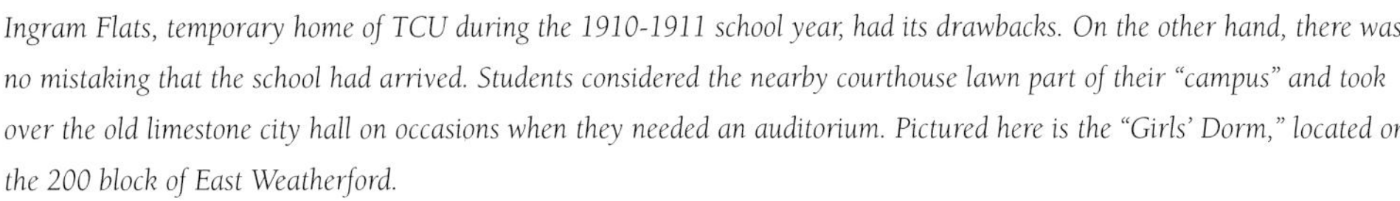

Ingram Flats, temporary home of TCU during the 1910-1911 school year, had its drawbacks. On the other hand, there was no mistaking that the school had arrived. Students considered the nearby courthouse lawn part of their "campus" and took over the old limestone city hall on occasions when they needed an auditorium. Pictured here is the "Girls' Dorm," located on the 200 block of East Weatherford.

COURTESY OF THE *FORT WORTH STAR-TELEGRAM* PHOTOGRAPH COLLECTION, SPECIAL COLLECTIONS, UNIVERSITY OF TEXAS AT ARLINGTON LIBRARIES, ARLINGTON, TEXAS, AR 406 1-63-18.

J. Frank Norris.

COURTESY OF THE FORT WORTH PUBLIC LIBRARY.

shockwave through the city—Norris, the police charged, had set fire to his own church. Claiming that he was the object of a conspiracy, the preacher produced some threatening letters he claimed to have received before the fire. Behind the plot were "the president of the Board of Trade and 156 prominent men," whom he alleged, "gave me 30 days to get out of town."

At the trial, a milkman provided damning evidence that he had plainly seen Norris running from the church just as flames were erupting from the building. While Norris's attorneys picked away at the antagonistic witness, prosecutors, it seemed, found positive proof that Norris had manufactured his tale of a conspiracy. A scrap of paper the police pulled from the preacher's pocket fit the torn corner of one of the threatening letters. The type print, moreover, matched the machine confiscated from Norris's home. In the end, however, the smoking gun had been loaded with blanks. When the judge rendered his verdict of "not guilty," the courtroom burst into a spontaneous revival meeting of hymns and hosannas.

Certainly, Norris had not cornered the market on that "Old-Time Religion." The *Fort Worth Record* reported in December 1918 that at the first meeting of his month-long campaign, popular revivalist Billy Sunday is "turning 'em away." Thousands converged on the Coliseum for a Saturday evening worship, packing the auditorium "from platform to exits." Other disappointed thousands returned to the city or stood outside to catch what they could. At the revival's conclusion, ten thousand people listened to Sunday's farewell sermon. Many in the crowd got so emotional that 983 reportedly "hit the sawdust trail," coming up to the platform to be saved at such a pace that ushers could barely take care of them all.

More quietly, several congregations built impressive houses of worship, lending a majestic diversity to the growing city. The Disciples of Christ erected a Neoclassical building of cast stone near the center of the

Students and supporters of TCU gather to lay the cornerstone for the school's Administration Building, 1911.

COURTESY OF TEXAS CHRISTIAN UNIVERSITY, SPECIAL COLLECTIONS, MARY COUTS BURNETT LIBRARY, FORT WORTH, TEXAS.

business district, while the Episcopalians established the medieval-inspired St. Andrew's just down the street. Also downtown, African Americans built both the Allen Chapel A.M.E. and the Mount Gilead Baptist Church. On the North Side, a small community of immigrants established the first Greek Orthodox Church, and as the Hispanic population there grew, it organized the Iglesia de San Jose. To the black, the brown, and the immigrant, their houses of worship provided a wealth of services such as day nurseries, gymnasiums, sewing rooms, and even swimming pools, that would otherwise be unavailable.

During the 1910s a significant foreign enclave emerged on the North Side. Greeks, Bulgarians, Russians, Serbs, Romanians, Hungarians, Poles, Czechs, Spaniards, and Mexicans transformed the area surrounding

✧

The Metropolitan Hotel, where a deadly scandal unfolded.

COURTESY OF THE *FORT WORTH STAR-TELEGRAM* PHOTOGRAPH COLLECTION, SPECIAL COLLECTIONS, UNIVERSITY OF TEXAS AT ARLINGTON LIBRARIES, ARLINGTON, TEXAS, AR 406 4-7-10.

✧

On January 13, 1913, Amarillo rancher Beal Sneed strode purposefully into the marble and mahogany lobby of the Metropolitan Hotel (above), where he spotted cattleman A. G. Boyce sitting in a chair reading a newspaper. According to witnesses, Sneed then drew his revolver and made quick work of the "Captain," as the seventy-year-old rancher was called. The killer had directed his incendiary temper at the elderly man for helping his son, Al Boyce, escape criminal charges for abducting Sneed's estranged wife. Sneed had confined her to an Arlington Heights sanitarium for mental problems, yet it appeared to observers that she was merely crazy in love. Mrs. Sneed, in fact, had confessed to her husband that she planned to run away with Al Boyce to South America. A few weeks earlier, she had telegraphed a message to her paramour: "For God's sake, come and get me." He did. With $100,000 Boyce withdrew from the bank, the fleeing lovers made their way to Winnipeg, Canada, where Sneed caught up with them. The wife was sent back to the sanitarium, and Boyce was held for abduction, the charge for which his father had extricated him. Incredibly, Sneed was acquitted of the killing. Even more fantastic was a second acquittal following his slaying of Al, on whom he reportedly unleashed both barrels of a shotgun on September 14, 1922, in Amarillo.

COURTESY OF THE *FORT WORTH STAR-TELEGRAM* PHOTOGRAPH COLLECTION, SPECIAL COLLECTIONS, UNIVERSITY OF TEXAS AT ARLINGTON LIBRARIES, ARLINGTON, TEXAS, AR 406 2-103-33.

✧

Standing atop the roof of the Westbrook Hotel, revivalist Billy Sunday (right) accepts a generous check to help him spread the Gospel to the people of Fort Worth.

COURTESY OF THE *FORT WORTH STAR-TELEGRAM* PHOTOGRAPH COLLECTION, SPECIAL COLLECTIONS, UNIVERSITY OF TEXAS AT ARLINGTON LIBRARIES, ARLINGTON, TEXAS, AR 406 2-107-15.

Swift and Armour into an ethnic babble, each group adapting its traditions to the new environment. The Czechs, for example, founded the Fort Worth Sokol, an Old World institution that used gymnastics to impart the virtues of health, self-discipline, and patriotism to its young people. Like the Germans, imbibing formed part of their cultural fabric, and the Sokol saw no conflict joining with the SPJST, or Slavonic Benevolent Order of Texas, in building a lodge at 2400 North Houston Street. Originally created as an insurance agency, the SPJST had grown into a fraternal organization that provided a place for Czech immigrants to drink beer and socialize.

Many European immigrants saved their money and opened stores or developed truck farms and restaurants, eventually assimilating into the general Anglo culture. Social and material progress for African Americans and Hispanics, however, grew from within their own communities. The black population expanded into the Lake Como area after a flood forced families to move from the Trinity bottomland that adjoined Purina Mills. A lot sale at a dollar down created a modest building boom, and African-American leaders soon established the Industrial & Mechanical College there and built a Union Church, shared by Methodists and Baptists. Although the college soon failed, one of its remaining buildings became a grade school, where such teachers as Mrs. Tennessee Smith lovingly instructed students in the basic skills. Black commerce began to thrive, too. One of the most successful Como businessmen was Sebastian C. Crook. In 1915 he established a dairy and poultry business that thrived on its delivery service to Arlington Heights.

During these years, *barrios* also emerged around *la empaka*—packing plants. It was a logical migration for Mexicanos who traced their communal origins to the late 1880s and "Lower Calhoun," which lay roughly between the Acre and the first stockyards, about where I-35W and I-30 meet today. Other barrios emerged east of the stockyards and a few blocks west of the courthouse, north of West Belknap. These residents worked mainly as domestic and manual laborers, but they also opened businesses such as groceries, food stands, bars, and barber shops. After Swift and Armour arrived, however, the proportion of Mexicanos in North Side grew steadily as Eastern Europeans assimilated and found other places more inviting.

Although Hispanic Fort Worth can claim a presence as old as the founding of the military post—cavalryman Anthony Méndez was among the soldiers who arrived with Major Ripley Arnold—many, if not most, of the city's leading families trace their arrival to the turbulent revolutions that rocked Mexico during the 1910s. As the civil war heated up, and the United States became embroiled with Pancho Villa along the border, the *Fort Worth Record* in 1914 criticized local Hispanics for not doing their part. Of the "2,000 Mexicans" who lived in the city, "there is not one who has as yet expressed himself as being ready to fight." No doubt the caustic reporter knew little of the oppressive racial conditions on the border; otherwise he might have added that no one

✧

Mt. Gilead Baptist Church.

COURTESY OF THE SOUTHWESTERN MECHANICAL COMPANY COLLECTION, SPECIAL COLLECTIONS, UNIVERSITY OF TEXAS AT ARLINGTON LIBRARIES, ARLINGTON, TEXAS, 98-97-45.

was ready to fight for Uncle Sam. Indeed, another report passed the rumor that a recruiting officer in Villa's army had just left Fort Worth by train with a "squad of Mexicans" bound for El Paso.

A brief preoccupation with the revolutions in Mexico was soon eclipsed by the Great War. For three years Americans remained on the sidelines, most of them determined not to get involved in the European conflagration. Yet, when German aggression finally pulled the United States into the war, Fort Worth inserted itself into the middle of the action. While on a business trip to Austin, Chamber of Commerce President Ben E. Keith learned that the government was going to make Texas the home of several camps. Immediately he began working his contacts and phoned associates in Fort Worth, urging them to survey some prospective sites. Soon, he and former State Representative Louis J. Wortham were in Washington, D.C., boasting of the Panther City's advantages—splendid rail lines,

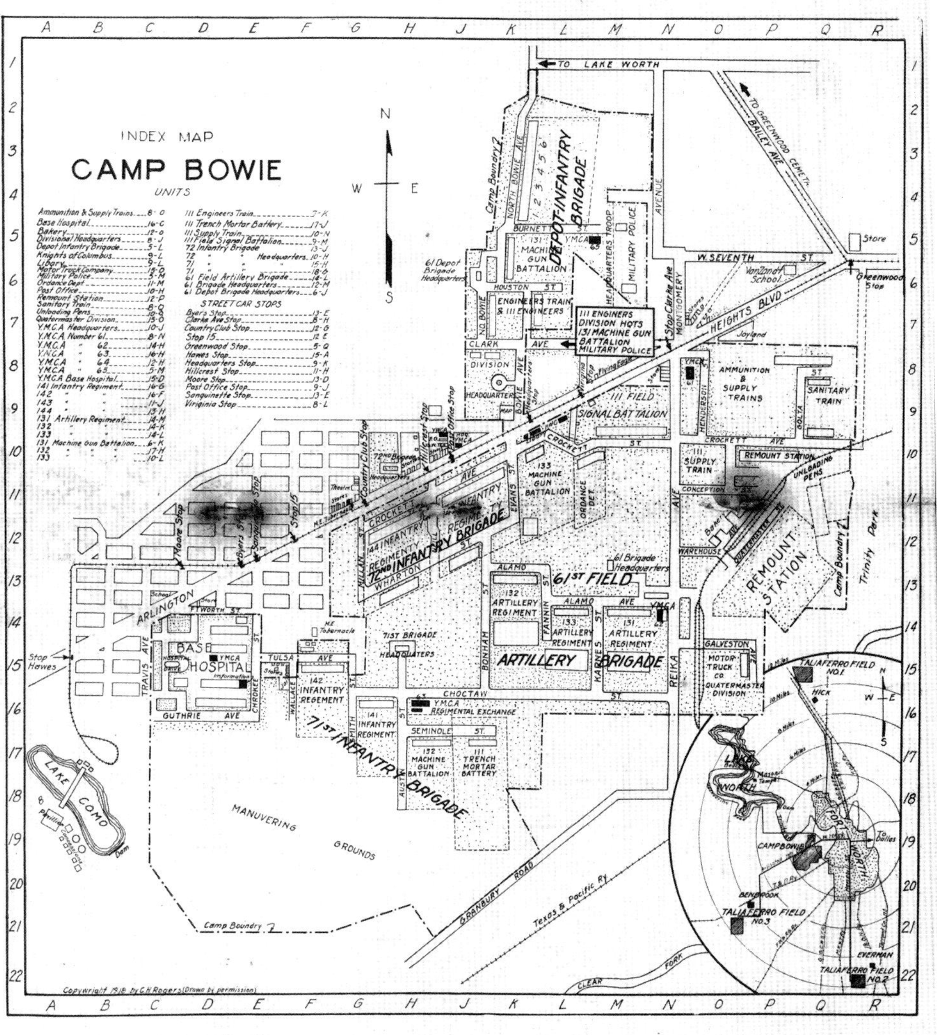

A map of Camp Bowie. Arlington Heights Boulevard was changed after the war to Camp Bowie Boulevard. Notice the inset map, lower right, with locations of the three airfields.

A SOUVENIR PROGRAM OF THE MILITARY REVIEW, PANTHER DIVISION. COURTESY OF SPECIAL COLLECTIONS, UNIVERSITY OF TEXAS AT ARLINGTON LIBRARIES, ARLINGTON, TEXAS, UA 473 1918 #1.

Perhaps the most experienced pilot who flew the skies above Fort Worth was Vernon Castle, Commander of the Eighty-fourth Canadian Training Squadron, Royal Flying Corps. Veteran of some three-hundred combat missions, he earned the Croix de Guerre for valiant service. Even before the Great War, Castle and his wife, Irene, had gained wide renown as an accomplished dance duo. Tragically, the pilot's life was cut short on February 15, 1918, when he crashed after avoiding a mid-air collision with a student pilot.

COURTESY OF THE AMON CARTER MUSEUM COLLECTION, FORT WORTH PUBLIC LIBRARY.

Before America's entry into the war, the Allies established three Taliaferro Fields, numbered 1, 2, and 3; when the U.S. Army took command, they became, respectively, Hicks, Benbrook (also known as Carruthers), and Barron. Wrecks were a common occurrence, and over a hundred pilots lost their lives in training.

COURTESY OF THE AMON CARTER MUSEUM COLLECTION, FORT WORTH PUBLIC LIBRARY.

✧

Camp Bowie during the war.

COURTESY OF THE LYNDON SIMPSON COLLECTION, FORT WORTH.

access to agricultural markets, a ready labor force, and a good year-round climate.

The enthusiastic pitch brought Army brass from San Antonio, who looked over the land around Lake Worth, a spot south of town near where the Seminary South shopping center would much later arise, and suburban Arlington Heights. A deluge that greeted the military's decision makers left the Fort Worth delegation nervous, but the heavy rain actually proved a blessing for Arlington Heights. The natural drainage there helped convince the Army that the site should be a serious contender.

To sweeten the pot, Fort Worth offered General Charles G. Morton land inducements for trench warfare training, a hard-surface road, a railroad spur, and municipal services. The city's commitment cinched the deal. After selecting a 1,140-acre site in Arlington Heights, the government named the grounds for James Bowie, co-commander of the Alamo. It took over five thousand laborers only a hundred days to erect fifteen-hundred buildings. When it was completed, the camp became the home of the fighting Thirty-sixth, appropriately named the Panther Division. The headquarters arose just west of where the Bowie Theater would be built.

At the same time Keith was vying with several other Texas cities for additional sites where the Air Corps could train fliers. His efforts took him back to the nation's capital. There he attended a going away party for General Benjamin D. Foulois, who was departing for the Western Front. America's first military pilot, Foulois had developed a fondness for Fort Worth when the city entertained him and his aero squadron in 1915 while they were en route to Fort Sam Houston in San Antonio. As they dined, the general scribbled a note on a cigarette paper, appealing to a counterpart in the British Royal Flying Corps: "Do what you can for this Texan." He did. Fort Worth beat Austin, Dallas, Midland, Waco and Wichita Falls for three aviation sites that eventually became Hicks, Benbrook, and Barron Fields.

The training facilities meant boom times for Fort Worth. The Army payroll alone neared $2 million a month, much of it redistributed throughout the city's business community. Just before Christmas, 1917, the *Fort Worth Record* published an account of the soldiers' "invasion" of the city on payday, describing the men as "a heavily cash-armed force" that advanced on the city "afoot, in automobiles, and in streetcars." The soldiers, read the report, "were repeatedly repulsed at the picture shows, public dance halls and other establishments put under temporary ban," but "they were never utterly defeated,

✧

The funeral of Vernon Castle.

COURTESY OF AMON CARTER MUSEUM COLLECTION, FORT WORTH PUBLIC LIBRARY.

due to fresh troops being rushed to the scene after each repulse."

Before the war was over, the entertainment fare was trimmed considerably when military authorities joined forces with city and county officials to kill Hell's Half Acre. The effort was praised as "the most sweeping anti-vice crusade ever put into execution in Texas." Reformers had made such boasts before, and the cancer-like Acre had always returned. This time, however, the military police and civil authorities went undercover, provoking complaints that the measures bordered on martial law. "Civil guarantees requiring warrants for arrest and for search and seizure have been virtually suspended," noted a reporter. The police station became a revolving door through which prostitutes and gamblers came and went twenty-four hours a day. At one time there were eighty men and women in jail and 150 more released on bond. Fortunately for the troops, most of them got the message.

The city had been a good host to the soldiers, and when the Panther Division paraded for the first time, banks, businesses, factories, and schools closed their doors. Almost 225,000 people turned out for four hours of marching and drills. The "Sammies"—Uncle Sam's boys—were outfitted in khaki, puttees, and broad-brimmed field hats, their rifles slung over shoulders that bore the "T-Patch." The insignia noted the origin of these recruits, composed almost exclusively from Texas and Oklahoma. Less than half a year later the Panther Division went into action in France. On the first day, one regiment suffered 691 casualties; by Armistice Day over twenty-six hundred had given their lives or were wounded.

While the Allies were prosecuting an end to the Great War, another enemy, the Spanish Influenza, marched relentlessly across the world's borders, threatening the lives of everyone in its path. In Fort Worth the *Record* announced "an appeal for mattresses, blankets, cots, and bedding of all kinds." The reports of individual suffering evoked more terror than pity. A twelve-year-old orphan who had been working in a dairy contracted the flu and was turned away by the hospital, because it did not have a contagion ward. At the orphan's home itself, ten of the forty-five children there fell ill. West of town, an entire family living in a tent was found sick, their mortal plight made even more perilous by a rain that had drenched their beds. The flu had claimed so many victims that doctors could not treat them all. Nurses, too, were stretched to the limit. Some fell ill themselves; others were rumored to have gone into hiding. Seeing the conditions at one home, where the flu had infected all five family members, a nurse simply refused to

✧

People from all over Texas and Oklahoma gathered on the streets of Fort Worth, April 11, 1918, and bid farewell to the well-trained Panther Division before it departed for France.

COURTESY OF THE DALTON HOFFMAN COLLECTION, FORT WORTH.

✧

General John J. Pershing decorates members of the Thirty-sixth Division on the battlefields of France. Note the "T-Patch" on the doughboy's shoulder (right).

COURTESY OF THE *FORT WORTH STAR-TELEGRAM* PHOTOGRAPH COLLECTION, SPECIAL COLLECTIONS, UNIVERSITY OF TEXAS AT ARLINGTON LIBRARIES, ARLINGTON, TEXAS, FWST H201.

stay. Then, as suddenly as it had come, the Spanish Influenza disappeared with the onset of winter.

At the same time another, more welcome, event would make Fort Worth a player in the lucrative petroleum industry. With the Allies desperate for oil, the price in 1917 had skyrocketed to $3.50 a barrel. Then, in October, black gold shot out of the derrick of a wildcat well near Ranger. Soon, it seemed as if all of old Northwest Texas was awash in oil as gushers came in at Desdemona, Burkburnett, Breckenridge, and Electra. In Fort Worth the lobbies of banks and hotels turned into oil stock exchanges as wildcatters solicited eager subscribers, many who put up Liberty Bonds for security. The Westbrook Hotel, in particular, commanded the center of the oil trade. The lobby, cleared of furniture, could not accommodate the throng of men who spilled onto the sidewalks buying and selling oil stock. The lone remaining fixture, a statue that watched impassively over the frenzied dealing, earned the nickname "The Golden Goddess."

By the end of the next year three refineries were operating in Fort Worth, with four others under construction or financed by builders. Before long, pipelines would connect the city with New Jersey. An almost unimaginable wealth of business showered the Panther City as new companies were formed to manufacture, warehouse, sell, and transport all manner of oilfield equipment and supplies. Will Fox, who produced *The World in Pictures*, stopped in Fort Worth on his way to West Texas to capture the oil boom on film and declared that its nightlife rivaled New York City's "Great White Way" for its crowds and attractions.

After all the confetti from the Armistice Day Parade was swept up, Fort Worth turned its attention to capitalizing on wartime developments. Camp Bowie itself left a ready-made site for homes and businesses that at last fulfilled the dreams of the failed developer who had envisioned it. Upon their discharge from the Air Corps, Russell H. Pearson and two fellow fliers founded the Fort Worth Aerial Transportation Company featuring thirteen Curtiss JN4 "Canucks." A publicity stunt in which the pilots delivered candy to mayors and oilmen throughout old Northwest Texas did not cultivate enough business to keep the company afloat. Still, Pearson predicted that "within a few years, we'll have planes flying as fast as 150 miles an hour, carrying passengers who sleep on the planes just as they do now in Pullman's." It was a vision sown in the seeds of the Great War, and one that Fort Worth would eventually make a reality. More immediate was the oil industry that transformed the economy and skyline of Fort Worth.

During the last days of the decade, Fort Worth boasted that it was the "fastest growing city in America." The cry is heard that "we are not building fast enough," declared the *Fort Worth Record*. "This cry is not coming from boomers or irresponsible persons. It comes from staid, conservative businessmen who have never been known to let loose a dollar unless they had two in sight." The newspaper claimed that a measuring of bank clearings, post office receipts, and building permits for the century's first two decades would show that "each year found the city a step in advance—some years she was a long stride ahead."

✧

The Westbrook Hotel.

COURTESY OF QUENTIN MCGOWN COLLECTION, FORT WORTH.

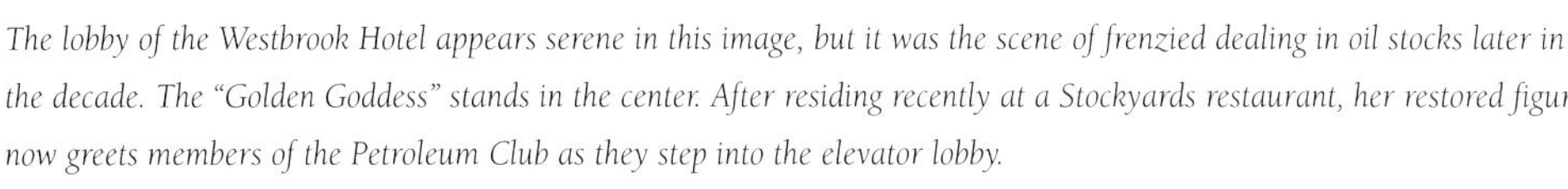

The lobby of the Westbrook Hotel appears serene in this image, but it was the scene of frenzied dealing in oil stocks later in the decade. The "Golden Goddess" stands in the center. After residing recently at a Stockyards restaurant, her restored figure now greets members of the Petroleum Club as they step into the elevator lobby.

COURTESY OF THE *FORT WORTH STAR-TELEGRAM* PHOTOGRAPH COLLECTION, SPECIAL COLLECTIONS, UNIVERSITY OF TEXAS AT ARLINGTON LIBRARIES, ARLINGTON, TEXAS, AR 406 1-31-5.

Rich strikes in West Texas, like this one in Burkburnett in 1918, made Fort Worth an oil capital for a multitude of speculators, equipment manufacturers, and salesmen.

COURTESY OF THE *FORT WORTH STAR-TELEGRAM* PHOTOGRAPH COLLECTION, SPECIAL COLLECTIONS, UNIVERSITY OF TEXAS AT ARLINGTON LIBRARIES, ARLINGTON, TEXAS, FWST H086.

In an age when barnstorming was all the rage, Fort Worthian Ormer Locklear reached the top of his profession. He first took to the air as a teenager, when he and his brother built a glider—its wings fashioned from bamboo fishing poles—that was lifted into the sky behind their father's Maxwell. When America declared war on Germany in 1917, Locklear enlisted in the U.S. Army Air Service and trained at Barron Field, near Everman. He became so proficient at maneuvering his Curtiss Jenny and making repairs in mid-flight that he was made an instructor, much to his dismay. Aces returning from the war remarked that his flying surpassed anything they had seen in France. After the Armistice, the retired Army pilot put together "Locklear's Flying Circus," which routinely brought all other activity to a standstill wherever they appeared. Locklear graduated from wing walking and boarding planes from a moving automobile, to jumping from one plane to another. His most daring stunt was called the "Dance of Death," in which he and another pilot would actually switch planes while in flight. In 1920, Locklear signed a lucrative Hollywood contract to perform stunts for a film, The Great Air Robbery. *In his next film,* The Skywayman, *his luck finally ran out. During a night-time scene, he nosedived toward a set of blinding spotlights that were supposed to be turned off as a signal for him to pull up. For whatever reason they remained on, and the camera kept rolling, capturing the crash that killed him and fellow pilot "Skeets" Elliott. Locklear was twenty-eight years old. Six days later, August 8, 1920, he was buried at Greenwood Cemetery in Fort Worth with fifty-thousand mourners in attendance. Afterward, a considerably larger number of people witnessed the double fatality on the big screen—the temptation to show the crash scene was too much for the producers to resist.*

COURTESY, NATIONAL AIR AND SPACE MUSEUM, SMITHSONIAN INSTITUTION, SI NEG 85-12327 AND SI NEG 85-12330.

Downtown Fort Worth, 1926. A distinctive skyline began to emerge during this decade. In the left foreground the Medical Arts Building is under construction, looking southeast over Burnett Park (see page 138). Its shadow, barely visible, falls toward the Neil P. Anderson Building (1921, eleven stories); just beyond it sits the Fort Worth Club (1925, twelve stories). The twenty-four-story Farmers & Mechanics Bank (top middle) towers over its neighbors. It opened at the beginning of the decade with bragging rights of being the state's tallest building—a crown that it quickly surrendered. Roughly a block farther south, the Hotel Texas (1921, thirteen stories) and the W. T. Waggoner Building (1919, twenty stories) create a canyon that dwarfs the six-story Wheat Building, hailed as a skyscraper itself by boosters when it was completed in 1901.

COURTESY OF THE FORT WORTH PUBLIC LIBRARY.

CHAPTER 3

THE FRONT PORCH OF WEST TEXAS

1920-1929

Around Fort Worth, the "roar" in the Roaring Twenties sounded more like the scream of a panther—bold, strong, and determined. The bountiful resources of West Texas stoked the city's economic engine, feeding industries with cotton and grain, oil and gas, and everything on four legs that bawled, whinnied, oinked, and bleated. This nature's metropolis was a magnet for the people of West Texas, too. Some came to shop, others to make money, and all to enjoy life in the city "Where the West Begins." For better and worse, the prosperous Twenties saw Fort Worth take great strides in the development of an urban society whose appetites and interests drew in part from its western and southern roots, but also from an emerging modern America.

Standing tall in the center of all the action was Amon Carter, publisher of the *Fort Worth Star-Telegram*. With the "glibness of a snake oil peddler, the dogmatism of a saved-again evangelist, and the sincerity of a first-term congressman," he played cowboy for America and put Fort Worth and West Texas on the nation's mental map. Typically Carter wore his Shady Oak Stetson hat whenever he traveled, often accented by a bandana held in place around his neck with a diamond stickpin. He stuffed his tailored pants into handmade purple and white boots—the colors of TCU—stamped with the horned frog mascot, and occasionally topped off the outfit with chaps and spurs and a holster that cradled two pearl-handled pistols. His biographer asserted that "the cowboy" was a "caricature, not a characterization, of the western Texan." It was something an enamored public far beyond the Red River did not know, and Carter played their gullibility for all it was worth. For the Panther City, that image was worth a fortune.

Bowie native Amon Carter had landed in Fort Worth just after the turn of the century and co-founded the interminably struggling *Star*. When the paper finally foundered, Carter "traded up," he later said, manipulating the purchase of the successful *Telegram*. With the forceful cowboy behind it, the combined daily would become one of the country's most influential newspapers well into the 1950s. By 1923 the *Star-Telegram*

✧

TCU's campus shows signs of growth.

COURTESY OF THE *FORT WORTH STAR-TELEGRAM* PHOTOGRAPH COLLECTION, THE UNIVERSITY OF TEXAS AT ARLINGTON LIBRARIES, ARLINGTON, TEXAS, AR 406-1-63-18.

had become the largest newspaper in the southern half of the United States.

It was West Texas that boosted the paper's circulation beyond those in such larger cities as Houston, New Orleans, and Atlanta. To West Texans the *Star-Telegram* was their equivalent of the *New York Times*. Most of them could care less about what was happening on the other side of the world. What they wanted to know was: "Could Bossy live on mesquite beans and cactus pods, and will the turkey plague in Cuero spread to San Saba?" Of course, the *Star-Telegram* covered the news of the world, but usually explained events as they related to West Texas. With Carter promoting the entire region, the newspaper led the fight for better roads and higher prices for crops and beef. It brought new industry into West Texas, and in 1923 it pushed the state to establish Texas Tech University in Lubbock.

Amon Carter cultivated his contacts from a suite at the Fort Worth Club, but did his most effective boostering at Shady Oak Farm on the shores of Lake Worth. Alva Johnston, in a *Saturday Evening Post* article, described it as "a sort of one-man Bohemian grove," where multimillionaires, politicians, and celebrities were always welcome. "It is hard for any financial or political giant to cross the country without finding himself making a stop-over at Shady Oak Farm and fishing from Amon Carter's black-bass pool," wrote Johnston. Important guests usually left wearing one of the publisher's signature Shady Oak Stetsons. He gave away thousands of them. When Lord Sidney Rothermere visited, his aides dryly informed Carter that the distinguished board chairman of the *London Daily Mail* would not "play cowboy with him." Yet, directly, there he was—plain 'ol "Sid" to Amon Carter—outfitted like one of the Sons of the Pioneers. When he departed, the delighted Rothermere was not only sporting the Stetson, but also one of Carter's pearl-handled six-shooters.

To Carter it was all about boostering. He reveled in the glow of friendships with

✧

Lord Sidney Rothermere, board chairman of the London Daily Mail, joins in the fun at Carter's Shady Oak Farm.

COURTESY OF THE *FORT WORTH STAR-TELEGRAM* PHOTOGRAPH COLLECTION, SPECIAL COLLECTIONS, UNIVERSITY OF TEXAS AT ARLINGTON LIBRARIES, ARLINGTON, TEXAS, AR 406 6-17-2.

✧

Oilman and rancher W. T. Waggoner, a regular contributor to the publisher's boostering schemes, holds up "the one dollar Amon Carter did not get," as he put it.

COURTESY OF THE *FORT WORTH STAR-TELEGRAM* PHOTOGRAPH COLLECTION, SPECIAL COLLECTIONS, UNIVERSITY OF TEXAS AT ARLINGTON LIBRARIES, ARLINGTON, TEXAS, AR 406 2-116-15.

✧

American Airlines can trace its beginnings to this airfield that critics described as a "weed patch."

COURTESY OF THE *FORT WORTH STAR-TELEGRAM* PHOTOGRAPH COLLECTION, SPECIAL COLLECTIONS, UNIVERSITY OF TEXAS AT ARLINGTON LIBRARIES, ARLINGTON, TEXAS, AR 406 1-44-25A.

✧

Fort Worth, for awhile, was home to the Army dirigible Shenandoah. *For a sense of perspective, note the truck parked at the base of the tower. Amarillo, which sat atop the world's most abundant supply of helium, had little trouble making a winning case for wresting the lighter-than-air craft from the Panther City. Both cities mourned the loss of the dirigible and most of its crew, when a violent storm broke it into three pieces over Ohio. Although thirteen crewmen lost their lives in the tragedy, Lieutenant Commander Roland G. Mayer was able to rescue others by maneuvering one of the fragments safely to the ground. He would return to Fort Worth at the onset of World War II as division manager of Convair—the "bomber plant."*

COURTESY OF THE *FORT WORTH STAR-TELEGRAM* PHOTOGRAPH COLLECTION, SPECIAL COLLECTIONS, UNIVERSITY OF TEXAS AT ARLINGTON LIBRARIES, ARLINGTON, TEXAS, AR AR 407 1-6-52.

1923

MID-WEEK PICTORIAL

Fort Worth Diamond Jubilee Echoed in New York

Fort Worth, Texas Diamond Jubilee

✧

In 1923 Fort Worth kicked off its Diamond Jubilee, which New Yorkers acknowledged with a wreath-laying ceremony. The caption read, in part: "Miss Dura Louis Cockrell, Daughter of Mayor Cockrell of Ft. Worth, Texas, Placing wreath on the Granite Monolith at Madison Square Garden, New York, which marks the burial place of General William Jenkins Worth, founder of Fort Worth, at ceremonies on Nov. 14 in connection with the Texas City's Diamond Jubilee. General Worth was a notable figure in the War of 1812, the Seminole War and the Mexican War."

COURTESY OF THE TOM RUSSELL COLLECTION, DALLAS, WWW.GENEALOGYIMAGESOFHISTORY.COM.

prominent men and women, but he always wanted something in return. Whether it was a business relocation, some money to fund a special project, or merely a good word for Fort Worth and West Texas, Amon Carter persisted until he roped in his prize. Once, when wealthy rancher-turned-oilman W. T. Waggoner posed for a *Star-Telegram* photographer, he held up a silver dollar: "Here, take a picture of this," he barked, "It's one dollar Amon Carter didn't get." One of the publisher's most significant coups was stealing Texas Air Transport from Dallas and winning a bid to deliver airmail from Meacham Field, a lonely spot north of town that observers described as a "weed patch." Within a year a hangar capable of sheltering fourteen aircraft housed a fleet of Curtiss passenger planes and Pitcairn Mailwings on the former pasture. Shortly afterward, TAT became Southern Air Transport—an ancestor of American Airlines.

Carter represented modernity, and progress meant that some older ways of life would

✧

Back in the Panther City, revelers celebrate the Diamond Jubilee in true western style.

COURTESY OF THE *FORT WORTH STAR-TELEGRAM* PHOTOGRAPH COLLECTION, SPECIAL COLLECTIONS, UNIVERSITY OF TEXAS AT ARLINGTON LIBRARIES, ARLINGTON, TEXAS.

disappear. During the decade the old commission form of government was retired, and in its place a city manager and council began calling the shots. In 1928 the Concho Wagon Yard was sold to a buyer who converted it—appropriately—into a parking lot. The last of about a dozen such facilities, the old stopover had taken up most of the 400 block of East Belknap since the 1850s. Greenwall's Opera House fared better. Remodeled and renamed the Palace Theater, it cast its lot with Hollywood, boasting a massive pipe organ touted as "second to none in any motion picture theater in America." When the new curtain drew for the first time, viewers delighted to Nazimova in the title role of *The Brat*. Down the Street, where patrons had fed coins into primitive nickelodeons, the old Lyric theater was razed, and in its place the Capitol Theater emerged. While the amusement park at Lake Worth enjoyed expansions and growing crowds, the boardwalks and pavilions at the old turn-of-the-century parks weathered into disrepair. Lake Erie, for example, once a popular spot for moonlit strolls and picnics under the shade of its arching willows, was unceremoniously drained as part of a campaign to rid the surrounding area of malaria-carrying mosquitoes.

✧

Students at Texas Women's College (now Texas Wesleyan University), dressed up for the Diamond Jubilee.

COURTESY OF THE *FORT WORTH STAR-TELEGRAM* PHOTOGRAPH COLLECTION, SPECIAL COLLECTIONS, UNIVERSITY OF TEXAS AT ARLINGTON LIBRARIES, ARLINGTON, TEXAS.

Change also engendered a sense of history, and in the autumn of 1923 Fort Worth celebrated its past with a "Diamond Jubilee." Several events and commemorations anticipated a weeklong pageant and carnival billed as the "biggest the state has ever seen." In New York City the Texas Club there supervised a ceremony at the grave of the city's namesake, General William Jenkins Worth. Back in Cowtown, a film of Fort Worth during earlier times pushed the box office gate at the Hippodrome past all of the first-run movies then showing. Also tied into the festivities were football games and polo matches, Indian war dances, and the usual kickoff parade, led by a chuck wagon with "Fat Stock Show, 1896" painted on its side.

As the date of the celebration approached, Mayor E. R. Cockrell issued a call for "all citizens of Fort Worth to enter into the spirit of the Diamond Jubilee by dressing in the styles of 50 and 75 years ago." They did not disappoint. Bewhiskered cowboys and women in poke bonnets and Mother Hubbard dresses filled downtown streets illuminated by flaming lights that flickered blue and yellow. A different activity unfolded on each block below Main Street. Between First and Second, Will Travis's "Negro Jazz Band" played; on the next block was the Wilbur Brown orchestra. Down other streets were minstrels and blackface comedians, snake charmers and fortunetellers, boxers and strongmen, and all kinds of singers and dancers. To Cockrell's chagrin, a few of the celebrants on the first night got carried away, discharging their firearms and setting off explosives that cost the city about $15,000 in repairs. Milling among the crowd the next evening was a body of cowboy-clad policemen.

The crowning touch of the Diamond Jubilee was a history pageant of ten episodes that unfolded on the grounds of Forest Park. Actors relived the founding of the military post, the defeat of Birdville for county seat, and the exodus of men who fought for the Butternut and Gray. Crowds experienced anew the coming of the Texas & Pacific, the discovery of an artesian well, and even such recent events as the explosion of commercial growth and army life at Camp Bowie.

Meanwhile, the big oil strikes, of which the late history was such a major part, flowed seamlessly into the oil fraud trials of the 1920s. Among the hundreds of

✧

As the oil boom continued to run its course during the Twenties, "The Texan" enjoyed brief popularity for its ability to maneuver the region's notoriously poor roads. Assembled by the Texas Motor Car Association of Fort Worth from a variety of standard parts, its special feature was oversized wheels that gave it a road clearance of 11 3/8 inches.

VEHICLE AT THE CENTRAL TEXAS MUSEUM OF AUTOMOTIVE HISTORY, ROSANKY, TEXAS; PHOTO BY THE AUTHOR.

✧

The Petroleum Building, arose at 210 W. Sixth Street in 1927.

COURTESY OF QUENTIN MCGOWN COLLECTION, FORT WORTH.

petroleum companies operating in Fort Worth during the boom were a host of suitcase operations, many of them rife with con men. Scores of hopeful millionaires eagerly turned over hard-earned assets to barkers peddling worthless stock on the street corners. Others ended up on sucker

✧

The Star-Telegram *Building.*

COURTESY OF THE *FORT WORTH STAR-TELEGRAM* PHOTOGRAPH COLLECTION, SPECIAL COLLECTIONS, UNIVERSITY OF TEXAS AT ARLINGTON LIBRARIES, ARLINGTON, TEXAS, AR 406 1-26-53A.

✧

As new radio stations signed on, the Star-Telegram's *"Station Log," featuring a roster of frequencies and programs, became a standard item in family living rooms during the Twenties.*

COURTESY OF THE DALTON HOFFMAN COLLECTION, FORT WORTH.

✧

From this small room inside the Star-Telegram *Building, WBAP broadcast its program to an ever-growing audience.*

COURTESY OF THE *FORT WORTH STAR-TELEGRAM* PHOTOGRAPH COLLECTION, SPECIAL COLLECTIONS, UNIVERSITY OF TEXAS AT ARLINGTON LIBRARIES, ARLINGTON, TEXAS, AR 406 1-74-8A.

lists and surrendered their cash only when promoters called in the middle of the night to announce they had struck oil and needed just a few thousand dollars more to finish drilling.

Most of the victims were shamed into silence, but Hale Center rancher Frank Norfleet refused to take his fleecing without a fight. In 1919 master swindler Joe Furey and four confederates in the lobby of the Westbrook Hotel gained his confidence by painting rosy visions of easy oil profits. At one point, just after turning over $45,000, Norfleet grew suspicious and drew his revolver. Reaching for a Bible, one of the grifters clutched it to his heart: "'I swear by my mother's grave that I am not trying to trick you...don't kill me." Satisfied, Norfleet agreed to meet the gang in Dallas the next day. Of course, by then, they were long gone. The story, however, was just beginning.

Into the early years of the 1920s, Norfleet pursued ringleader Furey, just missing him in places as far away as England, France, and Germany. Finally the swindler's luck ran out at a café in Jacksonville, Florida. There, Norfleet cornered Furey and held a gun on him. The quick-thinking conman started hollering, "Bandit! Robber!" and immediately a crowd mobbed Norfleet. Still, the rancher managed to grab Furey, who writhed violently, scratching and kicking his tormenter, even biting Norfleet and taking off a piece of a finger. After police arrived and sorted out the story, it took four of them to handcuff their prisoner. In the end Norfleet did not get his money back, but his satisfaction was worth far more. "I tricked the trickster," he declared. Furey later died in a Huntsville prison serving out his sentence.

For other swindlers the bubble burst when they turned to the U.S. Mail to market their schemes. Dr. Frederick A. Cook, self-proclaimed discoverer of the North Pole, had created quite a sensation when he came to Fort Worth, renting the entire twentieth floor of a downtown office building and combining 413 companies—each with a golden sucker list. At his trial, the prosecution used two hundred witnesses and submitted nine hundred exhibits to convince jurors of the doctor's overwhelming guilt. From the bench, federal judge John M. Killits gave the grand swindler a cold stare and decreed: "First we had Ananias. Then we had Machiavelli. The twentieth century produced Frederick A. Cook."

The W. T. Waggoner Building; the old Board of Trade's six-story tower (behind it, and to the right) looks tiny by comparison.

COURTESY OF THE *FORT WORTH STAR-TELEGRAM* PHOTOGRAPH COLLECTION, SPECIAL COLLECTIONS, UNIVERSITY OF TEXAS AT ARLINGTON LIBRARIES, ARLINGTON, TEXAS, AR 406 5-18-3.

A downtown "canyon" began to develop along West Seventh Street during the 1920s that grew into "Show Row" by the 1940s, so named for all the movie theaters whose towering signs lit up the canyon with a gaudy brilliance. In the foreground (left) is the Elks Hall, which would soon be razed.

COURTESY OF THE JACK WHITE PHOTOGRAPH COLLECTION, SPECIAL COLLECTIONS, UNIVERSITY OF TEXAS AT ARLINGTON LIBRARIES, ARLINGTON, TEXAS.

Important visitors often lodged at the Fort Worth Club, where the city's most influential businessmen kept private rooms.

COURTESY OF THE *FORT WORTH STAR-TELEGRAM* PHOTOGRAPH COLLECTION, SPECIAL COLLECTIONS, UNIVERSITY OF TEXAS AT ARLINGTON LIBRARIES, ARLINGTON, TEXAS, AR 406, 1-26-34.

New construction peaked with the completion of the Blackstone Hotel in 1929.

COURTESY OF THE *FORT WORTH STAR-TELEGRAM* PHOTOGRAPH COLLECTION, SPECIAL COLLECTIONS, UNIVERSITY OF TEXAS AT ARLINGTON LIBRARIES, ARLINGTON, TEXAS, AR 406 1-31-2A C685.

✧

At Arlington Heights the recently vacated Camp Bowie was quickly transformed into an upscale middle-class neighborhood. Its network of roads and trolley lines provided a ready-made site for developers. The skyline can be seen on the horizon (right).

COURTESY OF THE *FORT WORTH STAR-TELEGRAM* PHOTOGRAPH COLLECTION, SPECIAL COLLECTIONS, UNIVERSITY OF TEXAS AT ARLINGTON LIBRARIES, ARLINGTON, TEXAS, AR 406 5-23-1.

Another oil company found guilty had posted four hundred thousand letters a week for over two months and could barely keep pace opening envelopes full of cash, checks, and money orders that came in return. Its principals and hundreds of others went to jail or paid significant fines, but at least one swindler reportedly escaped the concerted sweep by actually drilling and hitting pay dirt. When he learned that postal inspectors were investigating his operation, the promoter determined to hustle a boiler to the site where his well was supposed to be. When the truck broke down, he ordered to a crew, "drill right where you are," and by luck or providence the roughnecks brought in a gusher. To play it safe, he later drilled at the original site, which coughed up nothing but dust.

The notoriety of the protracted oil fraud trials did little to slow legitimate drilling. Neither did it retard the building boom that transformed the skyline into a modern metropolis, pushing new businesses and residences into prairies where cows grazed. At its peak, Fort Worth was gaining five thousand new residents a month, and only six American cities could point to more new construction. The *Star-Telegram* exclaimed that Seventh Street "from Main west to Lamar resembles more some large industrial plant than an artery of traffic." Its own new building at Seventh and Taylor was among those that had policemen rerouting traffic. The eleven-story building of cotton broker Neil P. Anderson, built in 1921, soon looked modest sitting in the shadows of such giants as the twenty-story W. T. Waggoner Building and that of the Farmers and Mechanics Bank that scraped the sky at twenty-four stories. Briefly the F&M Building was the tallest in the state.

Still other structures added to the skyline. Lending an agrarian touch was Universal Mills. Along with competitors Bewley and Burrus, it bolstered Fort Worth's claim as the "grain hub" of the Southwest. In 1925 the city showcased its mills and sixteen elevators when the Texas Grain Dealers Association met there. New hotels such as the Texas and the Worth were joined by the new Fort Worth Club building, where many notable industrialists and celebrities stayed. But it was the Blackstone Hotel, completed in 1929, that became the focal heart of the city's social scene until after World War II. The imposing art deco building, with its vertical set-back form, copied the design of hotels that had recently been constructed in New York, Chicago, and Saint Louis.

Where there was building, of course, there was also commerce. Banking grew fat on oil and agribusiness wealth, as new institutions such as the Trinity State Bank and the Union Bank and Trust Company joined the First National, the Continental National, and the Fort Worth National. The latter bank in 1927 absorbed the F&M and put its name on the recently completed office tower. Together they bankrolled a host of businesses that provided jobs for the swelling population. During the decade manufacturers opened modest plants that produced such items as batteries, rubber products, bricks, boxes, shoes, and tools. With considerable fanfare, the Justin Boot Company of Nocona moved to Fort Worth in 1925. A perfect fit for Cowtown, Justin arrived in a caravan of about sixty trucks, greeted by "bands, banners, cheers, and éclat," as one reporter put it.

Early in the decade a series of strikes threatened to put the brakes on the feverish boom. A steel strike, leaving builders wanting for nails, inspired a correspondent to compare the situation to "the same problem that confronted the Children of Israel." Like making bricks without straw, builders confronted the problem of "making houses without nails."

Railroad workers during the summer of 1922 went on strike, too, disrupting timetables and provoking sabotage and violence. Because the nature of railroading left workers isolated, union men found it easy to capture strike breakers and spirit them away for a flogging. Typical was the experience of two T&P scabs kidnapped at gunpoint and forced into a car. On a rural lane the pair was told to strip off their clothing and lay on the ground. After a brutal whipping, the strike-breakers were ordered to put their clothing back on and run. Only a little luckier were four adolescents employed by the Frisco shops. As the boys approached the top of a hill by the Dreamland Dance Hall, a group of about twenty-five men seized them and drove to a spot outside of town, where they roughed them up. The boys got the message. The next morning they went to the shop, got their pay, and quit.

✧

The "Great Flood" of 1922 claimed over thirty lives and left over a thousand homeless. Yet, later it would be all but forgotten, and new construction along the Trinity River bottomland invited even more devastating floods.

COURTESY OF THE DALTON HOFFMAN COLLECTION, FORT WORTH.

Despite their violent tactics and adverse press, the striking railroad workers enjoyed no small measure of support. Local churches raised donations for the union men, and from the pulpit, pastors heartened them with instructive sermons. When September rolled around that year, Labor Day held more meaning than usual. The next day the *Fort Worth Press* reported: "Four thousand men and women who turn the wheels of industry in Fort Worth marched or rode in the parade Monday morning." Most of the men walked in shirtsleeves and work clothes; others, such as the spotlessly white bakers, wore the apparel of their trade. Many of the women marchers carried signs declaring such messages as: "We are homeowners and tax-payers." About two-hundred striking garment workers carried banners that read: "Do we look like outlaws?" Among the bands and marchers were several floats decorated in red, white, and blue carrying the wives and children of union men. On one of them sat children under the banner: "For these we are fighting." The parade ended at Trinity Park, where the workers enjoyed an all-day picnic and a program of concerts and contests.

The most serious strike, however, involved workers at the meat packing plants, who put pressure on Armour and Swift to close the open shop. This, the meatpackers would not do, and soon they refused to recognize the unions themselves. When Armour and Swift cut wages, John Malone, district president of the Butcher Workmen's Union, received an order from Chicago to join forty-five thousand workers in fifteen states for a general strike. About two thousand union men in Fort Worth walked off the job for the first time since 1904.

Then the situation grew ugly. The packers pitted black against white by recruiting African Americans to take over the jobs abandoned by the strikers. As tension mounted daily, a crowd of menacing union men met about a thousand workers leaving the plant on December 6, 1921. All along the line police opened spaces for the departing men, and just as quickly the strikers blocked their path. Just then, one of them grabbed African American Fred Rouse by the arm, and he reacted by jerking loose and firing a .32 pistol point blank into the crowd. Tom and Tracey Maclin happened to be the unfortunate ones to stop the bullets, but neither was seriously wounded. Rouse then fled, but was quickly overtaken and suffered a tremendous beating.

Rouse was carried to the City-County hospital, where he recovered for several days under the guard of a solitary policeman. The officer, perhaps tipped, stood down when a mob composed of young men wearing "handkerchief masks" brusquely shouldered aside a doctor and nurse and seized their victim. They carried the unclothed Rouse to a car and headed for Samuels Avenue, where a large hackberry tree provided a convenient

✧

North Side, dominated by Swift and Armour, looked peaceful from the air, yet during the Twenties the meatpackers became embroiled in a bitter strike when disgruntled union workers walked off the job.

COURTESY OF THE *FORT WORTH STAR-TELEGRAM* PHOTOGRAPH COLLECTION, SPECIAL COLLECTIONS, UNIVERSITY OF TEXAS AT ARLINGTON LIBRARIES, ARLINGTON, TEXAS, AR 406 1-61-26.

gallows. As he hung there, the mob riddled his body with bullets. Only after it was over did Police Chief Hamilton arrive on the scene. The affair brought condemnation on city and county officials for negligence, but a grand jury that conducted a lynching probe could find little evidence among a hundred subpoenaed witnesses to bring a case to trial.

Meanwhile the strike ran its course. Union men continued to intimidate scabs by derailing trolleys trying to enter the plants and occasionally administering a beating. One of the Maclin brothers, in fact, was back in the news for his part in assaulting a strikebreaker. Even though the local union remained willing, the strike ended when workers in Chicago, Omaha, and Oklahoma City threw in the towel. Both Armour and Swift said they would take back many of the skilled workers, but declared that the "strikers must act as individuals in seeking to get back their jobs," and only then "as vacancies occur."

✧

Rows of fresh beef await further processing.

COURTESY OF THE WILLIAM S. WOOD PHOTOGRAPH COLLECTION, SPECIAL COLLECTIONS, UNIVERSITY OF TEXAS AT ARLINGTON LIBRARIES, ARLINGTON, TEXAS, AR 320.

Soon a back-to-business attitude prevailed, and the consumer society that emerged during the decade demanded a range of goods and services that scarcely existed only a few years earlier. Filling stations, restaurants, and tearooms proliferated, and customers buying on the installment plan not only bought cars, but also lined up at dozens of shops for radios, refrigerators, and all manner of electrical products. While many retailers bellied up, long-time merchandisers Stripling's and Monnig's responded positively to changing consumer tastes and buying patterns and held their own with chains such as Woolworth's and the Dallas-based Sanger Brothers. Perhaps nobody, however, worked as conscientiously as the farsighted Leonard Brothers, Marvin and Obie. Just before the decade began their storefront had claimed just twenty-five feet of downtown space. During the 1920s they bought unclaimed railroad freight, fire stock, and the inventories of bankrupt competitors. Consequently, Leonard's peddled everything under the sun—from fur coats to tuna fish, and from pianos to tractors—setting the course for expansions that would eventually command parts of six city blocks.

Consumers also developed an appetite for leisure activities, and Fort Worth during the 1920s provided plenty of amusements. During the summer months, Lake Worth was the place to be. On a typical Fourth of July as many as thirty thousand people splashed into the water, raced their motorboats, or screamed into the dips and turns of a massive roller coaster hugging the shoreline. Added to the park's attractions, the Alvez, a 130-foot double-deck excursion boat, plied the waters of Lake Worth for the first time in 1925. Powered by two one-hundred-horse-power diesel engines, it could carry about six-hundred people with room enough left for dancing. "When the mercury becomes unbearable it will be the coolest spot in Texas," glowed its owners. "She is hemmed in by a line of windows that drink in the Lake Worth breeze."

As elsewhere, Fort Worth during the Roaring Twenties experienced its share of bootleg liquor. "There were a few people who neither bought, traded, or made liquor, beer, nor wine during the epoch," read a contemporary report, "But there were only a few." Peddlers sold illicit spirits from their trunks in dimly lit parking lots and made home

✧

The Leonard's block in the 1920s. At first there was little to distinguish the Leonard brothers' store from its many competitors. Hard work and vision, however, soon separated them from the pack.

COURTESY OF THE *FORT WORTH STAR-TELEGRAM* PHOTOGRAPH COLLECTION, SPECIAL COLLECTIONS, UNIVERSITY OF TEXAS AT ARLINGTON LIBRARIES, ARLINGTON, TEXAS, AR 406 1-30-18-C489.

deliveries, but it was the speakeasy that best characterized casual tippling among the partying crowd. Women, lately empowered by the vote, broke gender barriers by defying outdated moral codes that had kept them from smoking cigarettes, drinking liquor, and going on unchaperoned dates. At speakeasies off South Henderson, Summit Avenue, and the Lake Worth Road, flappers made merry right alongside men, dancing to the same jazz tunes that were all the rage in other big cities. In addition, "Exchange Avenue was loaded with speakeasies," recalled former police officer, Andy Fournier. "You know that prohibition law—well, that was a law that was never very popular."

However reluctant, the law responded to the call of duty. Fort Worth officers working with federal agents made many a raid on suspected bootleggers, although more got away than were caught. Most of them were small-timers anyway, such as the one who sold a bottle to a young Central High coed at a dance. Shortly afterward Principal R. L. Paschal caught her in the school basement passing around what was left. More serious was an episode where officers discovered a dozen fifty-gallon barrels containing about $10,000 worth of liquor. Some residents on Decatur Road had tipped off the police after noticing trucks going up and down the otherwise sleepy lane late at night. Officers probing the ground with pickaxes destroyed some of the evidence before finding the cache under a pile of hay, but the remaining barrels were sent to an evidence warehouse. There they aged, while police searched in vain for the bootleggers.

In the normal course of affairs, the Fat Stock Show set a new one-day attendance record in 1925, when fifteen thousand people passed through the turnstiles. An even larger throng visited the Fort Worth Zoo that year for a birthday party honoring Queen Tut, a five-year-old baby elephant. The zoo anticipated as many as twenty-five thousand children. The Yellow Cab Company donated five thousand bags of peanuts for the occasion, enough "to bring tears to the eyes of every circus elephant in the land," wrote a reporter. "Chefs at the Texas Hotel have baked the biggest birthday cake in the history of the universe. It is so tremendous that a truck has been chartered to transport it to the grounds." No doubt the party made up for some of the adverse press surrounding a settlement made to young Jack Wiggins. A few months earlier he had gotten too close to a bear that thrust a paw through its wire cage and mauled the boy's leg.

✧

With its sandy beach, a casino, and other attractions, Lake Worth was the place to be on hot summer days.

COURTESY OF THE *FORT WORTH STAR-TELEGRAM* PHOTOGRAPH COLLECTION, SPECIAL COLLECTIONS, UNIVERSITY OF TEXAS AT ARLINGTON LIBRARIES, ARLINGTON, TEXAS, AR 406 1-42-40A.

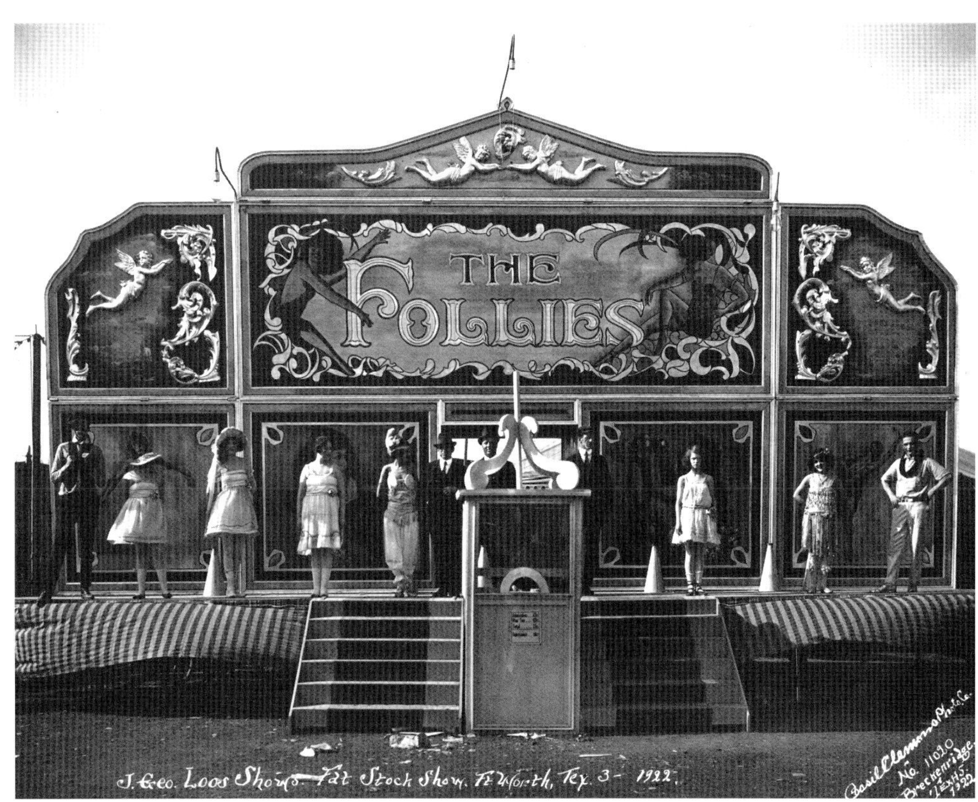

✧

On the Midway at the Fat Stock Show, 1922.

COURTESY OF THE BASIL CLEMONS PHOTOGRAPH COLLECTION, SPECIAL COLLECTIONS, UNIVERSITY OF TEXAS AT ARLINGTON LIBRARIES, ARLINGTON, TEXAS, AR 317 6-14.

Perhaps the greatest attendance records for an amusement were not even kept, divided as they were among all the movie houses across the city. By 1920 Texans were shelling out over $24 million dollars a year for tickets, or, about twenty movies per person. A great boost to summer business came after air conditioning was added. Yet, even during days when the temperature topped a hundred degrees, some patrons could hardly wait for the show to end. The early units were not equipped with thermostats, and audiences became so chilled that many people caught colds. The most popular innovation, however, made its Fort Worth debut at the Palace Theater on November 15, 1928. "A miracle occurred," declared house manager, Harry Gould, when *The Jazz Singer* opened. "Al Jolson came onto the screen and talked right out loud"—

✧

Queen Tut had long been a zoo favorite with children before this 1947 photograph. In 1925 her fifth birthday party reportedly attracted as many as twenty-five thousand youngsters.

COURTESY OF THE *FORT WORTH STAR-TELEGRAM* PHOTOGRAPH COLLECTION, SPECIAL COLLECTIONS, UNIVERSITY OF TEXAS AT ARLINGTON LIBRARIES, ARLINGTON, TEXAS, FWST 1893.

"Come on Ma, and listen to this," twittered the actor, as he led into a popular hit of the day, "Blue Skies."

Among the brightest stars in Hollywood during the Roaring Twenties was Rudolph Valentino. When he visited Fort Worth in 1923, a crowd mobbed the handsome actor, mostly young women "gasping about their hearts being weak." To get his interview a small crowd of reporters packed into a car to escape the chaotic scene. One of them breathlessly summed up her report: "He's a Prince!" Another clung to his manhood, claiming: "He failed to give me a thrill. He's certainly a nice young feller, but…the Sheik couldn't cause my gizzard to do a clog dance."

Of course, the 1920s was the "Golden Era of Sports," and the nation's pastime was also Fort Worth's. From 1919 to 1925 the city's beloved Cats enjoyed a seven-year run atop the Texas League. Five times they won over a hundred games, and their success floated the entire league into "Class A" ball. In 1921 the Cats forced the inauguration of a "Dixie Series" with the winner of the Southern Association, billed as the world series of the minor leagues. Special trains leased by Amon Carter—"Dixie Specials"—carried hundreds of Cats fans to games in Memphis, Mobile, Atlanta, and New Orleans. In five attempts, Fort Worth returned home with the championship trophy four times.

So successful were the Cats that fans bragged they could take on the New York Yankees. An exhibition game in Fort Worth gave them the chance. Three times Babe Ruth faced the Cats' Jimmy Walkup, and three times the "Sultan of Swat" struck out. Saving face, the slugger reminded: "I'm in the big leagues, and he ain't."

The Cats' answer to Babe Ruth was Clarence "Big Boy" Kraft. Between 1922 and 1924, he led the Texas League in home runs, hitting a record fifty-five during the 1924 season. Then, at the peak of his game, Big Boy announced his retirement. It would be many years before players began seeing lucrative contracts, and quite simply Kraft saw more security in owning a Ford

✧

The Fort Worth Cats and New Orleans Pelicans in 1923.

COURTESY OF THE JACK WHITE PHOTOGRAPH COLLECTION, SPECIAL COLLECTIONS, UNIVERSITY OF TEXAS AT ARLINGTON LIBRARIES, ARLINGTON, TEXAS, AR 407 1-7-37.

dealership than swinging a bat. Baseball great Bobby Bragan recalled that the showroom filled with customers, but it was baseball, not automobiles, they wanted to talk about. "Finally," Bragan said, Kraft "felt forced to post a notice that no one could come in and discuss baseball without purchasing a car first."

For some men and women who associated change with the erosion of their mores and social status, the Twenties were moving too fast. Sunday Blue Laws were passed by a city council feeling the pressure of religious groups wanting to return the Sabbath to a day of rest. The first Sunday when the law went into effect, crowds wandered aimlessly among the closed theaters, stores, and filling stations, discussing the terms of the order. Many motorists who had left their cars at garages on Saturday night were left stranded on Sunday morning. Among the notices posted on the door of a locked store read: "Hush, don't make any noise; Fort Worth is dead." Dallas, however, whose own Blue Laws had not yet gone into effect, managed briefly to drain the Panther City's entertainment dollar as interurban cars filled to capacity made the one-hour run to the city "Where the East Peters Out."

The harshest face of resistance to change covered itself under the white hood of the Ku Klux Klan. In 1921 Kleagle No. 101 set up shop in Fort Worth. As part of the larger movement, it rode a two-and-a-half-year wave of violence and intimidation aimed at monitoring morality and race relations. The Klan in Fort Worth was longer on talk than action, but across Texas, reports of lynchings, whippings, and even an acid tattoo—"KKK" emblazoned across the forehead of a black bellhop in nearby Dallas—had bootleggers, African Americans, "foreigners," and Catholics lying low.

A typical game day at LaGrave Field. Everyone loves a winner, and Fort Worthians turned out in droves to cheer for their Panthers.

COURTESY OF THE *FORT WORTH STAR-TELEGRAM* PHOTOGRAPH COLLECTION, SPECIAL COLLECTIONS, UNIVERSITY OF TEXAS AT ARLINGTON LIBRARIES, ARLINGTON, TEXAS, AR 406 5-14-15.

In February 1922 about eighteen hundred Klansmen from Fort Worth and North Texas answered the clarion of trumpeters blaring forth the "Ku Klux Kall." From the T&P Station the column headed up Main Street to the courthouse behind a horseman who carried an electrically lighted red cross. Following were drummers, cross and flag bearers, and hooded men, many whose masks were blown free by a strong wind. The almost surreal parade was met by an eerie silence broken only by hollow drumming, the flapping of robes, and by ripples of applause that competed with occasional jeers.

As elsewhere, a vocal bloc of Fort Worthians felt more threatened by the vigilantes than the forces the secret society was trying to protect them from. Members of the local Liberty League met at the Westbrook Hotel to condemn the Klansmen as "shysters…feasting on an innocent public and prostituting the offices and courts of this country under the blind guise of patriotism and one hundred percent Americanism." The demonstrators indeed had something to fear. At the four-thousand-seat Klavern Hall

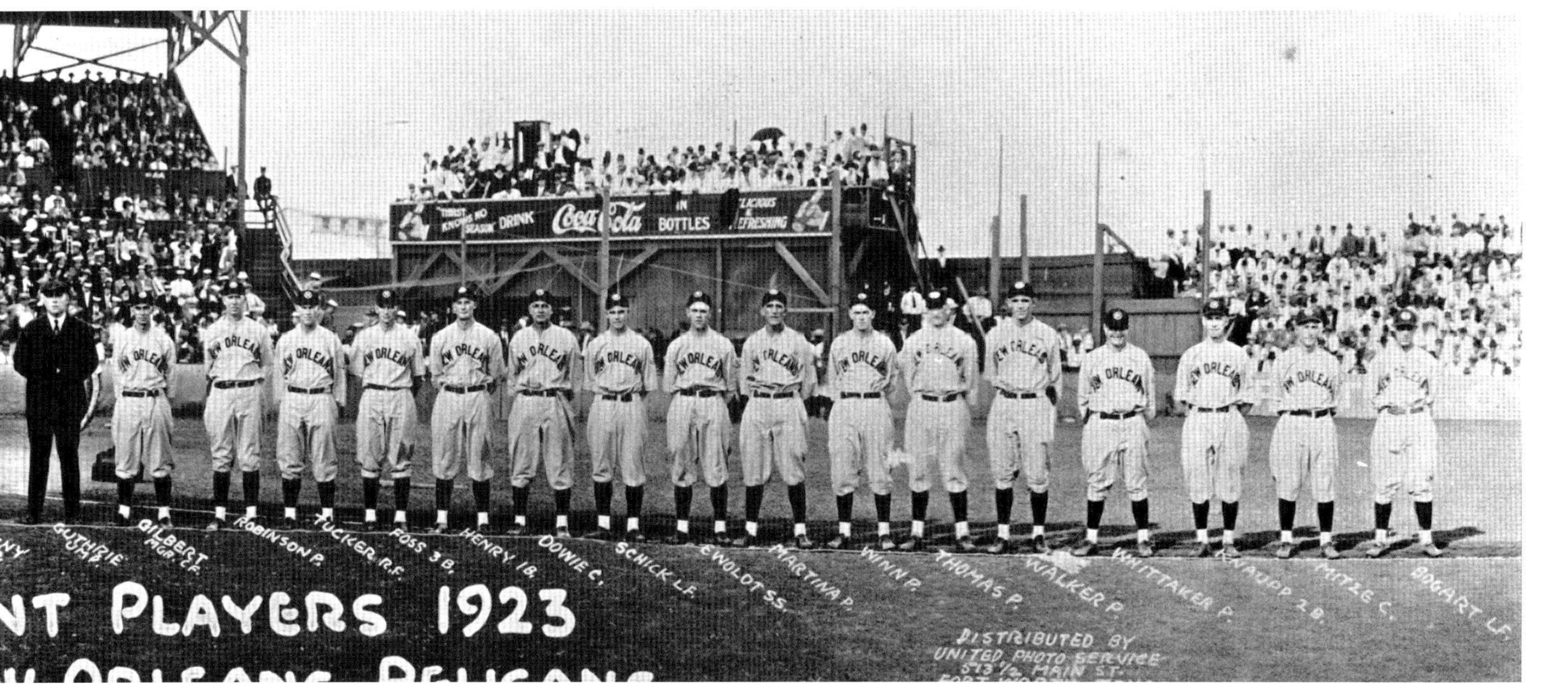

The 1920 football team of the Fort Worth Colored High School. The next year it would be renamed for long-time African-American educator I. M. Terrell.

COURTESY OF THE DALTON HOFFMAN COLLECTION, FORT WORTH.

on North Main a speaker from Atlanta boasted that the city's public offices were filled with its members. No doubt he was exaggerating, but his chilling pronouncement that "90 percent of the preachers, your leading lawyers and your social leaders are loyal klansmen" made it seem as if the secret society were taking over the machinery of society.

In the early summer of 1923, downtown traffic came to a standstill for two hours as seemingly everyone in Fort Worth turned out for what was promoted as the first official masked parade of Klan women. Just as the fifteen hundred marchers started through the business district, an airplane outfitted with red lights to resemble a fiery cross flew low over the parade route, briefly drowning out a chorus of "Onward Christian Soldiers."

The next evening the Ku Klux Klan lit a thirty-five-foot cross on Camp Bowie Boulevard to mark the opening of their grand "Beno Bazaar," featuring carnival attractions, vaudeville acts, and other amusements as well as the giveaway of sixteen new Fords. Organizers had scheduled events to last several weeks, but trouble over the lease of land and complaints about some of the games being used as devices for gambling forced Klansmen to end the bazaar early, with six of the new cars remaining in their possession.

Then, seemingly overnight, the Klan's prestige in Texas evaporated when "Ma" Ferguson defeated the secret society's gubernatorial candidate in 1924. That year the Klan headquarters in Fort Worth was bombed twice, and when an arsonist finally succeeded in burning the hall, the secret society was hard-pressed to muster the resources to rebuild. Leaders made one last dark rumble, though, when Klavern No. 101 asked for a recall of the city council and its manager, O. E. Carr, for discriminating against its members. "Forty 'protest crosses' blazed forth at various places in Fort Worth nearly all Friday night," reported the *Fort Worth Press*. Yet the fiery crosses burned and died, and their embers grew cold, and nobody seemed to care one way or the other. To underscore his authority, city manager Carr dismissed the men whom the Klan was supporting, and with that, the flap ended.

The nightmarish episode of white hoods and burning crosses was but an aberration in a decade in which the people of Fort Worth felt their way, sometimes with more emotion than sense, into a modern age. Business and ballyhoo better characterized Roaring Twenties life in the Panther City than Klan parades and labor strikes. It was a decade of adolescence, when the pockets of oilmen appeared as deep as the wells they drilled, and the thoughts of most men and women were occupied by movies and baseball and

Fort Worth's black community continued to thrive despite a climate of racial antagonism. Here, several citizens gather at a local soda fountain on Juneteenth, c. 1925.

COURTESY OF THE FORT WORTH PUBLIC LIBRARY, TARRANT COUNTY BLACK HISTORICAL & GENEALOGY SOCIETY COLLECTION.

A Klan parade in nearby Dallas, 1921. Fort Worth also had its share of these bizarre spectacles.

COURTESY OF THE *FORT WORTH STAR-TELEGRAM* PHOTOGRAPH COLLECTION, SPECIAL COLLECTIONS, UNIVERSITY OF TEXAS AT ARLINGTON LIBRARIES, ARLINGTON, TEXAS, AR 406 1-42-23A.

how they could scheme to acquire all the new gadgets and conveniences that were suddenly available.

The stock market that crashed so resoundingly on Wall Street that black Thursday of October 24, 1929, seemed like a faint echo in faraway Fort Worth. On the front porch of West Texas the commercial pulse beat to the ups and downs of petroleum and agribusiness. The headline of the evening *Star-Telegram* that day concerned a bank robbery in Brownwood that netted the holdup men $5,000. Only under a smaller banner warning of a possible freeze did the newspaper report "Near Panic in Stock Market." The next day the story took second place to the outcome of former Interior Secretary Albert Fall's guilty verdict for taking kickbacks in the oil patch. By Saturday the stock market collapse fell from the front page, and, for the moment, all seemed right in the Panther City.

✧

Perhaps the city's most controversial figure, the First Baptist's J. Frank Norris was a rabid reformer and leading supporter of the Ku Klux Klan. In his war against bootleggers, Norris once auctioned bottles of confiscated liquor to members of his congregation who delighted in smashing them to his exhortations. In 1924 he founded radio station KFQB (later KFJZ), which broadcast his fiery sermons from towers atop the church. Norris in 1926 shot to death church member D. E. Chipps, who had accosted the preacher in his office. Facing a murder charge, he nevertheless drew a host of supporters, both prominent and plain. L. P. Bloodworth, for example, a Methodist minister and grand dragon of the Texas Ku Klux Klan, vowed to do everything he could to assist "Brother Norris." The murder case ended like the previous decade's arson trial when a jury set him free.

COURTESY OF THE *FORT WORTH STAR-TELEGRAM* PHOTOGRAPH COLLECTION, SPECIAL COLLECTIONS, UNIVERSITY OF TEXAS AT ARLINGTON LIBRARIES, ARLINGTON, TEXAS, AR 406 2-82-43.

✧

Burnett Park as it appeared at the beginning of the decade; like many unimproved spots around the city, it would soon be transformed. *See p. 54.*

COURTESY OF THE *FORT WORTH STAR-TELEGRAM* PHOTOGRAPH COLLECTION, SPECIAL COLLECTIONS, UNIVERSITY OF TEXAS AT ARLINGTON LIBRARIES, ARLINGTON, TEXAS, AR 406 1-31-33.

✧

A view of the Fort Worth skyline, looking north at the beginning of the decade. Hell's Half-Acre once thrived in the area pictured in the foreground, but by the 1930s, warehouses and small businesses predominated. Old City Hall (left-middle), its once-commanding clock tower dwarfed by new neighbors, would soon be replaced with a modern structure (see page 78). There would be other changes as well, but the skyline would remain much the same until the 1950s.

COURTESY OF CAROL ROARK, FORT WORTH.

CHAPTER 4

DEPRESSION PAINS, NEW DEAL GAINS

1930-1939

As the pall of economic depression overspread the land, Fort Worth for a while watched nervously from a distance, hoping that its West Texas markets and a recent flurry of building would keep the local economy afloat until fiscal skies brightened. Yet all too soon, armies of the homeless and unemployed strained the city's resources, runs on its banks engendered panic, and a collapse in commodity prices threatened to sever its economic ties to West Texas. At the same time, the Great Depression brought out the best in a city whose leading citizens and solvent masses personified civic devotion and generosity. The Thirties was also a decade of happier events and even material progress. Magnified by the backdrop of hard times, Fort Worthians enjoyed a frontier centennial, gridiron victories, and New Deal programs that made the era a time to count blessings and even to do some celebrating.

To casual observers, the stock market crash that elsewhere pricked the bubble of business confidence showed few outward signs of deflating Fort Worth's buoyant optimism. In 1930 the city was riding a building boom cultivated in its Five Year Work Program. Far-sighted businessmen and politicians in the late Twenties had convinced voters to pass $100 million worth of bond issues to finance roads and bridges and erect new public-use buildings to replace facilities the city had outgrown. Coupled with another $50-million share from a state improvement program, Fort Worth led all Texas cities in new building in 1929 and 1930.

Despite all the construction dollars circulating in the local economy, neither investors nor consumers were blind to the deepening national crisis. As if laughing to keep up their courage, some conventioneers of an automobile industry meeting in Fort Worth scoffed at the idea that there was "anything depressing in the business outlook out where the West begins." More cautious onlookers worried out loud, their very concerns threatening to snap the tenuous threads that continued to pull businessmen along. In an effort to boost morale the Chamber of Commerce sponsored a campaign called "Prosperity Month" to bring attention to areas of the economy that seemed to be doing well, such as retail sales and manufacturing. Perhaps businessmen even felt heartened when the general manager of the National Association of Insurance Writers told a Fort Worth audience: "Texans don't know what a depression is. They ought to be in the East."

Yet already, undercurrents of the business collapse were pulling down the weakest members of society. A wave of transients drawn to the Panther City by reports of construction jobs applied for work that was already taken. When the *Star-Telegram*

✧

City fathers hoped their Five-Year Work Program, begun during the late Twenties, would keep the economy afloat until better times returned. Debuting in the first year of the new decade was the privately funded, nineteen-story Fair Building at Throckmorton and West Seventh that housed the eponymous department store and the Fort Worth Grain and Cotton Exchange.

COURTESY OF THE *FORT WORTH STAR-TELEGRAM* PHOTOGRAPH COLLECTION, SPECIAL COLLECTIONS, UNIVERSITY OF TEXAS AT ARLINGTON LIBRARIES, ARLINGTON, TEXAS, AR, 406 1-30-43.

✧

Shorter than the Fair Building by three stories, but eminently more elegant, was the Sinclair Building at Main and West Fifth. Standing against the sky like an art deco jewel, its eagle finials and green window panels became awash at night in a dazzling luminosity.

COURTESY OF THE *FORT WORTH STAR-TELEGRAM* PHOTOGRAPH COLLECTION, SPECIAL COLLECTIONS, UNIVERSITY OF TEXAS AT ARLINGTON LIBRARIES, ARLINGTON, TEXAS, AR, 406 1-30-43.

✧

The Medical Arts Building, here framed by Burnett Park, was a landmark on the west end of downtown. The building was completed in 1926.

COURTESY OF THE W. D. SMITH PHOTOGRAPH COLLECTION, SPECIAL COLLECTIONS, UNIVERSITY OF TEXAS AT ARLINGTON LIBRARIES, ARLINGTON, TEXAS, AR 430 53-396-1.

announced that engineers were ready to begin laying dams for Lakes Eagle Mountain and Bridgeport, local laborers had already filled every spot. Nevertheless, the headline proclaimed: "1,000 Unemployed Invade City to Seek Work on Two Dams." The fragile prosperity in fact seemed to work against the city. An editorialist complained that Fort Worth was "fast becoming a mecca for 'floating' laborers [and] drifters." Among the 165 unemployed men who took supper at the Union Gospel Mission early in 1930 were representatives of thirty-one states.

The first pitiful cases that attracted public attention drew immediate action. When a North Side family was evicted from their home, they set up camp in a covered wagon along the Trinity River. How strange it must have seemed to passersby who saw the old pioneer wagon resting in the shadows of modern skyscrapers. What the curious found inside, however, was quite alarming. Around a little stove was a family huddling against a blue norther that had rolled in, caring for their matriarch who lay sick and emaciated. Parked nearby was an El Paso family of eight who had been heading for Kansas when their money ran out. Too proud to beg, the ill-clothed parents and their children sat shivering in their car, pondering their limited options. Authorities responded to the plight of these unfortunates by arranging for the sick woman to spend a few days at the City-County Hospital. They also set up a makeshift tourist camp for the others and anyone else who might find themselves in similar circumstances.

All too soon such heartrending scenes became commonplace, stretching the resources of relief agencies and well-to-do individuals to the limit. When 1930 finally ended, the City-County Hospital reported that 7,510 free cases during that year had almost overwhelmed them. Little did they know that in 1931 the line of patients unable to pay for the hospital's services would grow to 36,433.

With so many men and women on the dole, city officials took measures to frustrate the "hobo, the panhandler, and the professional beggar." A Bureau of Welfare

✧

The Fort Worth Public Market briefly defied the bleak outlook for agriculture, opening its doors in 1930 to fourteen commercial vendors and renting out stalls to 132 hopeful farmers.

COURTESY OF THE *FORT WORTH STAR-TELEGRAM* PHOTOGRAPH COLLECTION, SPECIAL COLLECTIONS, UNIVERSITY OF TEXAS AT ARLINGTON LIBRARIES, ARLINGTON, TEXAS, AR, 406 5-8-13.

Investigation and Registration established a network to screen out unsavory characters thought to be milking the system. What they found was that the vast majority were simply desperate. On one particular morning thirty unemployed men and women called on the bureau seeking jobs. Most of them showed up in work clothes and carried letters of recommendation and military veteran credentials—anything to gain an edge. They also made it clear they wanted work, not relief. Most of them were supporting families, and a few shed bitter tears when officials coaxed them into providing details of their conditions.

Some of the jobs the bureau was finding for its virtually exclusive Anglo clients involved work that whites had traditionally shunned. African Americans and Hispanics had routinely filled such positions as yard workers, janitors, common laborers, and maids. Yet now they found themselves being shouldered aside. Churches and an extended kinship network cultivated support for the jobless in the black community, but the barrios were still developing. An increasingly hostile mood and the efficient work of the Immigration and Naturalization Service resulted in the exodus of roughly half of the estimated five thousand Mexicanos who lived in the city in 1930. But, when INS agents persisted in harassing one North Side alien, he told them they could deport him, but added, "I'm coming back, so come back in thirty days and get me again." The plucky response won the agents' admiration; then and afterwards, they left him alone.

While drifters had to fend for themselves, the Hotel Texas was more welcoming—at least to those who had the means to travel in style.

COURTESY OF THE *FORT WORTH STAR-TELEGRAM* PHOTOGRAPH COLLECTION, SPECIAL COLLECTIONS, UNIVERSITY OF TEXAS AT ARLINGTON LIBRARIES, ARLINGTON, TEXAS, AR 406 1-31-3.

By the spring of 1932 it became clear that prosperity was no longer "just around the corner." Some well intended programs crusading under such banners as the "War on Depression" and the "Job Finders Club" did not seem to be making the soup lines any shorter. For the first time, officials at City Hall locked the front doors "to prevent its passageways from being converted into a dormitory by the disinherited 'floaters.'" In the meantime a committee assembled by the Chamber of Commerce to assess the health of the city's economy reluctantly reported: "It is the consensus of the executive committee on unemployment that a real emergency crisis exists in Fort Worth."

To its credit, the Panther City responded. The Community Chest distributed thousands of meals to the destitute and organized a small army of volunteers to seek out those who were "too proud to beg." In its busiest month the City Health and Welfare Department provided

During the Depression, many people, such as this drifter, pausing in front of the post office, came to Tarrant County only out of a sense of desperation.

COURTESY OF THE LIBRARY OF CONGRESS, WASHINGTON, D.C.

A Civilian Conservation Corps camp, located at Lake Worth, provided relief for many unemployed Fort Worthians.

COURTESY OF THE *FORT WORTH STAR-TELEGRAM* PHOTOGRAPH COLLECTION, SPECIAL COLLECTIONS, UNIVERSITY OF TEXAS AT ARLINGTON LIBRARIES, ARLINGTON, TEXAS, AR 406 1-42-39.

assistance for 2,667 families and boarded a hundred transients above the old Central Fire Station, where they enjoyed a hot shower, mattresses, and heavy woolen blankets. On New Years Day 1931 the Lena Pope Home for orphans bedded down its first twenty-five occupants, secure from the sleet that was falling outside.

Of course, the list of religious charities and the kindnesses of individuals were endless. More lighthearted than poignant was the good work of a congregation in rural Keller. When it learned that transients at the Union Gospel Mission were going hungry, they donated a live steer. Fortunately, one of the perplexed volunteers knew someone at the Blue Bonnet Packing Company, who dressed and prepared the animal free of charge. In another unusual case an insurance executive arranged to return a $3,500 home to an inconsolable client whose foreclosure had swept away $2,000 worth of equity.

Yet, while many gave, others took. Holdups became almost commonplace, and more than once, victims reported that apologetic robbers demanded money, intoning: "I hate to do this, but I must." The level of desperation was marked by a willingness to risk life and freedom for a pittance. One frantic robber hit nine victims, but netted only $169.40 before his luck ran out.

✧

The "House of Mystery," the residence of O. D. Stevens in Handley.

COURTESY OF THE *FORT WORTH STAR-TELEGRAM* PHOTOGRAPH COLLECTION, SPECIAL COLLECTIONS, UNIVERSITY OF TEXAS AT ARLINGTON LIBRARIES, ARLINGTON, TEXAS, AR 406 2-105-36.

✧

Fort Worthians could briefly escape the troubled times by going to the theater at any of several opulent venues. The New Liberty on lower Main Street was not the equal of such spots as the Majestic or the Hollywood, but the air-conditioning was just as cold, and the popcorn every bit as fresh.

COURTESY OF THE W. D. SMITH PHOTOGRAPH COLLECTION, SPECIAL COLLECTIONS, UNIVERSITY OF TEXAS AT ARLINGTON LIBRARIES, ARLINGTON, TEXAS, AR 407 3-40.

One of Fort Worth's most spectacular crimes—involving a daring heist of the U.S. Mail and a double-cross that ended in murder—exposed the nefarious work of O. D. Stevens, "alleged head of a major 'crime corporation'" that operated throughout the Southwest. His first line of business was running a narcotics and bootlegging ring, but in February 1933 he and six associates held up the mailroom at the Texas & Pacific station, where they picked out several Federal Reserve currency sacks containing about $72,000. After lying low for a while, Stevens headed for New York City early in July and there laundered the money.

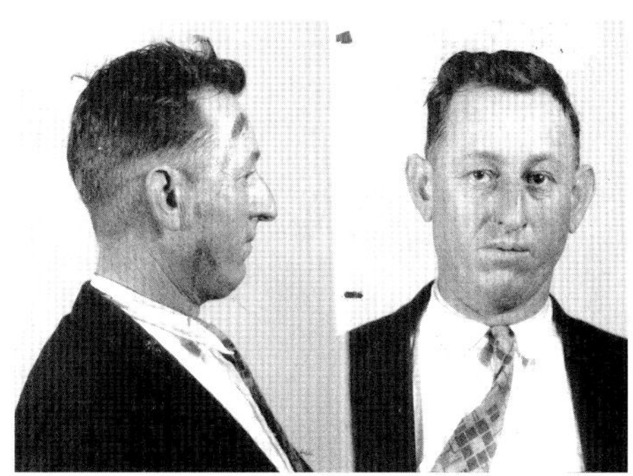

✧

O. D. Stevens' mugshot .

COURTESY OF THE *FORT WORTH STAR-TELEGRAM* PHOTOGRAPH COLLECTION, SPECIAL COLLECTIONS, UNIVERSITY OF TEXAS AT ARLINGTON LIBRARIES, ARLINGTON, TEXAS, AR 406 2-105-37.

A few days following his return, the gang was scheduled to meet at Stevens' Handley residence, described by a *Fort Worth Press* reporter as a "feudal estate" of fifty acres, the house itself standing "like a fortress on a knoll that overlooked every possible entrance." Three of the robbers, Jack Sturdivant and the Rutherford brothers, High and Shorty, showed up early and demanded their split of the loot, which no doubt antagonized their methodical-minded boss. The men's insistence, however, brought only a payment in lead issued at near point-blank range, rendering their faces almost unrecognizable.

After stripping the dead men and packing their clothes in a hogwire cage, Stevens and W. D. May, his neighbor and closest associate, along with the other two robber-murderers, brothers M. T. and M. D. Howard, fashioned a similar truss for the bodies. They added two one-hundred-pound sacks of concrete for good measure. By the light of the moon, Stevens and his cohorts dumped the separate bundles into the Trinity River from bridges four miles apart. The scheme began to unravel when word filtered to police that the wives of Jack and Shorty were asking questions about their missing husbands. Directly, a seven-year-old boy spotted the bundle of clothing just beneath the surface where it was dropped. News of the discovery soon led a man living near the other bridge to report to police some suspicious activity

✧

W. A. Pulliam (left) and W. T. Evans, county investigators, display the clothes of Jack Sturdivant and High and Shorty Rutherford, the three men who fell victim to O. D. Stevens' double-cross.

COURTESY OF THE *FORT WORTH STAR-TELEGRAM* PHOTOGRAPH COLLECTION, SPECIAL COLLECTIONS, UNIVERSITY OF TEXAS AT ARLINGTON LIBRARIES, ARLINGTON, TEXAS, AR 406 2-105-35.

that he had earlier assumed was simply "spooners" enjoying a tryst. It was there, just beyond the Allbright Bridge at First Street, where police located the bound corpses. Piecing together what had happened, the lawmen soon rounded up the four remaining members of the gang and charged them with murder and robbery.

Following a series of trials, the court condemned Stevens and May to the electric chair; the Howards got long prison sentences. Eventually, May was put to death. Stevens, however, won a reversal, and for his part in the robbery spent only sixteen years of a twenty-seven-year stretch in federal penitentiaries at Alcatraz and Leavenworth.

The story did not end there, however. An immediate search of the premises exposed all kinds of secret compartments in the walls, concealed entrances and exits, and even a hidden room under a stairwell. And although police turned up an estimated hundred thousand dollars in narcotics, only half of the loot from the T&P robbery was ever found. Over time, as the actual events grew dim, stories of ghosts and lucre grew in their place. The "house of mystery" for decades afterward continued to draw curious teenagers, treasure hunters, and junkies who plagued the succession of hapless owners.

Every bit as malicious were several outlaws on the FBI's "Most Wanted" list who passed through Fort Worth during the decade. "Machine Gun" George Kelly hid out for a while at his mother-in-law's house at 857 Mulkey Street, where neighbors occasionally spotted his sixteen-cylinder automobile rolling into the driveway. Later he used a shanty northwest of the city in the little community of Paradise, where he held a kidnapped Oklahoma oilman. When the dragnet began to center on North Texas, the FBI and local law enforcement officials met at the Blackstone Hotel to plan their strategy. Kelly got away that time, but he and his wife were later caught in Memphis, Tennessee. There, FBI agents burst into their hotel room, prompting Kelly to throw up his hands and plead, "Don't shoot. It's G-Men." In that way, another euphemism entered the popular lexicon.

Bonnie and Clyde were also occasional Cowtown visitors. Once, the couple reportedly checked in at the Stockyards Hotel and occupied a strategic corner room overlooking North Main and Exchange. Just up the highway, outside of Grapevine, they had recently slain a motorcycle patrolman, provoking a *Star-Telegram* headline that referred to Bonnie Parker as a "Cigar-Smoking Woman." So incensed was her psychotic companion that he mailed a death threat to publisher Amon Carter, warning that "Another remark about my underworld mate and I will end such men as you might quick."

Although none of the era's most notorious outlaws made any gunpoint withdrawals from banks in Fort Worth, there were nevertheless two attempted holdups of the Stockyards National Bank. The first one came on a "dog day" August afternoon. A nervous, fidgety man, later identified as shop owner Nathan Martin, walked up to the counter and demanded $10,000: "I am desperate, I have a price on my head, and I don't care anyway." Under his arm he carried a satchel packed with nitroglycerin. While the bank's vice president, Fred Pelton, went to vault, president W. L. Pier managed to slip away and telephone the police. Just as Pelton was returning, Martin spotted some officers and panicked. Whether he dropped the satchel or, as one report said, spiked the bottle of nitroglycerin on the marble floor, one thing was certain. A deafening explosion rocked the building, stripping the leaves from trees as far as a hundred yards away. Inside the lobby lay the mangled bodies of the robber and banker Pelton amidst the debris of twisted steel and splintered wood.

In the second attempt, a gang of four would-be robbers mistook a motorcycle rider for a policeman and confused his

✧

The Stockyards National Bank and its lobby, much the same as they looked on the day an attempted robbery went tragically awry.

TOP IMAGE COURTESY OF DALTON HOFFMAN COLLECTION, FORT WORTH. BOTTOM IMAGE COURTESY OF THE SPECIAL COLLECTIONS DIVISION, THE UNIVERSITY OF TEXAS AT ARLINGTON LIBRARIES, ARLINGTON, TEXAS, AR406 1-29-52.

✧

Broadcasting live from Fort Worth, Wilbert Lee "Pappy" O'Daniel began seducing the masses in 1928 with his homespun radio program, sponsored by Light Crust Flour. The show, which reached an audience that covered much of the state, also launched the music career of Bob Wills, the "King of Western Swing," who soon left to form the legendary Texas Playboys. Riding his radio popularity, O'Daniel founded his own Hillbilly Flour Company in 1935 and filed for governor three years later at the urging of his listeners. "Pass the biscuits, Pappy!" became his campaign slogan; the Ten Commandments his platform. While he posed as a man of the people, he was in reality a product of public relations men and reneged on his most of his Populist promises. Nevertheless, Texans again elected him governor in 1940, and in 1941 he narrowly defeated Lyndon B. Johnson in a special election for a vacant U.S. Senate seat. O'Daniel's folksy style proved an ill fit for that august chamber. Shunned by his colleagues and suffering a seven percent public approval rating, his political career ended in 1948.

COURTESY OF THE *FORT WORTH STAR-TELEGRAM* PHOTOGRAPH COLLECTION, SPECIAL COLLECTIONS, UNIVERSITY OF TEXAS AT ARLINGTON LIBRARIES, ARLINGTON, TEXAS, FWST 719 NEG #2.

backfiring engine for gunshots. Abandoning the heist, they piled into a black sedan and lit out for Saginaw, north of the city. After knocking out the back window they fired blindly at their phantom pursuer. By the time several citizens and a policeman actually did give chase, the outlaws had peppered the road with tacks they had brought along to cover their getaway. The only winners in the affair were local garages that specialized in fixing flats.

Rather than pariahs, the Depression-era bank robbers were heralded by many plain folk as heroes in the mold of the Wild Bunch. Like the Old West outlaws, these modern-day desperadoes were striking a blow for men and women who had lost their hard-earned savings when the institutions they had trusted became insolvent. The failure of one of the city's largest banks provided a bitter object lesson.

On the last day of January 1930, about a half hour before closing time, a run on the Texas National Bank emptied the vault, and soon it was discovered that the institution was $1.2 million in the red. Business leaders in the city tried to reassure the panicky customers of other banks that mismanagement, rather than general economic conditions, led to the failure. A judge agreed. After seizing their personal assets, he sentenced the bank's top two officers to the federal penitentiary at Leavenworth. The president, B. B. Samuels, learned of the verdict while in the hospital, recovering from an "acute heart condition" that saw the 170-pound man wither to a mere 70 pounds.

However repentant they were, the bankers got little sympathy in the wake of hardships suffered by former customers. One, a retired schoolteacher, was described as a "very gaunt woman with white hair pulled severely to the top of her head." For years she had lived frugally and saved $5,000 from a $100 monthly salary. Her loss forced her back into the classroom, where she taught the grandchildren of former students.

Even more tragic was the story of Louis B. Ward, a forty-seven-year old cashier of the failed bank. After losing his money he

✧

At a time when fascism was seizing hearts and minds in other parts of the world, "Pappy" O'Daniel pandered many of the same transparent themes to gullible Texans, who ate it up as readily as his Hillbilly biscuits.

COURTESY OF THE TEXAS STATE ARCHIVES AND LIBRARY, AUSTIN.

✧

Bob Wills, who got his break helping the future governor peddle his Light Crust Flour, developed a sound—"western swing"—that has proven far more enduring than the politics of his one-time employer.

COURTESY OF THE JACK WHITE PHOTOGRAPH COLLECTION, SPECIAL COLLECTIONS, UNIVERSITY OF TEXAS AT ARLINGTON LIBRARIES, ARLINGTON, TEXAS, AR407 1-7-68.

climbed the steps of the police station and pulled out a .38 revolver. In front of an unsuspecting crowd milling about the street, he pressed the gun against his temple and pulled the trigger. A suicide note on the Texas National's letterhead read: "To whom it may concern....My health is gone, my job is gone, and probably many of my friends. This is my only way of providing for my family—that is, by making available to them my life insurance money, that they may have something to live on."

The failure of the Texas National inspired rumors that other Fort Worth banks were close to tanking, but once again the response by city leaders led to one of the decade's finest hours. Bill McDonald, whose Fraternal Bank and Trust Company lost $209,500 that it had deposited in the Texas National, put an abrupt end to questions about the health of the institution on which the black community depended. "I was responsible for placing the loan," he said, and, to his enduring credit, McDonald dipped into his own fortune and unceremoniously paid it back. The *Fort Worth Star-Telegram* did its part by focusing on the health of the financial community in general. It regularly highlighted reports of "all-time deposit records" and published lists of "cash balance on hand" along with gross deposits that showed the assets of local banks in the tens of millions.

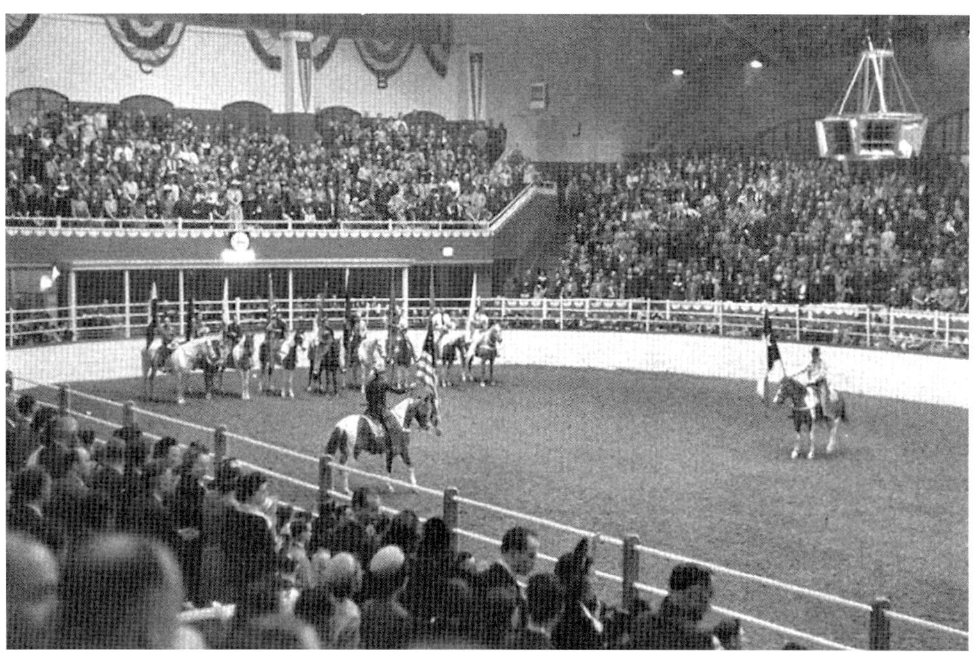

✧

The Southwestern Exposition and Fat Stock Show provided a welcome distraction during these hard times.

COURTESY OF THE FORT WORTH PUBLIC LIBRARY.

After overcoming one last crisis early in 1931, it seemed as if Fort Worth had become inoculated against the grippe of panic that elsewhere continued to infect the industry like a fever it could not entirely shake. The month after the Texas National disaster, rumors began flying that the First National Bank was in similar trouble. At two o'clock on February 18 a herd of agitated customers invaded the lobby demanding their money. It was a classic "bank run," or, in the Texanese of the institution's largest depositor, W. T. Waggoner, a "money stampede."

With the distressed crowd threatening to get unruly, directors of the First National Bank and city leaders such as Amon Carter and merchant William Monnig emerged from a quick, but decisive conference and announced that the institution would remain open all night to serve its depositors. For five hours the drama unfolded. Speech after speech importuned customers to remain calm. The arrival of armed guards carrying in sacks of coin and currency from the Federal Reserve Bank in Dallas underscored the message. It was "Pappy" Waggoner, however, who finally won the depositors' confidence. Promising to sell every cow and oil well, he raised a hand in oath: "I hereby pledge to you every cent I own and possess in this world that you will not lose a single dollar in this bank."

Hesitant applause turned to light cheering when Waggoner repeated his vow. Then, the crisis turned into a party. Amon Carter had caterers bring in sandwiches and hot dogs, and two orchestras from the Hotel Texas filled the lobby with merry music. Officers looked the other way as customers passed around flasks of bootleg liquor, singing "Hail, Hail, the Gang's All Here." All the while cashiers serviced lines of men and women

✧

Fort Worth in 1936, looking east from West Seventh Street. By this time the worst of the Great Depression was over, and the local economy was beginning to show signs of vigor.

COURTESY OF THE JACK WHITE PHOTOGRAPH COLLECTION, SPECIAL COLLECTIONS, UNIVERSITY OF TEXAS AT ARLINGTON LIBRARIES, ARLINGTON, TEXAS, AR 407 9-35.

✧

Labor Day participants flaunt the fruits of the Twenty-first Amendment, which ended Prohibition.

COURTESY OF THE FORT WORTH PUBLIC LIBRARY.

redepositing their money. The next morning, there was more cash in the vault of the First National Bank than the previous day when the run began.

By the time newly inaugurated president Franklin D. Roosevelt announced his historic "banking holiday" in March 1933, an air of composure already prevailed in Fort Worth. The occasion even found most of its citizens in good spirits, many of them devising artful ways to barter. Hens were traded for gasoline and wheat for haircuts. A golf course manager swapped two apples he had just received on credit to a newsboy for a paper. At Leonard's Department Store, brothers Obie and Marvin endeared themselves to their customers and eased the currency shortage by cashing checks partly in paper scrip that was redeemable at their new store. When a client called on a banker and remarked how "quiet and serene" it seemed in the empty lobby, the official replied: "Yes...things are so quiet that you can hear the interest accumulate."

At Texas Women's College, the former co-ed Polytechnic, trustees were also searching for creative solutions to save their own troubled institution. They even tried selling one-by-eight-foot plots for a dollar apiece; in return contributors would have their names inscribed in a "Book of Life." Faced with a declining enrollment, one administrator later claimed that the school's tangible assets by 1932 consisted of "a side of hog meat [and a] cupboard of home-canned blackeyed peas." TWC, it seemed, owed everybody in town. The principal argument against liquidation was that the property value was insufficient to make it worthwhile for prospective receivers to foreclose. Still, trustees were ready to throw in the towel, save for one dissenting vote—that of Reverend T. W. Brabham. In the end they decided to keep the school open on the condition that Brabham would become president. He agreed.

Miraculously, the good reverend led his flock across the Red Sea of ink that separated the college from solvency. One of his first decisions was to open the school to men as well as women. When the first mixed class enrolled during the fall of 1934, trustees had not yet changed the name to reflect the new status. Nevertheless, the *Star-Telegram* reported that the "boys enrolled at Texas Women's College...are rapidly making their presence felt." Several freshmen among them had pried the "W" and the "O" from the school's sign, leaving "Texas Man's College" to greet those arriving to the campus. By also refinancing its debt and convincing most of the faculty to stay on, the refashioned Texas Wesleyan College survived the crisis. By the end of the decade the enrollment was pushing four hundred, and the school was beginning to thrive.

Although hard times lingered, the worst seemed to be over. Fort Worth held its held its Southwestern Exposition and Fat Stock Show during the banking holiday, yet there was little evidence of an economic pall. "Fort Worth has spirit," wrote an enthused reporter who visited the Stockyards fair. "To see a town with its banners flying; a town which went right ahead in spite of moratoria and mourners, hell and high water, to stage its big annual show, one of the biggest shows of its kind in the United States. It demonstrates something unique in the form of civic spirit and undiscouraged civic enterprise—a first class, first hand demonstration of what America needs."

What America also needed about that time was a stiff drink. In 1933 the passage of the Twenty-first Amendment repealing Prohibition injected some liquid cheer into the bleak despair of the times. On the evening when alcohol once again became legal in Fort Worth, raucous crowds packed the streets, while bands played *How Dry I Am* and strangers embraced like it was Armistice Day all over again. Chanting "We want beer," throngs of merrymakers anxiously monitored the ballroom clocks at the Hotel Texas, the Blackstone, and Westbrook, waiting for midnight.

Within an hour after the stroke of twelve, bar owners were racing through the streets with permits to sell the forty five carloads of suds that had rolled into town for the momentous occasion. With light ceremony, Assistant City Manager D. W. Carlson popped the top on the first legal beer that Fort Worth had seen in more than a decade. When the day was over, wholesalers estimated that Fort Worthians had knocked off 30,000 cases and guzzled another 12,800 gallons off of local taps. FDR's popular edict also resulted in a modest construction boom and added to the public purse with the building of taverns and the collection of tax receipts. Among the winners was

✧

The Black Horse Troop of the U.S. Second Cavalry, linear descendants of the soldiers who founded Fort Worth, parade in the uniforms of the old dragoons for the Frontier Centennial.

COURTESY OF THE FORT WORTH PUBLIC LIBRARY.

✧

City fathers and distinguished guests enter the Frontier Centennial grounds in grand fashion to kick off the festivities. Elliott Roosevelt sits behind Amon Carter who is "riding shotgun."

COURTESY OF THE *FORT WORTH STAR-TELEGRAM* PHOTOGRAPH COLLECTION, SPECIAL COLLECTIONS, UNIVERSITY OF TEXAS AT ARLINGTON LIBRARIES, ARLINGTON, TEXAS, AR 406 2-19-17.

Ben E. Keith whose distributorship grew into a successful wholesaling firm, propelling the tireless booster into the presidency of the Chamber of Commerce.

The same irreverent spirit that attended the repeal of Prohibition reached new heights in 1936 when the city openly thumbed its nose at Dallas by hosting what it called the Frontier Centennial. A kind of outlaw exposition, it was thrown in defiance of its neighbor's state-sanctioned observance of the Texas Republic's hundredth anniversary. Neither Fort Worth nor Dallas existed in 1836, a fact that even Amon Carter appreciated by assuming that San Antonio or Houston would be awarded the site. In the end, Dallas amassed a war chest that outweighed any historical merit.

The unsuspected coup jolted the Panther City's leadership out of their armchairs at the Fort Worth Club. Until then, society women had been planning a centennial fair that would have scarcely rivaled the Diamond Jubilee of the previous decade. The new circumstances now demanded a Texas-sized rebuttal. Amon Carter, William Monnig, and a handful of other Fort Worth millionaires swung into action. After gaining promises from the Public Works Administration for construction dollars, they recruited Broadway producer Billy Rose, who in the space of three months transformed a one-time horse pasture into a cross between a Ziegfeld extravaganza and the Buffalo Bill Wild West Show. The battle cry "Fort Worth For Entertainment; Dallas For Education" exploded across billboards and barns around the Southwest, skimming off some of the multitudes whose tourist dollars would otherwise have fattened the gate at the State Fair Grounds in Dallas.

The Frontier Centennial opened a month late, but in grand style, trumpeting a four-month run that would give its well-heeled neighbor to the east all the competition it could handle. Packed aboard a Wells Fargo stagecoach, triumphant city fathers accompanied by Governor James Allred and a bevy of other Texas politicians and notables—all elaborately outfitted in Shady Oak Stetsons and gaudy western gear—whoopied onto the show grounds, hollering and waving. Perched on top beside the moneybox was the president's son, Elliott Roosevelt. Three thousand miles away, fishing off the coast of Maine, his father pressed a button, and by the magic of twentieth-century technology FDR cut the ribbon that officially opened the festivities.

As it shaped up, the Frontier Centennial was an odd mixture that spanned the range of entertainment from county fair sideshows to Broadway musicals. Appropriately, workers recreated a frontier village, "Sunset Trail," to occupy the center of the exposition grounds. Otherwise, Rose lined up agricultural exhibits and "freak shows" that included such oddities as a mind-reading dog and a 7'5" giant. He also put together a kind of variety show, "The Last Frontier," that featured a herd of bison, cowboys and Indians, and sixty-eight teams of square dancers. On a nearby rise, 180 monkeys frolicked; a lucky eight comprised an all-simian band directed by one "Joe Peanuts." Jumbo, a colossal

✧

Inside Casa Mañana, the musical productions beggared description. A powerful motor submerged below the lagoon turned the revolving stage, giving it the illusion of floating on water.

COURTESY OF THE *FORT WORTH STAR-TELEGRAM* PHOTOGRAPH COLLECTION, SPECIAL COLLECTIONS, UNIVERSITY OF TEXAS AT ARLINGTON LIBRARIES, ARLINGTON, TEXAS, AR 406 1-26-19.

musical circus, commanded its own building with state-of-the-art sound and lighting. Then, there were the "Six Tiny Rosebuds," a chorus line of ample women who could have out see-sawed TCU's starting linemen. The drawing cards that pulled in the crowds, though, were Sally Rand and Casa Mañana.

The provocative Rand had made the fan dance an artistic, if controversial, expression of interpretive dance. But the mobs of men who packed the Pioneer Palace each night left it to others to quibble over what was art and what was entertainment. They came to see the show. In Fort Worth, Rand traded the plumes for balloons. Bathed in a blue spotlight, she teased audiences by dancing gracefully behind the large bubbles, occasionally betraying flashes of her voluptuous body. Rand was also hostess of her own "Nude Ranch." Inside the "exhibition" hall, fifteen beauties wearing nothing but cowboy hats and boots, and holstered guns and bandanas, tossed beach balls and pitched horseshoes behind a floor-to-ceiling wire screen to keep the more enthusiastic patrons from joining them in the fun.

As titillating as the flesh shows were, the crown jewel of the Frontier Centennial was Casa Mañana. It boasted the world's largest revolving stage, turned by a 450-horsepower motor that took almost two minutes to complete a revolution. Built on tracks submerged in a man-made lagoon, the stage appeared to be floating. Along the rim, forty-three fountains shot up a curtain of water colored by a rainbow of lights. The stage sets were just as elaborate. As the massive wheel turned, renowned bandleader Paul Whiteman conducted two orchestras while recreated scenes from such venues as the 1904 St. Louis World's Fair, the Paris Exposition of 1925, and the 1933 Chicago Century of Progress Exposition overawed spellbound audiences. Even Dallas reporters openly called the show "staggering," admitting that it "beggars description." Expressing apologies to Julius Caesar, the *Dallas Journal*'s Fairfax Nisbet wrote: "We went to Fort Worth, we saw, and will break down and confess we were conquered."

Despite losing almost a hundred thousand dollars, the Frontier Centennial gave Fort Worth a boost that could not be measured in hard currency. The exposition drew over a million visitors who sorely needed a respite from the psychological doldrums of the Great Depression. For one shining moment the national spotlight turned on Fort Worth. Attending the festivities were such notables as novelist

✧

The ever-winsome Sally Rand and pugnacious Billy Rose.

COURTESY OF THE *FORT WORTH STAR-TELEGRAM* PHOTOGRAPH COLLECTION, SPECIAL COLLECTIONS, UNIVERSITY OF TEXAS AT ARLINGTON LIBRARIES, ARLINGTON, TEXAS, FWST NEG. # 2.

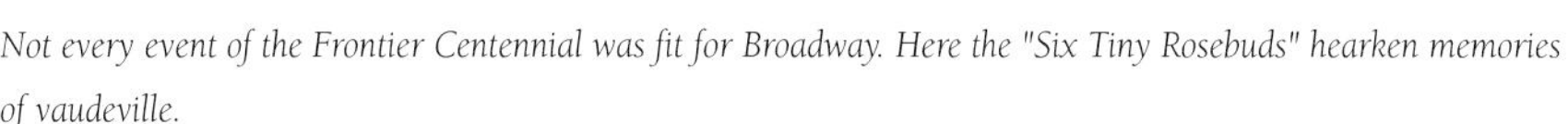

✧

Not every event of the Frontier Centennial was fit for Broadway. Here the "Six Tiny Rosebuds" hearken memories of vaudeville.

COURTESY OF THE *FORT WORTH STAR-TELEGRAM* PHOTOGRAPH COLLECTION, SPECIAL COLLECTIONS, UNIVERSITY OF TEXAS AT ARLINGTON LIBRARIES, ARLINGTON, TEXAS, AR 406 1-26-25.

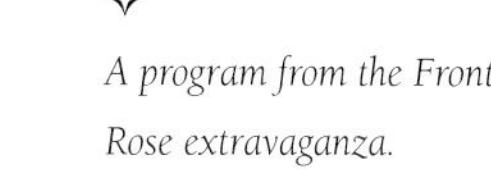

✧

A program from the Frontier Centennial promoting a Billy Rose extravaganza.

COURTESY OF THE DALTON HOFFMAN COLLECTION, FORT WORTH.

Ernest Hemmingway, Vice-President John Nance Garner, FBI Director J. Edgar Hoover, flying ace Jimmy Doolittle, and legions of politicians, show business personalities, and columnists of every leading newspaper in the country. In later years William Monnig reflected: "Fort Worth was flat on its back until we put on that show."

Ironically the Will Rogers Memorial Center, considered by planners to be the key to the exposition's success, did not open until after the season ended. The sole physical survivor of the centennial, the complex combined the Will Rogers Coliseum, Auditorium, and Memorial Tower, highlighted with ornate tile friezes, brightly colored bas-relief murals, and stunning geometric designs. To secure funding from the Public Works Administration, Amon Carter in 1935 had traveled to Washington, D.C., and told anyone who would listen that such a venue would be a perfect home for the city's Southwestern Exposition, Fat Stock Show, and Rodeo. When PWA director Harold Ickes turned down the project, Carter went straight to his intimate friend, the president. As the story went, Postmaster General James Farley told Carter to wait outside the Oval Office, but purposely left the door ajar, knowing the publisher would be eavesdropping. Raising his voice, Farley exclaimed: "Amon wants to build a cowshed." To which FDR bellowed, "Cowshed!" Just then Carter burst through the door to object, but hardly got a word out before Roosevelt and Farley doubled over with laughter. A few months later Carter received a note from Jesse Jones, director of the New Deal's Reconstruction Finance Corporation: "Your cowshed has been approved."

The PWA also provided funds to build roads and bridges, the Botanical Gardens, a new library, a sanatorium, and thirteen new schools and an athletic stadium. The Gardens, started in 1933, was the first federal relief project of the many developments that helped revive the city's flagging employment. Inspired by some of the finest European parks, the gardens transformed a former gravel quarry into one of the city's most enduring amenities. Queen

✧

Snow covers the deserted Frontier Centennial grounds. Soon, all that remained was the Will Rogers Memorial Center (top). Ironically, planners considered it to be the key to the event's success, but it did not open until after the exposition ended.

COURTESY OF THE FORT WORTH PUBLIC LIBRARY.

✧

The demolition of the old City Hall made room for its New Deal successor.

LEFT IMAGE COURTESY OF THE *FORT WORTH STAR-TELEGRAM* PHOTOGRAPH COLLECTION, SPECIAL COLLECTIONS, UNIVERSITY OF TEXAS AT ARLINGTON LIBRARIES, ARLINGTON, TEXAS, AR 406 1-26-32. RIGHT IMAGE COURTESY OF THE *FORT WORTH STAR-TELEGRAM* PHOTOGRAPH COLLECTION, SPECIAL COLLECTIONS, UNIVERSITY OF TEXAS AT ARLINGTON LIBRARIES, ARLINGTON, TEXAS, AR 406 1-26-32.

✧

TCU's Davey O'Brien arrives at New York's Downtown Athletic Club to claim the 1938 Heisman Trophy.

COURTESY OF TEXAS CHRISTIAN UNIVERSITY, SPECIAL COLLECTIONS, MARY COUTS BURNETT LIBRARY, FORT WORTH, TEXAS.

Tut the elephant, which had grown considerably larger since her fifth birthday party during the previous decade, aided in the construction effort by wallowing out a clay seal for an otherwise porous manmade lagoon. The piecemeal additions of the zoo and Trinity Park, the Botanical Gardens, and the Will Rogers Memorial Center laid the foundation for a sprawling cultural district that in later decades would come to rival much larger American cities.

If New Deal spending and the Frontier Centennial helped ease the pain of the Great Depression, football provided a transcendent glory all its own. No group of high school gridders was more worthy of adoration during these years of want than the boys of Masonic Home, an institution for orphans and dependents of widows. Always outmanned and outnumbered the "Mighty Mites," as they were called, earned a Davidic reputation for playing—and beating—much larger schools. Whether at home or some faraway venue, a Masonic Home game was an event. On occasion police had to shuttle players from the courthouse to Northside's LaGrave Field, because game traffic had turned the streets into a parking lot. The boys did not field a band, but the Shriners' fez-and-tasseled drum and bugle corps filled in admirably.

During a four-season stretch, from 1930 to 1933, the Home lost only one game, and that to a junior college. Their small-school classification played only to the regional level during those years, but in 1934 they were "voted up" and seized the opportunity by going all the way to the state finals. At Corsicana they fought the brawny home team to scoreless tie. Over 12,000 fans crowded into the 8,000-seat stadium, and at one point a section of overpacked bleachers collapsed under the weight. Although obviously outmatched, the Mighty Mites held back five Corsicana scoring threats deep in their own territory. The game ended, in fact, with the home team on the six-inch line.

Other Fort Worth schools—North Side, Paschal, and Arlington Heights—also drew large crowds, which won the city a PWA contract for a new stadium, Farrington Field. Named for recently deceased Fort Worth I.S.D. Athletic Director Ervin Stanley Farrington, the twenty-thousand-seat facility opened in time for the 1939

✧

A post parade at Arlington Downs. Until pari-mutuel betting in Texas was outlawed, the track was a popular entertainment destination.

COURTESY OF THE *FORT WORTH STAR-TELEGRAM* PHOTOGRAPH COLLECTION, SPECIAL COLLECTIONS, UNIVERSITY OF TEXAS AT ARLINGTON LIBRARIES, ARLINGTON, TEXAS, AR 406 5-9-8.

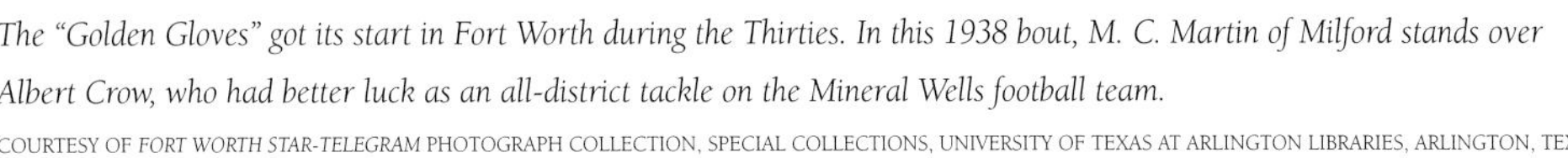

The "Golden Gloves" got its start in Fort Worth during the Thirties. In this 1938 bout, M. C. Martin of Milford stands over Albert Crow, who had better luck as an all-district tackle on the Mineral Wells football team.

COURTESY OF *FORT WORTH STAR-TELEGRAM* PHOTOGRAPH COLLECTION, SPECIAL COLLECTIONS, UNIVERSITY OF TEXAS AT ARLINGTON LIBRARIES, ARLINGTON, TEXAS, FWST 989, 2.

During the spring of 1939 Fort Worth enjoyed The Story of Vernon and Irene Castle, *starring Fred Astaire and Ginger Rogers. The movie was the first of several world premiers for the city. It was also a homecoming of sorts for the popular actress. Early in the 1920s she was introduced as eight-year-old singer Virginia Rogers to Fort Worthians tuned into WBAP radio.*

COURTESY OF THE *FORT WORTH STAR-TELEGRAM* PHOTOGRAPH COLLECTION, SPECIAL COLLECTIONS, UNIVERSITY OF TEXAS AT ARLINGTON LIBRARIES, ARLINGTON, TEXAS, AR 406 2-21-10.

football season and instantly gained recognition as one of the finest public school stadiums in the Southwest.

TCU likewise broke ground for a new stadium in 1930. Eventually it would be renamed for Amon Carter, its biggest fan and the man most responsible for pushing the bonds that built it. Carter, sporting those omnipresent purple and white boots, followed the team everywhere, occasionally bursting into the dressing room to give half-time pep talks and exhorting the players to victory from the sidelines. In 1936 the Horned Frogs traveled to San Francisco for a game with undefeated Santa Clara, and there the publisher led the school band down Market Street to the team's hotel, where he was guest of honor for the welcoming banquet. Carter's bragging compelled his hosts to badger him into backing up the tall talk with his checkbook. Ordering the hotel staff to bring out a No. 2 washtub, Carter challenged the Californians to fill it up, pledging: "I'll cover anything you bet." Over ten thousand dollars flowed over the top and onto the floor, eventually landing in Carter's pockets when TCU upset the "unbeatable" Broncos, 9-0.

It was on the arm of "Slingin' Sammy" Baugh, however, that TCU rose to national prominence. The tall, lean West Texan, behind the blocking of I. B. Hale and fellow All-American Ki Aldrich, earned the reputation in many circles as the greatest quarterback ever to play college football. In one of those frequent "games of the century" Baugh and TCU hosted an SMU team at the end of the 1935 season that matched the Horned Frogs' perfect 10-0 record. Long after fans packed the new thirty-thousand-seat stadium, men were still leaping over wire fences from the tops of automobiles to get into the game. Sportswriting giant Grantland Rice of the *New York Sun* covered the contest, declaring it was "the most desperate football this season has known from coast to coast."

With seven minutes left to play and the scored tied 14-14, SMU's Bob Finley heaved a fifty-yard bomb out of punt formation to a leaping, twisting Bobby Wilson who pulled in the game winning pass. Behind 20-14, Baugh twice led his teammates deep into the Mustangs' end of the field only to see his receivers drop precision-drilled passes, which cost them the game. Despite the loss to SMU, on a cold but glorious New Year's Day, 1936, with diagonal sheets of rain pelting the Sugar Bowl field, TCU salvaged a share of the national championship, besting LSU 3-2.

As good as Baugh was, it was his understudy Davey O'Brien who led TCU to its only undisputed national championship at the end of the 1938 season. His gritty play and the team's almost magical success won the 5'7", 150-pound quarterback the Heisman Trophy. With Amon Carter sitting atop a stagecoach beside O'Brien, the normally unflappable New Yorkers watched agog as the cowboy-clad contingent of the publisher and the quarterback, the TCU coaching staff, and the team captains waved and hollered as they made their way down the middle of Broadway to the Downtown Athletic Club.

Riding the wave of gridiron success and New Deal construction, Fort Worth rejoiced in 1938 when *Forbes Magazine* reported that the Panther City also resided in the economic center of the "No. 1 territory of the Nation." City leaders declared that in Fort Worth the Great Depression was officially over. If this dark chapter had obscured progress in the march of time, its evidence was nevertheless everywhere to be seen and felt. In 1930 the last of Fort Worth's founding fathers, Khleber Van Zandt, died peacefully in his sleep. Also passing from the scene during the 1930s was the old Carnegie Library, over which local women's clubs at the turn of the century had fought so valiantly to acquire. Gone, too, was the vitriol that attended the emergence of the Ku Klux Klan. In its place, local religious leaders Hastings Harrison, Ernest May, William Margowski, and I. E. Horwitz headed a local chapter of the National Conference of Christians and Jews, organized in 1939 to "promote justice, amity, understanding and co-operation" among the city's several active faiths.

In the material culture, motor use continued to grow. The first traffic signals, featuring bells that rang each time a light changed, began regulating the movement of cars, buses, and motorcycles in 1931. Fully enclosed vehicles equipped with radios necessitated a switch to silent signals in 1937. Downtown, parking meters began popping up along the sidewalks in 1936, steadily growing in number from three hundred to about two thousand within a decade.

Finally, on New Year's Day 1939 "Old Number 270," the city's officially designated last streetcar, "rumbled down Main Street…and on to the car barns and oblivion." A sense that the Panther City was closing a quaint chapter in its record of development gripped those who came to watch, but most everyone was in agreement that it was time for the slow and virtually riderless lines to go the way of the old nickelodeons and vaudeville that disappeared a generation earlier.

In 1925 a newspaper report had boasted that together the city's streetcars logged the improbable distance of 18,000 miles a day "or the distance from Fort Worth to Hong Kong and back again." Yet the very next year, when passenger demands called for a new transportation artery between Oakhurst and downtown, officials heralded things to come by adding a bus service, rather than laying new rails. Within a few years the city council was regularly ordering the removal of track, attributing several fatal accidents to poorly maintained rails. By 1938 a fleet of 140 buses was serving riders, and officials of the Fort Worth Transit Company were peddling the last of their serviceable cars to other cities.

Aboard that final trip was one J. M. Higgins, who, as a boy of thirteen had appeared on the scene at the precise moment when the Panther City's first electric trolley made its maiden run. He and some other boys had been fishing, Higgins recalled. "We passed the barn and saw the electric car moving out. I jumped on it." A few blocks later he was "put off" for not paying a fare. Like the first time, his last ride was also free.

The Fort Worth of streetcars, silent movies, and bootleg liquor had matured on the breadlines and government teat of the Great Depression. Future generations would look back fondly at the Frontier Centennial, the illustrious football teams, and even the era's character building experience with the same sense of nostalgia that had attended the last streetcar ride. As the decade came to an end, it was becoming clear that another great test lay before America and Fort Worth.

✧

Fort Worth remained an important air center during the decade. On January 14, 1935, the Star-Telegram *heralded American Airlines' new transcontinental service, "The Southerner," a direct route to Washington, D.C. and New York: "A big twin-motored monoplane roared across the Municipal Airport Monday morning, its propellers biting into a brisk north wind…."*

COURTESY OF THE LIBRARY OF CONGRESS, WASHINGTON, D.C.

✧

The intersection of Seventh Street and avenues Camp Bowie, Bailey, and University at the end of the decade.

COURTESY OF THE *FORT WORTH STAR-TELEGRAM* PHOTOGRAPH COLLECTION, SPECIAL COLLECTIONS, UNIVERSITY OF TEXAS AT ARLINGTON LIBRARIES, ARLINGTON, TEXAS, AR 406 1-22-5.

Downtown Fort Worth, c. 1940.

COURTESY OF THE W. D. SMITH COLLECTION, SPECIAL COLLECTIONS, UNIVERSITY OF TEXAS AT ARLINGTON LIBRARIES, ARLINGTON, TEXAS, AR 430 42-122-1.

CHAPTER 5

"LOOK—UP IN THE SKY!"

1940-1949

Just as apprehensive Fort Worthians proceeded into the depression years with cautious hope, the advent of the new decade had them clinging to another kind of uncertain optimism, one that would keep them out of the world war that was already engorging much of Europe and Asia. Of course, it was beyond the ability of Fort Worth to escape something so pervasive as the economic depression of the Thirties, and once again it could not avoid being touched by the larger events of the Forties. Yet, just as the federally funded New Deal projects had provided an unexpected boost that lifted the city's fortunes, the war effort brought another round of government spending. Once more the face and fortunes of the Panther City would be forever changed.

In the fall of 1940 almost every edition of the *Star-Telegram* heralded the movements of German troops and the Nazi's bombing of London. But ever so briefly the war clouds parted as Fort Worth showcased *The Westerner*, starring Gary Cooper. "Everybody but Hitler Here for Premier," trumpeted one of several headlines. The "City Where the West Begins" rolled out the red carpet for the show's stars, Cooper and Doris Davenport, as well as the movie's director, William Wyler, and its producer, MGM mogul Samuel Goldwyn. Other luminaries included comedian Bob Hope and America's favorite sidekicks Walter Brennan and Chill Wills.

Organizers whipped up enthusiasm for the star-studded event by staging a parade. In front, on horseback, was the tall, handsome Cooper; beside him rode a beaming Amon Carter. Davenport trailed behind them in a buggy and delighted in talking to adults and children alike, who crowded around her as the procession cut a slow path along the route.

As hundreds of spectators leaned out of the windows of office buildings for a commanding view, thousands of others lined the streets, many dressed in range attire, waving cowboy hats and kerchiefs. Several times the parade ground to a halt, but the effervescent Cooper took the delays as an opportunity to sign autographs—mostly on the hats of admirers—until he was forced to move along. A *Star-Telegram* reporter surmised that he "accumulated enough fuzz off of ten-gallon hats to stuff a pillow."

The parade ended at the Will Rogers Auditorium, where *The Westerner* premiered at 2 p.m. It rolled again that evening at both the Worth and Hollywood theaters. Outside, the reconstructed street took on the appearance of a western movie set. Crowning the day of festivities was "The Westerner Movie Star Ball," an invitation-only event where well-heeled patrons danced alongside their screen idols at the Hotel Texas' Crystal Ballroom.

If Gary Cooper took Fort Worthians minds off of world events, the 1940 publication of a best-selling fiction, *The Inheritors*, caused another kind of sensation. The provocative novel by Philip Atlee, pen name of James Young Phillips, rocked Fort Worth society a generation before Grace Metalious's *Peyton Place* would cause the blue blood of New Englanders to run cold. Phillips had spent his teenage years growing up at a Crestline Drive home on the prosperous west side, where most of the city's movers and shakers then resided. The peccadilloes of their silver-spooned children provided plenty of grist for a story filled with prodigious drinking, gratuitous sex, and favors due the privileged. "Her kiss was soft and searching, an insinuating pleasure that moved warmth over my mouth and shook me," read a lurid passage. "Desire stiffened in me like wonder, and I put her down on the bed, looked at her rounded loveliness..."

The wagging tongues of gossipers guessed at the thinly veiled identities of the characters, while the real-life subjects recoiled in indignation. At the library, so many books disappeared from the shelves that the sole remaining copy was kept under lock and key, its readers assigned a place near the eyes of watchful staff members.

The early 1940s also saw the Jim Hotel, located at 413 East Fifth Street, hit stride as a center for an emerging jazz and blues culture. The Cooper brothers—Levi, Bob, and Oscar—acquired the complex from Bill McDonald during the Depression and nurtured its College Inn nightclub into an underground institution. By the 1940s white

Gary Cooper rides alongside a beaming Amon Carter, just in front of a banner that read "Where the Westerner Begins."

COURTESY OF THE *FORT WORTH STAR-TELEGRAM* PHOTOGRAPH COLLECTION, SPECIAL COLLECTIONS, UNIVERSITY OF TEXAS AT ARLINGTON LIBRARIES, ARLINGTON, TEXAS, AR 406 1-29-47.

Fort Worth had shrugged off the social risks of packing into the cramped Jim alongside the regular African-American clientele to see such performers as Louis Armstrong, Cab Calloway, Count Basie, and Billie Holiday. Even white entertainers like Sarah Vaughan, Chick Webb, and Paul Whiteman played to

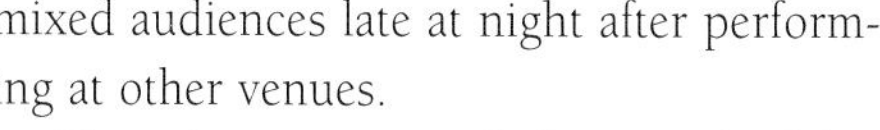

mixed audiences late at night after performing at other venues.

The white owners of those nightclubs, however, complained that the Jim, which did not usually start hopping until after midnight, was siphoning off their late night business and appealed to local authorities to impose a 1 a.m. curfew. About a day or so

Former TCU All-American Sammy Baugh made a better Indian than a cowboy. At the beginning of the decade, the Washington Redskins quarterback and future Hall-of-Famer tried his hand at acting. Here, Baugh poses for a still shot publicizing his starring role in the serial, King of the Texas Rangers.

COURTESY OF THE *FORT WORTH STAR-TELEGRAM* PHOTOGRAPH COLLECTION, SPECIAL COLLECTIONS, UNIVERSITY OF TEXAS AT ARLINGTON LIBRARIES, ARLINGTON, TEXAS, FWST C517.

Fort Worthians loved a parade and enjoyed a steady procession during the Forties. This one celebrated the dedication of the Will Rogers Memorial Coliseum, just before the decade's first Thanksgiving.

COURTESY OF THE *FORT WORTH STAR-TELEGRAM* PHOTOGRAPH COLLECTION, SPECIAL COLLECTIONS, UNIVERSITY OF TEXAS AT ARLINGTON LIBRARIES, ARLINGTON, TEXAS, AR 406 1-29-18.

A generation before Peyton Place, *high society in Fort Worth recoiled in indignation over* The Inheritors.

JACKET COVER FROM *THE INHERITORS* BY JAMES PHILIP ATLEE. USED BY PERMISSION OF THE DIAL PRESS/DELL PUBLISHING, A DIVISION OF RANDOM HOUSE, INC.

✧

The entrance to the Jim Hotel (left).

COURTESY OF THE FORT WORTH BLACK HISTORICAL & GENEALOGY SOCIETY COLLECTION, FORT WORTH PUBLIC LIBRARY.

✧

While Fort Worth was always quick to roll out the red carpet for visiting celebrities, the African-American community took the lead in greeting heavyweight boxing champion Joe Louis.

COURTESY OF THE FORT WORTH BLACK HISTORICAL & GENEALOGY SOCIETY COLLECTION, FORT WORTH PUBLIC LIBRARY.

after the edict had been handed down, the Jim's staff got a call from prominent socialite Anne Burnett, who said she was bringing along a little group that night. "I told her she couldn't do that because the police wouldn't let us play music late," remembered Bob Cooper. "She said not to worry about the police, that she'd take care of the police. She did. We never had a problem with the police after that."

Record crowds also packed the once-cavernous coliseum for the Southwestern Exposition and Fat Stock Show in 1941, but the next year it was clear that war was on everyone's mind. Those who attended the parade saw a martial theme overshadow the traditional western fare as various military units marched, pausing occasionally to perform close-order drills. Red, white, and blue was everywhere, and patriotic songs filled the air.

Despite the emotional display and the appearance of America's number one box office cowboy Gene Autry, the show lost money in 1942. When officials wondered aloud whether to continue holding the North Side tradition, nature itself provided the answer. A few weeks after the show closed, the one-two punch of a flash flood ended any hope that it would continue to enjoy its Stockyards home. The first wall of water rose five feet over the banks of Marine Creek, the second one over seven. Small buildings became battering rams that caved in the brick walls of more substantial structures. Entire inventories from store shelves, the contents of desks and file cabinets, and even trophies and loving cups swept from the Livestock Exchange Building swirled among cars and trash and dead animals as the flotsam mass hurtled toward the swollen Trinity.

Efforts to rebuild the heart of North Side focused on meeting the needs of a city at war, and in 1943 the Southwestern Exposition and Fat Stock Show failed to open its gates for the first time in forty-seven years. "There is a strange quiet hovering over Exchange Avenue...these mid-March days," read a Chamber of Commerce brochure in 1943. "Back of it all, of course, are the same three fellows who have been causing all of the trouble of late—Hitler, Tojo and Mussolini." John B. Davis, the show's secretary-manager, stated: "the entire energy and equipment of the livestock industry should be devoted to the task of increased production in line with our Government's request."

By that time, of course, Fort Worth and America were in the thick of the conflict. On December 7, 1941, Dave Naugle was the first man in town to get the news of Pearl Harbor. He was on duty at radio station KFJZ, when suddenly the bells on the teletype machines started going crazy. "Flash—Japs Attack Oahu." Government wires conveying the news at first ordered radio staff not to give the identity of the island town that was under attack, nor to give the local weather—presumably in the event that another wave of Zeros had targeted the mainland. Soon, however, Americans were poring over globes and atlases looking for the small dot on the map that denoted Pearl Harbor.

Amon Carter sent his own cable to his friend President Franklin D. Roosevelt. Looking for a silver lining, the publisher calculated that the sneak attack might be "a blessing in disguise." With the country unified as never before, he declared that Pearl Harbor would at least "silence those damned isolationists and America

✧

A scene from the Stockyards' last Southwestern Exposition and Fat Stock Show, 1942. Declining revenues and the war put the annual event in mothballs the next year; it would reopen in 1944 at the Will Rogers complex.

COURTESY OF THE *FORT WORTH STAR-TELEGRAM* PHOTOGRAPH COLLECTION, SPECIAL COLLECTIONS, UNIVERSITY OF TEXAS AT ARLINGTON LIBRARIES, ARLINGTON, TEXAS, AR 407 7-14.

✧

Opening night at the Haltom Theater, December 8, 1941. What normally would have provided an escape from routine cares could not outweigh the events of the previous day, when the Japanese attacked Pearl Harbor.

COURTESY OF THE *FORT WORTH STAR-TELEGRAM* PHOTOGRAPH COLLECTION, SPECIAL COLLECTIONS, UNIVERSITY OF TEXAS AT ARLINGTON LIBRARIES, ARLINGTON, TEXAS, AR 406 1-37-10.

First sons-of-bitches...If they open their mouths again they should be put in a concentration camp."

Carter's diatribe was not the idle talk of a rabble-rouser. Fort Worth, largely behind the boostering of the publisher and American Airlines' founder C. R. Smith, became what the *Star-Telegram* called the "fountainhead of America's air might." In 1940 the city won an Army contract to transform a pasture south of Lake Worth into a bomber plant and airbase. Downtown, the T&P Building became headquarters for the Army Air Force Training Command in July 1942. From its offices Lt. General Barton K. Yount and his 250 officers directed the activities of almost one-eighth of all the entire Army, overseeing the supervision of every air training facility in the country. Fort Worth took note of that fact, boasting that it was home to the single largest educational institution in the world.

On the outskirts of the city, the groundbreaking at sleepy little White Settlement unfolded on April 18, 1941. At the ceremony, Major General Harry C. Brant turned the earth with a silver spade, then looked resolutely upon the crowd: "We're starting to dig Hitler's grave this afternoon," he declared. The factory, built for the Consolidated-Vultee Aircraft Corporation (Convair), was to be identical to ones in Oklahoma and Georgia. In fine Texas fashion, however, an extra twenty-nine feet was added to the Cowtown site, making it the longest aircraft plant in the nation. Just one day short of a year after construction began, the first B-24 Liberator rolled off the mammoth assembly line. More than thirty thousand men and women built over three thousand B-24s before switching to B-32 production at the end of 1944.

Next door, at the Tarrant Field Airdrome, over four thousand World War II pilots of the Army Air Force Training Command earned their wings. The base underwent several name changes before finally adopting Carswell Air Force Base in 1948 to honor local hero Horace S. Carswell, Jr. One of many Fort Worth men to contribute the ultimate sacrifice during the war, the former TCU gridiron star commanded the 308th Bombardment Group in the Pacific Theater.

Among the accomplishments that won Carswell a Distinguished Service Cross in 1944 were the separate sinkings of a Japanese cruiser and a destroyer. A week after the second score, anti-aircraft fire crippled his B-24 as he was bearing down on a Japanese convoy. One-by-one his four

The Consolidated-Vultee Aircraft Corporation, or Convair, as it was popularly known.

COURTESY OF THE JACK WHITE PHOTOGRAPH COLLECTION, SPECIAL COLLECTIONS, UNIVERSITY OF TEXAS AT ARLINGTON LIBRARIES, ARLINGTON, TEXAS, AR 407 5-18) ARLINGTON, TEXAS, AR 407 7-14.

Amphibious landing craft test the waters at Lake Worth.

COURTESY OF THE *FORT WORTH STAR-TELEGRAM* PHOTOGRAPH COLLECTION, SPECIAL COLLECTIONS, UNIVERSITY OF TEXAS AT ARLINGTON LIBRARIES, ARLINGTON, TEXAS, AR 406 1-42-38.

Horace Carswell, Jr., of Fort Worth, recipient of the Medal of Honor.

COURTESY OF THE *FORT WORTH STAR-TELEGRAM* PHOTOGRAPH COLLECTION, SPECIAL COLLECTIONS, UNIVERSITY OF TEXAS AT ARLINGTON LIBRARIES, ARLINGTON, TEXAS, AR 406 2-18-50 C848.

engines failed, all the while fuel leaking from a puncture in the tank. Somehow Carswell managed to make it over land so that his crew could bail out. When his bombardier reported that flak had ruined his parachute, the pilot remained in the cockpit, hoping to glide to safety. Luck ran out, however, and the plane crashed into a mountain and exploded. His hero's death earned Carswell the Medal of Honor and the condolences of a grieving city.

The war effort in Fort Worth, as in other American cities, was total. Its citizens bought rationed goods and participated in scrap iron drives. They worked in military factories and daily scanned the papers for news of Allied progress. They sent sons and even daughters to distant theaters of action in every corner of the globe. They also bought war bonds out of proportion to their numbers.

In the summer of 1942 Ben E. Keith chaired a bond drive that netted $5,314,000 in pledges ranging from $50 to $50,000. Fitting tradition, city fathers organized a parade to whip up enthusiasm for the sale, while high rollers met with Texas Governor Coke Stevenson at the Fort Worth Club for a private fundraiser. The Panther City donated twenty planes, one bearing a gold plate with the name "City of Fort Worth," and another "County of Tarrant."

As legions of young Fort Worth men left for basic training and war, a labor shortage created unprecedented job opportunities for Mexican immigrants and women, mostly Anglo. Hispanic jobseekers, many returning

Major General Roger Ramey salutes widow Virginia Carswell at the dedication of Carswell Air Force Base, home of the Eighth Air Force and the Seventh Bombardment Wing, 1948.

COURTESY OF THE *FORT WORTH STAR-TELEGRAM* PHOTOGRAPH COLLECTION, SPECIAL COLLECTIONS, UNIVERSITY OF TEXAS AT ARLINGTON LIBRARIES, ARLINGTON, TEXAS, AR 406 2-18-50.

Fort Worth did not waste any time going to a wartime economy. To conserve precious fuel, the Star-Telegram *early in 1942 began delivering newspapers to downtown customers by wagon. The horse, "Normandie," was kept in a makeshift stable in back of the* Star-Telegram *Building.*

COURTESY OF THE *FORT WORTH STAR-TELEGRAM* PHOTOGRAPH COLLECTION, SPECIAL COLLECTIONS, UNIVERSITY OF TEXAS AT ARLINGTON LIBRARIES, ARLINGTON, TEXAS, AR 406 1-26-53A.

Even window shoppers got a dose of patriotism when they walked past Striplings Department Store.

COURTESY OF THE FORT WORTH PUBLIC LIBRARY.

to the Panther City after being forced back across the Rio Grande during the Depression, found the INS in a more relaxed mood. The new reality did not erase racial barriers, but a kind of social thaw nevertheless encouraged *tejano* families and immigrants to test de facto segregation.

At the beginning of the decade, land east of North Main comprised the so-called "Mexican side," where dirt roads led to rude shacks within clear view of spacious homes and well manicured lawns on the thoroughfare's west side. Youthful probes across the divide normally invited fights and rock tossing; inquiries from Tejanos about property brought cold stares and stoned silence. Population pressure and the prosperity of war, however, pushed the burgeoning barrio across North Main and into Diamond Hill. Hispanic families began to make inroads into other once-forbidden neighborhoods scattered around town as well.

For women, the image of "Rosie the Riveter" came alive in the Convair plant and other war-related industries. Even if society was not quite ready for gender equality, it nevertheless welcomed women who did their part by toiling behind welders' masks and driving forklifts. The burdensome

A labor shortage during the war years and continuing prosperity afterwards encouraged Hispanics to test segregation. The brown faces among an otherwise white Christmas crowd at Leonard's toy department in 1948 evidence the beginnings of racial tolerance.

COURTESY OF THE *FORT WORTH STAR-TELEGRAM* PHOTOGRAPH COLLECTION, SPECIAL COLLECTIONS, UNIVERSITY OF TEXAS AT ARLINGTON LIBRARIES, ARLINGTON, TEXAS. AR 406 1-30-19.

A Panther City "Rosie" places rivets in a Liberator.

COURTESY OF THE LIBRARY OF CONGRESS, WASHINGTON, D.C.

The Fort Worth "Guardettes," attached to the Texas National Guard, drill with wooden rifles.

COURTESY OF THE *FORT WORTH STAR-TELEGRAM* PHOTOGRAPH COLLECTION, SPECIAL COLLECTIONS, UNIVERSITY OF TEXAS AT ARLINGTON LIBRARIES, ARLINGTON, TEXAS. AR 406 1-26-38.

✧

Downtown on the eve of the war, looking north from the lower end of Main Street; the Bowen Bus Station is at the left, foreground.

COURTESY OF THE LIBRARY OF CONGRESS.

demands of wartime production allowed them, however briefly, to prove they could maintain a man's pace on the factory floor.

On the other hand, the headline "2 New Bus Conductors Never Shave!" did raise a few eyebrows. After the transit company hired the two women in September 1943 to make change on buses that transported hundreds of workers between the business district and the bomber plant, several nervous customers called, wondering if the company was planning on putting them behind the wheel. Spokesmen remained noncommittal, even though women were already driving buses in Dallas and other cities.

No doubt a recent near-catastrophe in Fort Worth raised some concerns. In that incident the brakes had failed on an inbound bus, forcing the male driver to zigzag through the intersection at Seventh and Penn and across a service station parking lot, where it left a spewing gas pump in its wake. It finally crashed into a retaining wall, leaving fifty customers dazed and shaken.

Yet, with bus fares doubling from fifteen million a year to over thirty million between 1941 and 1943, it was just a matter of time before labor demands put that first woman in the driver's seat. Soon, customers grew used to the "lady drivers," just as they had grown accustomed to women occupying so many other previously male-only jobs. The next year, when a bus rolled over twice on a slippery stretch of White Settlement Road injuring fifty-four people, no one asked about the driver's gender.

White-collar jobs also went begging during the war years. The North Fort Worth State Bank, for example, made Eve Randle the city's first woman bank officer. Over at the *Star-Telegram*, Managing Editor Jim Record hired seven women reporters during one month in 1942. Soon they were known as "JRR's Harem." With the blessings of their male counterparts the women mortified the puritanical staff boss at an office party by arriving bare-bellied in sheer harem costumes. Record finally had

✧

A jubilant Amon Carter greets his son upon the young man's release from a German prisoner-of-war camp.

COURTESY OF TEXAS CHRISTIAN UNIVERSITY, SPECIAL COLLECTIONS, MARY COUTS BURNETT LIBRARY, FORT WORTH, TEXAS)

✧

With France liberated but beaten down in 1944, nationally syndicated columnist Drew Pearson originated the idea of a "Freedom Train" to provide relief. With Amon Carter's backing, Fort Worth responded with fifteen carloads of food. Once the country began to recover, they returned the kindness with a "Gratitude Train" filled with French wines and cuisine.

COURTESY OF THE *FORT WORTH STAR-TELEGRAM* PHOTOGRAPH COLLECTION, SPECIAL COLLECTIONS, UNIVERSITY OF TEXAS AT ARLINGTON LIBRARIES, ARLINGTON, TEXAS, AR406 1-26-37.

River Oaks, incorporated in 1941, registered explosive growth during the decade. Most of its working class population depended on industrial jobs at places such as the bomber plant and the Stockyards. Note the downtown skyline in the distance.

COURTESY OF THE *FORT WORTH STAR-TELEGRAM* PHOTOGRAPH COLLECTION, SPECIAL COLLECTIONS, UNIVERSITY OF TEXAS AT ARLINGTON LIBRARIES, ARLINGTON, TEXAS, AR 406 1-29-49.

enough and fled down the hall when a porter—dressed like a palace eunuch—gunned a motorcycle through the city room.

It was a more somber office when the immediacy of the war left the newspaper's owner with a sense of impending mortality. Lieutenant Amon Carter, Jr., was reported missing in action in North Africa on Valentine's Day, 1943. The same Amon, Sr., who could seemingly move mountains—or at least enough dirt to raise a mile-long building, plus twenty-nine feet—suddenly found himself helpless. Frantic phone calls and telegrams to the Red Cross, the Army, and even the White House failed to turn up any information on the whereabouts of his precious "Cowboy," as Carter always called his son. In return, reams of sympathy notes, including one from Eleanor Roosevelt, as well as a resolution from the Texas Legislature only left the newspaper giant more despondent.

Then, after two agonizing months, Lieutenant Carter finally got word to his father that he was being held at a POW camp in Gdansk, Poland. Later, it was learned that Carter and a sergeant were left

Texas Christian University toward the end of the decade reflected the area's growing affluence and a renewed emphasis on higher education.

COURTESY OF TEXAS CHRISTIAN UNIVERSITY, SPECIAL COLLECTIONS, MARY COUTS BURNETT LIBRARY, FORT WORTH, TEXAS.

on a mountaintop observation post when the tanks of German field marshal Erwin Rommel broke through American lines. For ten days the pair made their way across the rugged terrain, holing up in caves and splitting apart cactuses for their sustenance. Hiding in a clump of that plant so familiar to the West Texan, shotgun-wielding Bedouins rousted them from sleep. After being beaten and stripped by the nomads, Carter and the sergeant were sold to a German patrol that soon had them shipped to Italy. From there they were herded aboard a cattle car and sent to the concentration camp.

As the war wound to its conclusion the lieutenant was moved to Luchenwalde Prison, not far from Berlin, where he again scratched off a note to his father. Immediately, the publisher wrangled a seat aboard a Paris-bound airplane. From the French capital, he made his way by jeep toward the recently liberated prison camp, stopping at the makeshift headquarters of the Eighty-third Division. As he was climbing back into the vehicle, Carter heard a familiar voice yell: "Dad, here I am." In a storybook ending conveyed almost immediately to anxious *Star-Telegram* readers who had been following the saga in faraway Fort Worth, father and son shared a weeping embrace. For the Carter men the war was over, and on August 14, 1945, the rival *Fort Worth Press* declared it official for the rest of the world, its own banner headline shouting: "IT'S OVER!"

✧

Fears that the end of the war would bring a return to times of economic depression quickly proved groundless. The Eagle Mountain Yacht Club reflects the new consumer-driven prosperity, 1947.

COURTESY OF THE *FORT WORTH STAR-TELEGRAM* PHOTOGRAPH COLLECTION, SPECIAL COLLECTIONS, UNIVERSITY OF TEXAS AT ARLINGTON LIBRARIES, ARLINGTON, TEXAS, AR 406 1-21-45.

✧

The transformation back to a peacetime economy was not entirely smooth. In 1948, packinghouse workers went on strike to protest wages that seemed to be shrinking in the face of postwar inflation.

COURTESY OF THE *FORT WORTH STAR-TELEGRAM* PHOTOGRAPH COLLECTION, SPECIAL COLLECTIONS, UNIVERSITY OF TEXAS AT ARLINGTON LIBRARIES, ARLINGTON, TEXAS, AR 406 1-61-1.

Those who returned found a different Fort Worth than the one they had left. "Since you went off to war, Texan, Fort Worth's metropolitan population has jumped 85,000," crowed reporter Hugh Williamson. Not long before he wrote that piece in 1946, the city limits encompassed little more than sixty-five square miles; within just two years the boundary would embrace over a hundred. As returning servicemen and others came seeking jobs and housing, industrialists responded by developing tracts of land adjoining the city and then filing for annexation.

In response, many of the outlying communities incorporated during the decade to avoid being roped in by Fort Worth and saddled with its burdensome taxes. Yet they grew so fast that new residents clamored for the benefits of city services. Soon, their own local governments began raising taxes almost annually to satisfy the demands of homeowners and builders. In this way, a patchwork of incorporated places emerged during the 1940s. White Settlement, Westworth Village, and River Oaks gained that status in 1941. In 1944, Haltom City joined them. The next three years saw Everman, Forest Hill, Kennedale, and Benbrook Village answer the roll call. In the decade's final year Dalworthington Gardens, Pantego, Lake Worth Village, Sansom Park, and Saginaw incorporated as well.

The effect of such sudden growth thrust upon the city by a mobile population that came from every point on the compass radically altered the city's demography. "The encroachment of damyankees and airplanes has got the old-timers confused," Williamson observed. To illustrate his point, the writer related how a group of Eastern women in town for a fashion show were privately making fun of some local cowboys walking toward them. But when the men got a load of the latest women's styles, they turned the tables on the visitors and doubled over laughing.

Guffaws and merrymaking also radiated from a three-and-a-half mile strip along Jacksboro Highway, but what was going on there was no laughing matter. The short stretch of road bristled with beer joints and liquor stores as well as red-light tourist courts and clubs that provided a thin veneer for gambling. Lying snug between the Stockyards and the military reservation, Jacksboro Highway catered to the needs of workers in both industries, but also attracted its share of high rollers, politicians, and the partying crowd from the city. Moreover, it was a choice destination for oil field workers and cowboys who drove in from the "dry" counties of old Northwest Texas to get drunk and raise Cain. Like Hell's Half Acre of an earlier generation, Jacksboro Highway earned its reputation on the winks of compliant lawmen and the inevitable killing when the leash ran slack.

At such high-tone venues as the 2222 Club, Coconut Grove, or the appropriately named Casino, big band leaders such as Benny Goodman and Harry James played for dancers who hung around after the city-mandated curfew to sip on liquor, while in the back rooms patrons rolled dice and played cards. At some of the lowbrow dives, bar owners stretched chicken wire across the stage to protect musicians from flying beer bottles.

B. M. Kudlaty, a wrecker driver whom police also enlisted to take pictures of occasional murder victims, declared that on Jacksboro Highway "you could get into anything you were big enough to handle."

✧

Part of the Strategic Air Command's superbomber fleet on the runway at Carswell AFB.

COURTESY OF THE *FORT WORTH STAR-TELEGRAM* PHOTOGRAPH COLLECTION, SPECIAL COLLECTIONS, UNIVERSITY OF TEXAS AT ARLINGTON LIBRARIES, ARLINGTON, TEXAS, AR 406 1-11-46.

Learning where that line lay could be hazardous. When two thugs robbed and beat a leading underworld figure at knifepoint outside the Scoreboard Lounge, the man used his connections to track them down. Reportedly, he lured one of the muggers into his car, parked outside a beer joint, and there collected a handful of teeth and an eyeball. He then kneecapped the unfortunate hoodlum and dumped him in front of a hospital and stolidly drove away.

It was a new kind of Cowtown to be sure, but the wide-open reputation that Fort Worth had cultivated in its lusty frontier days seemed fitting to distant observers. Reporter Hugh Williamson conceded as much, but added: "Nowadays you hear more about airplanes than cows." The arrival of six thousand transfers from the flight base at Sioux City, Iowa, under the direction of the newly formed Strategic Air Command punctuated the continued importance of the city's military sector. At the Stockyards, total receipts shattered old records, peaking at five-and-a-quarter million animals in 1944, yet boom times there could not match the industrial might of the bomber plant. By the end of the decade aircraft manufacturing replaced meatpacking as the city's economic cornerstone.

The ending of the war did little to slow production at the bomber plant. Although layoffs cut deeply into Convair's workforce, thousands of laborers continued to churn out B-29s. Still others busied themselves with developing the B-36, a secret project that set an ominous tone for the postwar era. When the bomber was unveiled at the newly christened Carswell A.F.B. during the summer of 1948, Fort Worth moved into the national spotlight. Here, the Air Force boasted, was a plane that could fly ten thousand miles before refueling in mid-air, making it capable of delivering a nuclear bomb to any spot on the planet. Soon the flight logs of the B-36 listed destinations as far away as Europe, Asia, and the Arctic Circle. In February 1949 Fort Worth marked another milestone when the *Lucky Lady II*, a production model B-50 with a regular crew piloted by James G. Gallagher, rose from the Carswell runway, circled the globe and returned home, becoming the first airplane to record a nonstop round-the-world flight.

A fear of communist Russia made the bomber necessary and heightened security around the military reservation. Commander Alan D. Clark issued orders that all civilian traffic would be subject to search and interrogation. No one was beyond suspicion. "Intensive undercover checking" became routine to screen Air Force personnel reporting for duty at Carswell. In a statement that would become familiar in the emerging Cold War, Colonel Clark vowed to "weed out" any men "with known communistic leanings or known to have been associated in the past with persons of communist or subversive activities."

Nothing led ordinary citizens to wonder more what was going on behind the big fence than the role the Strategic Air Command played in the mysterious events that centered on Roswell, New Mexico, in

✧

The Lucky Lady II *is greeted by a battery of newsreel cameramen upon returning from the first nonstop around-the-world flight.*

COURTESY OF THE *FORT WORTH STAR-TELEGRAM* PHOTOGRAPH COLLECTION, SPECIAL COLLECTIONS, UNIVERSITY OF TEXAS AT ARLINGTON LIBRARIES, ARLINGTON, TEXAS, FWST NEG. 2191, #5.

✧

Major Jesse A. Marcel shows off the debris of a high altitude weather balloon in a Carswell office. Stationed at Roswell, New Mexico, with the 347th Bomber Group, he had taken part in the recovery of an alleged flying disk.

COURTESY OF THE *FORT WORTH STAR-TELEGRAM* PHOTOGRAPH COLLECTION, SPECIAL COLLECTIONS, UNIVERSITY OF TEXAS AT ARLINGTON LIBRARIES, ARLINGTON, TEXAS, FWST NEG. 2026, #3.

✧

Participants line up for a postwar Juneteenth Parade.

COURTESY OF THE FORT WORTH BLACK HISTORICAL & GENEALOGY SOCIETY COLLECTION, FORT WORTH PUBLIC LIBRARY.

July 1947. After headlines declared that a flying disc had crashed outside the small New Mexican town, SAC moved quickly to quash the story. Under a cloak of secrecy Air Force personnel loaded the debris into a B-29 and flew it to Fort Worth, where military brass displayed the wreckage of a high altitude research balloon. The "aliens" who went down with the supposed flying saucer, they insisted, were merely anthropomorphic test dummies used in the experiment. Yet the tight security surrounding the Roswell incident as well as the way the Air Force controlled the release of news forever linked Fort Worth to the most bizarre conspiracy tale in the nation's history.

Everyday life would never quite be the same. Officials of the Southwestern Exposition and Fat Stock Show managed to resume the annual event in 1944, but at a new site, the Will Rogers Memorial Coliseum and Auditorium. Over the protests of a few die-hards at North Side, voters passed a $1.5-million bond package that expanded the exposition facilities and provided a year-round administration building. In 1946 the show turned the corner, kicking off its golden anniversary with a parade that drew a large share of the city's thirty-two-thousand-plus students who were given a holiday.

A few months later, along those same downtown streets, black pride manifested itself in the observance of the eighty-second anniversary of the Emancipation Proclamation. None were more aware of the sense of postwar change than African Americans, who were loath to return to the racial status quo after doing their part to defeat totalitarianism abroad. The Juneteenth celebration brought together almost every church and civic organization in Fort Worth's black community. The parade featured six floats, twenty-two horse-back riders, and no small measure of patriotic music to underscore the message that they too were loyal Americans. Following the parade, groups split up to enjoy picnics, toss horseshoes, and play softball games.

Quietly, African-American leaders pressed the city government to post some real gains. While black Fort Worthians saw city services improve modestly and enjoyed new funding for public schools, the city council left them disappointed when it rejected a request to hire African-American police officers. "If these people were employed as policemen," concluded Chief R. E. Dysart, "they would have to work only as an isolated group, and would be restricted to work among the Negro race." A police officer, he added, "should be able to work among all groups of people." In the 1940s that was simply a concept that white Fort Worth was not ready to grasp.

Seemingly, the only constant in a decade of change was the performance of Fort Worth golfer Ben "Hawk" Hogan. The one-time Glen Garden caddy dominated the Professional Golf Association in the 1940s, standing atop the money board five times despite serving a three-year hitch in the Army Air Force. In 1948 the PGA named Hogan "Player of the Year."

✧

Ben "Hawk" Hogan drives off the seventeenth tee at the Colonial Country Club.

COURTESY OF *FORT WORTH STAR-TELEGRAM* PHOTOGRAPH COLLECTION, SPECIAL COLLECTIONS, UNIVERSITY OF TEXAS AT ARLINGTON LIBRARIES, ARLINGTON, TEXAS, FWST 3133, NEG. #3.

✧

Hogan being loaded into an ambulance outside of Van Horn, Texas, 1949.

COURTESY OF THE *FORT WORTH STAR-TELEGRAM* PHOTOGRAPH COLLECTION, SPECIAL COLLECTIONS, UNIVERSITY OF TEXAS AT ARLINGTON LIBRARIES, ARLINGTON, TEXAS, AR 406 3-33-34.

WBAP was on hand for a 1947 speech by President Harry Truman, where it telecast the state's first remote broadcast.

COURTESY OF THE JACK WHITE PHOTOGRAPH COLLECTION, SPECIAL COLLECTIONS, UNIVERSITY OF TEXAS AT ARLINGTON LIBRARIES, ARLINGTON, TEXAS, AR 407 7-16.

Then, in February 1949, the Hawk suffered a life-changing tragedy. On their way home from the Phoenix Open, Hogan and his wife, Valerie, crashed head-on into a bus that had crossed into their lane outside of Van Horn, Texas. Just as the two vehicles were about to collide, the quick-thinking golfer covered his wife, saving them both. The wreck left him shattered, however, and an ambulance transported Hogan to an El Paso hospital, where he almost died. The decade ended with the once-great golfer struggling just to grip a club. His brilliant career, it seemed, had met an untimely end.

Television, the medium that would one day popularize professional golf among the masses, debuted publicly in the Panther City on September 29, 1948, when Carter pitchman Frank Mills faced the camera and announced: "This is WBAP-TV, Fort Worth." So began the first regular broadcast in the Southwest. The city had previously laid claim to the first demonstration of this technological marvel back in 1934 as one of that year's expositions at the Stockyards fair. But this time the potential viewing audience was ready for it.

Earlier, in June, the station had previewed a closed-circuit feed for an excited crowd of local dignitaries, representatives of RCA Victor, and prospective television dealers at the Hotel Texas. What they expected to see was a professional program featuring the singing Flying X Ranch Boys. What they saw instead was a bunch of musicians clowning in front of the camera, telling lame jokes, and falling down laughing. Up in the studio, master of ceremonies Frank Mills had been waiting interminably for his cue from the red recording light. Mills finally asked a floor man, "What's going on?" To which the man replied, "I haven't heard from the truck." So, in the spirit of the moment, Mills mugged at the camera: "Okay Amon, you got all those tin-horns down there…"

Suddenly a frantic, red-faced crewman burst through the door: "You're on the air! You're on the air!" Realizing that both the camera light and the studio telephone were not working, Mills gathered his equanimity, faced the camera and intoned: "I'm sorry, Mr. Carter. We're just up here rehearsing…we'll take it from the top now." The mortified emcee just

Frenchman's Well, then thought to be the only remaining physical evidence of the old military post. It was moved to another location and subsequently disappeared. There is some speculation that the well was destroyed when a garbage truck backed over it.

COURTESY OF THE *FORT WORTH STAR-TELEGRAM* PHOTOGRAPH COLLECTION, SPECIAL COLLECTIONS, UNIVERSITY OF TEXAS AT ARLINGTON LIBRARIES, ARLINGTON, TEXAS, AR 406 H190.

A view from the flood water's edge in 1949 shows the "six-points" intersection (where avenues Camp Bowie and University come together at West Seventh and Bailey streets) completely under water.

COURTESY OF THE FORT WORTH PUBLIC LIBRARY.

✧

WBAP was on hand to record footage of the "Great Flood of '49."

COURTESY OF THE JACK WHITE PHOTOGRAPH COLLECTION, SPECIAL COLLECTIONS, UNIVERSITY OF TEXAS AT ARLINGTON LIBRARIES, ARLINGTON, TEXAS, AR 407 7-3.

✧

An aerial photograph shows the extent of the damage. This unique view, looking south (downtown is to the left, the arts district to the right), shows Farrington Field in the upper right-hand corner; West Seventh Street on the other side of Montgomery Ward is entirely under water. The bridge in the background is part of West Lancaster Avenue.

COURTESY OF THE FORT WORTH PUBLIC LIBRARY.

knew his first day in front of the camera would be his last, but graciously, Carter never mentioned the incident.

By the end of the year WBAP-TV—Channel 5 to generations of local couch potatoes—signed the first dual network affiliation in the nation, tapping both NBC and ABC. Sports and movies provided the main programming, since both took up a lot of time while producers experimented with how best to exploit the new medium. Station officials became so desperate that they begged the Fort Worth I.S.D. to broadcast high school games on Thursday, Friday, and Saturday nights.

The decade ended with the commemoration of Fort Worth's centennial. With the occasion came the sober reflection that few physical reminders had survived the formative days when the mythical panther took its nap on Main Street. Aroused citizens began surveying the remnants of their past and determined to save what they could from the ravages of time, and commemorate the vestiges already lost. The *Star-Telegram*'s Oliver Knight, gathering information that would soon be used for his classic *Outpost on the Trinity* (1953), lamented the "decay, neglect and destruction" that was then "erasing the imprints left by the era of frontier adventure."

The newspaperman-author admonished that Fort Worth might come to be known as "the city with much history and few markers." He observed that within the past two years the last standing relic of the old Army fort, Frenchman's Well, had been reduced to rubble when a garbage truck crashed into it. The loss left a mott of trees in front of the County Health Center as the only first-hand witnesses to the founding of the city. According to Tom Slack, an old pioneer banker, Major Ripley Arnold and his Second Dragoons had tethered

✧

Just before the memorable flood, Fort Worth suffered another kind of disaster when the grandstand at LaGrave Field burned.

COURTESY OF THE *FORT WORTH STAR-TELEGRAM* PHOTOGRAPH COLLECTION, SPECIAL COLLECTIONS, UNIVERSITY OF TEXAS AT ARLINGTON LIBRARIES, ARLINGTON, TEXAS, AR 406 3-1-12.

their horses there at the fort's aborning moment. Among the few remaining historical objects still capable of being rescued was a painted sign in an alley near the courthouse. The old shingle had advertised the detective agency of former city marshal Timothy "Longhair Jim" Courtwright.

Into the vacuum stepped the newly formed Tarrant County Historical Society, which planned to begin marking important sites. Among the first was the pool at the Botanic Gardens. There, early in the 1840s it was then believed, the first two white men in the area, Arkansas trappers Edward S. Terrell and John P. Lusk, camped and traded with local Indians.

The Fiesta-cade, another of Fort Worth's Texas-sized celebrations, also marked the hundredth anniversary. More reminiscent of the Diamond Jubilee than the Frontier Centennial, this one commemorated many of the same events as the 1923 pageant. Appended to the arrival of U.S. dragoons, Civil War days, the long trail, and the coming of the railroad were more recent milestones as the emergence of the bomber plants, and even Casa Mañana.

Margaret Woodruff, a great-great-granddaughter of city namesake General William Jenkins Worth, made her first visit to the Panther City as the invited guest of the pageant's organizers. "I've been wanting to see Fort Worth all my life," the gray-haired matron told a reporter. "After all these years, I'm glad I finally made it here at last." From her fifty-yard-line box, Woodruff seemed pleased with the way script writers portrayed Worth as a gentle spirit that cantered through the Fiesta-cade's founding scenes.

✧

Lacking another venue, the Cats continued to play at LaGrave until the flood completed the destruction that the fire began.

COURTESY OF THE *FORT WORTH STAR-TELEGRAM* PHOTOGRAPH COLLECTION, SPECIAL COLLECTIONS, UNIVERSITY OF TEXAS AT ARLINGTON LIBRARIES, ARLINGTON, TEXAS, AR 406 3-1-12.

She also registered some amusement when a stubborn pony pitched its "Indian" rider directly in front of her. Grinning, she exclaimed: "He got policed…as we say in the Army." Then, as a spotlight searching the crowd finally landed on her box, Woodruff rose hesitantly and waved to the crowd, which returned her blessing with a long, rolling round of applause.

The year 1949, however, would not be remembered for the Fiesta-cade. Long after the celebration grew dim in the city's collective mind, the great flood of 1949 would remain a vivid memory. There had been some monumental trash movers before, but this one killed eleven people and left some thirteen thousand others homeless. At its crest, the floodwaters reached the second story of the Montgomery Ward building on West Seventh Street and cut off the west side from downtown.

On a night that also brought tornadoes and fifty-mph straight-line winds, a horrified Mrs. Ira Adams watched helplessly as the swirling waters carried away her husband and eighty-year-old mother. Momentarily she saved herself by clinging to a Forest Park Ferris wheel, only to be knocked loose by drifting wreckage. Somehow she managed to reach a tree, where her screams attracted some railroad workers who managed to rescue her.

Yet just as city officials saw the great fire of 1909 as a kind of blessing, so too, did proponents for new area lakes see this latest disaster as opportunity in disguise. In the name of flood control city fathers convinced Congress to pass emergency funding for the U.S. Army Corps of Engineers to begin construction for Lakes Benbrook and Grapevine. Earlier projects had already resulted in Lake Worth, Eagle Mountain, and Lake Bridgeport. Such a bountiful resource on the edge of the arid West led to open-ended possibilities. During the next half century a new generation of boosters would prove as adept as their predecessors in touting the natural assets of a city that possessed all the ingredients for greatness.

✧

A veneer of snow presents a scene of tranquility on downtown's west side as the turbulent decade came to an end.

COURTESY OF THE *FORT WORTH STAR-TELEGRAM* PHOTOGRAPH COLLECTION, SPECIAL COLLECTIONS, UNIVERSITY OF TEXAS AT ARLINGTON LIBRARIES, ARLINGTON, TEXAS, AR 406 1-32-5.

✧

Downtown Fort Worth, from the air at least, looks much the same as it did before World War II. At ground level, however, the wear of age was beginning to show. Soon, the effects of well-intended federal policies would further diminish the once-vibrant heart of Fort Worth and Tarrant County.

COURTESY OF THE TEXAS CHRISTIAN UNIVERSITY, SPECIAL COLLECTIONS, MARY COUTS BURNETT LIBRARY, FORT WORTH, TEXAS.

CHAPTER 6

GREATER FORT WORTH

1950-1959

The postwar Fifties for America and Fort Worth were prosperous, but precarious, times. The Panther City, as a center for national defense, enjoyed a windfall in federal contracts. But for men and women who drew a paycheck from Uncle Sam, the thought that their work had placed a nuclear bull's-eye over North Texas was never far from the back of their minds. Living where the West begins also meant being on the hither edge of the Old South, and Fort Worthians—often clumsily—came to grips with the problems of integration. The collective mind, however, would remember the decade more for the rise of the suburbs and the flourishing arts district that propelled Fort Worth into the first tier of American high culture. The homogenizing influences of television, mass markets, and popular culture diluted the "Cowtown" identity that city fathers over the years had alternately embraced and pushed away. Yet a new personality and a new Fort Worth was emerging—part western and fully cosmopolitan—that would set a tone for cultivating the best aspects of both cultures.

During the 1950s the population of Tarrant County beyond the corporate limits of Fort Worth grew faster than the city itself. While Fort Worth added about seventy-seven thousand new souls, suburban growth registered almost a hundred thousand, transforming once-rural pastures and dirt roads into grids of tract homes and busy streets and highways. Commercial growth in the new suburbs at first struggled to adjust to changing patterns of life. "You could fire a cannon down a busy thoroughfare at midday and not hit anyone," one Hurst businessman complained of his bedroom community.

Everyone, it seemed, had driven into Fort Worth to begin the workday. At suburban strip centers that sprang up like mushrooms along major highway arteries, entrepreneurs wrung their hands, hoping that weekend shoppers would make up for the lack of business during the workweek. Consequently, that figurative cannon would have found few targets on downtown streets at night. "In by eight and out at five" became the routine for most men and women who worked at the oil and financial companies that dominated the downtown business district.

The failed Gruen Plan, named for Viennese urban planner Victor Gruen, was a visionary concept that promised to turn downtown into a futuristic maze of shops and offices. Perhaps it might even have saved the central business district from the inner city decay that became particularly noticeable during the 1950s. Texas Electric President J. B. Thomas championed this model of urban efficiency, painting serene images of landscaped plazas where visitors and workers could stroll beneath arches and enjoy the gurgling of waterfalls and fountains without the irritating din of downtown traffic. Yet the prospect of a leisure city dominated by electric shuttles and skywalks seemed too far-out

✧

Suburban strip center in Richland Hills

COURTESY OF THE *FORT WORTH STAR-TELEGRAM* PHOTOGRAPH COLLECTION, SPECIAL COLLECTIONS, UNIVERSITY OF TEXAS AT ARLINGTON LIBRARIES, ARLINGTON, TEXAS, AR 407 3-44.

for automobile-dependent Texans, whose practical sense leaned more toward getting in and getting out than stopping to smell roses.

Nevertheless the skyline did change significantly for the first time since the commercial building boom of the 1920s. In 1956 the Continental National Bank constructed a thirty-one-story tower capped with an enormous revolving clock—the time lit up on two sides and "CNB" emblazoned on the other two faces—that squinting eyes could make out even from the distant ridges far beyond the central business district. Down on the streets, however, plywood gradually replaced many of the windows in the recently vibrant heart of the city. The big department stores such as Leonards and Monnigs managed to keep old customers and attract new ones, but other retailers and entertainment managers came to recognize that people shopped and played where they lived.

✧

"The Gruen Plan for a Greater Fort Worth Tomorrow"—a vision that went unfulfilled—promised to resurrect the declining business district.

COURTESY OF THE *FORT WORTH STAR-TELEGRAM* PHOTOGRAPH COLLECTION, SPECIAL COLLECTIONS, UNIVERSITY OF TEXAS AT ARLINGTON LIBRARIES, ARLINGTON, TEXAS, FWST 3584.

Fort Worth was far from dead, however. Just across the Trinity River its social pulse registered a strong beat inside the developing arts district. In the spring of 1953 the Fort Worth Art Museum staged its "Groundbreakers' Ball," arguably the most imaginative kickoff in the city's history. Five hundred industrialists and society mavens turned out in costume—some as laborers, some as picketers, other as parts of buildings, and even a group who comprised a prison chain gang. Ted Weems and his orchestra supplied the music, while the guests danced and sipped cocktails and, with a fine Cowtown flair, feasted on gourmet cuisine served from the back of a chuck wagon.

Even as the art museum was breaking ground, the newly christened Children's Museum next door was captivating groups of youngsters with a model of its neighbor-to-be. From its modest beginnings at the De Zavala School in 1945, the museum quickly outgrew two stately old mansions on Summit Avenue. In 1950 the city council passed a bond issue to build a permanent home just west of the Will Rogers complex.

In the weeks before the opening, a tax measure came before voters asking them to provide even more money for maintenance. An open house, anxious officials hoped, would silence critics and swing the vote in their favor. The two-hour walkthrough succeeded beyond their expectations. Nearly four thousand children and parents lined up outside, some five hours before the doors opened, waiting for the chance to be among the first to experience the wide array of exhibits and hands-on activities from the worlds of natural science and history as well as art and astronomy. To the relief of museum officials, the tax bill passed.

The Fifties was an exciting time to be a child in Fort Worth. At the Forest Park Zoo they could take in just about everything that swims, slithers, walks, and flies. Among the new features included an aquarium, a reptile house, and an aviary that enhanced the park's growing collection of land animals.

For a brief, shining moment Queen Tut pushed all the new exhibits from the forefront of publicity. The baby elephant that

✧

With the construction of the Continental National Bank in 1956, the giant revolving clock added a distinctive touch to the city's skyline.

COURTESY OF THE *FORT WORTH STAR-TELEGRAM* PHOTOGRAPH COLLECTION, SPECIAL COLLECTIONS, UNIVERSITY OF TEXAS AT ARLINGTON LIBRARIES, ARLINGTON, TEXAS, AR 407 8-46.

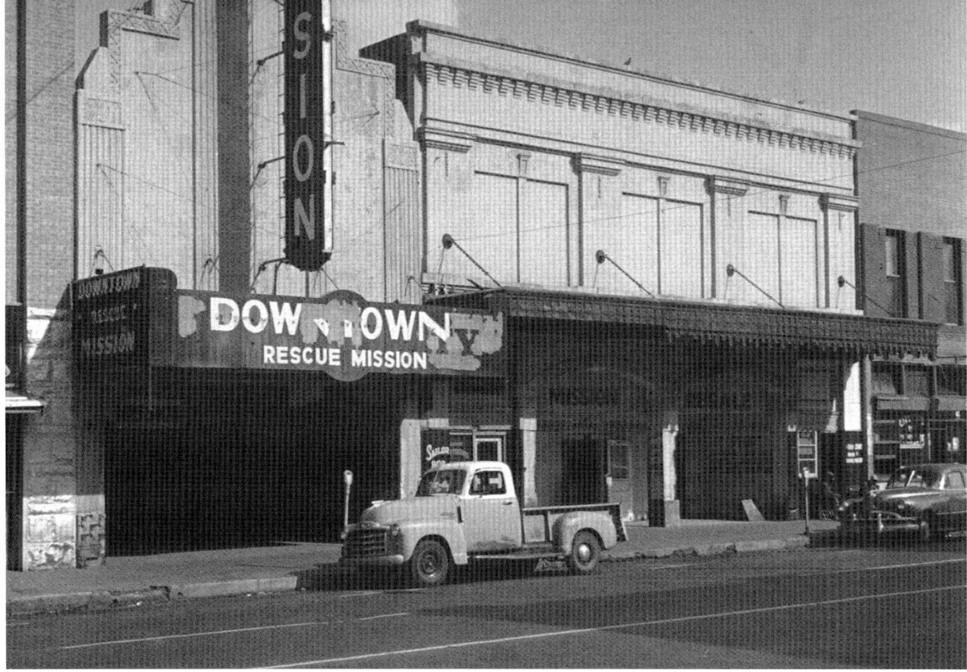

Two faces of downtown. The view at Main and Fourth Street (left). Farther down Main Street the Downtown Rescue Mission (right) operated out of the once-cheerful Liberty Theater (see page 71).

LEFT IMAGE COURTESY OF THE *FORT WORTH STAR-TELEGRAM* PHOTOGRAPH COLLECTION, SPECIAL COLLECTIONS, UNIVERSITY OF TEXAS AT ARLINGTON LIBRARIES, ARLINGTON, TEXAS, AR 407 9-27. RIGHT IMAGE COURTESY OF THE *FORT WORTH STAR-TELEGRAM* PHOTOGRAPH COLLECTION, SPECIAL COLLECTIONS, UNIVERSITY OF TEXAS AT ARLINGTON LIBRARIES, ARLINGTON, TEXAS, AR 407 3-40.

had gorged on peanuts at her fifth birthday party in the Twenties and wallowed out a lagoon at Trinity Park the next decade had grown into a venerable old monarch by 1956. When a rogue elephant felled her longtime handler, Jim Brown, Queen Tut charged in and shoulder-blocked the crazed animal, gingerly keeping the zookeeper safe beneath her giant haunches. She then absorbed two vicious assaults before a frantic team of park workers could pull the near-lifeless man to safety. Now, concluded Texana columnist Frank X. Tolbert, "you can understand why the biggest animal at the Fort Worth zoo is the biggest favorite with Jim Brown."

Running a close second among park-goers was the "Tiny T&P," the labor of love created by former railroader Bill Hames. A miniature streamliner with eight blue and silver coaches, and another model of a wood-burning locomotive with a like number of antique-looking cars, ran a course that stretched along a scenic five-and-a-half mile

Winning the first Tchaikovsky International Competition in Moscow catapulted Fort Worthian Van Cliburn into stardom. He made the cover of Time Magazine *as "The Texan Who Conquered Russia" (May 19, 1958). Inside, a photograph of him receiving the gold medal was accompanied by the caption: "He may be Horowitz, Liberace and Presley all rolled into one." On his return, Cliburn received a hero's welcome. New York City commemorated the achievement with a tickertape parade (illustrated here). Afterward he traveled to Washington, D. C. and met with Presdident Eisenhower before giving a command performance at Carnegie Hall, which he followed with a string of concerts in Boston, Philadelphia, London, and Paris. Cliburn's recording of Tchaikovsky's Piano Concerto No. 1 became the first classical recording to sell a million copies.*

COURTESY OF THE VAN CLIBURN FOUNDATION.

Queen Tut.

COURTESY OF THE *FORT WORTH STAR-TELEGRAM* PHOTOGRAPH COLLECTION, SPECIAL COLLECTIONS, UNIVERSITY OF TEXAS AT ARLINGTON LIBRARIES, ARLINGTON, TEXAS, FWST, NEG. # 499.

Bill Hames shows off his "Tiny T&P" to six-year-old Rodney Lane of Denton, 1959.

COURTESY OF THE *FORT WORTH STAR-TELEGRAM* PHOTOGRAPH COLLECTION, SPECIAL COLLECTIONS, UNIVERSITY OF TEXAS AT ARLINGTON LIBRARIES, ARLINGTON, TEXAS, FWST NEG. # 4044.

roadbed through Forest and Trinity parks from a station at the zoo. On the occasion of the ride's debut, the *Fort Worth Press*'s Jack Gordon chortled: "Gloomy rail moguls who keep taking off passenger trains, in listless surrender to other modes of transportation, should see what Mr. Hames is doing."

At the time, the Tiny T&P was billed as the longest miniature train in the world. Hames had a worker walk the track at San Antonio's Brackenridge Park with an odometer, just to make sure. During its first weekend the amusement drew 10,500 riders. Another three thousand long-faced children and adults had their money refunded as the sun lowered in the sky on the train's final runs. There would be other weekends, though. In its first year and a half the little engines pulled over a half-million passengers.

Perhaps nothing in the emerging cultural district, however, generated more excitement than the new Casa Mañana. A wistful John Ohendalski informed *Press* readers in the fall of 1957 that the "dream-memory" of Fort Worth's "closest brush with big-time show business was waking up." The announcement credited local oilman J. H. Snowden as the project's chief backer. As envisioned, two imposing Kaiser Aluminum Geodesic Domes would comprise the new Casa—one that would house a theater-playhouse, the other for hosting banquets and conventions.

Upon its completion in 1958, Casa Mañana was only half as big as originally planned, but under its single dome there was "plenty to whoop about," declared columnist Gordon. The first season—opening with *Can-Can* and closing with *Call Me Madam*—played to eighty-four percent of capacity, "a remarkably high figure in any league," the newspaperman continued.

Of all the shows that summer and fall, the most memorable single performance, according to Casa producer Melvin Dacus, came on a night when a fierce storm cut off the building's electricity just as Beverly Sills began singing "Villa" in *The Merry Widow*. The audience at first began to stir, but, as Sills continued, they settled into their seats and drank in the beautiful melody that had taken on an emotional quality amid the darkened playhouse.

Billy Rose, no doubt, would have loved it. The creator of the original Casa Mañana never returned to see his legacy. He did, however, visit Fort Worth once, in 1954, to attend a testimonial luncheon. Among those gathered to honor him were thirteen of the old Frontier Centennial board. "Almost everything good that's happened to me since stemmed from what happened here," Rose confided.

For old-times sake the showman accompanied a smaller group to the grounds. There, he found only one building left standing, the Pioneer Palace. It all must have seemed so far away. Where once the multitudes ooh'd-and-ah'd to Rose's overblown extravaganza, the bubble dances of Sally Rand, and the music of

The new Casa Mañana.

COURTESY OF THE *FORT WORTH STAR-TELEGRAM* PHOTOGRAPH COLLECTION, SPECIAL COLLECTIONS, UNIVERSITY OF TEXAS AT ARLINGTON LIBRARIES, ARLINGTON, TEXAS, AR 406 1-11-49.

Producer Melvin Dacus, the force behind much of Casa's success, promoting The Student Prince, *one of the venue's hits of 1959.*

COURTESY OF THE *FORT WORTH STAR-TELEGRAM* PHOTOGRAPH COLLECTION, SPECIAL COLLECTIONS, UNIVERSITY OF TEXAS AT ARLINGTON LIBRARIES, ARLINGTON, TEXAS, AR 406 2-28-15.

Paul Whiteman and His Orchestra, there was little left of the original Casa but a single star-shaped fountain and the rusting skeleton of the revolving stage.

The march of time also trod past some of the city's leaders, men whose lives had shaped the economic and social landscape of the Panther City. In 1950 Fort Worth mourned the passing of Bill McDonald. Two years later the First Baptist's fiery J. Frank Norris died. Joe T. Garcia, only fifty-four, followed him the next year, but his name survived in the restaurant that continued his legacy. Then, on June 23, 1955, *Star-Telegram* subscribers awoke to read: "Amon Giles Carter died at 8:20 p.m. Thursday."

From across the country, an outpouring of calls, letters, and telegrams flooded the newspaper's offices. Lyndon Johnson, whom Carter had once snubbed, praised the publisher on the floor of the Senate: "[H]e walked with cattleman and kings, with crop farmers and with presidents…." Such was the provenance of all those condolences. Upwards of fifteen thousand people turned out for the funeral. Among a sea of flowers was an arrangement sent by Billy Rose in the shape of a Shady Oak Stetson. Then, with a magnificent West Texas sunset for a backdrop, the man who had played cowboy for Fort Worth and America was lowered into his final resting place.

Even before Carter's passing, it appeared as if his own success had begun to outgrow him. The economic scope and social diversity attending all the ventures he had fostered also bred mavericks who determined to break free of his lasso, men unintimidated by the size of the loop or how tight it promised to close on them. One of those rare individuals was a young man of unflagging fortitude, a thirty-one-year-old veteran B-24 bombardier from Weatherford with thirty combat missions to his credit. In the midterm congressional election of 1954, he challenged the publisher's handpicked incumbent in the Democratic primary, House Representative Wingate Lucas. With the rival candidate gaining ground as the summer date of the plebiscite neared, Carter began trying to bully him from the political stage. On one hand, the *Star-Telegram* passively ignored his candidacy. Shaking a figurative finger, the upstart scolded the publisher for giving a wildly successful political dinner "less space than an obituary of [a] Chinese laundryman in Seattle who once passed through Fort Worth." On the other hand, the challenger felt Carter's full force land on him two days before the election in the form of a front-page

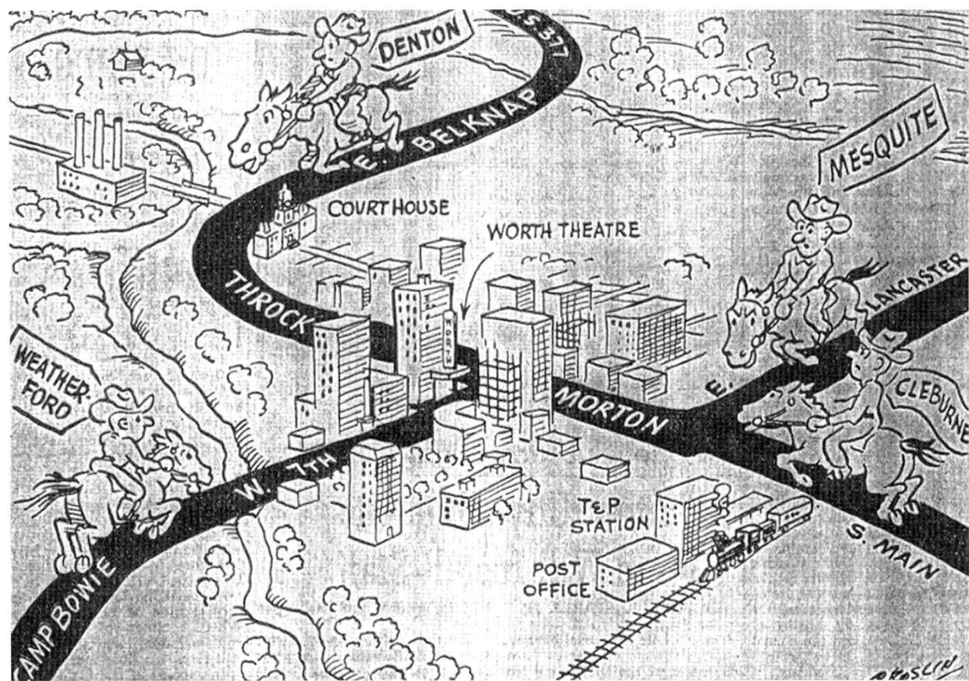

✧

All roads lead to Fort Worth along the race's routes.

COURTESY OF THE *FORT WORTH STAR-TELEGRAM* PHOTOGRAPH COLLECTION, SPECIAL COLLECTIONS, UNIVERSITY OF TEXAS AT ARLINGTON LIBRARIES, ARLINGTON, TEXAS.

✧

To help promote the 1951 world premier of the movie Fort Worth, *starring Randolph Scott, Cowtown promoters organized a unique horse race. As four contestants converged on the theater district from each compass point, updates via radio apprised those lining the routes of their progress, while loudspeakers near the finish line kept the multitudes assembled there in a state of anxious anticipation. Veteran rodeo star Bob Rothel of Weatherford (above) broke the tape in less than twenty-four minutes. The movie star himself, dressed in the black outfit he wore in the film, presented Rothel with a three-foot trophy and a new saddle donated by the Leddy Boot and Saddle Company. After the presentation, seven thousand jubilant moviegoers streamed into the Worth, Hollywood, Palace, and Majestic Theaters to enjoy the show.. At the time, it was the largest crowd ever to attend a movie premier.*

COURTESY OF THE *FORT WORTH STAR-TELEGRAM* PHOTOGRAPH COLLECTION, SPECIAL COLLECTIONS, UNIVERSITY OF TEXAS AT ARLINGTON LIBRARIES, ARLINGTON, TEXAS, FWST 2632.

editorial extolling Lucas' record, while dismissing his own detailed agenda as nothing but "vague promises."

The very next day, the inspired challenger published an eloquently tenacious editorial of his own, one for which he had to dig into his own pocket to pay the advertisers' rate of almost a thousand dollars. On July 23, 1954, in "An open letter to Mr. Amon G. Carter and the *Fort Worth Star-Telegram*," the candidate declared: "You have at last met a man…who is not afraid of you." While striking a balance between castigating the publisher for "printing only that which you WANTED the people to read" and praising him for "the many wonderful things you have done for Fort Worth and our area," he reminded him that others also "aspired…to try to do things for our area and our people." Closing with the promise that "I will be YOUR Congressman, just as I will EVERYONE'S Congressman," the challenger closed: "Very sincerely yours, Jim Wright."

The next day the people spoke with their ballots, and Wright came away the winner. The victorious election launched a thirty-four-year career that saw him rise to the speaker's chair of the lower chamber. He also won over Amon Carter. To the publisher's credit, he did not have to run the letter that was so critical of him and his newspaper. Neither did he have to pen a congratulatory editorial following the defeat of the man Wright had called his "personal, private Congressman." But he did. Perhaps Carter saw a bit of himself in Wright, admonishing the young man to take to his new job, "and hop to it in full force and good humor." Carter, of course, would soon pass from the scene, leaving Wright to continue building on his legacy by bringing home billions of dollars and thousands of jobs to Fort Worth and its constituent region in the form of government contracts and business development.

✧

The funeral for Amon Carter, 1955.

COURTESY OF THE JACK WHITE PHOTOGRAPH COLLECTION, SPECIAL COLLECTIONS, UNIVERSITY OF TEXAS AT ARLINGTON LIBRARIES, ARLINGTON, TEXAS, AR 407 10-2-45.

Like death, change, of course, was inevitable and not without its own peculiar pain. It went by many names, but as suburbia transformed the recently bucolic countryside, its appellation became "progress." Azle turned into a haven for blue-collar defense workers, putting such a strain on the school that administrators were forced to divide the auditorium into four classrooms. Little Benbrook, home to about thirty people—mostly farmers—during the recent war grew by 548 percent during the decade. Across Little Fossil Creek from Haltom City the brand new community of Richland Hills carved out a spot in the awakening countryside. Everywhere, noted an alarmed columnist, the "little cities about Fort Worth are gobbling up everything in sight, stretching miles from their legitimate boundaries."

Within the corporate limits of the Panther City itself Cass Edwards II ended years of speculation when he announced that the 4,020-acre ranch his great-grandfather had founded on the southwestern edge of the city would be broken up by a master plan of subdivisions and strip centers. "We hope to make this the most outstanding exclusive development in the Southwest," he said, "one that the city can be proud of." Opening up the sprawling ranch, lying between Westcliff and Ridglea, removed the barrier that separated TCU and Arlington Heights. During the Fifties it would quickly begin to fill in.

At Arlington the familiar sight of the well house at Center and Main was replaced in 1951 by a traffic signal. Community leaders believed the mineral tap from which generations of townsfolk had sipped and filled jugs had simply become a hazard. The well whose rich mineral crystals were once packaged and distributed across the country was unceremoniously capped; plans to pipe the water to a sidewalk fountain never materialized.

As Arlington grew into a bedroom community for both Fort Worth and Dallas during the late 1940s it took action to plan its future. City Manager Albert S. Jones

✧

An ebullient Jim Wright (facing the camera) celebrates with his campaign staff upon winning his first congressional election in 1954.

COURTESY OF TEXAS CHRISTIAN UNIVERSITY, SPECIAL COLLECTIONS, MARY COUTS BURNETT LIBRARY, FORT WORTH, TEXAS.

✧

Industry and homes continue to take over erstwhile farmlands in the outlying areas as shown in this photograph of Richland Hills. In the next decade construction of the new Airport Freeway would separate the plant and housing development.

COURTESY OF THE *FORT WORTH STAR-TELEGRAM* PHOTOGRAPH COLLECTION, SPECIAL COLLECTIONS, UNIVERSITY OF TEXAS AT ARLINGTON LIBRARIES, ARLINGTON, TEXAS, AR 407 6-35.

in 1950 marketed the strategically located suburb as a "growing city where real estate is big business and industry is not wanted." Reality, however, soon dictated otherwise. Two years later General Motors announced that it had selected Arlington for the site of a million-square-foot assembly plant.

Shortly afterwards, at the former Arlington Downs where legal horseracing had enjoyed a brief heyday in the 1930s, H. C. Miller bellowed to his wrecking crew atop the weathered grandstand: "Rip it up, and throw it down." The site soon became home to another massive industrial development, the Great Southwest Corporation, which joined GM as well as recent arrivals American Can, Menasco Aircraft, and a host of smaller businesses that manufactured everything from dolls and ceramics to furniture and an item that the Atomic Energy Commission would not reveal.

Orchestrating most of the action was "Boy Mayor" Tommy Vandergriff. Only twenty-five years old when he won the job in 1951, this son of local powerbroker Hooker Vandergriff soon made his own name. Critics had predicted that the flashy USC grad, whose business experience centered mostly around promoting sports contests and beauty pageants, would be a "playboy mayor concerned with nothing but fluff."

He quickly proved them wrong. A tireless booster for Arlington, Vandergriff guided the well-planned and deliberate growth of an infant city poised to explode. The eight-thousand-odd souls who inhabited Arlington when Vandergriff became mayor topped 120,000 by the time he retired in 1977. With characteristic modesty, a manner that would endear him to fellow citizens, Vandergriff shrugged to an interviewer in 1957: "I'm not going to take credit for any of it." Citing geography, timing, and harmony he declared: "Arlington grew because of an amazing civic spirit, a community-wide desire."

Land prices in Arlington during the 1950s skyrocketed in some places from $300 an acre to over $3,000. The rigorously zoned city shone like a beacon to fastidious residential developers. During the decade over a hundred subdevelopments took root on Arlington's bald prairies and cut into dense stands of post-oaks where the picturesque Cross Timbers intruded. At one point the city water department was connecting upwards of five hundred new homes a month. Supermarkets and shopping centers sprang up at the crossroads of major intersections that were dirt roads only a few years earlier.

At local schools, growing faculties greeted more than a thousand new students annually, compelling the Arlington I.S.D. to push a $3-million building bond in 1955, the first of several mammoth packages. To facilitate the sudden, but not entirely unexpected growth, the city dammed up Village Creek in 1956. The site where county namesake General Edward H. Tarrant had fought bands of Caddos, Tonkawas, and other Indians living in extended settlements along the bottomland that gave the creek its name, soon lay all but forgotten beneath the waters of the new Lake Arlington.

Anticipating the rural growth just to the north of Arlington, Bill Austin moved his

For as long as most Arlington citizens could remember, the well house had been a fixture at the intersection of Central and Main streets. Growth and increased traffic, however, compelled city planners to cap it and pave over the site in 1951 (see page 29).

COURTESY OF THE *FORT WORTH STAR-TELEGRAM* PHOTOGRAPH COLLECTION, SPECIAL COLLECTIONS, UNIVERSITY OF TEXAS AT ARLINGTON LIBRARIES, ARLINGTON, TEXAS, FWST 1476.

"Boy Mayor" Tommy Vandergriff and Chamber of Commerce secretary Dorothy Wallace admire the symbolism of a new street sign, purchased with funds from one of the organization's campaigns.

COURTESY OF THE *FORT WORTH STAR-TELEGRAM* PHOTOGRAPH COLLECTION, SPECIAL COLLECTIONS, UNIVERSITY OF TEXAS AT ARLINGTON LIBRARIES, ARLINGTON, TEXAS, AR 406 2-115-10.

The "avenue" in Collins Avenue might have seemed pretentious when the decade was new and the road was little more than a dirt trail. During the Fifties, however, it would grow into a busy thoroughfare.

COURTESY OF THE *ARLINGTON CITIZEN-JOURNAL* PHOTOGRAPH COLLECTION, SPECIAL COLLECTIONS, UNIVERSITY OF TEXAS AT ARLINGTON LIBRARIES, ARLINGTON, TEXAS, ACJ 96-10-9.

family from Fort Worth to Hurst in 1949, where he traded the log book in his commercial truck for an apron. There he managed Emma's Café, a roadside eatery that served drivers who plowed the route along Highway 183 (now Highway 10) that connected Fort Worth and Dallas. It became a busier road in 1950, when work crews replaced the pocked asphalt with a new concrete surface.

Nevertheless, the dusty lanes that fed into 183 betrayed few hints of the suburban phenomenon that was about to develop. In the Hurst of 1950, phone service was not yet a year old, and men and women still drew water from family wells. The teenagers who befriended Bill Austin's young daughter anticipated country and western dances and bragged on the animals they were grooming for the 4-H Club.

All of that was about to change. Holding up a copy of the *Star-Telegram*, Principal C. C. Bodine on March 27, 1951 announced to his student body that the Bell Aircraft Corporation had bought a fifty-five-acre tract of land just up the highway that would soon become the site of a $3-million helicopter factory. "Take a good look at Hurst," Bodine intoned dramatically, "It will never be the Hurst as you have known it."

An Arlington housing development, 1953.

COURTESY OF THE *ARLINGTON CITIZEN-JOURNAL* PHOTOGRAPH COLLECTION, SPECIAL COLLECTIONS, UNIVERSITY OF TEXAS AT ARLINGTON LIBRARIES, ARLINGTON, TEXAS, ACJ 96-9.

The announcement by company President Lawrence D. Bell came on the heels of a countrywide search that settled on Fort Worth, as he put it, "because of its strategic location, its large population...and our company's excellent relations with Convair...and other aircraft and industrial organizations in the region." As envisioned the plant would employ two thousand local people as well as a cadre of managers who would swap the frigid winters at Buffalo, New York, for the sweltering summers of North Texas. At the time, the conflict in Korea was raging, and Bell helicopters were gaining wide and favorable publicity for evacuating wounded soldiers and taking part in reconnaissance missions. Adding Cold War imperatives into the mix assured that new government contracts would make the plant a growing force in the emerging economy of "Greater" Fort Worth.

Sure enough, Bell during the 1950s posted new orders in the tens of millions of dollars from the Army, Navy, and Marines. Within three years after turning out its first whirlybird, the Hurst plant grew into a $15-million factory with 3,500 employees. It also earned a promotion, as one correspondent reported, when workers pulled down the Bell Aircraft sign that signified its division status and placed in its stead a new logo proclaiming the Bell Helicopter Corporation, an independent subsidiary of the booming transportation giant.

As Bell churned out its turbine-powered HU-1's, the first generation of "Hueys," it also developed new models and experimented

✧

The Bell Helicopter Corporation in Hurst helped Tarrant County keep its edge as one of the country's leading centers for aircraft production.

COURTESY OF THE JACK WHITE PHOTOGRAPH COLLECTION, SPECIAL COLLECTIONS, UNIVERSITY OF TEXAS AT ARLINGTON LIBRARIES, ARLINGTON, TEXAS, AR 407 5-3.

with other designs that were better left on drawing boards. The most radical project proposed an atomic-powered helicopter the length of a football field. A close match was the Dynasoar—short for "dynamic soaring"—a joint effort between Bell and Convair that was touted as more of a spaceship than a jet airplane. Its engineers foresaw a craft that would be boosted into the fringes of the earth's atmosphere by rockets. There, in the rarified air, it would be capable of reaching a speed of 17,500 mph and circle the globe in the stunning time of an hour and a half. Yet another experiment, the XV-3, produced a "convertiplane" prototype that passed wind tunnel tests at Moffett Field in California. The tilt-wing aircraft showed much promise, but its designers never quite worked out the bugs. Stubbornly, it remained on the planning horizon, to the regret of some who saw the project grow into the troubled V-22 Osprey.

The same year that Bell opened its factory gates, the first passenger flight touched down at the ill-fated Greater Fort Worth International Airport, midway between the Panther City and Dallas. Just after World War II, businessmen and local officials in Fort Worth became convinced that Meacham Field was simply inadequate for the traffic generated by American Airlines, Braniff, and Delta. Dallas, on the other hand, chafed at the way its upstart neighbor was trying to stack the economic deck on what was supposed to be a cooperative venture. Petty bickering over the proposed location of the terminal finally provoked Dallas to back out and concentrate on improving Love Field. Meacham, meanwhile, languished.

Briefly it looked as if Fort Worth had pulled off its greatest coup over Dallas since staging the Frontier Centennial back in 1936. After the Civil Aeronautics Administration approved Fort Worth's application for federal funds to build the colossal airport, Dallas congressman Frank Wilson convinced the House Appropriations Committee to kill it. Yet, like so many times before, a delegation of the Panther City's "Who's Who" descended on Washington, D.C. and convinced senators to revive the bill. Seemingly Fort Worth had won the contest, when, on April 25, 1953, a welcoming committee herded the sleepy passengers from a late night New York-to-Los Angeles flight onto the tarmac, where they were feted with a barbecue to inaugurate the field and terminal building named for its champion, Amon G. Carter.

In many respects, the grand opening proved to be the airport's high water mark. Originally it was scheduled to open in 1950, but poor weather and shaky financing delayed construction for almost three years. In 1951 and again in 1952 voters had to approve expensive bond issues just to keep the earthmovers rattling. When the airport was completed, the number of daily flights

✧

The Hurstview Addition, shown here in 1951, became home to many Bell employees.

COURTESY OF THE *FORT WORTH STAR-TELEGRAM* PHOTOGRAPH COLLECTION, SPECIAL COLLECTIONS, UNIVERSITY OF TEXAS AT ARLINGTON LIBRARIES, ARLINGTON, TEXAS, AR 406 1-38-26.

never came close to its potential—in part because it could never attract Dallasites who preferred the conveniences of Love Field. Fort Worth businessmen conceded as much when they testified before a Civil Aeronautics Board hearing in 1956. It was a bitter pill to swallow.

The next year the *Star-Telegram* took a shot at its rival, predicting that improvements at the Greater Fort Worth International Airport would attract new passengers dissatisfied with the "hemmed-in and overcrowded Love Field." While admitting that the "glamorous, giant lobby of the Carter Field terminal building [was] almost empty of customers," it nevertheless glowed that "things are looking up." Citing new runway construction, additional safety features, and a momentary upward trend in traffic, airport officials promised a turnaround—"and this time," continued the newspaper, "they seem to really believe it when they say it."

Giving the airport another boost was the opening of American Airlines' "Stewardess College" nearby, the first of its kind in the nation. The luxurious complex, designed to train a thousand flight attendants annually, featured "country-club like surroundings of stone, glass, beautiful scenery and swimming pool." Laborers constructed the façade largely out of West Texas fencing stones that early-day ranchers had used to enclose pastures on the near-treeless plains.

At a speech delivered at Carter Field, House Speaker Sam Rayburn dedicated the college as American Airlines President C. R. Smith and the first class of prospective

✧

American Airlines flight attendants pose at the company's Stewardess College under construction.

COURTESY OF THE *FORT WORTH STAR-TELEGRAM* PHOTOGRAPH COLLECTION, SPECIAL COLLECTIONS, UNIVERSITY OF TEXAS AT ARLINGTON LIBRARIES, ARLINGTON, TEXAS, AR 406 1-36-16.

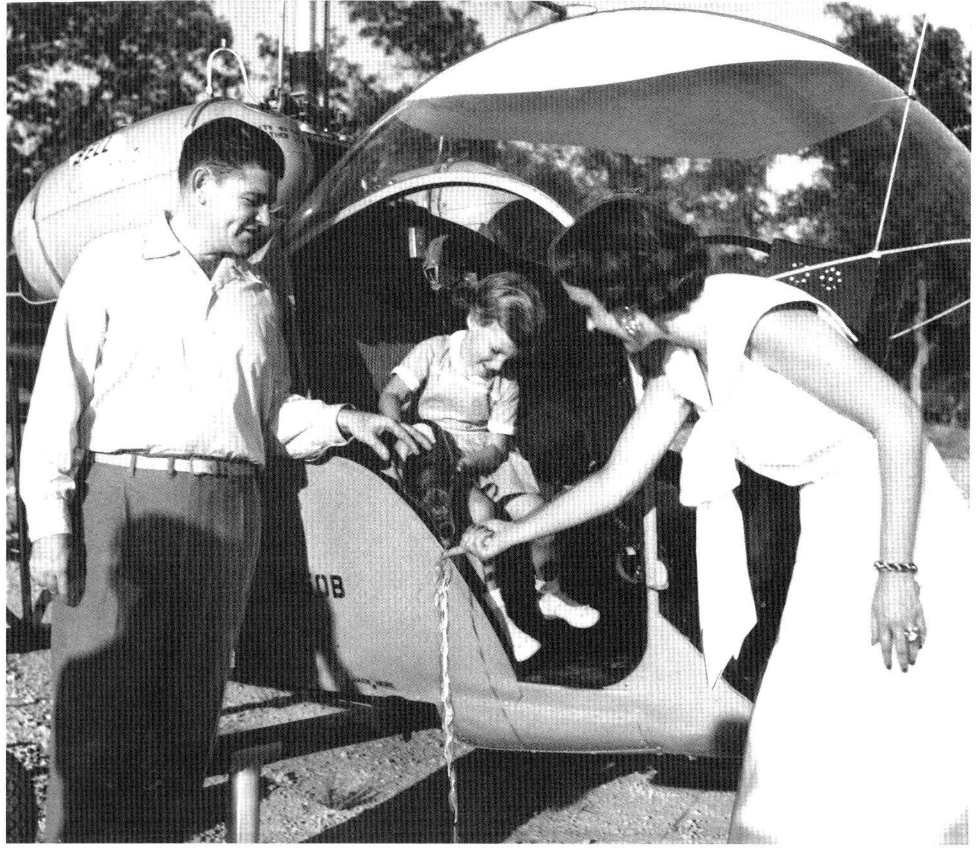

✧

Civilian uses for helicopters never fulfilled the hopes of Bell's managers. Yet, for awhile, talk of ubiquitous heliports and commuter choppers excited the imagination of forward-looking executives. Here, young George Ann Ambrose and her parents check out the first helicopter to land at Eagles Nest Resort on Eagle Mountain Lake.

COURTESY OF THE *FORT WORTH STAR-TELEGRAM* PHOTOGRAPH COLLECTION, SPECIAL COLLECTIONS, UNIVERSITY OF TEXAS AT ARLINGTON LIBRARIES, ARLINGTON, TEXAS, AR 406 1-21-46.

✧

The Texas Tech Red Raider football team stops over at the new Amon Carter Field to celebrate its 1954 Gator Bowl victory with local fans.

COURTESY OF THE *FORT WORTH STAR-TELEGRAM* PHOTOGRAPH COLLECTION, SPECIAL COLLECTIONS, UNIVERSITY OF TEXAS AT ARLINGTON LIBRARIES, ARLINGTON, TEXAS, AR 406 5-16-4.

✧

The aptly named "Mixmaster" alongside the older network of rails.

COURTESY OF THE JACK WHITE PHOTOGRAPH COLLECTION, SPECIAL COLLECTIONS, UNIVERSITY OF TEXAS AT ARLINGTON LIBRARIES, ARLINGTON, TEXAS, AR 407 1-15.

graduates looked on. A few weeks later fifty-one young women received their wings, each polishing her pin with the same velvet cloth. The graduates started another tradition by dropping a personal item into the wishing well by the Kiwi monument, dedicated to the organization of former American Airlines flight attendants.

The breathtaking pace of suburban growth could not have been achieved without the new system of federally funded freeways, reinforced by immense state spending on secondary highways. During the decade a network of divided roads brushed the edges of the central business district, affording easy access to downtown businesses and government offices while routing other traffic away from the city's nerve center. Where I-35W and the Dallas-Fort Worth Turnpike (now I-30) were joined by feeder roads, the "Mixmaster" directed often-confused drivers over a system of cloverleafs and bridges.

✧

The new toll road promised to make traffic jams like this one on Lancaster Avenue in the early Fifties a thing of the past..

COURTESY OF JACK WHITE PHOTOGRAPH COLLECTION, SPECIAL COLLECTIONS, UNIVERSITY OF TEXAS AT ARLINGTON LIBRARIES, ARLINGTON, TEXAS, AR 407 10-2-32.

✧

Before and after: the Dallas-Fort Worth Turnpike near Oakland Boulevard.

TOP IMAGE COURTESY OF THE JACK WHITE PHOTOGRAPH COLLECTION, SPECIAL COLLECTIONS, UNIVERSITY OF TEXAS AT ARLINGTON LIBRARIES, ARLINGTON, TEXAS, AR 407 9-45. BOTTOM IMAGE COURTESY OF THE HASKINS PHOTOGRAPH COLLECTION, SPECIAL COLLECTIONS, UNIVERSITY OF TEXAS AT ARLINGTON LIBRARIES, ARLINGTON, TEXAS, H 1250.

✧

The Texas Progressive Youth Cup, an African-American organization that took its name from the Biblical verse "my cup runneth over," successfully picketed several Fort Worth businesses during the 1950s. Here, protesters target the Coca-Cola Bottling Company, demanding that management hire black truck drivers.

COURTESY OF THE FORT WORTH PUBLIC LIBRARY, TARRANT COUNTY BLACK HISTORICAL & GENEALOGY SOCIETY COLLECTION.

On the turnpike's opening day, a reporter cheerily remarked: "After 117 million half-dollars are dropped into the toll-takers' hands, the road will be toll-free." The only incident that marred the opening came when a South Texas woman hauling a load of pigs to the Panther City got lost. Ending up at the tollbooth, she scorched the attendant: "To blazes with this paying money to ride on a road." With traffic stacking up, the angry "pig lady" tried to make a U-turn, but her trailer was too long.

The experience that changed the face of Fort Worth and the unsuspecting farming communities on its fringes was a nationwide phenomenon. Yet, for all its good intentions, the colossal Federal Highway Program fostered suburban growth at the expense of their urban cores. Similarly, an expanded Federal Housing Administration program seeded the development of suburban communities, but its reluctance to extend loans for apartment construction and home improvements in older neighborhoods assured the decay of inner cities.

To African Americans, it seemed as if once again the blessings of democracy were eluding them. Against the backdrop of the growing Civil Rights movement, many black leaders in Fort Worth cried "Enough!" They went to city hall when the north freeway cut two of their parks in half—one that provided African-American golfers with the only course that welcomed them. When the board voted to close public swimming pools rather than desegregate, NAACP Spokesman Clifford Davis ridiculed their illogic: "Everybody will have equal access—to nothing." Even as whites were boasting in 1956 that $8 million allocated toward recent building programs had given Fort Worth "the state's [most] outstanding system of Negro schools," local NAACP President Dr. G. D. Flemmings pointed out that the Board of Education was nevertheless "violating the law and they'll find it out very soon."

For the time being, however, it was a hollow threat. The previous year black leaders themselves had learned just how steep a climb they faced in reaching that white schoolhouse. Going into the 1955-56 school year, three African-American students in the southeast Tarrant County town of Mansfield challenged the status quo in court. Local tradition meant that after the eighth grade, black students would have to complete their secondary education at Fort Worth's I. M. Terrell High School. It also meant they would have to catch a Trailways bus that left Mansfield at 7:15 in the morning, then wait two hours after school

Mansfield High School students on the first day of classes in 1955 arrive to see an African-American effigy hanging over the schoolhouse door.

COURTESY OF THE *FORT WORTH STAR-TELEGRAM* PHOTOGRAPH COLLECTION, SPECIAL COLLECTIONS, UNIVERSITY OF TEXAS AT ARLINGTON LIBRARIES, ARLINGTON, TEXAS, FWST 3663 NEG. #1.

During the fall of 1956 teens gathered outside the home of Lloyd G. Austin to protest the family's attempt to integrate the Riverside neighborhood.

COURTESY OF THE *FORT WORTH STAR-TELEGRAM* PHOTOGRAPH COLLECTION, SPECIAL COLLECTIONS, UNIVERSITY OF TEXAS AT ARLINGTON LIBRARIES, ARLINGTON, TEXAS, FWST 3662, 1.

ended at 3:30 to return. If they played sports or were in the band or some other after-school activity, they had to find rides and might not get home until nine o'clock.

Despite a stunning victory in federal court, the black community in Mansfield knew it was still too soon to celebrate. On the first day of school, an angry mob blocked the path of the three students, punctuating threats with effigies they had hanged from the flagpole and over the school's front entrance. Others, with the connivance of the mayor and police, set up a checkpoint on the edge of town, where they roughed up and turned back suspected sympathizers.

The action of Governor Allen Shivers and the inaction of President Dwight D. Eisenhower sealed the students' fate. Texas Rangers, called in by Shivers, sided with the rabble. Eisenhower, facing reelection, chose not to intervene. So, it came to pass that *Brown v. The Topeka Board of Education*, which promised to end public school segregation, would cut its teeth at Little Rock, Arkansas; the Mansfield affair would be little more than a sordid footnote to the history of the American Civil Rights movement.

Other manifestations of white resistance emanated not so much out of hatred, but from a kind of pocketbook racism. About 325 Handley residents, for example, united to lobby the FHA against approving a 650-unit apartment complex for African Americans just east of Stop-Six and Rosedale Park. Later that same year, a woman speaking on behalf of the Forest Park Civic League drew applause when she protested the development of a housing project in North Mistletoe Heights. "We don't object to Negroes having comfortable homes," the woman bleated, "but when it happens out here our property value deteriorates."

Complaining led to impending violence when African American Lloyd G. Austin moved his wife and infant daughter to Riverside in 1956. Once more effigies decorated the limbs of trees, but this time the mob—composed mostly of teenagers—burned crosses and called for blood. "Stay away and stay alive," read the placard of one protester, as others hollered such epithets as "Hang the n[------]" and "Go back to the Congo." Nervous policemen, unable to convince the protesters to break up, at least stood watch until the heckling cabal grew weary enough to call it a night.

There was another side of white Fort Worth, however, that wanted to move forward. Black and white citizens in 1944 had formed the Fort Worth Urban League, dedicated to improving the conditions of local African Americans. While it shied away from overt

Despite racial tensions, Fort Worth's black community enjoyed a vibrant social life as this group of revelers at a segregated nightclub illustrates.

COURTESY OF THE FORT WORTH PUBLIC LIBRARY, TARRANT COUNTY BLACK HISTORICAL & GENEALOGY SOCIETY COLLECTION.

crusades, the organization nevertheless attacked head-on the problems of education, crime, and housing. In 1954, in fact, the Urban League's efforts to build and repair homes in black neighborhoods funneled $5 million into the local economy and earned recognition for the top black housing program in the nation.

Fort Worthians marked progress in other ways as well. Early in the decade the black community finally got the policemen they had asked for just after the war. By 1958 there were more openings than applicants. When the first black golfers in 1955 hit the links at formerly all-white Rockwood, the *Press* reported that "nothing out of the ordinary happened." The next year city buses desegregated just as quietly. A minor stir attending the realization that mixed-race baseball games were being played at Greenway Park served only to pack the stands. "We've been playing white teams down here for nine years," yawned African-American Athletic Director T. O. Busby. "It never attracted any attention before, but it sure helped the crowd."

Those at the top of American society who continued to fight integration charged that communism lurked behind black unrest. Such voices were not as virulent in the Panther City as in some other places; nevertheless one thing remained clear-during the Fifties, Fort Worthians took the threat of communism and nuclear war seriously. Like their counterparts elsewhere, local teachers and government workers were compelled to take loyalty oaths, and the Red-baiting superpatriots who feasted on society's pinkish fringe never lacked for popular support.

One visitor to the Fort Worth Public Library, upon noticing the writings of Karl Marx shelved alongside those of America's Founding Fathers, expressed his outrage in a letter to the editor. "We have within our walls an evil Trojan horse," he warned. "I ask that the public be informed as to [the] identity of [the] person or persons responsible." The culprit, of course, was Melvin Dewey, who had conceived his decimal system in the 1870s. The only thing "red" in this instance was the letter writer's face when he finally learned how it all worked.

Given the Cold War rhetoric of the day, it was no wonder that some men and women were seeing Reds behind every tree. The speech that House Speaker Sam Rayburn delivered to the first graduates of the Stewardess College was just as much an occasion to "warn against complacency" as it was to honor the young flight attendants. Praising the women for spreading good will, "Mr. Sam" contrasted a world in which there was "less good will than there has ever been [since] anyone now living can remember.... Our civilization and freedom are in danger," he warned, "and let nobody tell you they are not."

Then, there was the problem of Jacksboro Highway—a strictly American-made nuisance. Doing his part to kindle the rivalry between the two regional giants, a *Dallas Morning News* correspondent toured the strip three times during the fall of 1950. His report made page one. The sensational story charged: "Wide open gambling—dice, horse race bookmaking, slot machines or roulette—has been running unmolested in Fort Worth and Tarrant County." Indignant, District Attorney Stewart Hellman remarked that at least the Panther City "has been singularly blessed by being free of violence that has marked gambling activity in Dallas."

Locals share a slice of the "Fabulous Fifties" at Lake Grapevine. If they were like most middle-class Americans, the tumultuous events of the decade that unfolded around them might as well have been happening in another part of the world.

COURTESY OF THE *FORT WORTH STAR-TELEGRAM* PHOTOGRAPH COLLECTION, SPECIAL COLLECTIONS, UNIVERSITY OF TEXAS AT ARLINGTON LIBRARIES, ARLINGTON, TEXAS, AR 407 8-14.

Little more than a month later a spectacular bombing had the lawyer eating his words. Someone who knew what they were doing had rigged gambler Nelson Harris's car to a charge of nitroglycerin that ignited when he turned the key. The blast blew his eyes right out their sockets and left his mangled body embedded in the seat. Tragically, he was not alone. Sitting beside him was his pregnant wife, who died on the operating table along with their unborn child.

It would be the first of several grisly underworld slayings that rocked Fort Worth during the decade. Wells, shallow graves, and the bottom of Lake Worth all provided convenient dumping grounds for the hoodlums who so viciously guarded their underworld turf. It would take a string of federal grand juries to bring the freewheeling strip under control. In the course of reform, several careers were broken, and any number of high-toned men and women saw their reputations sullied.

✧

U.S. House Speaker Sam Rayburn of Texas chose the occasion of the Stewardess College dedication to warn area citizens of an imminent Communist menace.

COURTESY OF THE *FORT WORTH STAR-TELEGRAM* PHOTOGRAPH COLLECTION, SPECIAL COLLECTIONS, UNIVERSITY OF TEXAS AT ARLINGTON LIBRARIES, ARLINGTON, TEXAS, AR 406 2-90-25.

Despite all of society's ills, average Fort Worthians were too busy making a living and having fun to become involved in matters that did not affect them directly. For the first time since the 1920s, a youth culture emerged that produced its own music, its own lingo, its own interests. Let the grown-ups worry about communism, their sons and daughters had more pressing concerns. Turning their backs on the problems of the world, teenagers in Fort Worth as elsewhere focused on congregating in parking lots, going to drive-in movies, and collecting the latest 45-rpm recordings of their favorite rock n' roll stars.

At the North Side Coliseum, which had turned to promoting wrestling matches and trade shows, Elvis Presley played before a packed house in 1956. The venue's manager, R. G. McElyea, had earlier booked the rock n' roller for a mere $500 just before a string of hits propelled Presley to the top of the Pop charts. Despite the protestations of the

✧

A Fort Worth policeman surveys the damage to mobster Nelson Harris' car. The blast broke windows and scattered debris across three adjoining lots. It also propelled a car battery through a neighbor's window, which sprayed acid on a baby in its crib.

COURTESY OF THE *FORT WORTH STAR-TELEGRAM* PHOTOGRAPH COLLECTION, SPECIAL COLLECTIONS, UNIVERSITY OF TEXAS AT ARLINGTON LIBRARIES, ARLINGTON, TEXAS, AR 406-2-51-3.

✧

Elvis Presley plays his $500 date at the North Side Coliseum, April 20, 1956.

COURTESY OF THE *FORT WORTH STAR-TELEGRAM* PHOTOGRAPH COLLECTION, SPECIAL COLLECTIONS, UNIVERSITY OF TEXAS AT ARLINGTON LIBRARIES, ARLINGTON, TEXAS, FWST 3605, 1.

✧

TCU All-American Jim Swink offers tips to some young admirers.

COURTESY OF THE JACK WHITE PHOTOGRAPH COLLECTION, SPECIAL COLLECTIONS, UNIVERSITY OF TEXAS AT ARLINGTON LIBRARIES, ARLINGTON, TEXAS, AR 407 7-62-5.

star's manager, Colonel Tom Parker, McElyea refused to renegotiate the contract. Sullen or not, "The King" gyrated before a sea of screaming girls, while envious boyfriends looked on. It was a memorable evening, and one that would not come again for sixteen years.

In the world of college football, TCU also enjoyed a good run in the Fifties. It had been a long wait for fans who longed for the glory days of Sammy Baugh and Davey O'Brien. The Horned Frogs finished in the Top Ten four times during the decade and produced nine All-Americans, including running back Jim Swink, the 1955 runner-up for the Heisman Trophy. In 1956 the Frogs were eyeing a national championship, but their hopes were gigged and drowned at College Station in what became known as the "Hurricane Game." Back then, coaches did not delay a contest because of bad weather. On this day the sky turned black, sheets of rain turned to hail, and gusts of wind threatened to snap the light standards at A&M's Kyle Field. Behind 7-6 and facing the gale and a fourth-and-one at the Aggie goal line, the Frogs failed to find the end zone. TCU would never again come so close to a national crown.

It was a happier ending for Ben Hogan. Just sixteen months after his near-fatal accident, the Hawk-turned-Phoenix staged one of the most inspiring comebacks in sports history. In the summer of 1950 he captured the National Open, and that fall won the second of his four "Player of the Year" titles. Critics, who had once found Hogan aloof and even unfriendly, came to view him as a quiet and determined underdog.

His story soon attracted Hollywood, which cast Glenn Ford as Hogan in *Follow the Sun*. After the Cowtown world premiere, Marvin Leonard hosted a reception for almost five-hundred guests at the Fort Worth Club. To the amazement of the crowd, the normally reserved Hogan got so caught up in the moment that he joined fellow golfer Jimmy Demaret in a chorus of "The Sun's Going to Shine."

For all the problems of race, Reds, and crime, it seems ironic that the decade would be remembered in the popular culture as the "Fabulous Fifties." Yet many of the problems that seemed so great at the time either worked themselves out or metastasized into bigger problems that characterized later decades. Certainly, measured by what loomed on the horizon, those who lived through the Sixties and beyond would look back nostalgically at the 1950s as an age of near-innocence.

✧

The Fort Worth skyline, looking east, 1968.

COURTESY OF THE *FORT WORTH STAR-TELEGRAM* PHOTOGRAPH COLLECTION, SPECIAL COLLECTIONS, UNIVERSITY OF TEXAS AT ARLINGTON LIBRARIES, ARLINGTON, TEXAS, AR 406 1-29-49.

CHAPTER 7

A NEW MODERNITY

1960-1969

The Vietnam War, race riots, and a rebellious youth culture threatened to turn many American cities inside out during the Sixties. Fort Worth, by comparison, seemed almost quiet. Its frontier legacy had nurtured a sense of God and country that dovetailed tightly with conservative business attitudes, especially in the defense industries. Socially, it discovered a liberal heart that largely accepted integration. Yet the Panther City was not without its own upheavals, even if they were mostly demographic. West Texas began fading in importance as Fort Worth started looking to all points on the compass to boost its population and business growth. The rush to suburbia accelerated, too, leaving the inner city to scramble for its viability. In the outlying communities, national chains settled in, compelling homegrown retailers to compete against an impersonal bottom line. It was a new Fort Worth to be sure, but one that drew successfully on the same kind of far-visioned leadership that had brought it this far.

The pace of life during the decade seemed to be gaining a step at every turn, and the passing of personalities and landmarks from bygone days provided occasional reminders. In 1961 Fort Worth mourned "Westerner" Gary Cooper, who had thrilled so many local people at the movie's premier two decades earlier. Billy Rose died in 1966. At the zoo, the seventy-five-hundred-pound Queen Tut, a favorite there since 1923, collapsed suddenly and keeled over in 1964.

Materially, Fort Worth gave up on a number of once-thriving downtown hotels and theaters. The last picture shows flickered at the Worth, the Hollywood, the Palace, and the Majestic in once-opulent halls that had been left to age with neither dignity nor grace. The turn-of-the-century Metropolitan Hotel came down in 1960, and its contemporary, the Westbrook Hotel, lay vacant by the end of the decade, awaiting the wrecking ball. The old blues institution, the Jim, preceded it into oblivion, its site turned into a parking lot. At the Blackstone a series of new owners were left frustrated by low occupancy rates, and by the end of the decade "Fort Worth's Hotel of Distinction" stood empty, its once grand entrances boarded up to keep out vandals and wandering derelicts.

If Fort Worthians mourned the vanishing symbols of downtown's glory days, the demise of the strip on Jacksboro Highway brought more sighs of relief than cries of anguish. City officials seized the right of eminent domain to scrape from the landscape considerable swaths of former nightclubs and seedy motels as part of a road-widening project. Other places, such as the once-hopping Skyliner fell to wrecking crews or found new, if even lowlier, uses.

With the passing of so many landmarks many Fort Worthians wondered aloud if the city's best days were behind them. When the decade began, the outlook presented more pitfalls than opportunities. To image-sensitive leaders, the appellation "Cowtown" seemed the mark an ignoble heritage, rather than an industry whose economic might had carried the city well into the twentieth century. It was an industry, however, that clearly lived on borrowed time. Early in 1962 the *Fort Worth Press* published the obituary of the sixty-year-old Armour and Company with the headline: "Death of a Giant." With it went twelve hundred jobs. Bemoaning the plant's astronomical overhead, one observer noted: "They could buy meat from the independent packer cheaper than they could process it themselves." Modernizations at Swift allowed that plant to hold on for a few more years, but the demise of its amicable competitor signaled the end of an economic era.

Structural changes in the petroleum industry had also left the self-described "Oil Capital of West Texas" with another sobriquet that rang hollow. Even the defense industry was suffering troubled times. In June 1960, seventeen hundred union workers at Bell Helicopter staged a walkout to gain leverage for negotiating better wages, more holidays and vacations, and beefier pension plans. Over at General Dynamics—formerly Convair—the imminent fulfillment of several contracts had economists predicting that employment would fall to six thousand by the end of 1962, a faint echo of busier times when thirty thousand men and women had kept the mile-long plant humming. It was during such crises as these that Amon Carter had so often come running, but now he was gone.

✧

The Mallick Tower, 1968. The building was the first downtown high rise west of Henderson Street.

COURTESY OF THE FORT WORTH STAR-TELEGRAM PHOTOGRAPH COLLECTION, SPECIAL COLLECTIONS, UNIVERSITY OF TEXAS AT ARLINGTON LIBRARIES, ARLINGTON, TEXAS, AR 406 1-29-49.

Despite the dire outlook, Fort Worth businessmen remained optimistic. An encouraging word came, of all places, from the *Dallas Morning News*, which late in 1962 praised the Panther City for its resilience during many dark times in the past. Fort Worth, it marveled, "has demonstrated a strong capacity to change—and to continue growing." Suburban construction and retail sales made up for the industrial downturn, the article noted, signaling that the economy *de jour* would be consumer driven.

The power vacuum left by Amon Carter was being ably filled by a cooperative leadership that worked more like a team than the clique of millionaires that had always set the city's course from smoke-filled rooms at the Fort Worth Club. In contrast to the old wheeler-dealers, the new leadership in 1963 threw open the doors of the Will Rogers Auditorium for the first of the decade's three Town Hall meetings, broadcast live on WBAP radio and televised by KTVT's Channel 11.

Two thousand men and women turned out to offer hundreds of ideas that ranged from practical needs like attracting new industry to such chimerical suggestions as bringing the Gruen Plan out of mothballs. Continued support for cultural activities, branch libraries, and additional parkland gained wide support. The Reverend Douglas Olson voiced the General Ministers Association's desire to root out pornography, clean up the slums, and bridge the gap between the races. Yet, without question, a proposal already in the works to build a downtown convention center and market hall generated the most excitement.

Like the old North Side Coliseum, the Will Rogers complex had become inadequate to accommodate the country's lucrative convention traffic. A massive civic center, proponents argued, would not only bring business back to Fort Worth, but if situated downtown, it could help reverse the decline that marked the core business district. A delegation of several dozen Panther City officials and civic leaders then began a cross-country tour of the latest facilities in places such as Pittsburgh, Miami, Las Vegas and other popular convention destinations to find out what made the best ones successful and to spot any avoidable flaws. When the

✧

The 1500 block of Main Street reveals the ragged edge of the downtown business district in 1964.

COURTESY OF THE *FORT WORTH STAR-TELEGRAM* PHOTOGRAPH COLLECTION, SPECIAL COLLECTIONS, UNIVERSITY OF TEXAS AT ARLINGTON LIBRARIES, ARLINGTON, TEXAS, AR 406 1-61-46.

✧

The Texas Boys Choir always showed Cowtown's best face to admiring audiences. The group moved its headquarters in 1956 from Denton to Fort Worth, where it reached new heights of acclaim. Their tours took the boys to cities throughout North America and Europe. Here, during the summer of 1963, Director George Bragg leads the group into Wales, where they sang at the International Music Eisteddfod.

COURTESY OF THE *FORT WORTH STAR-TELEGRAM* PHOTOGRAPH COLLECTION, SPECIAL COLLECTIONS, UNIVERSITY OF TEXAS AT ARLINGTON LIBRARIES, ARLINGTON, TEXAS, AR 406 1-63-2.

✧

On Public School Day, children enjoying the Midway at the Fat Stock Show do not appear to have many reminders of the heritage that marked the occasion.

COURTESY OF THE *FORT WORTH STAR-TELEGRAM* PHOTOGRAPH COLLECTION, SPECIAL COLLECTIONS, UNIVERSITY OF TEXAS AT ARLINGTON LIBRARIES, ARLINGTON, TEXAS, AR 406 1-27-12.

advisory board put the bond issue before Tarrant County voters on April 25, 1964, the vote was not even close. Downtown would have its convention center.

The fourteen-block site, south of the Hotel Texas, targeted the remaining physical remnants of Hell's Half Acre. Workers prepared for the demolition by carrying away all manner of fixtures, furniture, and junk left behind by the evicted tenants. Rumors abounded with regard to some spectacular finds, especially rare coins—"enough to make numismatics drool," wrote the *Star-Telegram*'s Roger Summers. Lewis Gribble, an Abilene salvage dealer, supposedly walked away with a 1787 half-dollar inscribed "United States Federation of America." Another story told of a laborer who suddenly quit his job upon finding a wad of bills that had rolled out of a piece of furniture he was hauling away. "The last they saw of him," continued Summers, "was his north side headed south."

On the eve of the demolition, the bloated section of squalid shops, warehouses, and hotels stood eerily silent. Reporters likened the doomed blocks to a ghost town and speculated about the stories its buildings could tell. Indeed, as the walls came tumbling down, the jaws of a massive clamshell crane exposed to the sunlight many long-hidden or forgotten sights and artifacts of the city's headiest days. Here, the rooms of a second-story hotel erected on top of another building gaped open for the first time since closing during the Great Depression; there, a football board betrayed the once lively activity of a bookmaking operation.

Then, there was the old Majestic Theater, for which columnist Jack Gordon waxed nostalgically. Through its stage entrance door had walked the likes of Mae West, Harry Houdini, the Marx Brothers, Helen Hayes, and other stars, some equal, most lesser. Surveying an alleyway littered with wine bottles, he lamented: "The once lovely playhouse has been beaten to its knees. By tomorrow, it will be no more."

Four years later the Tarrant County Convention Center opened officially just before Thanksgiving, 1968, with a ten-day "Action Spectacular," featuring all manner of shows, special events, and celebrities. The cooperative effort in 1965 had earned Fort Worth the National Municipal League's All-America City award. It was the largest of the eleven U.S. cities that gained similar recognition that year among 121 competitors. The plaque, reading in part, "In recognition of progress achieved through intelligent citizen

✧

KTVT's "Big Red" mobile television studio parked outside the Will Rogers Auditorium. The unit regularly filmed such events as the "Cowtown Jamboree" at Panther Hall and the "Miss Texas Pageant" as well as going to Dallas to cover the State Fair.

COURTESY OF THE *FORT WORTH STAR-TELEGRAM* PHOTOGRAPH COLLECTION, SPECIAL COLLECTIONS, UNIVERSITY OF TEXAS AT ARLINGTON LIBRARIES, ARLINGTON, TEXAS, AR 406 1-62-29.

action," certainly captured the spirit of the broad grass-roots support that had filtered up from the Town Hall movement.

After a weeklong siege of hard spring rain, the skies parted for the celebration that attended the award. Spectators lined up ten-deep along the parade route and began cheering as Carswell's color guard turned the first corner. Following close behind, members of civic groups smiled broadly and waved to the crowd, while lines of convertibles carrying suburban dignitaries idled behind their high school marching bands. Predictably, an ear-piercing rock ensemble proved the favorite among the many teenagers who attended.

Among dozens of floats was a model of General Dynamics' F111. Leonard's too promoted its business with a papier mâché version of its recently introduced M&O Subway car. The Texas Electric Service Company rolled out Reddy Kilowatt, a jolt of electricity in each hand, under the banner: "More power to Fort Worth." NBC affiliate, WBAP Channel 5, also played the double-entendre with its rainbow-spectrum slogan, "Proud as a peacock."

As in times recently past, the parade ended at the Will Rogers Coliseum. There, Governor John Connally exhorted an overflow crowd to "face the future with the same faith that brought you here tonight. Make no small plans. Dream no timid dreams. Reach boldly for the destiny of your time with vision and determination."

Even before the governor took the dais, nine-year-old Joe Irwin had elbowed his way up to the platform, where he took a seat among the distinguished guests. The boy soon drew the attention of a curious reporter to whom he confessed that he did not belong on the stage. He justified his actions, however, by

✧

Workers salvage the empty buildings on the east side of Main Street between the 13th and 14th blocks, prior to the demolition.

COURTESY OF THE *FORT WORTH STAR-TELEGRAM* PHOTOGRAPH COLLECTION, SPECIAL COLLECTIONS, UNIVERSITY OF TEXAS AT ARLINGTON LIBRARIES, ARLINGTON, TEXAS, AR 406 1-61-46.

✧

Three Casa Mañana actresses oversee the Tarrant County Convention Center groundbreaking, July 15, 1966.

COURTESY OF THE *FORT WORTH STAR-TELEGRAM* PHOTOGRAPH COLLECTION, SPECIAL COLLECTIONS, UNIVERSITY OF TEXAS AT ARLINGTON LIBRARIES, ARLINGTON, TEXAS, AR 406 1-61-48.

The TCCC under construction.

COURTESY OF THE *FORT WORTH STAR-TELEGRAM* PHOTOGRAPH COLLECTION, SPECIAL COLLECTIONS, UNIVERSITY OF TEXAS AT ARLINGTON LIBRARIES, ARLINGTON, TEXAS, AR 406 1-61-48.

Dignitaries line up to cut the block-long ribbon that officially heralds the completion of the TCCC, November 21, 1968.

COURTESY OF THE *FORT WORTH STAR-TELEGRAM* PHOTOGRAPH COLLECTION, SPECIAL COLLECTIONS, UNIVERSITY OF TEXAS AT ARLINGTON LIBRARIES, ARLINGTON, TEXAS, AR 406 1-62-3.

exclaiming: "I wanted to see Governor Connally real bad." The reporter quoted one of the guests, impressed with young Joe's pluck and determination, as predicting that someday he might grow to be governor himself.

Despite the Convention Center and the goodwill cultivated by the Town Hall meetings, downtown did not suddenly spring back to life. Retailers and restaurateurs continued to go under, and conventioneers from out of town preferred to stay at places like the sprawling Green Oaks Inn in Arlington Heights or the Western Hills in suburban Euless. Yet from the expansive portico of the Amon Carter Museum of Western Art, visitors beginning in 1961 could enjoy a panoramic view of the ever-inspiring skyline and pretend that on the street the city was as vibrant as it had always been. Certainly the foot traffic inside the Arts District grew busier during the decade.

Inside the rugged fossil-limestone edifice was the publisher's collection of western paintings and sculptures. Since the late Twenties he had been accumulating them, mostly the works of his favorite artists, Frederick Remington and Charles Russell. Amon Carter no doubt would have approved of his museum. After all, he had picked the site himself, and his daughter, Ruth Carter Stevenson, ably led the foundation to which he had bequeathed $7 million. Under her direction the museum board soon broadened its mission to include art that represented all periods of the American frontier. It also began accumulating a wealth of old newspapers, photographs, and historical documents that made the Amon Carter a nationally recognized research facility as well.

Dorothy Taylor, representing the Great Southwest Corporation, waves to the crowd atop the Inn of the Six Flags double-decker bus as the All-America City parade makes its way down Houston Street.

COURTESY OF THE *FORT WORTH STAR-TELEGRAM* PHOTOGRAPH COLLECTION, SPECIAL COLLECTIONS, UNIVERSITY OF TEXAS AT ARLINGTON LIBRARIES, ARLINGTON, TEXAS, AR 406 1-29-50.

At the Children's Museum, a new wing was added that made it the world's largest of its kind. With new exhibits, a library, and meeting rooms, the range and scope of the

✧

Nine-year-old Joe Irwin commandeers a spot on the platform next to former Chamber of Commerce President Raymond Buck.

COURTESY OF THE *FORT WORTH STAR-TELEGRAM* PHOTOGRAPH COLLECTION, SPECIAL COLLECTIONS, UNIVERSITY OF TEXAS AT ARLINGTON LIBRARIES, ARLINGTON, TEXAS, AR 406 1-29-50.

facility soon obligated directors to change its name to the Museum of Science and History. Not many youngsters had a use for the eight-thousand-volume science and medical research library. Nor could they intelligently follow the proceedings of the Audubon, astronomical, and archaeological societies that met there. Nevertheless, inside the main halls the hands-on displays and visual exhibits still focused on educating the children for whom the museum was originally intended.

Amon Carter Square. On the left is the Will Rogers Auditorium and Coliseum; across the parking lot, above, is the Museum of Science and History; farther right, on the same lot, is the Fort Worth Art Center; across the street, right, is the Amon Carter Museum. Before long, the empty spaces would begin to fill, making the city's arts district the largest municipally owned group of entertainment and cultural buildings in the United States.

COURTESY OF THE *FORT WORTH STAR-TELEGRAM* PHOTOGRAPH COLLECTION, SPECIAL COLLECTIONS, UNIVERSITY OF TEXAS AT ARLINGTON LIBRARIES, ARLINGTON, TEXAS, AR 406 1-29-49.

Beyond the Arts District, other museums opened. The short-lived Heritage Hall, presenting the life story of Fort Worth in a series of ten dioramas, took over the old Kress Building on Main Street in 1966. It attracted Interior Secretary Stewart Udall and western character actor Slim Pickens to the opening, but the museum fetched only a fraction of the three hundred thousand annual visitors predicted by the Downtown Fort Worth Association. Neither a general store, nor live entertainment and silent movies, could save the museum, and it soon folded.

More enduring was the Pate Museum of Transportation, fourteen miles beyond the Weatherford traffic circle near the community of Cresson. Marie Pate, wife of Texas Refinery Corporation founder A. M. Pate, Sr., used the business's recreation ranch as an outlet for her obsession with various modes of travel. The idea formed as her collection of antique automobiles grew. "People began to come to see them anyway," Mrs. Pate explained, "so we decided the logical thing to do was to open it to the public."

So she did in July 1969. In addition to automobiles formerly owned by celebrities and wealthy businessmen, Mrs. Pate obtained a railroad passenger car, a mockup of a Gemini space capsule, a Korean tank, several airplanes, and even an old stagecoach. Her most cherished prize, however, was a 1917 Premier, the only automobile left of its kind.

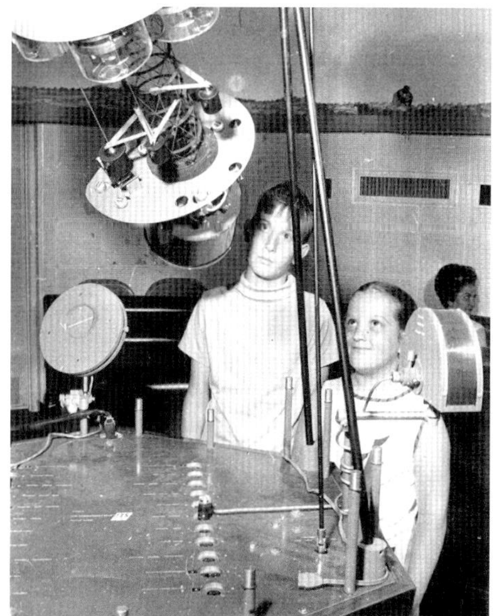

✧

Young visitors to the Noble Planetarium, located in the Museum of Science and History, examine the "Thingamajig." The instrument was designed to coordinate the movements of the planets, moons, and stars and project them on the facility's domed ceiling.

COURTESY OF THE *FORT WORTH STAR-TELEGRAM* PHOTOGRAPH COLLECTION, SPECIAL COLLECTIONS, UNIVERSITY OF TEXAS AT ARLINGTON LIBRARIES, ARLINGTON, TEXAS, AR 406 1-31-28.

✧

Scenes from the short-lived Heritage Hall museum, located on Main Street, opposite the Blackstone Hotel. The maze of artifacts and dioramas failed to attract the crowds predicted by its promoters, and the venture soon folded.

LEFT IMAGE COURTESY OF THE *FORT WORTH STAR-TELEGRAM* PHOTOGRAPH COLLECTION, SPECIAL COLLECTIONS, UNIVERSITY OF TEXAS AT ARLINGTON LIBRARIES, ARLINGTON, TEXAS, AR 406 1-31-32. RIGHT IMAGE COURTESY OF THE *FORT WORTH STAR-TELEGRAM* PHOTOGRAPH COLLECTION, SPECIAL COLLECTIONS, UNIVERSITY OF TEXAS AT ARLINGTON LIBRARIES, ARLINGTON, TEXAS, AR 406 1-31-32.

Across University Drive from the Forest Park Zoo, the Log Cabin Village brought pioneer days to life for a generation of youths who passed many a Saturday watching TV westerns. The driving forces behind the park were Fred Cotten, a civic leader from nearby Weatherford, and local advertising executive Mickey Schmid. The men shared an alarm over the disappearing vestiges of the area's frontier days. Their mission to relocate and restore area cabins found like-minded supporters who solicited funds, researched the history of each structure, and enlisted the help of restoration architects.

Yet, as piles of weathered and rotted logs accumulated, the project came under fire by residents in the adjoining neighborhood around the exclusive Colonial Country Club. One irate homeowner complained to Mayor Tom McCann that the entire collection was nothing but a "bunch of junk and trash," adding: "Let the people who started this monkey business come and tell us what they proposed to do and when they are going to do it." Soon enough, teams of carpenters, engineers, and grounds workers transformed the village into a treasured landmark of furnished cabins, enhanced by a natural wooded setting dotted with period items such as wells and wagons, and tools and grinding stones.

Along with the two-story Harold Foster home, claimed Park Manager Betty Regester, came an unexpected surprise. In the corner of an upstairs bedroom they often felt an overwhelming presence, accompanied by the scent of fresh lilacs and a sudden drop in temperature. On several occasions staff members swore they actually saw the apparition of an attractive middle-aged woman with long, dark hair, dressed much like the period docents themselves. Wide-eyed visitors, too, occasionally came barreling down the stairs, which finally prompted park officials to close the second floor to the public.

If the ghost of the Log Cabin Village raised skeptical eyebrows, the "Lake Worth Monster" left others rolling their eyes. Those who claimed to have seen the mystery beast, on the other hand, stuck passionately to their stories. It all began during the decade's final summer, when the creature—described as "half-man, half-goat, with fur and scales"—terrorized a car carrying six people. After a local radio station reported the encounter, crowds of curiosity seekers flocked to the site opposite Greer Island, a few of them armed and determined to bag the "goatman." Surveying the dizzy mob, police Sergeant A. J. Hudson remarked: "I'm not worried about the monster so much as all those people wandering around out there with guns."

The only shooting, however, came from the camera of a hopeful shutterbug whose errant aim failed to capture its subject. "I was too busy rolling up my window," explained resident Jack Harris, whose sudden

✧

Descendants of Harold Foster assess the site on which the old pioneer's log home came to rest. Docents and visitors at the Log Cabin Village claimed the dwelling was haunted.

COURTESY OF THE *FORT WORTH STAR-TELEGRAM* PHOTOGRAPH COLLECTION, SPECIAL COLLECTIONS, UNIVERSITY OF TEXAS AT ARLINGTON LIBRARIES, ARLINGTON, TEXAS, AR 406 1-31-32.

✧

"The Lake Worth Monster," a musical by Johnny Simons, played before enthusiastic crowds at the Art Museum's Solarium shortly after a rash of "goatman" sightings ended.

COURTESY OF THE *FORT WORTH STAR-TELEGRAM* PHOTOGRAPH COLLECTION, SPECIAL COLLECTIONS, UNIVERSITY OF TEXAS AT ARLINGTON LIBRARIES, ARLINGTON, TEXAS, AR 406 1-31-11.

encounter with the beast left him shaken. Authorities dismissed the monster as a prankster or even a bobcat. A crowd of about thirty or forty witnesses, however, would have none of that. Despite the creature's imposing presence—one observer estimated that it was "7 feet tall and must have weighed 300 pounds"—some daring souls bragged they would "get mean" with it. It was then that the monster showed up and reportedly picked up a tire, heaving it toward the crowd from a distance of five hundred feet.

"Earlier there were some sheriffs deputies there," said Harris, "and one of them was sort of laughing like he didn't believe it." But the tire toss and a pitiful, inhuman howl sent the officers scrambling. "Those sheriff's men weren't any braver than we were," continued the would-be cameraman, "they ran to get in their car." As quickly as the rash of sightings began, they abruptly ended, leaving Fort Worthians forever to speculate just what it was that had terrorized the shores of Lake Worth during the summer of '69.

Such frivolity stood in stark contrast to the weighty issues that involved Fort Worth during one of the country's most turbulent decades. If America ever enjoyed a measure of innocence, it ended November 22, 1963, a day that began for President John F. Kennedy at the Hotel Texas. The previous evening Air Force One had dipped low over the city, its skyscrapers outlined in Christmas lights turned on to honor the president and his wife, Jackie. On the roof of St. Joseph's Hospital, a sign in lights beamed a special message: "Welcome JFK." Thousands of local citizens had turned out to greet their leader at Carswell Air Force Base; hundreds of others lined the route to the city.

As the president waded through well-wishers at the Hotel Texas, he heard someone cry out: "Shafty!" Kennedy, responding to his World War II nickname, recognized the voice and made his way over to Edward Miller, a Marine whom the former captain of the PT-109 had rescued from an enemy beachhead in the Pacific Theater. After a warm embrace, the Kennedys made their way up to Suite 850, its walls decorated with priceless paintings borrowed from the Kay and Velma Kimbell, Ruth Carter Johnson, and other local collectors.

The next morning the president flipped through the *Dallas Morning News* and ate his breakfast, which lost some of its spice when he spotted a black-bordered, paid-for message accusing him of cozying up to the Communists. In front of the Hotel Texas there were no critics among a crowd of about five thousand mostly local people who waited in a drizzling rain to hear JFK make a few remarks. The president's last speech was delivered to an invitation-only audience inside. By eleven o'clock, Kennedy was ready to take the short hop to Dallas, where his destiny awaited.

About an hour later, Fort Worth, like the rest of the country, stood frozen in shocked disbelief when reporters broke the news that an assassin had murdered the charismatic young president. By evening police had flushed out the suspected triggerman, Lee Harvey Oswald. Newsmen did not take long to discover his close ties to the Panther City.

✧

President Kennedy speaks to a crowd outside the Hotel Texas on the morning of November 22, 1963, while Congressman Jim Wright (immediate left) enjoys the moment

COURTESY OF TEXAS CHRISTIAN UNIVERSITY, SPECIAL COLLECTIONS, MARY COUTS BURNETT LIBRARY, FORT WORTH, TEXAS.

A former Marine and the son and brother of service veterans, the Arlington Heights dropout had made news when he emigrated to the Soviet Union in 1959 and again when he returned to the United States in 1962. His brother, R. L., had speculated upon Lee Harvey's defection that it might all have been a ruse so that he could write a book about his experiences. Tragically, it was anything but a stunt, and shortly, the former defector too, would be cut down by an assassin's bullet. At Oswald's funeral in Fort Worth, newsmen sent to cover the burial found themselves mustered into service as pallbearers.

In matters of race, the mixed bag that had alternated between progress and inertia during the Fifties opened up to significant gains in the Sixties. Nevertheless, if segregationists in Fort Worth had become less vocal, many whites remained indifferent to the cause. Encapsulating their sentiments, one Fort Worth man shrugged: "My grandparents lived in Tennessee…when the slaves were freed….The Negroes went wild. That's what they're doing now."

Yet, in the Panther City and elsewhere, the Christian love and non-violence practiced so dutifully by such black organizations as the Southern Christian Leadership Conference had chipped away at a white society that professed to own spiritual stock in those same principles. In contrast to the "boisterous and bloody demonstrations in other cities," gloated *Fort Worth Press* reporter Delbert Willis, "a quiet revolution in integration has gone almost unnoticed in Fort Worth."

Indeed, whether in church groups or as part of loosely organized programs such as "Operation Fellowship," the white and African-American communities began con-

✧

Earlier, in 1959, R. L. Oswald learned about his brother's defection to the Soviet Union. He thought at the time that Lee Harvey must have been involved in some kind of undercover plot.

COURTESY OF THE *FORT WORTH STAR-TELEGRAM* PHOTOGRAPH COLLECTION, SPECIAL COLLECTIONS, UNIVERSITY OF TEXAS AT ARLINGTON LIBRARIES, ARLINGTON, TEXAS, FWST 4118, 8, 10/31/59.

sciously to bridge the gap of race by interacting socially. The Mayor's Commission on Human Relations reported during 1963 that most of the city's restaurants, hotels, department stores, theaters, athletic events, and churches had already integrated—and without soliciting any self-congratulations.

Arguably, the zenith of the movement in Fort Worth followed closely on the heels of violence at Selma, Alabama. Over six hundred black and white marchers in the Panther City joined hands early in 1965 for a peaceful march on City Hall. Anticipating hecklers after a bomb threat proved to be a hoax, seventy-five extra-duty policemen ringed a recreation building where the march began. Not one incident, however, marred the rally, described as more of "a church service rather than a protest." As they gathered, the marchers rang out "My Country 'Tis of Thee," then started toward City Hall, singing the movement's anthem, "We Shall Overcome." At their destination, ministers, both black and white, spoke uninterrupted from the steps.

✧

Spectators and reporters outnumber mourners at the funeral of Lee Harvey Oswald.

COURTESY OF THE *FORT WORTH STAR-TELEGRAM* PHOTOGRAPH COLLECTION, SPECIAL COLLECTIONS, UNIVERSITY OF TEXAS AT ARLINGTON LIBRARIES, ARLINGTON, TEXAS, FWST 4816, 35- 28, 11/25/63.

Nowhere, of course, had segregation been so adamantly defended or so passionately attacked as in the public school system. Nevertheless, a decade that began with the Board of Education meeting behind closed doors seeking to buck court-ordered race mixing, ended with a matter-of-fact acceptance of a new status quo. As the 1963-64 school year approached, the district put a gradual desegregation plan into effect. The smooth transition soon rendered the plan's continuation pointless, and, by the 1967-68 school year, Superintendent Eldon Busby was able to report that the Fort Worth I.S.D. was totally desegregated.

Already most suburban schools had stopped paying transportation and tuition fees for their black students who had traditionally attended high school at I. M. Terrell. Even in Mansfield, where about thirty African-American students pre-enrolled for the 1965-66 school year, integration proved uneventful. Most citizens there were simply trying to forget the problems that brought ignominy to the community just nine years earlier. "They weren't ready for [integration]," explained Superintendent Willie Pigg. "Attitudes have changed particularly because the people in Mansfield have changed."

In the Hispanic community, men and women did not press for civil rights as intensely as in black Fort Worth. Nevertheless, Orra Compton, with the city's Community Relations Committee, expressed bitterness over being "the forgotten minority." Fort Worth Tejanos were also frustrated that schools seemingly denigrated the state's Spanish-Mexican heritage as a matter of course and felt that the city ignored their neighborhoods when it came to developing parks and playgrounds.

The "crux of the problem," according to *El Sol de Texas* Editor G. L. Duarte, was a "total lack of leadership and organization." As the Fort Worth newspaperman saw it, the city's Hispanic community was divided by cliques, its spokespeople jealous of one another's power and fearful they would lose their influence if various groups combined their strength. He also complained that successful Tejanos quickly moved into white suburbs, leaving the problems of the barrios to others. Such problems, once exposed to public discourse, soon helped consolidate an ascending leadership that achieved rapid progress during the next decade.

Blatant racism in Fort Worth did not disappear, of course, but when it did show itself, the old specter popped up from the radical margins of a more tolerant society. "Little Sid" McGoodwin found out as much in 1966, when he wantonly killed black shoeshiner John Hughes Wallace at a North Side dive. Assistant D.A. Grady Hight made what observers called the most impassioned final argument of his career. "Texas is part of the old Confederacy," he began. "A suspended sentence will make everyone ashamed except those people who think like this man [McGoodwin] does." Calling for a new era of justice, he rang out: "Let the beginning be here and now!" An affected jury agreed and condemned "Little Sid" to a life sentence at the state penitentiary.

The Vietnam War also stirred the emotions of Fort Worthians. Materially, the city quite naturally supported the war effort by churning out all kinds of jets and helicopters, ending any concerns that General Dynamics and Bell Helicopter would be a drag on the local economy. Rarely was there a time during the day when a quick scan of the sky did not reveal some kind of flying weapon out for a test run. The crescendo of the plodding choppers, doors wide open, never failed to attract the attention of schoolchildren, but it was the F-111s that froze them in place as they anticipated the sonic boom that usually followed the rip and whoosh of the low-flying aircraft.

Far from the massive protests that rocked some other American cities, most Cow-towners were loath to give up on the police action without getting something in return for the sacrifice of so many young men. They were also generous with their moral support. In response to a lonely Marine's letter, the city poured out its heart in a correspondence campaign. Virtually every school was involved in sending care packages along with their words of encouragement. In an open letter of thanks, Lance Corporal Gene Malone of Fort Worth admitted he figured that "maybe we would get a few 'pen pals' out of it," but "I should have known Texans better than that."

The stories of local heroes also boosted the cause. The *Fort Worth Press* lauded gunner's mate Jack Wright, for instance, whose tiny Coast Guard cutter engaged a ninety-nine-foot trawler carrying a hundred tons of weapons and munitions headed upriver into North Vietnam. Strapping himself into the harness of a fifty-caliber machine gun, Wright fired and ducked for two-and-a-half hours. Despite absorbing a piece of shrapnel that seared into his leg, he also helped storm the ship's deck, rousting out the survivors with his .45-caliber Colt automatic drawn and ready.

✧

University of Texas at Arlington students turn out to observe "Vietnam War Moratorium Day" in October 1969.

COURTESY OF THE *FORT WORTH STAR-TELEGRAM* PHOTOGRAPH COLLECTION, SPECIAL COLLECTIONS, UNIVERSITY OF TEXAS AT ARLINGTON LIBRARIES, ARLINGTON, TEXAS, AR 406 1-20-40.

✧

Later in the month UTA students protested the use of the rebel flag. Student activism soon resulted in changing the school's mascot from the "Rebels" to the "Mavericks."

COURTESY OF THE *FORT WORTH STAR-TELEGRAM* PHOTOGRAPH COLLECTION, SPECIAL COLLECTIONS, UNIVERSITY OF TEXAS AT ARLINGTON LIBRARIES, ARLINGTON, TEXAS, AR 406 1-20-40.

Just as Amon Carter had sent *Star-Telegram* reporters to World War II battlefields and camps to seek out Texans, the newspaper became the state's first major daily to humanize local men who found themselves on the front lines in Vietnam. The assignment fell to promising twenty-eight-year-old North Side and TCU graduate Bob Schieffer.

✧

Star-Telegram correspondent Bob Schieffer poses before taking off on a combat mission.

COURTESY OF THE *FORT WORTH STAR-TELEGRAM* PHOTOGRAPH COLLECTION, SPECIAL COLLECTIONS, UNIVERSITY OF TEXAS AT ARLINGTON LIBRARIES, ARLINGTON, TEXAS, AR 406 2-98-30.

During his four-month tour the newspaperman filed reports about soldiers such as former quarterback Gray Mills, calling the shots for a much different team than the one he had directed at TCU. He interviewed Master Sergeant Paul Hudak, a former employee of the newspaper, who had driven off a flight line just as an explosion rocked a row of twenty-two planes. Then, there was forty-year-old boot camp instructor-turned-combat sergeant Robert Bedwell.

So tough had the Fort Worth native been on his recruits, that one of them wrote a letter of complaint to his congressman. The hindsight afforded by a tour of combat duty, however, made the carping young Marine see things more clearly. Schieffer noted that the recruit reacted well under fire, risking his life to drag out his wounded comrades. Bedwell, he pointed out, also demanded as much of himself. During Operation Utah the sergeant had "crawled under heavy…machine gun fire for 100 yards with one of his wounded men hanging on his back." Then, the reporter added, "He went back and got out two more."

The war, of course, unfolded alongside happier times, led by an easily distracted suburban society. Jimmy Stewart and Maureen O'Hara packed the Palace Theater for the world premier of *The Rare Breed* in 1966. On the small screen, local TV stations were still enjoying the heyday of live children's shows in the Sixties, and virtually anyone who grew up in Fort Worth during that time got a steady dose of Icky Twerp and *Slam Bang Theater* on KFJZ-TV Channel 11, and the rival *Mr. Peppermint Show* on WFAA-TV Channel 8. Their live schtick, woefully unsophisticated by today's standards, nevertheless delighted a generation of baby boomers.

✧

Bill Camfield, known to adoring children as "Icky Twerp," hosted the wildly popular Slam Bang Theater on KTVT Channel 11.

COURTESY OF PAUL CAMFIELD, FREDERICKSBURG, TEXAS.

Bill Camfield, better known as the frenetic Icky Twerp, got children out of bed in the morning and greeted them when they came home from school in the afternoon. With his comically undersized cowboy hat and horn-rimmed glasses, he threw pies and broke up fights between his ape companions Ajax and Delphinium. Together they hammed it up while technicians got the next episode of *The Three Stooges* ready to roll. Many were the parents who worried aloud about the effects this nutty fare might have on their kids, which, of course, simply made the daily spectacle that much more appealing.

✧

Angus G. Wynne, Jr. (right), creator of Six Flags Over Texas.

COURTESY OF THE *FORT WORTH STAR-TELEGRAM* PHOTOGRAPH COLLECTION, SPECIAL COLLECTIONS, UNIVERSITY OF TEXAS AT ARLINGTON LIBRARIES, ARLINGTON, TEXAS, AR 406 1-59-14.

✧

The Butterfield Stage was a popular ride when Six Flags Over Texas opened in 1961. The park's three-hundred-foot-tall landmark Oil Derrick now occupies this spot.

COURTESY OF THE *FORT WORTH STAR-TELEGRAM* PHOTOGRAPH COLLECTION, SPECIAL COLLECTIONS, UNIVERSITY OF TEXAS AT ARLINGTON LIBRARIES, ARLINGTON, TEXAS, AR 406 1-59-15.

In contrast, the low-keyed Jerry Haynes more presaged Mister Rogers. In his trademark straw hat and peppermint-striped sport coat, he conversed with inanimate guests and showed cartoons such as *Bennie and Cecil*. Among Mr. Peppermint's most popular cast members were hand puppet "Bun E. Rabbit" and "Mr. Wiggly Worm," which was nothing more than a puppeteer's finger, painted with dot-eyes and a smile, poking up through the bottom of a box. To his adoring audience, such details did not matter.

In the 1960s, Arlington became the playground for both Fort Worth and Dallas with the opening of Six Flags Over Texas and Turnpike Stadium. For local families and visitors, trips to the two parks would provide lasting memories far removed from the weightier issues of the day. For the business community, it helped seed a booming tourist and convention industry and cultivated an already growing sense of cooperation among the many suburban communities and the two great cities that anchored either end.

As first announced by the *Star-Telegram* in 1957, the former Waggoner DDD Stock Farm at the Turnpike and Watson School Road would give way to a "Disneyland-like Great Southwest Land," with all kinds of rides and attractions. At the center would be a one-hundred-thousand-square-foot retail store carrying all kinds of sports and camping equipment, motorcycles, and clothing. Target ranges, casting ponds, and

✧

The slide at Skull Island.

COURTESY OF THE *FORT WORTH STAR-TELEGRAM* PHOTOGRAPH COLLECTION, SPECIAL COLLECTIONS, UNIVERSITY OF TEXAS AT ARLINGTON LIBRARIES, ARLINGTON, TEXAS, AR 406 1-59-12.

Youngsters line up to enlist in the park's Confederate section, a new twist for the second season, 1962.

COURTESY OF THE *FORT WORTH STAR-TELEGRAM* PHOTOGRAPH COLLECTION, SPECIAL COLLECTIONS, UNIVERSITY OF TEXAS AT ARLINGTON LIBRARIES, ARLINGTON, TEXAS, AR 406 1-59-16.

More appropriate, and still a Six Flags favorite, was the Old West shootout in the Texas section.

COURTESY OF THE *FORT WORTH STAR-TELEGRAM* PHOTOGRAPH COLLECTION, SPECIAL COLLECTIONS, UNIVERSITY OF TEXAS AT ARLINGTON LIBRARIES, ARLINGTON, TEXAS, AR 406 1-59-16.

other demonstration facilities would crown the project.

The park—minus the giant retail center—opened in August 1961 as Six Flags Over Texas. Over fifteen thousand people turned out for the opening. Taking part in the ceremony were mayors Tom Vandergriff of Arlington, John Justin of Fort Worth, Earle Cabell of Dallas, and their counterparts from Grand Prairie and Irving. The park's chief owner and developer, Angus G. Wynne, Jr., cut the ribbon, declaring that Six Flags would be "as a shining beacon" for the millions of visitors whom he predicted would come to enjoy good old-fashioned Texas hospitality and wholesome family fun.

Befitting the theme of the six flags, the park was divided into sections representing each era of the state's history, complete with miniature period towns and attractions. For $4.50 for adults, a dollar less for children, parkgoers got full access to all the rides and attractions. Aboard the Butterfield Overland Stage they braved the attacks of painted Indian warriors and cowboy bandits; rowing in long canoes, friendlier Indians guided them across a shallow lagoon; in the "Astrolift's" gondola cars they glided from one end of the park to the other; they serried into fiberglass logs that floated along a serpentine plume set among the trees, ending with a long slide and a splash; they also set out in a river boat to rescue the lost expedition of French explorer La Salle. This last ride endured such hazards as Spanish cannons and a man-sucking whirlpool. When it appeared as if the boat would crash into the face of a rock cliff, a secret tunnel opened, revealing treasures and the skeletons of those who died trying to claim it. At the Southern Palace, live shows struck a patriotic theme, and when the entire cast assembled to sing "You're a Grand Old Flag," it never failed to bring the crowds to their feet.

Each season brought new attractions. When guests wandered into the Confederate section during the park's second summer, they passed through four Greek Revival columns that had once supported the portico of a Southern plantation house. There, a band blared "Dixie," signaling a Confederate recruitment rally, while a strolling troubadour entertained the park's guests until they learned that he was really a "Yankee spy." Skull Island, the Runaway Mine Train, a giant smoking volcano, Boom Town, the Spelunkers' Cave, and a three-hundred-foot-tall oil derrick all debuted as the decade progressed.

Six Flags immediately became the most popular business in the region for college students seeking summer employment. Each year about ten thousand of them applied for jobs, yet nine out of ten would walk away disappointed. The lucky ten percent, according to Public Relations Director David Blackburn, got their jobs largely on appearance and personality. "It's hard to beat that pretty girl flashing that smile," he chirped. Before she put on the bright whites and candy stripes, however, she and other successful applicants would have to know sixty pages of the "do's and don'ts" that made Six Flags, as the manual said, "the friendliest place on earth."

There was no question that Wynne's park exceeded even his own visions. The Texas Tourist Development Agency reported in 1964 that Six Flags Over Texas had topped the Alamo as the state's most popular tourist destination. The millionth visitor had spun the turnstile sometime during the 1962 season, a year that attracted parkgoers from every state in the Union and forty foreign countries. Soon it was bringing in that many and more in a single season.

✧

Young Six Flags employees, winners of the first Six Flags Educational Scholarship in 1966, read their letters of congratulations from donor Angus G. Wynne, Jr.

COURTESY OF THE *FORT WORTH STAR-TELEGRAM* PHOTOGRAPH COLLECTION, SPECIAL COLLECTIONS, UNIVERSITY OF TEXAS AT ARLINGTON LIBRARIES, ARLINGTON, TEXAS, AR 406 1-59-16.

Seeking a complement to Six Flags, Arlington announced that it was making a bid to bring big league baseball to North Texas. The majors were then expanding, and Mayor Vandergriff once more found himself in the thick of the hunt. Officials, including those of Fort Worth and Dallas, targeted a spot near the old Arlington Downs site as a perfect place to build a thirty-one-thousand-seat domed stadium. The coterie hoped to beat Houston to the punch, which had also announced plans for a dome. Anticipating another bond election, local minor league official Allen Russell warned: "If the majors should bypass this area on the first go-round it might be years before big league baseball would become a reality here." Only one thing was certain, wrote a reporter: "If and when you do see major league baseball here, you'll see it in the air-conditioned comfort of a [domed] stadium."

In the end Houston got the dome and the Astros; Arlington ended up with Turnpike Stadium and the minor league Dallas-Fort Worth Spurs. Both the Houston and North Texas facilities opened for the 1965 season. While the Astros welcomed the New York Yankees to town, the Spurs played host to the Albuquerque Dodgers. Fans paid $1.25 to sit on a grassy right-field burm; for seventy-five cents more they could get a seat behind home plate. It was fun, but major league baseball, it was not.

Although the people of Fort Worth and North Texas missed baseball's brass ring, there were few other laurels they failed to seize during the Sixties. Going into the decade, such issues as race, leadership, inner city decay, and even a sense of regional identity loomed ominously. Those same problems lingered as the period ended, yet they did not seem quite as imposing. Fort Worthians looked to the future undaunted, buoyed by the indomitable western spirit of a truly "All-America City."

✧

"Alan Bean Day," December 22, 1969. Somewhere in the middle of this crowd the hometown hero, Alan Bean, recently back from the first mission to the moon, enjoys a tickertape parade. It provided a fitting end to a decade that presented so many changes.

COURTESY OF THE *FORT WORTH STAR-TELEGRAM* PHOTOGRAPH COLLECTION, SPECIAL COLLECTIONS, UNIVERSITY OF TEXAS AT ARLINGTON LIBRARIES, ARLINGTON, TEXAS, FWST 5925, 33A, 12-22-69.

Fort Worth, early in the 1970s, framed by the Water Gardens.

COURTESY OF THE *FORT WORTH STAR-TELEGRAM* PHOTOGRAPH COLLECTION, SPECIAL COLLECTIONS, UNIVERSITY OF TEXAS AT ARLINGTON LIBRARIES, ARLINGTON, TEXAS, AR 406 1-31-39.

CHAPTER 8

THE "METROPLEX"

1970-1979

For many Americans, the Seventies represented a time of "malaise." Even President Jimmy Carter intimated as much. The decade certainly had its lowlights, from Richard Nixon resigning in disgrace, to the U.S. pulling out of Vietnam. To describe the condition of the economy, pundits created a new word"—"stagflation"—an unsettling combination of stagnation and inflation that set orthodox Keynesian theory on its ear. Then, there was the energy crisis, characterized by long lines at gas stations.

By contrast, Fort Worth seemed almost to exist in another America. The Panther City sat smack-dab at the buckle of what demographers were beginning to call the "Sunbelt," the swath of air-conditioned states that suddenly appealed to jaded Northerners and others looking for brighter prospects. The Seventies also presented an opportune time for civic and business leaders in Fort Worth to join their counterparts in Dallas. Together they transformed an old rivalry into an alliance that benefited all of North Texas. In the process, developers began to revive downtown Fort Worth and discovered a bankable mystique in their Cowtown heritage. "Malaise?" Not here, partner, not in the city "Where the West Begins!"

In 1971 all of North Texas at last celebrated the victory of bagging a major league franchise. With the announcement that the Washington Senators were headed for the nearby city of Arlington, baseball fans in the Panther City talked about a return to the glory days of the Cats and saw visions of American League pennants. The *Star-Telegram* predicted that the Senators, who would be going by a new name yet to be determined, "could be revered like Fort Worth's finest of yesteryear—Clarence "Big Boy" Kraft and

✧

Former Boston Red Sox Hall-of-Famer Ted Williams appears as if he might be wondering what he has gotten himself into as he accepts a pair of cowboy boots outfitted with baseball cleats.

COURTESY OF THE TEXAS RANGERS BASEBALL CLUB.

✧

Eighteen-year-old David Clyde, not even three weeks out of high school, stands on the mound in front of the Rangers' first sellout crowd. He rewarded them by pitching a one-hitter against the Minnesota Twins.

COURTESY OF THE TEXAS RANGERS BASEBALL CLUB.

Jake Atz, who led the Cats on the field and Paul LaGrave and W. K. Stripling, who masterminded the city into an exciting baseball town." The new lineup would include Cy Young winner Denny McLain and longball hitter Frank Howard, along with their manager, Hall-of-Famer Ted Williams.

A players' strike delayed the 1972 season, but when the recently christened Texas Rangers finally hit the home field against the Angels on April 21—San Jacinto Day—it seemed to be worth the wait. First baseman Frank Howard inaugurated the new era with a four-hundred-foot homerun in the first inning. The promising beginning soon turned sour, however, and when the season ended, the Rangers were looking up from the cellar, 38 ½ games out of first place.

After the disastrous debut, Ted Williams called it quits. The following season, manager Whitey Herzog would be the next in a long line of helmsmen who came to town with impressive resumes and promises of pennants. Yet none could deliver, and the Rangers became the laughingstock of the American League. "Did you hear the one about the man who took his wife to pantyhose night?" went one joke. "The women's hosiery got more runs than the Rangers."

The closest thing to a pennant in North Texas came during the 1979 season, when the fictitious "Fort Worth Strangers" claimed a Western Division championship. The lighthearted ruse was the creation of *Star-Telegram* staffers who gave the alter ego Strangers ample coverage, complete with box scores and photographs. Even the *New York Times* and world news anchor Walter Cronkite picked up on the short-lived sensation. Capping the two-week season was a "live" broadcast of the 12-8 title win over the California Angels.

Despite so many disappointments, there were nevertheless some precious moments to savor. The first sellout on June 27, 1973, provided the decade's high water mark, courtesy of eighteen-year-old pitcher David Clyde. His one-hit victory over the Minnesota Twins came just twenty days after his high school career ended at suburban Westchester outside of Houston. Hailed as the savior of the franchise, he soon threw out his arm and found himself struggling in the minor leagues, while the Rangers returned to grappling with an omnipresent lineup of the same old diamond-demons.

Other issues and episodes with roots in earlier decades also played out during the Seventies. As the Vietnam War wound to a close, five crewmembers of a downed Carswell B-52 returned to Fort Worth in 1973 from captivity at a Hanoi prison. Unlike most other veterans who came back unapplauded, the POWs stopped over at Sheppard AFB in Wichita Falls, where about two thousand cheering well-wishers and tearful family

✧

Fort Worth was not a hotbed of antiwar protest, but with the Vietnam War still raging in 1970, this group of about two hundred marchers made their way through downtown for a rally at Burnett Park.

COURTESY OF THE *FORT WORTH STAR-TELEGRAM* PHOTOGRAPH COLLECTION, SPECIAL COLLECTIONS, UNIVERSITY OF TEXAS AT ARLINGTON LIBRARIES, ARLINGTON, TEXAS, AR 406 1-20-41.

✧

Edward Guinn, Fort Worth's first black city councilman, confers with Sharkey Stovall (left), Watt Kemble, Jr. (right), and Howard McMahan (back to camera).

COURTESY OF THE *FORT WORTH STAR-TELEGRAM* PHOTOGRAPH COLLECTION, SPECIAL COLLECTIONS, UNIVERSITY OF TEXAS AT ARLINGTON LIBRARIES, ARLINGTON, TEXAS, AR 406 1-30-31A.

✧

For all the good intentions of integration, one unforeseen consequence proved to be destructive of the African-American community—the closing of traditionally black schools. Principal Walter Day of the historic I. M. Terrell High School is pictured here at the end of the 1972-73 academic year, after which the school closed its doors.

COURTESY OF THE *FORT WORTH STAR-TELEGRAM* PHOTOGRAPH COLLECTION, SPECIAL COLLECTIONS, UNIVERSITY OF TEXAS AT ARLINGTON LIBRARIES, ARLINGTON, TEXAS, FWST 6397, 31A, 6-2-73.

members greeted them. On the racial front, Fort Worth during the decade would elect African Americans and Hispanics to the school board, the city council, and the municipal court—again, with little self-congratulation. Both the Metropolitan Black Chamber of Commerce and the Fort Worth Mexican American Chamber of Commerce got their starts in the Seventies as well.

Sally Rand, from an even earlier era, stepped back into the spotlight briefly in 1976, fans in hand. Although on the long side of seventy, she took the stage at Casa del Sol, still adept at teasing the audience with flashes of the legendary body that had so captivated audiences at the Frontier Centennial. Speculating that she had gone to packing her flesh into a body suit, one young woman in the crowd jeered to her tablemate: "At her age, you can bet she's not really working nude behind those fans."

Backstage, columnist Jack Gordon passed on the remark to the dancer and gathered the gumption to ask her whether it was true. Rand just smiled. Allowing a lace robe to fall to the floor, she retorted with her own query: "What do *you* think?" Standing before him, "completely bare," Gordon gaped, "was one of the world's most famous bodies," still "flawless" in his estimation. The Cowtown date would be one of her last appearances. Later in the year Sally Rand died of heart failure at a Los Angeles hospital.

Nothing, however, marked the passing of time more than the fiery purge of the vacant Armour complex in 1971. The long-tottering Swift plant had just closed its own doors,

✧

Fire engulfed the vacant Armour plant in August 1971. The spectacular inferno signaled the end of the meatpacking era in Fort Worth.

LEFT IMAGE COURTESY OF THE *FORT WORTH STAR-TELEGRAM* PHOTOGRAPH COLLECTION, SPECIAL COLLECTIONS, UNIVERSITY OF TEXAS AT ARLINGTON LIBRARIES, ARLINGTON, TEXAS, AR 406 1-23-43. RIGHT IMAGE COURTESY OF THE *FORT WORTH STAR-TELEGRAM* PHOTOGRAPH COLLECTION, SPECIAL COLLECTIONS, UNIVERSITY OF TEXAS AT ARLINGTON LIBRARIES, ARLINGTON, TEXAS, AR 406 1-23-44.

leaving the packing plants a near ghost town. A wrecking crew that had taken Armour's six floors down to the second level provided about the only activity. Somehow the remaining wood and cork insulation caught a spark.

By the time the station house received the first alarm at about 11 p.m., the blaze had already spread out of control, tapping into the decades-old accumulation of lard and grease that had saturated the plant's thick floors and walls. More than a hundred firemen were on the scene by midnight, futilely pouring water into the unquenchable inferno. The entire Stockyards district glowed eerily as crowds of silent onlookers beheld one-hundred-foot flames and immense billows of dense smoke that a northern breeze sent spiraling over the city. It would be two weeks before the great fire finally exhausted itself.

Another, more salacious, drama unfolded in public view when flamboyant Fort Worth oilman T. Cullen Davis during the summer of 1976 became "the richest man in America ever accused of murder." Three eyewitnesses fingered him as the shooter in a late evening bloodbath that left two dead and two others wounded. He certainly possessed a motive. Earlier that afternoon the judge in Davis' divorce case had boosted the monthly payment to his estranged wife, Priscilla, from $3,500 to $5,000 and ordered him to give her an additional $52,000 to cover bills that had piled up.

According to Priscilla, Cullen waited for her and her new boyfriend, former TCU basketball player Stan Farr, in the darkened kitchen of the Davis's nineteen-thousand-square-foot mansion, which the judge had earlier compelled the oilman to vacate. Dressed in black and wearing a shoulder-length black wig, Cullen calmly walked up to Priscilla, she insisted, and said "Hi." He then shot her in the chest and pumped four slugs into Farr, killing him. Outside, Bubba Gavrel and Beverly Bass were coming to the front door as Priscilla beat a path to a neighbor's house to call the police. When the officers arrived they found Gavrel shot, paralyzed from the waist down. In the basement they discovered the body of Priscilla's daughter, Andrea Wilborn, who was left there to writhe in agony before dying from a chest wound.

Enter Houston trial attorney Richard "Racehorse" Haynes. In an Amarillo courtroom, the renowned lawyer spent several days grilling Priscilla and working to portray the defenseless Farr as a drug abuser. His ace-in-the-hole, however, was a surprise witness—a nursery owner who had purportedly sneaked onto the grounds to repossess some plants. The man testified that he saw the man in black, and that it was definitely not T. Cullen Davis. After deliberating for two days, the jurors stunned the trial's followers with a verdict of "not guilty."

Nine months later T. Cullen Davis was back in the news, this time accused of arranging a mass murder-for-hire. His plan, much of it caught on tape by FBI agents, targeted fifteen people, among them Priscilla, the judge in their divorce case, and even one of his own brothers. So, once again the oilman called on Racehorse Haynes, whose strategy was to convince jurors that Cullen believed he was working with the FBI to ensnare Priscilla. It was she, the attorney contended, who had actually initiated the bizarre episode by issuing a hit on her ex-husband. His client had simply been duped. Somehow, that side of the story came from conversations that went unrecorded. The average wag who had followed every detail of this public soap opera regarded the cover story preposterous. Of course, it was not they who mattered. When the jury reached its final conclusion, they read their verdict: "Move for acquittal." For a second time Davis left the courtroom with a smug expression of satisfaction, and once more the collective jaw of society dropped in disbelief.

✧

"Racehorse" Haynes (left) and his client, Fort Worth oil millionaire T. Cullen Davis, emerge confidently from the Potter County Courthouse in Amarillo.

COURTESY OF THE *FORT WORTH STAR-TELEGRAM* PHOTOGRAPH COLLECTION, SPECIAL COLLECTIONS, UNIVERSITY OF TEXAS AT ARLINGTON LIBRARIES, ARLINGTON, TEXAS, FWST 7168, 17A, 7-10-79.

The news of the decade, however, focused on development. Road construction—especially such vital links as the Turnpike, an extension of I-35W to Denton, and U.S. 183—began to yield a regional network connecting the cities and towns within roughly an 8-to-10-county area of North Texas. Like a double-bull's-eye, Fort Worth and Dallas sat somewhat unevenly in the center of it all. As a more mobile society emerged, employers and workers took little notice of county lines and professed no stake in decades-old rivalries. Bell Helicopter, Six Flags Over Texas, the Great Southwest Corporation, General Motors and dozens of smaller concerns had already conjoined the destiny of both big cities even before they began openly proclaiming their newfound union.

The realization that together Fort Worth and Dallas comprised one of the nation's largest inland metropolitan centers induced civic leaders to pool their strategic resources. In 1970, chamber of commerce Presidents

✧

T. Cullen Davis, appearing entirely at ease, passes time with supporters while the jury sits through deliberations during a second trial in which he was charged with murder-for-hire.

COURTESY OF THE *FORT WORTH STAR-TELEGRAM* PHOTOGRAPH COLLECTION, SPECIAL COLLECTIONS, UNIVERSITY OF TEXAS AT ARLINGTON LIBRARIES, ARLINGTON, TEXAS, FWST 7286, 18A, 11-10-79.

✧

Dallas Mayor Erik Jonsson (center) and J. C. Pace of Fort Worth (right) accept a $34.6 million check from banker James W. Alston to finance the D/FW airport.

COURTESY OF THE *FORT WORTH STAR-TELEGRAM* PHOTOGRAPH COLLECTION, SPECIAL COLLECTIONS, UNIVERSITY OF TEXAS AT ARLINGTON LIBRARIES, ARLINGTON, TEXAS, AR 406 1-20-7.

Harry Werst of Fort Worth and Morris Hite of Dallas helped lead a successful movement to join the two cities into one giant Standard Metropolitan Statistical Area (SMSA). After a non-profit consortium of businesses, chambers, universities, and economic development associations created the North Texas Commission the next year, they charged it with the responsibility of branding the region with a marketable label. By combining the words "metropolitan" and "complex," the NTC's marketing consultants came up with a catchy, descriptive term: the "Metroplex." Copyrighted in 1972, it gained immediate acceptance and quickly endowed the region with a recognizable name.

Joining forces formally was an idea whose time was long overdue. The two camps had already pooled their chips on building the colossal Dallas/Fort Worth Airport, seventeen miles from the center of both downtowns. When completed, the sprawling hub would encompass an area nine miles long and eight miles wide—larger than Manhattan Island. Financing the venture had committed the municipal credit of both cities and put the jobs of several area bankers on the line. No less than eight different airlines had underwritten others costs. Contracts were let in the hundreds of millions of dollars, and a "no work stoppage" agreement was secured with all the trade unions involved with the project. With so much riding on the venture, there was no room for the kind of quibbling that had dogged the ill-fated Greater Southwest Airport. So Cowtowners sucked up their pride, pursed their lips, and got accustomed to saying "Dee-F-Dubya."

Just after midnight on January 13, 1974, the first commercial flight touched down, long before workers put the finishes touches on the new facility. Despite the staggering achievement and a welcoming crowd so raucous that it drowned out the ceremonial speech, the media seemed more concerned

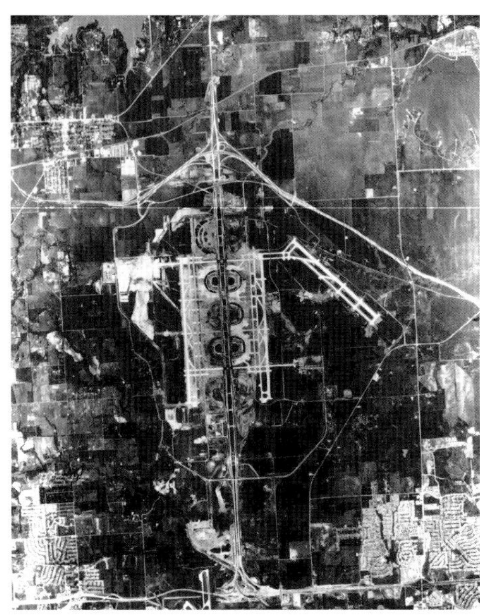

✧

An aerial view of D/FW from three miles up as it neared completion.

COURTESY OF THE *FORT WORTH STAR-TELEGRAM* PHOTOGRAPH COLLECTION, SPECIAL COLLECTIONS, UNIVERSITY OF TEXAS AT ARLINGTON LIBRARIES, ARLINGTON, TEXAS, AR 406 1-20-3.

✧

Closer to the ground, the "people mover" makes a trial run.

COURTESY OF THE *FORT WORTH STAR-TELEGRAM* PHOTOGRAPH COLLECTION, SPECIAL COLLECTIONS, UNIVERSITY OF TEXAS AT ARLINGTON LIBRARIES, ARLINGTON, TEXAS, AR 406 1-20-4.

✧

While D/FW grew accustomed to a daily welter of activity, the Greater Southwest Airport became the haunt of teenagers who raced their cars on the runways and ran amok through empty halls at the old terminal. Authorities scattered tires and posted patrols to discourage the fun.

LEFT IMAGE COURTESY OF THE *FORT WORTH STAR-TELEGRAM* PHOTOGRAPH COLLECTION, SPECIAL COLLECTIONS, UNIVERSITY OF TEXAS AT ARLINGTON LIBRARIES, ARLINGTON, TEXAS, AR 406 1-36-13. RIGHT IMAGE COURTESY OF THE *FORT WORTH STAR-TELEGRAM* PHOTOGRAPH COLLECTION, SPECIAL COLLECTIONS, UNIVERSITY OF TEXAS AT ARLINGTON LIBRARIES, ARLINGTON, TEXAS, AR 406 1-36-13.

with the plight of a honeymoon couple that could not locate their luggage. If Amon Carter had still been alive, several newsmen would have been looking for other jobs. But it was a new day, and in the months to come, few snafus escaped the attention of carping reporters. There was no eluding the fact, however, that the futuristic airport was everything its boosters said it would be, and soon D/FW was transforming the broad, bald prairie around it into a driving economic force.

Nothing did more to prove the wisdom of the airport's backers than the relocation of American Airlines' headquarters from New York City to Fort Worth in 1978. It was something of a homecoming, to be sure. At Meacham Field in the Twenties, both Texas Air Transport and Texas Airways got their start before the merger that created the transportation giant.

The windfall that brought American Airlines to Fort Worth actually started out as a jest as far as D/FW Director Ernest Dean was concerned. Meeting with AA chairman Albert V. Casey about the corporation's reservation center, Dean jovially asked his guest when he was going to go ahead and move its entire outfit to the Metroplex. To his surprise, Casey was already amenable to the idea. The bond package that Fort Worth and Dallas soon put together was more than even the Big Apple could offer. After suffering a blistering rebuke from New York Mayor Ed Koch, Casey left the city, turning down a final offer that would have given the airline space in the World Trade Center.

D/FW and American Airlines had a tremendous impact on outlying communities. Several, such as Hurst, Euless, and Bedford—the Mid-Cities—had already mushroomed in the Fifties and Sixties and kept growing until drivers could pass from the city limits of one to another without even realizing it. In other places subdevelopments and shopping centers that had excited new residents just a decade or so earlier were now becoming liabilities for

✧

Northeast Mall under construction.

COURTESY OF THE *FORT WORTH STAR-TELEGRAM* PHOTOGRAPH COLLECTION, SPECIAL COLLECTIONS, UNIVERSITY OF TEXAS AT ARLINGTON LIBRARIES, ARLINGTON, TEXAS, AR 407 3-41.

community planners who wanted to continue riding the cutting edge of growth.

In Northeast Tarrant County for example, Richland Plaza had seemed like a shopper's paradise in 1962 when it was new. But, when the Northeast Mall in Hurst opened in 1971, the once-trendy shops at the plaza began moving to new strip centers or went out of business. The anchor, JCPenney, opened an even bigger store at the new mall and turned the former location into an outlet shop for slow-moving merchandise.

Over in Hurst, boys like Buddy Hamm liked to wile away lazy afternoons shooting BB-guns and riding bikes down the narrow trails in a lush thicket of post oaks where the mall would arise. Then, one day, Hamm recalled, "I topped the hill and just came to a stop. They had scraped it all." Over the next year local kids watched concrete mixers, cranes, and an army of construction workers turn the land into something unfathomable. While Hamm and the other boys found new places to play, kids too young to remember "the woods" would become the first generation of mall rats.

The same scene had already unfolded at Seminary South Mall, a short drive down I-35W, and it repeated itself at Ridgmar Mall on the west side and at Six Flags Mall and Forum 303 in Arlington. Each of the new complexes boasted enormous department stores that anchored the end of a spoke. Down the great halls were restaurants such as Wyatt's Cafeteria or El Fenix, and stores with catchy names such as Chess King, Sound Town, Oshman's, Coach House Gifts, Picadilly Fair, and Miss Bojangles. Shoppers could drop off their children at game rooms like the Space Sport or let them pick out a movie to watch at the malls' multiscreen theaters. At the center the halls came together at cavernous atriums illuminated by natural light and dotted with fountains and full-sized trees, beside which shoppers rested. It was the Gruen Plan, moved to the 'burbs and all under one roof.

In the city itself, specifically at Amon Carter Square, the announcement by the Kimbell Foundation in 1964 that it would open a multimillion dollar gallery to house the collection of its founder, the late Kay Kimbell, brought unparalleled praise from every corner of the art world. Despite the breathtaking strides the Arts District had taken during the Sixties, Mayor Sharkey Stovall called the Kimbell "the greatest thing that has happened to Fort Worth in the field of culture for many years." It was a tall boast—and true.

The grounds at the Kimbell Museum.

COURTESY OF THE *FORT WORTH STAR-TELEGRAM* PHOTOGRAPH COLLECTION, SPECIAL COLLECTIONS, UNIVERSITY OF TEXAS AT ARLINGTON LIBRARIES, ARLINGTON, TEXAS, AR 407 3-27.

A view inside the Kimbell's South Gallery.

COURTESY OF THE *FORT WORTH STAR-TELEGRAM* PHOTOGRAPH COLLECTION, SPECIAL COLLECTIONS, UNIVERSITY OF TEXAS AT ARLINGTON LIBRARIES, ARLINGTON, TEXAS, AR 406 1-31-18.

The building itself was designed by Philadelphia architect Louis Kahn, who came to Fort Worth to sign his contract. "Man has no other reason than to express," he told an assembly. "It's the measure of a city when acts of its citizens make art available to all."

Kimbell's gift capped a near rags-to-riches story. He went from helping his father operate a flourmill in the Northeast Texas town of Whitewright to serving on the boards of seventy corporations by the time of his death in April 1964. He and his wife Velma bought their first painting in 1931. In time their priceless collection grew to some two hundred works, most of them centuries old. The artists comprised a Who's Who of the great masters—among them Rembrandt, Gainsborough, Romney, Rubens, Van Dyck, and Goya.

The Fort Worth Art Museum briefly shared the spotlight with the Kimbell when it expanded. Here, looking as if they had wandered over from the Children's Museum, Director Henry Hopkins (left) examines the model along with Art Association President Edward Hudson, Jr.

COURTESY OF THE *FORT WORTH STAR-TELEGRAM* PHOTOGRAPH COLLECTION, SPECIAL COLLECTIONS, UNIVERSITY OF TEXAS AT ARLINGTON LIBRARIES, ARLINGTON, TEXAS, AR 406 1-31-10.

Five-year-olds Jennifer Taylor and Michael Hume receive instruction from Roger Pool, who held a class for preschoolers.

COURTESY OF THE *FORT WORTH STAR-TELEGRAM* PHOTOGRAPH COLLECTION, SPECIAL COLLECTIONS, UNIVERSITY OF TEXAS AT ARLINGTON LIBRARIES, ARLINGTON, TEXAS, AR 406 1-31-20.

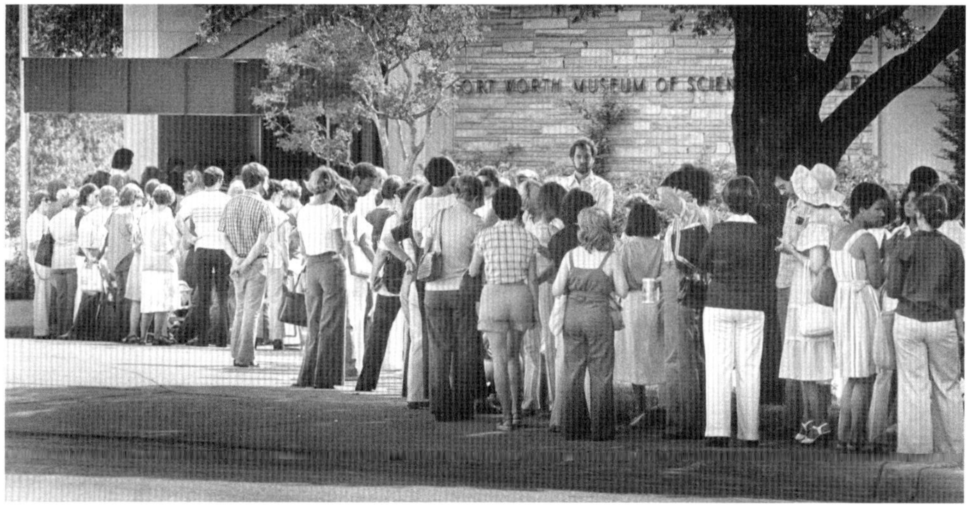

Aspiring artists wait to register for basic drawing classes at the Fort Worth Museum of Science & History; the line began forming at 1:30 a.m.

COURTESY OF THE *FORT WORTH STAR-TELEGRAM* PHOTOGRAPH COLLECTION, SPECIAL COLLECTIONS, UNIVERSITY OF TEXAS AT ARLINGTON LIBRARIES, ARLINGTON, TEXAS, AR 406 1-31-29.

To draw attention to the city's cultural amenities, performers Nancy Holland, Vanecka Benton, and Amy Arnst (left to right) in 1975 staged "A Dance of the Equinox" on the front lawn of the Art Museum and later at the Water Gardens.

COURTESY OF THE *FORT WORTH STAR-TELEGRAM* PHOTOGRAPH COLLECTION, SPECIAL COLLECTIONS, UNIVERSITY OF TEXAS AT ARLINGTON LIBRARIES, ARLINGTON, TEXAS, AR 406 1-1-31-20.

The museum opened in 1972 under the direction of Richard F. Brown. Upon his death, Edmund Pillsbury took charge. The renowned art historian expanded the collection by continuing to acquire paintings of the European masters. His generous loans of the museum's art as well as bringing exhibits to Fort Worth helped boost the Kimbell's prestige, earning it world-class recognition.

If Cowtown seemed an unlikely seat of high culture, the thought did not appear to register with local patrons. Just as Fort Worth loved its art, it also embraced the theater. In addition to Casa Mañana, live performances found enthusiastic audiences at the Hip Pocket Theater, the Community Theater, Sojourner Truth Players, Shakespeare in the Park, and the Windmill Dinner Theater.

They also enjoyed ballet and the symphony. "It isn't unusual, nor is it frowned upon," asserted one commentator, "when many of the operagoers in Fort Worth show up for a performance in jeans and T-shirts. Culture and Cowtown have made compatible bedfellows."

Yet Fort Worth would not be Cowtown without its country and western music. Its popularity ebbed and flowed, of course, but at the core there always remained a die-hard following that frequented honkeytonks like the Long Branch Saloon with its deep shag carpet and the Watering Trough, its dim

TCU could point to all kinds of development projects during its centennial decade. Here, Perry Bass presents the Annie Richardson Bass Building to the school in 1971.

COURTESY OF THE *FORT WORTH STAR-TELEGRAM* PHOTOGRAPH COLLECTION, SPECIAL COLLECTIONS, UNIVERSITY OF TEXAS AT ARLINGTON LIBRARIES, ARLINGTON, TEXAS, AR 406 1-63-25.

lights set in wagon wheels that illuminated a sign heralding: "Cowtown USA."

When WBAP 820 acquired a clear channel in 1970 and adopted a "Country Gold" format, it soon became the nation's number one country music station. Down the long, dark stretches of highway from well beyond the Ozarks into New Mexico and from Old Mexico to Canada truckers and travelers tuned in to hear Bill Mack—the "Midnight Cowboy"—spin tunes and talk country.

At the same time, a new "progressive" country sound found a home at the refurbished Panther Hall when singers like Chet Atkins and Charley Pride were not filling the venue. Willie Nelson, who had once cut an album at the venue during its heyday, played at the reopening of the east side institution. Other bands—Commander Cody and the Lost Planet Airmen, Augie Myer and the Cowboy Headband, and Asleep at the Wheel—also attracted devoted fans. If the sound had a new twist, the audience, men with long hair and tattered blue jeans and women with shag haircuts and haltertops, also reflected the changing times.

As the Baby Boom generation began to reach maturity, leisure activities gained a new importance. That fact was not lost upon a new civic leadership that seemed suddenly to discover the forty-eight miles of untapped riverfront meandering through the county. With its announcement of the inaugural Trinity River Festival, the *Star-Telegram* in 1973 predicted: "The merry, merry month of May will be a lot merrier this year along the banks of the Trinity."

Mayfest, as the event came to be called, combined the efforts of the city's Streams and Valleys Committee and Parks and Recreation Department along with the Junior League and the Tarrant County Water District. The tens of thousands who came to dance around the maypole, browse the booths of arts and crafts, enjoy rides, and listen to music, spent a lot of money, most of it earmarked for further improvements along the Trinity.

A product of that first festival was a one-hundred-foot lighted waterspout situated in the middle of the river, just north of the West Freeway bridge. As Mayfest grew into a much-anticipated annual event, the riverfront came to life. Workers beautified expansive stretches of the Trinity, planting of thousands of trees along banks that flood control crews

Certainly, TCU possessed one of the nation's most unique collegiate mascots. "Super Frog" was an instant hit with children in the stands.

COURTESY OF THE *FORT WORTH STAR-TELEGRAM* PHOTOGRAPH COLLECTION, SPECIAL COLLECTIONS, UNIVERSITY OF TEXAS AT ARLINGTON LIBRARIES, ARLINGTON, TEXAS, AR 406 1-63-29.

Richard Jensen helps restore Texas & Pacific Engine 610, known afterward as the "Freedom Train." It made its way across the United States during the country's Bicentennial in 1976.

COURTESY OF THE *FORT WORTH STAR-TELEGRAM* PHOTOGRAPH COLLECTION, SPECIAL COLLECTIONS, UNIVERSITY OF TEXAS AT ARLINGTON LIBRARIES, ARLINGTON, TEXAS, AR 406 1-62-48.

had earlier denuded; they constructed several low water dams to assure the river's level flow; they poured ever-growing miles of concrete strips over which growing legions of outdoor enthusiasts ran and cycled.

Even before Mayfest became such a hit, local families were already enjoying Oktoberfest, the autumnal fundraiser for the Symphony League. In 1970 the organization's projects chairman, Lorene Cecil, put together a festival at the T&P Station that attracted a crowd of eight thousand. By the end of the decade the two-day event moved to the Convention Center and was pulling in over a hundred thousand people annually. The money raised by Oktoberfest enabled the orchestra to perform at Fort Worth area schools and provided scholarships for the Youth Orchestra.

Fort Worth was coming of age, and each passing decade marked new milestones. Texas Christian University in 1973 celebrated a century of existence. Two years earlier, the Fat Stock Show counted seventy-five. The Seventies, of course, was also the decade of the country's Bicentennial, and the Panther City played an important role in preparing for the year-long commemoration. In anticipation, the American Freedom Train Foundation chose a Fort Worth locomotive—the sole survivor of the 600 series steam engines built during the 1920s—to pull its twenty-two-car Freedom Train across the country during the Bicentennial year.

When the Fourth of July rolled around, city officials who planned a city-wide celebration anticipated that as many as forty-five thousand people would defy the ninety-degree-plus weather; it was estimated that over three times as many thinly clad patriots actually showed up to pay tribute to the occasion. A parade and festival, marked by cannon salutes, music, and other activities, were capped off by a pyrotechnics display at Heritage Park featuring a 175-pound "shell of a million flowers"—the state's largest single firework to that date.

Unexpectedly, a fierce but brief thunderstorm swept through Heritage Park just as the sun was setting. Sharp claps of thunder sent people scurrying for nearby cars and underpasses, while others huddled beneath blankets, newspapers, and even

The "Spirit of '76 Bicentennial Bus" never left town, but racked up some impressive mileage, educating local students. Here, a group of Western Hills High School students listens to a lecture as the bus sits at the corner of Sixth Street and Houston.

COURTESY OF THE *FORT WORTH STAR-TELEGRAM* PHOTOGRAPH COLLECTION, SPECIAL COLLECTIONS, UNIVERSITY OF TEXAS AT ARLINGTON LIBRARIES, ARLINGTON, TEXAS, AR 406 1-8-13.

Parade-goers make their way through Heritage Park after viewing the downtown Bicentennial Parade (left), while a worker prepares the fireworks for the evening's main event.

LEFT IMAGE COURTESY OF THE *FORT WORTH STAR-TELEGRAM* PHOTOGRAPH COLLECTION, SPECIAL COLLECTIONS, UNIVERSITY OF TEXAS AT ARLINGTON LIBRARIES, ARLINGTON, TEXAS, AR 406 1-8-12. RIGHT IMAGE COURTESY OF THE *FORT WORTH STAR-TELEGRAM* PHOTOGRAPH COLLECTION, SPECIAL COLLECTIONS, UNIVERSITY OF TEXAS AT ARLINGTON LIBRARIES, ARLINGTON, TEXAS, AR 406 1-8-13.

The Tarrant County Convention Center became a popular venue for rock concerts during the Seventies. Here, a crowd swarms the box office for Led Zeppelin tickets, which resulted in a near-riot.

COURTESY OF THE *FORT WORTH STAR-TELEGRAM* PHOTOGRAPH COLLECTION, SPECIAL COLLECTIONS, UNIVERSITY OF TEXAS AT ARLINGTON LIBRARIES, ARLINGTON, TEXAS, AR 406 1-62-5.

A more orderly crowd, ironically, jams the center for a hockey game between the short-lived Fort Worth Wings franchise and the Dallas Black Hawks.

COURTESY OF THE *FORT WORTH STAR-TELEGRAM* PHOTOGRAPH COLLECTION, SPECIAL COLLECTIONS, UNIVERSITY OF TEXAS AT ARLINGTON LIBRARIES, ARLINGTON, TEXAS, AR 406 1-62-1.

garbage can lids. By the time the fireworks show began, however, the crowd had returned, standing in places almost shoulder-to-shoulder in ankle-deep water. Lightning, still visible on the western horizon, continued to play in harmony with the fireworks display as the last rockets burst in the sky.

Also enjoying larger-than-expected crowds was the Tarrant County Convention Center. Truly, it had exceeded the wildest dreams of its backers. When journalist Nancy Madsen found herself on the Turnpike in bumper-to-bumper traffic long after rush hour, her writer's curiosity got the better of her. "Had everyone in Dallas decided to move to Fort Worth?" she wondered. Sensing a good story, she followed the line of creeping cars down an exit ramp. "I stopped, rolled down my window and asked a pedestrian what was happening." The reply came matter-of-factly: "Emerson, Lake, and Palmer." Another concert date, another sellout, and Madsen had her story.

Performance magazine, the insiders' rag for the rock world, named the Tarrant County Convention Center America's "Outstanding Arena" in 1977. The site attracted the hottest stars of the day—Kiss, the Eagles, Led Zeppelin, Foreigner, Neil Diamond, Peter Frampton, and others. Often, when promoters announced they would play just one Texas stop, they already had Fort Worth and its state-of-the-art facility circled on their maps.

For officials and staff, some who had worked the Fat Stock Show for years, the eccentricities of rock performers must have seemed bizarre. George Harrison demanded three identical kitchens at different locations for the convenience of his Indian cooks. Others ordered rare wines, gourmet food, and even M&M's of particular colors. A couple of artists had the convention staff redecorate dressing rooms into which they never set foot. Another "redecorated" his own room with uneaten meals that

The completed Water Gardens provided an enlightened complement to the modern Convention Center.

COURTESY OF THE *FORT WORTH STAR-TELEGRAM* PHOTOGRAPH COLLECTION, SPECIAL COLLECTIONS, UNIVERSITY OF TEXAS AT ARLINGTON LIBRARIES, ARLINGTON, TEXAS, AR 406 1-31-39.

✧

The Fort Worth National Bank building rises behind the debris of the demolished Westbrook Hotel, demolished in 1978.

COURTESY OF THE *FORT WORTH STAR-TELEGRAM* PHOTOGRAPH COLLECTION, SPECIAL COLLECTIONS, UNIVERSITY OF TEXAS AT ARLINGTON LIBRARIES, ARLINGTON, TEXAS, AR 406 1-31-5.

custodians had to scrape from the walls and ceilings. Then, there was Elvis. All he wanted was a six-pack of Coca-Cola—that and a considerably larger check than the $300 he split with his agent, Colonel Parker, after his first Cowtown gig in the Fifties.

Other than The Keg, a popular restaurant across the street from the convention center, not much else kept concertgoers and conventioneers downtown after the show. There was, however, the futuristic Water Gardens that at least made the trip to the central city a more pleasant experience. A gift of the Amon Carter Foundation, the full block of fountains, reflecting pools, and waterfalls was greeted at once as "both useless and splendid." At the ribbon cutting, local woman Marion King spoke like a true Fort Worthian. Surveying the central plaza, she smiled to a reporter: "[This] would make a wonderful place for a square dance."

The mind's eye of movie director Michael Anderson, however, beheld a different vision. Just after midnight one Sunday morning in July 1975, a series of explosions and the sight of a panic-stricken crowd scrambling over the walls of the Water Gardens alarmed motorists on the overhead bypass. To the relief of those who called in reports, they learned that it was all part of a movie, *Logan's Run*, set appropriately in the twenty-third century.

Downtown was beginning to come alive, even if it was reawakening more slowly than business and civic leaders wanted. Nevertheless, a number of projects gave Fort Worth its greatest downtown building boom since the 1950s. Covering four-and-a-half blocks, the thirty-seven-story Fort Worth National Bank building became the city's tallest structure when its first occupants began hauling boxes up to their new offices in 1974. A stunning example of modern architecture, the building held enough glass panels to cover five acres. Since each piece was twelve feet tall, a special machine had to be manufactured to set them into place. The *Star-Telegram* called it a "mechanical octopus with suction cups strong enough to pick up [Dallas Cowboy lineman] Bob Lilly."

On hand to help open the giant padlock symbolizing the building's dedication was three-year-old Kate Johnson, the great-great granddaughter of Khleber Van Zandt, who

✧

Prior to the demolition of the Worth Hotel in 1972, its ornate furnishings were sold at auction. Here, Betty Bronstad (top) and Betty Jordan claim their purchase.

COURTESY OF THE *FORT WORTH STAR-TELEGRAM* PHOTOGRAPH COLLECTION, SPECIAL COLLECTIONS, UNIVERSITY OF TEXAS AT ARLINGTON LIBRARIES, ARLINGTON, TEXAS, AR 406 1-32-7.

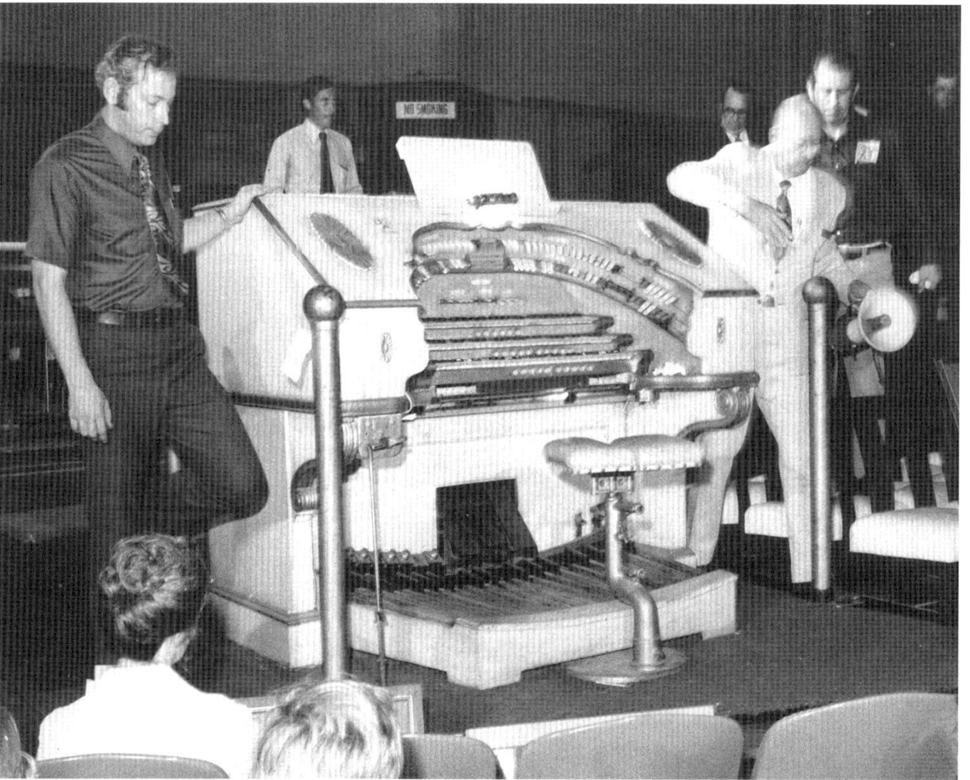

✧

The theater's organ would find a new home at Casa Mañana.

COURTESY OF THE *FORT WORTH STAR-TELEGRAM* PHOTOGRAPH COLLECTION, SPECIAL COLLECTIONS, UNIVERSITY OF TEXAS AT ARLINGTON LIBRARIES, ARLINGTON, TEXAS, AR 406 1-32-6.

✧

The elegant Medical Arts Building also fell victim to the times in 1973. During the next decade the forty-story Burnett Plaza would arise on that site.

COURTESY OF THE JACK WHITE PHOTOGRAPH COLLECTION, SPECIAL COLLECTIONS, UNIVERSITY OF TEXAS AT ARLINGTON LIBRARIES, ARLINGTON, TEXAS, AR 407 3-35.

✧

Anne Windfohr Marion at the dedication of a statue erected in her stepfather's memory, April 1981. Like the man being honored, it was larger-than-life.

COURTESY OF THE *FORT WORTH STAR-TELEGRAM* PHOTOGRAPH COLLECTION, SPECIAL COLLECTIONS, UNIVERSITY OF TEXAS AT ARLINGTON LIBRARIES, ARLINGTON, TEXAS, FWST 7482, 6-6A, 4-16-81.

served as bank president from 1874 to 1930. Inside, the bank's chief executive officer, Lewis H. Bond, assembled a collection of art that included two massive tapestries suspended in the five-story lobby. Outside, sculptor Alexander Calder's sixteen-ton red-orange abstract stabile, *The Eagle*, stood sentinel at the entrance.

Equally impressive was the construction of City Center (now the Charles D. Tandy Center), its bookend towers—which opened in 1976 and 1978—straddling a mall distinguished by an indoor skating rink. With its completion came a new Cowtown tradition of Christmas candles in lights running up the length of each tower. The mixed-use complex of office and shopping space arose on one of the blocks occupied by the old Leonard's Department Store, which the rising business giant bought in 1967 and later razed. The project in many respects became an extension of the man who built it.

By the 1970s, Charles D. Tandy had parlayed a Fort Worth leather crafts business founded by his father in 1918 into a retail empire that would eventually comprise more than twenty major companies and subsidiaries. It was the city's first firm to be listed by the New York Stock Exchange. A broad smile and easy manner that disarmed even the most lowly office worker belied an intensely aggressive salesman. Tandy pioneered modern methods of mail ordering and direct advertising. Among his many interests were Tandy Computers, RadioShack, Tandycrafts, Pier 1 Imports, and Color Tile. He also set up a profit-sharing plan for his employees and gave unstintingly to philanthropic causes, mostly around Fort Worth.

Just when it looked as if he might begin to fill Amon Carter's considerable boots, he died suddenly at the age of sixty. After a typical day full of meetings with business associates and civic leaders, he and wife Anne headed to the Ridglea Country Club where they danced until midnight. He was still partying long after she called it quits, laughing with friends, playing backgammon, and smoking his ever-present cigars before turning in at dawn.

At mid-afternoon a maid, who had gone into Tandy's bedroom to awaken him, instead found him dead. The next day flags across the city flew at half-staff. A shaken Mayor Hugh Parmer expressed everyone's regret: "He was a fine gentleman who has given a lot to the city.... His death is a great loss to us all."

Led by far-sighted developers such as Charles Tandy and Clark Nowlin, business and government had taken great strides in revitalizing the central city, yet entrepreneurs had not kept pace. The Tandy Center and Nowlin's two-level strip of shops and eateries at 600 Houston Street provided many of the same amenities as the suburban malls, but there were too many dead spaces, and visitors hesitated to take the long walk uptown from the Convention Center. "Any time there's a convention in town," groused the Chamber of Commerce, "it's a common sight to see a couple or group standing on a downtown corner, their convention ribbons fluttering forlornly in the breeze, looking up and down the street for something to do." On the other hand, perhaps they were simply wary. The ravages of time—weathered façades of derelict buildings, boarded-up windows, litter blowing down the streets, grass growing through cracked and uneven sidewalks—left the impression that downtown was not a safe place to be after the sun went down. But all of that was about to change.

✧

Despite the loss of several landmarks, other timeworn buildings managed to avoid the wrecking ball. The Land Title Building at Fourth Street and Commerce would soon be revived.

COURTESY OF THE *FORT WORTH STAR-TELEGRAM* PHOTOGRAPH COLLECTION, SPECIAL COLLECTIONS, UNIVERSITY OF TEXAS AT ARLINGTON LIBRARIES, ARLINGTON, TEXAS, AR 406 1-30-42)

✧

Downtown Fort Worth, c. 1980.

CHAPTER 9

RENAISSANCE

1980-1989

At the beginning of the decade, between the venerable, but deteriorating Tarrant County Courthouse and the modern Convention Center, stood a nine-block collection of tired old buildings that had once heralded the wealth of earlier generations. Yet even before the 1980s had run its course, it became clear that downtown and indeed, Fort Worth itself, was beginning to stir from its long lethargy. The heart of the metropolis pumped anew, its asphalt and concrete arteries, recently atrophied by cracks and potholes, was transplanted with fresh paving bricks aglow on dewy evenings in the soft ambiance of period lighting. Reconstructed turn-of-the century buildings stirred ghosts of Butch Cassidy and the Sundance Kid. Here and there, restored art deco skyscrapers awakened images of the heady and unsettling days of oil booms, depression, and war. New glass and steel towers among the masonry, however, kept mindful the brisk economy that fueled the revival, despite a mid-decade bust in oil prices.

Members of the larger body similarly thrived: urban frontiers emerged in weathered neighborhoods; the maturing arts district continued to fill in the empty lots of Amon Carter Square; hoofbeats and the gunfire of six-shooters echoed again in the Stockyards, but this time for the delight of tourists; and, out in the ever-burgeoning suburbs, city planners refined identities that earlier developers and high school football teams had created. It was a phenomenon that other American cities enjoyed during the Eighties, but nowhere was the renaissance so swift, so thorough, so stunning.

In the waning days of 1979, the bang that rang in the new decade leveled the last traces of the old Leonards blocks, making room for the Americana Hotel. Developer Sid Bass, joined by fellow industrialists Phil R. North and Hal Milner, orchestrated the demolition from Two Tandy Tower, overlooking the site between their top-floor vantage and the courthouse. On Bass's order from a walkie-talkie, a multicolored plume of sparklers burst from a mushroom cloud of smoke, from which about five thousand helium-filled balloons then began rising, many carrying gift certificates redeemable at Tandy Center shops. The trapezoidal hotel—soon renamed The Worthington—opened two years later.

At the other end of downtown, facing the Convention Center, the old Hotel Texas reopened as the new Hyatt Regency/Fort Worth (now the Radisson Plaza Hotel). In the years after it opened in 1921, its register had routinely included the signatures of celebrities and on rarer occasions, even presidents. While the façade was restored to near its original condition, the inside was gutted and refashioned, its six-story atrium boasting a cascading wall of water that fed its hanging gardens and emptied into pools where Japanese carp swam among the coins of wish-makers.

In the wee hours of Sunday morning on December 8, 1986, another explosion—this one unanticipated—helped clear the last blighted buildings across the street from the Worthington. Just a couple of hours after five hundred wedding guests at the hotel's grand ballroom had called it a night, a natural gas leak wafted over a spark, "turning the city's retail hub into a sea of broken glass." At least thirty structures suffered damage, including about a million dollars worth at the Worthington. Littered across the ballroom floor, a coating of shards was all that remained of a thirty-foot-tall plate glass window.

Miraculously, the explosion claimed no lives. The only injury, in fact, was a minor cut inflicted on former Dallas I.S.D. Superintendent Nolan Estes, who lay sleeping in his eleventh-floor hotel room. Also asleep, but just a precious few yards from the center of the blast, was Gregg Dugan, who ran the Caravan of Dreams nightclub and stayed in a backroom apartment.

A deep roar, followed by a numbing concussion, presented a rude awakening. Instinctively, the disoriented Dugan stumbled over the rubble and through a thick haze until he made his way to what remained of the alley. "I'm lucky, extremely lucky to be alive," he so rightly concluded.

After the cleanup, the owners of the flattened buildings decided it was a good time to sell their lots, and a happy Ed Bass came into possession of the entire block. His plans for further developing it dovetailed neatly with the vision of Bass Brothers Enterprises, a consortium composed of Ed, his older brother Sid, and their two younger siblings, Robert and Lee. Together with their parents, Nancy and Perry, the Basses had

Perry Bass (right), with guide, shows off the catch of the day while taking a well-deserved break in 1987.

COURTESY OF THE *FORT WORTH STAR-TELEGRAM* COLLECTION, SPECIAL COLLECTIONS, THE UNIVERSITY OF TEXAS AT ARLINGTON LIBRARIES, ARLINGTON, TEXAS, FWST AR 368, 84-14.

The Hyatt Regency, formerly the Hotel Texas, reopened in 1981 after operating as the Sheraton Fort Worth to serve convention traffic across the street. The Sheraton's owners destroyed the original lobby to squeeze in another floor; the Hyatt restored the space, but had to settle for a redesigned interior.

COURTESY OF THE *FORT WORTH STAR-TELEGRAM* COLLECTION, SPECIAL COLLECTIONS, THE UNIVERSITY OF TEXAS AT ARLINGTON LIBRARIES, ARLINGTON, TEXAS, FWST 7329, 25, 2-24-80.

The scene at Throckmorton and Second Streets on the morning of December 8, 1986, following an unanticipated explosion caused by a natural gas leak.

COURTESY OF THE *FORT WORTH STAR-TELEGRAM* COLLECTION, SPECIAL COLLECTIONS, THE UNIVERSITY OF TEXAS AT ARLINGTON LIBRARIES, ARLINGTON, TEXAS, FWST 8446, 12-8-86.

Ed Bass.

COURTESY OF THE *FORT WORTH STAR-TELEGRAM* COLLECTION, SPECIAL COLLECTIONS, THE UNIVERSITY OF TEXAS AT ARLINGTON LIBRARIES, ARLINGTON, TEXAS, FWST AR 368, 84-4.

Fire Station No. 1, part of the City Center Development and home to the 150 Years of Fort Worth Museum.

COURTESY OF JOHN T. ROBERTS, FORT WORTH, WWW.FORTWORTHARCHITECTURE.COM.

become, by 1980, the wealthiest family in Texas. Heirs of Fort Worth oilman Sid Richardson, their responsible stewardship of his fortune maintained the continuity of philanthropy and development such earlier civic benefactors as Amon Carter, Pappy Waggoner, Richardson himself, and Charles Tandy had established.

Before the decade began, Sid Bass had considered the alternatives of moving his part of the growing financial empire to New York City or remaking Fort Worth into a place that could attract the same kinds of business leaders who normally landed in the Big Apple. "He chose the latter," commented his brother, Ed. It would be a decision of monumental consequence for the material fortunes of Fort Worth.

The Bass Brothers Development Corporation wasted no time in swinging a deal that would have wowed the old coterie down at the Fort Worth Club. Together with the Dallas-based Woodbine Corporation, the consortium bagged a multimillion-dollar Urban Development Action Grant that beautified the downtown infrastructure between the two anchor hotels. The creation of Sundance Square, in fact, became an integral part of the plan. It was a dreamily appropriate name for a development that featured rows of Victorian-Styled business buildings. Described by economic analysts as a high-risk, low-yield venture, it nevertheless quickly attracted trendy shops and restaurants as well as a variety of office tenants.

Sundance Square earned Sid Bass rich praise for its innovative approach of blending old and new. But it was Ed, often seen as the maverick in the family, who turned the most heads with his appropriately named Caravan of Dreams, located behind Sundance Square at 312 Houston Street. The man who introduced the Biosphere to America unleashed on Fort Worth a $5.5 million neon-trimmed nightclub/restaurant/theater with a cactus garden that looked as if it had been plucked out of a rocky desert and laid upon the roof; integrated into the landscape was a geodesic dome and a grotto bar. Inside the club were murals and paintings that captured the best features of *avant-garde* and modern art.

One reviewer likened the Caravan's effect on "the usual Fort Worth leisure fare as, say, an Andy Warhol appearance might have on the Tarrant County Commissioner's Court." Despite the misgivings of critics, the Caravan developed a loyal following that became part of the blues and jazz scene that emerged there. Ed also introduced Cowtown to the kinds of cutting edge acts that played venues in New York and Los Angeles as well as resurrecting such controversial personalities as *Naked Lunch* author William Burroughs, whose Beat Generation poetry still resonated among off-beats of the "Me Generation."

Dominating Sundance Square were the Basses' City Center Towers, paternal twins that in 1982 and 1984 cut the skyline at 33 and 38 stories, respectively. At the foot of the project block lay Fire Station No. 1. Rather than tear it down, the Basses integrated the 1907-vintage hall into City Center, converting it into a museum to showcase images and artifacts from Fort Worth's past.

Unfortunately, several downtown icons surrendered to developers whose plans did not include historic preservation. At Main and Seventh the art deco Aviation Building, once home to American Airlines, fell to the wrecking ball to make room for the forty-story Continental Plaza (now Carter+Burgess Plaza). The emerald rhomboid became the new home of the Petroleum Club that occupied the top floor. Also sacrificed was the elegant Medical Arts Building, imploded during the previous decade, to accommodate the First United Tower,

Aztec Indians and eagles decorate the elaborate entrance of the sixteen-story Aviation Building. It was demolished to build Continental Plaza, which opened in 1982. Originally, this outstanding example of Zig Zag Moderne was the corporate headquarters of Southern Air Transport, a forerunner of American Airlines. Its last tenant, Trans American Life, erected a gaudy seven-story neon sign on the building's corner at Main and Seventh streets; an even tackier sign covered most of the façade facing east. The old art deco masterpiece deserved better.

COURTESY OF JOHN T. ROBERTS, FORT WORTH, WWW.FORTWORTHARCHITECTURE.COM.

✧

Democratic Congressman Jim Wright, Speaker of the House of Representatives, enjoys a friendly meeting with the Republican leadership at the executive mansion's Rose Garden in 1987. Such visits among members of rival parties would be fewer as American politics began to polarize in the ensuing years. One of the first victims of this internecine contest, Speaker Wright stepped down, as he said, to "end the mindless cannibalism" that had disrupted the work of Congress. His resignation came in the face of partisan furor that followed a year of investigations and strategic press leaks over charges that he had violated House ethics rules. The most damaging revelation was that a supporter had illegally purchased bulk copies of his book, Reflections of a Public Man*—to be precise, the royalties earned Wright exactly $7,700 spread out over three years. By contrast, the cloud that formed over Newt Gingrich, his chief antagonist and eventual successor as House Speaker, produced a storm that rained substantiated charges of lying to the House Ethics Committee, using tax-exempt foundations for political purposes, committing adultery—and, ironically—accepting the offer of a multimillion dollar advance for writing a book that brought a chorus of indignation from his own Republican colleagues. He reluctantly dropped the book deal. As for Wright, he could take comfort in his record of service to Fort Worth and Tarrant County over a thirty-four-year career that brought home millions of dollars in government contracts and many thousands of jobs that helped seed the area's renaissance. The livelihoods of approximately thirty-thousand families alone by the mid-1980s depended on aerospace appropriations he supported on behalf of General Dynamics and Bell Helicopter. Flood control projects, freeway construction, the creation of recreational areas, and landing the Fort Worth Federal Center are also among his achievements. Other orchestrations included obtaining $9 million in federal grants to revitalize downtown Fort Worth that triggered a half-billion-dollar avalanche of private construction; similarly, $8 million in federal seed money boosted the transformation of the Stockyards and North Side; he also helped assure the preservation of historic structures through the creation of tax breaks for renovation and maintenance. Wright, moreover, an original proponent of D/FW, led efforts that netted almost $100 million in federal funding to make the airport a reality; he interceded with the White House directly to initiate direct flights to Europe; he also paved the way for returning American Airlines to its founding home, winning the praise of AA chief Albert Casey, who called Wright's work "a miracle." The Speaker protected the massive investment by sponsoring the controversial Wright Amendment. Love it or loathe it, there is no denying that D/FW avoided the same fate as the Greater Fort Worth International Airport and has grown into one of the country's most important transportation facilities.*

COURTESY OF TEXAS CHRISTIAN UNIVERSITY, SPECIAL COLLECTIONS, MARY COUTS BURNETT LIBRARY, FORT WORTH, TEXAS.

✧

With its centennial approaching in 1985, the Tarrant County Courthouse received a long-needed restoration.

COURTESY OF THE *FORT WORTH STAR-TELEGRAM* COLLECTION, SPECIAL COLLECTIONS, THE UNIVERSITY OF TEXAS AT ARLINGTON LIBRARIES, ARLINGTON, TEXAS, FWST 8656, 3-1-88.

✧

Looking up from the first floor of the courthouse rotunda.

COURTESY OF JOHN T. ROBERTS, FORT WORTH, WWW.FORTWORTHARCHITECTURE.COM.

another forty-story skyscraper, completed in 1983 (now Burnett Plaza).

The rapid expansion of the central business district unfolded under the watchful eyes of other players—some big, some small—who possessed special interests. Women and men from old Fort Worth families cared deeply about preserving the physical remnants of the city that their grandparents and great-grandparents had called home. In 1980 the Junior League of Fort Worth funded the Historical Preservation Council of Tarrant County that unfolded an umbrella broad enough for forty organizations to huddle under.

Downtown property owners who wanted to cash in on the revitalization also pushed a positive agenda. In 1981 the nonprofit corporation Downtown Fort Worth, Inc. (DFWI) began operating on membership dues. One of its signal accomplishments was staging the Main Street Arts Festival. More controversial was the creation of a Public Improvement District in 1986 that levied taxes on downtown businesses to provide additional security, parking, and maintenance as well as marketing support to stimulate the budding tourist industry.

Momentum for judicious growth and preservation had gained steam as the Tarrant County Courthouse approached its centennial.

A poseur cowboy poses with the Chisholm Trail *mural by Richard Haas as a fitting backdrop.*

COURTESY OF PEGGY CASHION.

Outside, a thick coat of silver paint concealed its copper cupola from which each face of its four clocks gave different times. It was inside, however, where neglect and thoughtless expediencies took their greatest toll. At each level, flooring cut off the view of the once-breathtaking rotunda. Wood paneling covered marble wainscoting. Window units connected to electrical wiring dating back to World War I clattered from the transoms. Every other trace of the interior's original design was erased by dropped ceilings and makeshift walls.

To the rescue came Judge Mike Moncrief, who in 1980 responded to those whose solution was simply to replace the worn and weathered masterpiece with a new courthouse. "Over my dead body," he declared. With his backing, a $9.2-million series of bond packages to restore the originally priced $500,000-building passed. Under the direction of architect Ward Bogard the three-year project returned the Beaux Arts landmark to its former state of grandeur. Architects cobbled their blueprints from historic photographs and from drawings left over from the addition of a steam heating system that was installed in 1917. The subtle touches of such modern conveniences as elevators and central air did little to detract from the original features. Once again visitors would stop to admire the rotunda, walk the grand staircase, and generally gain a sense of being overawed by the cavernous hall of justice.

As long as the seemingly Soviet-inspired Tarrant County Civil Courts Building sat next door, however, the downtown development crowd would never fully achieve the combination of traditional, chic, and postmodern ambiance that it was striving so hard to cultivate. Most local people referred to the drab, modernistic box as "the Radiator Building" for the lengths of louvers running up its height. County Judge Roy English called it "the worst architectural accident to ever happen in Tarrant County."

The problem, in the end, turned out to be as illusory as the solution itself. With the support of a $1.5-million grant from the Sid Richardson Foundation, New York artist Richard Haas turned the building into a grand canvass. His *trompe l'oeil* masterpiece began with a stripped surface onto which he applied a second skin of cement and sand-gravel. The few functional features, such as porthole windows carved out of the new surface, blended into such painted-on "architectural" details as ornamental brick clusters and sculpted capitals, creating an intricate three-dimensional appearance that truly "fooled the eye" as the French-translated term for the genre indicated.

The Stockyards came alive during the 1980s as Fort Worthians at last embraced their western heritage without reservation.

COURTESY OF THE *FORT WORTH STAR-TELEGRAM* COLLECTION, SPECIAL COLLECTIONS, THE UNIVERSITY OF TEXAS AT ARLINGTON LIBRARIES, ARLINGTON, TEXAS, FWST FWST 8638, 1-22-88.

So successful was his Texas-sized optical illusion that Haas was enlisted to put a quick facelift on other bland and blighted downtown facades even before his work on the Civil Courts building was finished. Some of his art jazzed up featureless surfaces with cornices, columns, and simple bas-reliefs. Others were murals that celebrated the city's frontier heritage. In particular, his *Chisholm Trail*, on the south-facing wall of the 1902-vintage Jett Building at 400 Main Street (that once housed the Northern Texas Traction Company) became his signature work—even more so than the Civil Courts Building. Countless photographs of longhorn cattle seemingly bursting out of the mural behind smiling tourists so testified.

Not everybody hailed *trompe l'oeil*, however. Its detractors thought it became overdone and contributed to an emerging image of Fort Worth as a western Disneyland. "Sure it has great entertainment quality," remarked local art historian Judith Cohen, "but if you are entertained too much it becomes kitschy…like wearing too much jewelry." Apologists, though, like Sundance Square developer Bill Boecker insisted that "what it does is blend art and architecture and…helps knit together the fabric of downtown." For better or worse, *trompe l'oeil* left its mark on Cowtown in the 1980s, inspiring officials in other Texas cities to bring "the Fort Worth look" to their own restoration projects.

Building a unique modern culture on the foundation of its western heritage allowed Fort Worth at last to shed the negative connotation surrounding the term "Cowtown." "We're through denying our heritage to prove we've made progress," proclaimed Stockyards promoter "Cowboy" Steve Murrin. "Now we can say 'You bet, this is where the West begins!'" So it came to pass that "Panther City" would be heard less often as enthusiastic boosters began hanging the newly preferred nickname "Cowtown" on businesses, visitors' brochures, and locally sponsored events.

Backers of the Cowtown Marathon embraced the western handle to promote the inaugural event just before the decade began. On that February day in 1978 sleet-packed streets greeted only four hundred of the thousand registered runners. The slight turnout did not matter to founder Joel Alter. A veteran of races in cities whose scenery paled against the compact business and cultural districts of Fort Worth, the surgery professor at the Texas College of Osteopathic Medicine knew that Cowtown and the growing popularity of marathons were a perfect match.

As the event began attracting runners from most every state as well as Canada and Mexico, so too did it increasingly draw on the city's claim to the title "Where the West Begins." In 1980 the Tarrant County Sheriff's Posse took control of holding back the crowd that gathered at the Stockyards where the 26.2-mile trot and the shorter, but still grueling 10K run, began and ended. Two mounted cowboys fired their six-shooters to start the race, while another cowboy smiling on the participants from posters hanging all along the route admonished "You can do it!"

As the crowd waited to hear updates between country songs on the mobile unit of radio station KXOL, the two starters—seemingly at odds with each other—climbed off their mounts. To settle their mock argument, the pair shot it out to the delight of children whose yards-length attention spans did not match the miles-length races. By the end of the decade, six thousand runners bulged forward at the gun.

More than two-thousand marathoners begin the grueling 26.2-mile run from the starting line at the Stockyards.

COURTESY OF THE *FORT WORTH STAR-TELEGRAM* COLLECTION, SPECIAL COLLECTIONS, THE UNIVERSITY OF TEXAS AT ARLINGTON LIBRARIES, ARLINGTON, TEXAS, FWST 7346, 18, 2-24-80.

All along the route the rows of spectators lining the streets grew, too. The vast majority cheered them on, many handing out cups of water and halves of oranges. Still, an occasional sadist could be spotted reveling in the agony of runners dragging oxygen-depleted legs toward their goal. Yale Youngblood expressed what many of the participants surely felt as they wondered why they were so intent on punishing themselves. Five hundred yards from the finish line a seven-year-old boy darted up beside him and cocked: "Wanna race, Mister?" "Wanna die before you reach driving age buster?" Youngblood growled back. At the finish line, the weary man assured his own young sons that he and Pheidippides, the original marathoner, had parted ways for good. Reminding his father that he had said the same thing the year before, Youngblood smiled: "You have my word *as a runner*."

While most local people perceived "Cowtown" as largely symbolic, Tarrant County during the Eighties could still boast

Dr. Joel Alter, surgery professor at the Texas College of Osteopathic Medicine across from the Amon Carter Museum, and founder of the Cowtown Marathon.

COURTESY OF THE *FORT WORTH STAR-TELEGRAM* COLLECTION, SPECIAL COLLECTIONS, THE UNIVERSITY OF TEXAS AT ARLINGTON LIBRARIES, ARLINGTON, TEXAS, FWST 7346, 1, 2-22-80.

The building that is home to Billy Bob's Texas has an interesting history. It started out in 1910 as open-air cattle barn. The city enclosed it in 1936 for the Southwestern Exposition and Fat Stock Show, converting it into an exhibit building. During World War II the Globe Aircraft Corporation turned it into a factory and built planes there. After the war it became a department store.

COURTESY OF JOHN T. ROBERTS, FORT WORTH, WWW.FORTWORTHARCHITECTURE.COM.

three ranches of ten thousand acres or more within view of the skyline. Other material links also continued to tie the traditional livestock industry to the livelihoods of genuine stockmen. At a time when Texas was exporting the image of the Urban Cowboy across the face of the globe, over a half-million people annually mobbed the Southwestern Exposition and Fat Stock Show. Alongside dudes who bellied up to the bar at trendy Fort Worth saloons were men and women whose boots were no strangers to the droppings of cows and horses. All kinds of livestock organizations called Cowtown home. The National Cutting Horse Association (NCHA), formed at the 1946 Fat Stock Show, established itself on Benbrook Highway and annually held three of its six national competitions in Fort Worth. Similarly, associations that bred and registered Texas Longhorns, American Paint horses, and Texas Angus cattle maintained headquarters in Fort Worth.

Perhaps the most storied group was the Texas and Southwestern Cattle Raisers Association. From its beginnings at the town of Graham, where theft-plagued cattlemen in Old Northwest Texas met under the branches of a post oak tree in 1877, the organization eventually settled on West Seventh Street in Fort Worth. The approximately fifteen-thousand-member TSCRA had long since made its monthly magazine, *The Cattleman*, a staple on coffee tables across Texas, New Mexico, and Oklahoma. The association grew into an industry force that lobbied for favorable legislation, provided insurance for its members, and even opened a research library and first-rate museum to cultivate awareness.

Nothing, however, said Cowtown quite like Billy Bob's Texas. Nobody, save for its co-developers, could have envisioned rescuing the sprawling tin-covered structure that lay rusting and dented behind the Coliseum and Stockyards offices. To rancher and former Texas A&M football star Billy Bob Barnett and urban cowboy Spencer Taylor, however, the three-acre former cow barn was going to be the place where the West would begin *and* end. They saw in its sloping floor—constructed by the original owner for the convenience of his manure shovelers—an easy vantage for crowds viewing the band stage. They knew, too, that behind all that tin the department store had laid over the original façade was a sturdy building protected from the elements.

On opening night, in April 1981, Billy Bob's Texas could not have provided a starker contrast to the otherwise moribund North Side business district. Six-thousand-plus first-nighters converged on the searchlights, passing along rows of boarded-up and seedy buildings lining North Main. On the other side of the giant saloon lay the catacombs of dark, empty cattle pens; beyond them, the packing plants loomed wraith-like against the night sky. Only an occasional gaudy sign hanging over such Stockyards institutions as the Cattleman's Steakhouse and Theo's Saddle and Sirloin belied the district's decline.

Back at Billy Bob's, none of that mattered. Men and women who parked in the club's seven-acre lot climbed into stagecoaches and atop buckboards for a ride to the front door. Among reporters from *People* magazine and the *Washington Post* and crews from the morning shows at ABC and NBC, screen stars and high rollers mixed with cowboys, both real and imagined. They gawked at the eye patch that John Wayne wore in *True Grit* and admired the ambiance of the roughed-out cedar walls and the expansive bars with their brass rails and well-stocked shelves. Mostly they tried to grasp the scale of the "World's Largest Honky Tonk."

What emerged from the gutted shell was a breathtaking array of cow country commerce. The tens of thousands of customers who pushed through the louvered doors of the "saloon" could eat there, get a haircut, have an old-time photograph made, and outfit themselves in just about anything under the sun, so long as that sun shined in western skies. They could two-step to live music on either of the twin seven-thousand-square-foot dance floors; shoot pool at any of two dozen tables; watch a live rodeo; or, just sit and sip...all under one roof.

Billy Bob's Texas was certainly the most prominent, but not the only, pioneer in the refashioned Stockyards. Others, such as Steve Murrin, became vocal about the district's potential. In its long vacant or underused buildings potential investors saw a worn-out, but "constant reminder of our history, a way of authenticating the past for the present," as Murrin put it. Here, he insisted, the roots of the city's past awaited the same kind of rebirth that Chicago enjoyed in its Old Town and Denver at Larimer Square.

With Amonesque enthusiasm, a posse of investors transformed the Stockyards into a first-class tourist trap—in the most positive sense of the phrase. Once again the Coliseum hosted rodeos. Music filled the air along Exchange Avenue. Both dudes and ranch hands strode the covered boardwalk on their way to watering holes such as the White Elephant Saloon and the Pickin' Parlor; at the Brown Derby and the Lone Star Chili Parlor they waited for booths to open up. The massively comfortable Stockyards Hotel, a fine example of "Cattle Baron Baroque," came to anchor the block at one corner of Exchange and Main. North Side soon became the place to go, and not just for locals. Striking a pose that would have made the old *Star-Telegram* publisher proud, Murrin stood in full western regalia before a travel industry meeting in

✧

Van Cliburn, just before leaving for Washington, D.C., where he would entertain President Ronald Reagan and Soviet Premier Mikhael Gorbachev.

COURTESY OF THE *FORT WORTH STAR-TELEGRAM* COLLECTION, SPECIAL COLLECTIONS, THE UNIVERSITY OF TEXAS AT ARLINGTON LIBRARIES, ARLINGTON, TEXAS, FWST 8618, 12, 11-26-87.

London and ended a pitch with: "Y'all come to Fort Worth!"

Van Cliburn also did his ambassador's duty for his adopted hometown, returning to Russia, where the spotlight of world fame had first fallen upon him. At the invitation of President Mikhail Gorbachev and his wife Raisa, Cliburn's jet entered Soviet airspace without a Russian navigator—only the second time such a flight had been permitted. After rhapsodizing the Moscow audience with Tchaikovsky and Liszt, he met the first couple backstage, where they accepted a silver Tiffany plate and T-shirts with "Fort Worth Club" emblazoned on the keepsakes in block letters. The pianist also presented a generous check to the Russian Cultural Foundation. Returning the favor, the Moscow Conservatory at Rachmaninoff Hall feted the pianist with its first-ever master of fine arts degree. It was Cowtown diplomacy at is best.

Back in Fort Worth a new sound assaulted the airwaves. Coming in just below the radar of American popular culture, punk rock was about as foreign to both classical music and C&W as a field hand at the Petroleum Club. For those who danced to a different drummer, Zero's New Wave Lounge on East Lancaster became a short-lived, but vibrant underground scene. The stark hall attracted more curious spectators than it did devotees in leather and spiked hair. Nevertheless, bands such as The Hugh Beaumont Experience, The Ralphs, and The Telefones played regularly to enthusiastic audiences. Another popular band, The Fort Worth Cats, never broke the charts, but their album *Earthquake at the OK Corral* became a cult favorite. It was fun while it lasted, but all too soon the genre entered the mainstream in a more palatable form called alternative music.

✧

Fort Worthian King Coffey (top, middle) started his career as drummer for the Hugh Beaumont Experience, and then hit it big with Butthole Surfers, one of the enduring titans of punk rock.

COURTESY OF THE BUTTHOLE SURFERS. PHOTOGRAPH BY KERI PICKETT.

Until the Eighties, Fort Worth's Tejanos did not enjoy many media outlets. Then, KFJZ, a staple of local radio since the 1920s, switched to a Spanish language format and became *La Pantera*—The Panther. The transition heralded the prominence of Hispanic Fort Worth. The heart of the community beat in North Side, where the culture became dominant in the schools and churches. In 1983 business leaders of the reorganized Fort Worth Hispanic Chamber of Commerce doubled their efforts to cultivate small business growth. They also initiated a youth program that placed an emphasis on education. A $600 scholarship awarded to eighth-graders, redeemable with interest only upon graduation from high school, provided a creative incentive for students to further their education.

The growth of North Side's Mexican Independence Day celebration—*Diez y Seis de Septiembre*—cultivated a citywide awareness of the growing tejano community. The first parade during the late Sixties consisted of only two floats and several groups strung out along a couple of blocks. By 1980, more than twenty-five thousand people watched the mile-long parade of floats, high school bands, and local organizations. In addition to a fiesta at North Side's Marine Park, organizers arranged a celebration at Burnett Park. "The downtown fiesta is aimed primarily at the noon lunch crowd and that means mostly Anglo people," explained coordinator Rudy Renteria. By the end of the decade, one Mexican holiday was not enough to satisfy the increasingly diverse crowds of partiers, and *Cinco de Mayo* was added to the city's rites of spring.

✧

Dancers celebrate Mexican Independence Day at Burnett Park, 1980.

COURTESY OF THE *FORT WORTH STAR-TELEGRAM* COLLECTION, SPECIAL COLLECTIONS, THE UNIVERSITY OF TEXAS AT ARLINGTON LIBRARIES, ARLINGTON, TEXAS, FWST 7403, 20, 9-17-80.

A group of Fort Worthians, black and white, gathers in southeast Fort Worth in 1981 to commemorate the dedication of the Martin Luther King Freeway, which begins downtown as U.S. Highway 287 and ends at Village Creek Road. Noted columnist Bob Ray Sanders (left) stands with suit coat over his shoulder.

COURTESY OF THE FORT WORTH PUBLIC LIBRARY, TARRANT COUNTY BLACK HISTORICAL & GENEALOGY SOCIETY COLLECTION.

Certainly Fort Worth was large enough to accommodate a multiethnic population with a variety of cultures and interests. During the Eighties the population of Tarrant County passed the million mark, and by the time the decade ended, it had become home to over 309,000 more people than when it began. Of these newly counted souls, fewer were West Texans that those whom they had always referred to as "Yankees." Yellow T-shirts sporting "University of Michigan" logos seemed as common in some suburbs as burnt orange or maroon. In their own estimation, these Rust Belt refugees saw Texas as immune to the economic shockwaves of the so-called "Reagan recession" that rippled through the industrialized North early in the decade. With oil commanding a premium, Texas was awash in investment capital and bristling with high-paying jobs.

It came as no surprise then, that not a single Tarrant County savings and loan association appeared on a "problem list" issued by the Federal Home Loan Bank Board in 1981. At the time, astronomical inflation and usurious interest rates troubled investors and compelled the board to monitor closely the nation's thrifts. Richard Greene, president of Arlington Savings, nevertheless assured: "I'll tell you what's on the horizon. In Washington right now there are many savings incentive bills." Pointing to a spirit of bipartisanship, he predicted that legislators would create all kinds of opportunities for investors.

Greene was speaking for the little man; legislators, plied with the dollars of special interests, had another class of investor in mind. In Texas, at least, millions of dollars and the promise of many more millions hinged on oil profits and a continuing building boom. The deregulated thrifts began signing off on loans that would have provoked earlier bank officers to give applicants the bum's rush through the door they entered.

Then, all at once, in January 1986, a meteoric plunge in oil prices crashed down upon the shaky thrifts. At the end of the first business quarter that year Texas American Bancshares—owner of Fort Worth's largest bank (the former Fort Worth National, by then renamed Texas American Bank-Fort Worth)—announced a $22 million loss. By the end of the year that figure had climbed to $115.2 million. Those losses soon paled beside the numbers that accrued once the dominoes began to tumble. In the second quarter of 1988 alone, the bank announced it had lost $135 million. TAB stock that had traded for $42 a share during the heady days of the Eighties oil boom fell to $1.50.

For a while it looked as if the bank would fare better than many of its competitors. At one point twelve of Tarrant County's thirty-six thrifts—fully one-third—were technically insolvent. An FDIC bailout of TAB, assisted by a merger, promised to rescue what little shareholder equity remained. Charlie Hillard, local Ford dealer and a customer of the bank for forty years, emerged from a meeting of the board and moaned to a reporter: "I'm not happy about [the outcome], but it's kind of like the girl said about her husband, 'It's better than nothing.'" The next year the new financial house of cards fell in again, and once more another institution—this time Bank One—picked up the pieces.

For customers, the industry shakeup left them facing a confusing game of musical chairs. Familiar signs came down and new signs went up with every failure, bailout,

Freedman, *part of an exhibit of African-American art on display at the Fort Worth Public Library.*

COURTESY OF THE FORT WORTH PUBLIC LIBRARY, TARRANT COUNTY BLACK HISTORICAL & GENEALOGY SOCIETY COLLECTION.

and merger. Even before the oil bust, each of Fort Worth's "big three" had departed its old quarters along Seventh Street for a more fashionable address. Fort Worth National, of course, took the name of its holding company, TAB; First National became Interfirst; Continental National changed its name to MBank. In River Oaks, where the Security State Bank had operated for over a quarter of a century, customers were notified before it joined InterFirst. Before long, however, it became First RepublicBank. That name lasted only a few weeks before the NCNB Corporation of North Carolina ordered yet a new sign to grace the street corner. At least the sign companies were happy. On average, they charged about $5,000 for every name change at the small suburban banks; high-rise urban banks brought as much as $50,000.

Measured in human terms the financial catastrophe claimed some notable victims. Among investors who had reached beyond their grasp was Billy Bob Barnett, forever afterward referred to as "the former owner of Billy Bob's Texas." His ambitious plans to renovate and put into use other buildings in the Stockyards ran headlong into the debilitating bust. With more than twelve hundred creditors lined up with their hands out, Billy Bob's closed its doors in January 1988. Three months later Landmark Bank bought the nightclub at auction.

No one, however, illustrated the fall of the petroleum industry more vividly than Fort Worth oilman Eddie Chiles. The irascible business giant was at the top of his profession when the decade began. His well servicing outfit, The Western Company of North America, had gained an industry-wide reputation for feats of drilling, particularly from platform rigs. His crews punched holes into ocean floors from the Gulf of Mexico to the Gulf of Suez, and from the North Sea to the South China Sea. He also gained controlling interest of the Texas Rangers baseball franchise.

But it was radio that gave Chiles a public platform for stirring the apathetic masses to take action against runaway federal bureaucracy. His trademark greeting that began each broadcast on 650 stations across fourteen states announced: "This is Eddie Chiles, and I'm mad!" With that fact firmly established, he would roll into a prepared tirade. Everywhere, it seemed, red and white bumper stickers affirmed, "I'm mad, too, Eddie."

Yet all too suddenly the downward spiral in oil prices forced The Western Company into bankruptcy. His ties to arguably the worst team in baseball seemed to magnify the buffoonish quality of his fire-eating appeals. Soon, new bumper stickers could be seen across the land, taunting that indeed, Eddie *was* mad. By the end of the decade, Chiles had stepped down as CEO of The Western Company, its remnants absorbed by a Houston outfit that left the once busy Western headquarters vacant. Over in Arlington, a group of businessmen that included oil scion George W. Bush, snapped up the remaining pieces of Chiles' business empire.

✧

Eddie Chiles, looking neither mad nor angry.

COURTESY OF THE *FORT WORTH STAR-TELEGRAM* COLLECTION, SPECIAL COLLECTIONS, THE UNIVERSITY OF TEXAS AT ARLINGTON LIBRARIES, ARLINGTON, TEXAS. FWST AR 368, 88-1.

Just before the oil and thrift fiasco, a catastrophe of far greater human consequence unfolded at D/FW. No tragedy in the city's history would come even close to matching the solitary failure of Delta Flight 191 that was arriving at D/FW from Florida, August 2, 1985. Exactly fourteen seconds before 6 p.m. a radar controller casually reported "a little bitty thunderstorm sitting right on the final." Co-pilot Rudy Price added: "We're gonna get our airplane washed." A minute later another controller noted a rapid change in the direction of the wind.

Wreckage from the crash of Delta Flight 191, a disaster unparalleled in the history of Tarrant County.

COURTESY OF THE *FORT WORTH STAR-TELEGRAM* COLLECTION, SPECIAL COLLECTIONS, THE UNIVERSITY OF TEXAS AT ARLINGTON LIBRARIES, ARLINGTON, TEXAS, FWST 8193, 8-3-95.

At 6:03, as 191's captain Edward Connors reduced his speed, a pilot on Delta Flight 963 watched the thunderstorm grow into a roiling green-black monster. "Is that a water spout out there?" he asked, "I've never seen anything like it." Nevertheless, the tower asked Connors to continue reducing his speed. At 6:04 the 191 pilot reported lightning straight ahead. Then, at 6:05, the violent microburst of a wind shear pressed down on the plane. "Push it up, push it way up...Way up, way up, way up," commanded the desperate Connors.

Amid the sounds of the driving rain and the roaring of the jet's engines, all the helpless people in the tower could do was listen as Connors and Price wrestled for control of their aircraft. From the cockpit an unidentified voice sounded, "Oh [shit]..." as the flight touched down in a field north of Highway 114. Still traveling at 212 knots, it skimmed over the road and clipped the top off a car, killing instantly commuter William Mayberry, who had just moved from Mississippi to Grapevine the previous week. In another heartbeat the plane crashed into two four-million-gallon water storage tanks, and the radio went dead. From start to finish, it was all over in five minutes.

Of 165 passengers, only two walked away unhurt; 134 others were killed, and another fifteen suffered serious injuries. The tragedy brought attention to the microburst phenomenon, and small comfort that it was, the Delta crash led to improvements in air safety. Experts analyzed the disaster over and over to the benefit of pilots who would know better what to do when faced with the same situation. The crash also contributed to the immediacy of installing Terminal Doppler Weather Radar systems at airports across the country.

Fort Worth, and now the Metroplex to which it was attached, had suffered many calamities in the past and would be visited by killer hailstorms and even a tornado before the century ran its course. The fate of Flight 191, however, would stand alone in the collective memory. It was a tragedy that left permanent scars.

Although Fort Worth certainly lost its balance toward the end of the decade, it continued to focus on what lay ahead. The collapse of oil prices, ironically, had little effect on the Bass empire. A timely $400-million investment in Disney stock

The Fort Worth Cook Children's Medical Center.

COURTESY OF JOHN T. ROBERTS, FORT WORTH, WWW.FORTWORTHARCHITECTURE.COM.

early in the decade had grown to well over a billion dollars by 1989, more than offsetting any disappointments in oil and real estate. While other oilmen scrambled just to remain solvent, Robert Bass launched a $20-million capital fundraising campaign to combine the city's two children's hospitals into the Cook-Fort Worth CMC. Described as "a marvelous mix between a magic kingdom and the Mayo Clinic," the hospital bore the Bass mark of architectural distinction. A child's vision of the "inner court of an enchanted castle" inspired the six-story atrium, its view accessible out of an occasional balcony extending from the patients' rooms. Even the parking garage took on the look of a medieval castle. He called his effort to fund close to a third of the facility's cost "the most rewarding thing I have done."

Billy Bob's also returned under new management at the decade's "last call." In April 1989 the second inaugural attracted an almost capacity crowd that turned out for Willie Nelson. Many in the audience professed their ignorance of the bar's ten-month blackout. "Well, if this is the grand reopening, then I'm glad I'm part of it," remarked a mildly surprised first-timer. Others professed they had just come to see the "Red-Headed Stranger." If going to Billy Bob's was still an event in itself, it took a back seat to the larger experience of a Stockyards district that had taken on a life of its own.

Elsewhere, the development that would perhaps hold the longest-term significance came with the announcement of Fort Worth Alliance Airport, the vision of Ross Perot, Jr., son of the famous Dallas billionaire. What would become the world's first major industrial airport broke ground in 1988 on the immense rolling prairie about fifteen miles north of the city. Like so many other places in Tarrant County, this spot where cattle grazed and scissor-tailed swallows sang from strands of barbed wire fences was about to change. However, unique, it would be a familiar chapter in the story of Fort Worth and Tarrant County during the twentieth century.

✧

H. Ross Perot, Jr.

COURTESY OF THE *FORT WORTH STAR-TELEGRAM* COLLECTION, SPECIAL COLLECTIONS, THE UNIVERSITY OF TEXAS AT ARLINGTON LIBRARIES, ARLINGTON, TEXAS, FWST AR 368, 107H.

✧

Fort Worth Mayor Bob Bolen extends an official welcome to a crowd that gathered to break ground at the Fort Worth Alliance Airport.

COURTESY OF THE *FORT WORTH STAR-TELEGRAM* COLLECTION, SPECIAL COLLECTIONS, THE UNIVERSITY OF TEXAS AT ARLINGTON LIBRARIES, ARLINGTON, TEXAS, FWST 8704, 7-13-88.

The downtown skyline, 2005.

COURTESY OF JOHN T. ROBERTS, FORT WORTH, WWW.FORTWORTHARCHITECTURE.COM.

CHAPTER 10

COWBOYS & CULTURE

1990-2005

As one century came to an end and another began, Fort Worthians boasted that their hometown had grown into the state's most livable city. If their claim rested on amenities, then certainly they could make a strong case. A thriving tourist industry had emerged that was one part Cowtown and one part sophistication. The self-professed city "Where the West Begins" resonated with the bustle of earthy recreations at the Stockyards and more sublime activity of Sundance Square. As a cultural center Fort Worth possessed the kinds of museums, galleries, botanical gardens, live theater, symphony, ballet, and a zoo that much larger cities would gladly take in trade. It was also home to the Colonial National Golf Tournament and the Texas Motor Speedway; a short drive away were Texas Stadium and the Ballpark in Arlington.

The reemergence of downtown living, too, endowed Fort Worth with a cosmopolitan feel that some other Texas cities were hoping to achieve. An efficient transportation network linked the component parts of the metropolitan area to the growing suburbs and area lakes. Students from every state and dozens of countries attended institutions of higher learning in Fort Worth and Arlington—including a highly regarded medical school, the Texas College of Osteopathic Medicine (part of the University of North Texas Health Science Center), and the Texas Wesleyan University School of Law. A reputable community college system, too, had continued to add new branch campuses.

Backing up its bold proclamation as the state's most livable city, Fort Worth could point to an energetic and diversified economy that could survive without a dominant petroleum industry. The success of Fort Worth Alliance Airport, the acquisition of a U.S. Treasury Department printing plant, and the continued development of the central business district created a synergy that spun off in dozens of profitable directions. The *coup de grace* came in 2001 when Lockheed Martin, the descendant of Convair, won the largest single government contract ever awarded. The combined effect of so many public, private, and shared endeavors fashioned Fort Worth into an urban center that far surpassed its many parts.

Fort Worth no doubt could have survived without Carswell Air Force Base, too, but city officials were unwilling to give it up without a fight. As the Pentagon reassessed the nation's strategic arsenal in the years following the end of the Cold War, Congress ordered a number of bases around the country to close. Carswell, a victim of its own success, appeared to be among the losers in 1991. Colonel Richard Szafranski, commander of the Seventh Bomb Wing, certainly seemed resigned to the fact, declaring: "SAC's historic mission has been fulfilled."

All sorts of speculation about what would become of the property followed the creation of the Carswell Redevelopment Authority. The board heard plans that ranged from selling it outright to making it a reservation for the Tonkawa Indian tribe. In the end the federal government simply reconfigured Carswell's mission when it announced the creation of the Naval Air Station Fort Worth Joint Reserve Base in 1994. The conversion brought to town reservists from bases being shut down in Dallas, Tennessee, and Illinois.

In an earlier time the threat of losing the base would have thrown city leaders into a panic. By the 1990s, however, a new Fort Worth had emerged whose multiplicity of economic activities had chartered a new course. When Douglas Harman moved from his post as city manager to president and CEO of the Fort Worth Visitors & Conventions Bureau, he had a good idea of the kinds of assets at hand. His problem lay in tying together the disparate parts into a whole that would make Fort Worth a preferred destination for vacationers and conventioneers. Drawing on the concept of "heritage tourism," he sought to exploit Cowtown's rich frontier history and the tradition of philanthropy that resided in the arts community.

Certainly Harman enjoyed a head start on cities with similar aspirations. All he needed was a theme that would appeal to the imagination of prospective tourists. He found his mantra in "Cowboys and Culture." What distinguished Fort Worth from Dallas, Houston, or San Antonio, and especially cities beyond the borders of Texas, was that here the long drive to the railheads in Kansas took the great herds of cattle straight through the business district. The arrival of the railroad itself and the eventual emergence of the Stockyards made the city a final destination for all that walking stock. West Texans considered Fort Worth the market and social capital for their bovine-heavy economy, and second homes in the city became a mark of distinction for the region's great cattle barons.

Fort Worth, then, really *was* Cowtown. Through the years, many heirs of the old cattle empires found that underneath their ranges lay vast pools of oil. Those fortunes and others provided the endowment for the kinds of cultural outlets that helped Fort Worth overcome the "second city" inferiority of being so close to their better-heeled neighbor just downstream on the Trinity River.

✧

Sundance West, 333 Throckmorton, in 1991.

COURTESY OF JOHN T. ROBERTS, FORT WORTH, WWW.FORTWORTHARCHITECTURE.COM.

✧

Fort Worth Alliance Airport in northern Tarrant County.

COURTESY OF RON JACKSON, WWW.TEXASFREEWAY.COM.

✧

Comanche Indians perform at the Quanah Parker Pow Wow during the Stockyards' annual Chisholm Trail Roundup.

COURTESY OF AND COPYRIGHT BY ST. CLAIR NEWBERN III, WWW.STCLAIRPHOTO.COM

For most visitors as well as the average Fort Worthian, it was the Stockyards that best came to embody the city's identity. Those who never beheld the rows of empty cattle pens and ghostly silhouettes of the vacant packing plants could have scarcely comprehended the transformation. The geographic center of activity shifted from Billy Bob's Texas to the brick-paved Exchange Avenue. Friendly competition with the "World's Largest Honkey Tonk"—filled out mostly by cowboys of the drugstore variety—added immensely to the scenery that sightseers enjoyed. New family-friendly shops and restaurants filled in the spaces among the pioneers who had opened their businesses in the Eighties. Live rodeo and Wild West shows unfolded almost every weekend at the Coliseum. Next door a museum chronicling the district's history opened at the Livestock Exchange Building, and across the street the Texas Cowboy Hall of Fame honored the state's rodeo and cutting stars as well as featuring a gallery of antique wagons, buggies, and stagecoaches.

To commemorate the city's 150th anniversary the Fort Worth Herd was put together in 1999. Billed as the nation's only daily cattle drive, the mottled longhorns would bring traffic on Exchange Avenue to a standstill. Nobody seemed to mind waiting

Riding the Trinity Trail.

COURTESY OF THE FORT WORTH CONVENTION & VISITORS BUREAU.

The Grapevine Vintage Railroad (formerly the Tarantula Train) a division of the Grapevine Convention and Visitors Bureau, provides a crowning touch to the area's efforts to make a connection with its nineteenth-century heritage. A survey found that visions of hairy, many-legged spiders often frightened children when they learned they were going to "ride the Tarantula." "Puffy," as this engine is now called, has made a more favorable impression with the wee ones.

COURTESY OF THE GRAPEVINE VINTAGE RAILROAD.

as they watched the hard-looking cowboys drive the herd down the middle of the street. In the morning it was "head 'em up and move 'em out"; in the afternoon it was "bring 'em on in."

No attraction, however, could outdo the Stockyards Station. The former maze of covered hog and sheep pens reemerged as a pedestrian mall where tourists could eat and browse western boutiques, galleries, antique shops, and other kindred stores. There was even a livery stable there for horseback rides along the Trinity. When the faintest note of the distant, but distinctive whistle of the Tarantula Train wafted through the station, the effect was magical. Suddenly, young and old alike were transported to another time as the restored nineteenth-century steam locomotive puffed into the covered station, let out its passengers, and eased onto a massive turntable. The experience provided the crowning touch to a district that had strived mightily to recreate the bygone days of the frontier.

During the first month of 1992 the Fort Worth & Western Railroad's Tarantula Train pulled out of the austere gravel yard on Eighth Avenue for its inaugural trip to the Stockyards. The four-and-a-half-mile journey, as its bulletin promised, delivered "majestic views of the…skyline." Yet, it also revealed a scene of blight along the river bottoms of which even few longtime citizens were scarcely aware. Like the Stockyards itself, however, the route was a work in progress, and it improved with each passing year.

Four years later the Tarantula made another inaugural run to its new home at the Cotton Belt Depot in Grapevine, a growing suburb that also reaped dividends by refashioning its typical small-town Texas Main Street. All along the route traffic stopped and small crowds gathered to exchange waves with the passengers aboard the three antique passenger cars. When the locomotive pulled into the station, assembled delegates, including the Tarantula's owner Bill Davis and Grapevine Mayor William D. Tate, commemorated the occasion by smashing a bottle of champagne on the restored 1927-vintage turntable. Paeans to the many individuals who made the entire vision a reality greatly impressed those who heard the speeches.

✧

The Fort Worth Museum of Modern Art.

COURTESY OF JOHN T. ROBERTS, FORT WORTH, WWW.FORTWORTHARCHITECTURE.COM.

✧

Bass Performance Hall, Fourth and Commerce, in 1998.

COURTESY OF JOHN T. ROBERTS, FORT WORTH, WWW.FORTWORTHARCHITECTURE.COM.

✧

Ukrainian Lilian Akopova draws number three for her turn at the piano as Van Cliburn and John Giordano look on prior to the 2005 competition.

COURTESY OF THE VAN CLIBURN FOUNDATION; COPYRIGHT BY RODGER MALLISON.

The same kind of personal commitment to the city's welfare was reflected in the generosity of patrons who continued to develop Amon Carter Square. The publisher's namesake museum received a "subtle, yet substantial" makeover and expansion, earning the high praise of architectural critics, when it reopened in 2001. The following year, the same fastidious crowd gathered once more to admire the Museum of Modern Art's new home next door to the Kimbell. A creation of acclaimed Japanese architect Tadao Ando, the fifty-three-thousand-square-foot showcase was perhaps described best by one awestruck critic as "Modern Magic."

Joining the arts district in 2002 was the National Cowgirl Museum and Hall of Fame. The $21 million building, designed to complement the Wills Rogers complex, was a far cry from the library basement in Deaf Smith County where the museum got its start in 1975. Its Cowtown debut featured a wealth of artifacts, memorabilia, and exhibits that brought this overshadowed icon into the light of day.

Despite all the attention focused on Amon Carter Square, the crowning achievement of the arts community unfolded downtown with the completion of the Nancy Lee and Perry R. Bass Performance Hall, "the building with the angels." Critics hailed the center as "the last great concert hall of the twentieth century." The multipurpose facility, with its spacious lobby and grand center dome—three-quarters the size of the state capitol—would host live theater and the quadrennial Van Cliburn International Piano Competition in addition to a full schedule of concerts.

Unlike most other kindred venues, the Bass Hall enjoyed the advantage of private funding. That meant neither pressure groups nor city government could become the arbiter of moral standards in the event of controversial bookings. "The Modern Museum of Fort Worth," explained Sid Bass, "would bring in an exhibition with frontal nudity or a Mapplethorpe, and a handful of people would go down to the city council and complain, and one or two councilmen would threaten to withhold funding for upkeep or maintenance. It just wasn't worth it." At the Bass Hall, he continued, "we can bring in *Hair* if we want it."

Always near the top of the Bass's priority lists was the goal of continuing to revive the central city. Judging by the projects of other private developers and the public works of the city itself, they reached their goal, and then some. Cowtown native Joe Nick Patoski, who went on to become a feature writer at *Texas Monthly* magazine, glowed proudly when he wrote that "Downtown Fort Worth has become Texas' liveliest urban environment." Boasting "redbrick streets… lined with restaurants, nightclubs, and

✧

The Main Street Art Festival.

COURTESY OF THE FORT WORTH CONVENTIONS & VISITORS BUREAU.

✧

Cross Timbers Energy (XTO) emerged as a leading custodian of the city's material past. The W. T. Waggoner Building (1920), Petroleum Building (1927), Baker Building (1910), and Landmark Tower (1957) are counted among its real estate holdings. Here, the lobby of the W. T. Waggoner Building, home to such earlier tenants as the Continental National Bank, shines like new.

COURTESY OF THE JOHN T. ROBERTS, FORT WORTH, WWW.FORTWORTHARCHITECTURE.COM.

shops...the streets are jammed on weekends, and they bustle with activity from Monday through Friday." Some of the pedestrians even lived downtown or just off the bluff as condos and lofts made inner city living fashionable. After several failed efforts, the Blackstone Hotel was back, too, as the Courtyard Hotel by Marriott. There was also a spacious new bookstore, a corner deli, twenty movie screens, and four live-theater venues.

For a "city center that had been left for dead twenty-five years ago," wrote Patoski, what had been achieved was nothing short of a complete renaissance. The trend of refurbishing once-derelict hulks continued, and they reemerged even more elegant than when they were new. As developers planned additional downtown growth, they largely kept the architecture integrity of those earlier eras in mind.

Among the other notable triumphs of reinventing downtown Fort Worth was the removal of the I-30 overhead that rejoined West Lancaster Avenue to the central business district. For four decades the 1.4-mile stretch symbolized what one critic identified as "the conflict between the need to move traffic quickly and the desire to protect a city's character." The demolition was one of the last steps in a $173-million highway project that rerouted the obsolete and obtrusive mixmaster behind the Depression-era post office and T&P buildings.

The occasion brought together key city leaders and state highway officials, who had earlier come to loggerheads over the design. The transportation department's plans to double the size of the overhead motivated preservationists, neighborhood associations, and other concerned groups to form I-CARE, or I-30 Citizen Advocates for Responsible Expansion. Activism, backed up by a lawsuit, brought the two sides to the negotiating table, where they found common ground. On a rainy morning during the summer of 2001 there were no hard feelings among the former adversaries as they watched a jackhammer shake loose the first slice of concrete, marking the official beginning of the demolition.

✧

A line of coaches belonging to the Grapevine Vintage Railroad rests on a siding, waiting for the weekend, as a Budd RDC (Rail Diesel Car) of the Trinity Railway Express coasts by with a load of commuters. Soon, it too will be a relic as sleek new models are introduced.

COURTESY OF ERIC OLESEN, WWW.RAILPICTURES.NET.

West Lancaster, I-CARE proponents crowed, would soon become a people-friendly, tree-lined boulevard that would pull development to the lower end of downtown. The immediate future indeed looked promising. With the construction of a terminal for the Trinity Railway Express, the downtowns of Fort Worth and Dallas became linked, hearkening comparisons with the long-gone interurban line completed a century earlier. A renovated Convention Center and improvements to the Water Gardens were also hailed as catalysts for the anticipated revival.

The great hall that had seemed so modern and cavernous when it opened in 1968 felt drab and confining by the Nineties. Douglas Harman, from his new post at the Convention and Visitors Bureau, remarked that without giving the facility an overhaul, Fort Worth risked becoming a "fourth-rate convention city with a first-rate

✧

The Fort Worth/Tarrant County Convention Center commands fourteen downtown blocks. The city purchased the facility from Tarrant County in 1997, and then gave it a thorough makeover, poising itself to reclaim the share of convention traffic it enjoyed when it first opened in 1968.

COURTESY OF THE CITY OF FORT WORTH.

downtown." With every passing year, he noted, professional associations whose members had "fallen in love with the city," reluctantly dropped Fort Worth as a preferred destination.

Passing ownership from the county to the city allowed Fort Worth voters to issue bonds and raise hotel occupancy taxes to pay for the $75 million renovation and expansion of the re-christened Fort Worth/Tarrant County Convention Center. As fireworks burst in the sky over the lower end of downtown, the facility reopened its doors at the ninth annual "Party in Fort Worth" in April 2002. Visitors and dignitaries, who remembered the stark concrete floors and unadorned interior, marveled at the ballroom's twenty-one-color carpet featuring giant Texas wildflowers. Suspended on the ceiling were artful aluminum stars of various sizes. The distinguishing feature of the renovation, however, was a ten-sided glass and brick "Star Tower." The city's public events director, Kirk Slaughter, called it the "focal point of arrival," and a landmark for nighttime travelers passing along the interstate who would be attracted to its glow.

All of the positive changes that Fort Worth enjoyed as the millennium clock turned did not come in a helter-skelter string of successes. Going into the Nineties, city leaders recognized that a social and economic recalibration would be a necessary step in plotting a course for the future. In 1992, just as in 1963, the city council checked the pulse of its citizenry at a town hall meeting. And, as before, the forum led to the kinds of activities that earned Fort Worth its second All-America City Award.

Cowtown was among thirty finalist cities that sent a delegation to Tampa, Florida, to make its case before a National Civic League jury. The presentation went so well that one jurist threw out a good-natured barb about Fort Worth's rivalry with Dallas. When Chamber Vice-President Donna Parker pronounced: "We consider Dallas our strongest asset," the roar of laughter and applause left no doubt that the delegation would return a winner.

The next year Mayor Kay Granger headed a committee that put together more than two hundred events in an eleven-day celebration of its All-America City designation called "Fort Worth Open House." Many of the activities such as cleanup days and blood drives tapped into the well of civic pride. Others centered on entertainment, culture, and sports. One of the most popular attractions was "Fort Worth on the Move," a historical exhibit that demonstrated the progression of transportation that developed alongside the city. Everything from wagons and futuristic automobiles to vintage railroad stock and airplanes were gathered at the long-dormant T&P Building, which proved to be a draw in itself.

It was a new concept in transportation that spurred development in far northern Tarrant County. Less than a month before the new decade began the first jet cargo plane landed at the new Fort Worth Alliance Airport, erasing any skepticism that the world was ready for

✧

The convention center's ballroom.

COURTESY OF JOHN T. ROBERTS, FORT WORTH, WWW.FORTWORTHARCHITECTURE.COM.

✧

Looking up from inside the convention center's Star Tower.

COURTESY, JOHN T. ROBERTS, FORT WORTH, WWW.FORTWORTHARCHITECTURE.COM.

✧

The air traffic control tower at Fort Worth Alliance Airport.

COURTESY OF AND COPYRIGHT BY ST. CLAIR NEWBERN III, WWW.STCLAIRPHOTO.COM

such a facility devoted entirely to industry. Even before the airport opened, American Airlines had invested almost a half-billion dollars in a mammoth maintenance complex. During the Nineties, Federal Express, Nestle, Tech Data, Unison Industries, Texas Instruments, Zenith, Mitsubishi Motor Sales of America, JCPenney, Michaels Stores, and dozens of other corporations opened distribution centers enclosing millions of square feet of floor space.

The project far exceeded the expectations of its optimistic originator. Recalling what had been an immense rolling prairie scarcely a decade earlier, Ross Perot, Jr., expressed simple disbelief in what lay before his eyes at the century's end. In fact, there was no trace of immodesty when he honestly gawked: "We never envisioned anything this big."

Perot and his Hillwood Development Corporation associates had placed all their chips on aviation development, little expecting the synergy that set so many other plans in motion. While they were busy compiling lists of prospective clients gleaned from the World Aviation Directory, Santa Fe Railway made an unexpected call. Soon, the Gilded Age transportation giant was building an automobile unloading facility designed for the twenty-first century. It also joined with Burlington Northern and moved its headquarters into the vacant Western Company campus built during the Eighties oil boom by maverick businessman Eddie Chiles. Connections via ocean, rail, truck, and air soon had Alliance plugged into the global economy.

Other successes could be tracked by the announcements that rippled across the headlines of the *Star-Telegram* throughout the Nineties: the Drug Enforcement Administration was moving its air wing headquarters to Alliance; Galaxy Aerospace wanted to finish the interiors of its corporate jets there; the nearby Circle-T Ranch would become home to a corporate office park and new residential and retail developments. Most spectacularly, and farthest afield, the Texas Motor Speedway would become a next-door neighbor.

With over one hundred and fifty thousand seats, only the Indianapolis Speedway provided a larger venue. The number of spectators that congregated in the pit area for the annual NASCAR Winston Cup and music concerts almost doubled the capacity. Overlooking the track, the nine-story Speedway Club provided a fitting monument to this expensive sport. Inside the glass tower its members could work out, get a massage and relax in a Jacuzzi. The Starlight Room Restaurant with its cherry paneling and antique reproduction chairs became a meeting place for high rollers—many ferried in by helicopter to avoid the massive traffic jams—who came to town to enjoy the major events.

At one point, according to the Texas Workforce Commission, companies tied to the new growth in and around Fort Worth Alliance Airport accounted for one in every twenty civilian jobs in Fort Worth. The population pressure in northern Tarrant County set in motion a familiar transformation as developers set out to reinvent the area's small communities. In Westlake, residents waged a bitter but futile fight with Perot over his plans for the Circle-T Ranch. Keller and

✧

Texas Motor Speedway.

COURTESY OF THE FORT WORTH CONVENTION & VISITORS BUREAU.

✧

When the Cats brought home the Central Baseball League trophy in 2005, it was the modern team's first pennant and the Cats' first since 1948. They seemed to have already enjoyed a lock on one important category—going into the championship season they had led the league in attendance three years running.

COURTESY OF THE FORT WORTH CATS BASEBALL CLUB.

Southlake, discovered by developers during the previous decade, just wanted to assure that the new boost would be well planned. By the mid-1990s Keller had recorded four straight years of adding at least four hundred new homes that ranged between $130,000-to-$500,000 apiece. The pace at Southlake was not as brisk, but the half-million-dollar house was closer to the median price.

What happened to the Fechtel Farm in formerly rural Southlake could have happened just as easily at many of the family plots swallowed up by the emerging suburb. Joseph and Hazel Fechtel had bought the seventy-acre tract in the 1940s, where they cultivated a thriving egg hatchery and raised six children. Among their fondest memories were horse rides to Grapevine Lake for picnics, two weddings, and family gatherings that continued long after the kids grew into adults. Their decision to sell the land predictably stirred mixed emotions. "We love this place," said daughter Alicia, "but we're being crowded out by the city." The prospect of entering into an extraordinary partnership also made it an ideal time to concede to progress.

The farm that son Charles described as "the center of our family togetherness" became part of the new center of a community that had never known a traditional downtown. Designed by architect David Schwarz, who helped create much of Sundance Square, the $65 million Southlake Town Square echoed an old-fashioned downtown with shops built along street blocks, beyond which lay a tree-lined plaza. Brian Stebbins, who navigated the project through straits of red tape, predicted: "Five to ten years from now, when…the trees grow and the thing takes on some wear, it's going to be a real head-scratcher to figure out when this was built." On the very site where the old Fechtel farmhouse had stood, City Hall and the school district offices enjoyed a commanding view of the new town square.

✧

Droopy-eyed Dodger, the Cats' mascot, is anything but a sleepy panther. Here he livens up a home crowd; he also has competed in the Olympic Mascot Games in Orlando, Florida.

COURTESY OF THE FORT WORTH CATS BASEBALL CLUB.

✧

A scene from the 2004 All-Star game played at LaGrave Field. The Central League, to which the Cats belong, beat the Northeast League 9-4.

COURTESY OF THE FORT WORTH CATS BASEBALL CLUB.

Areas that had developed in earlier decades redoubled their efforts to compete with new rivals. The Ridgmar Mall on the city's west side spent $70 million trying to regain the loyalty of old customers. New tenants, an eighteen-screen theater, and a "playscape" over which a biplane was suspended from the ceiling helped the twenty-five-year-old mall make a successful comeback. Yet even at 1.3 million square feet it trailed in size behind the new Grapevine Mills; and, when the Northeast Mall followed suit with its own renovation, Ridgmar slipped to third place. From the west side of downtown, the competition did not seem threatening, however. Pointing to the county's explosive population growth, Ridgmar's marketing director, Jenelle Gossman, shrugged confidently: "The market can support [all] of us."

In its plans to help the Simon Property Group of Indianapolis expand the Northeast Mall and develop the land around it, the City of Hurst followed an ominous trend in using eminent domain to assist private enterprise. Almost all of the 128 homeowners whose residences were targeted for demolition gladly sold at a premium. The unwilling few, however, protested loudly. Theirs was a cause that engendered wide sympathy, but in the end it was a losing battle.

Fort Worth itself annexed vast tracks of land, and at the century's end the city encompassed over three hundred square miles, extending the fingers of its boundaries toward developments in every direction. The map of incorporated land came to resemble what reporter Valerie Fields described as "a humpbacked dragon—with lots of claws." Several pockets of resistors agreed that the predatory image was appropriate and formed a protest group that won some small victories. On the other hand, when owners of the Walsh and Sendera Ranches asked to be annexed, it became apparent that before long the area's big spreads would be no more.

Tarrant County itself added two hundred thousand people to the state's population during the Nineties, surpassed only by Harris and Dallas Counties. Increasing diversity and greater political representation and economic opportunities for minority citizens characterized the growth. Consequently, a sense of ethnic pride became manifest in any number of festivals and cultural contributions.

Fort Worth's African-American community, whose roots reached as far back as the city itself, projected its culture into the mainstream of life in a number of ways. Even before the decade began, city employees and many businesses and schools had already grown accustomed to taking a day off to commemorate the birthday of Martin Luther King, Jr. In 1992 the Jubilee Theater outgrew its storefront home on East Rosedale and moved to Sundance Square. That same year the city welcomed a national convention of more than seventy regional black chambers of commerce. At libraries and museums, patrons enjoyed exhibits that showcased the works of prominent African-American authors and artists. In 1996, the Central Library itself became the new home of the Tarrant County Black Historical and Genealogical Society, which moved its archival holdings from a tenuously maintained house on East Humboldt Street.

Earlier, in 1993, the black community invited members invited members of other races to come celebrate "Juneteenth," commemorating that day on June 19, 1865, when most Texas bondsmen learned of their emancipation. "When we chose 'Just for Today' as [this year's] theme, we mean that we want you to come on down, just for today," remarked the event's chairperson, Opal Lee. "Just for today, let's set aside our differences and celebrate our freedoms."

While many did, the overwhelmingly black crowds nevertheless revealed a reluctance on the part of Anglos to acknowledge the end of a historical chapter they had spent the better part of a century forestalling. Black History Month itself exposed some other wounds that refused to heal. With each passing February the well-meaning effort did bring an increasing media emphasis to the culture. Yet some of the area's most distinguished black intellectuals criticized it as "belittling" and "perfunctory."

✧

The recently completed Gaylord Texan Resort & Convention Center on Lake Grapevine offers guests miniature re-creations of the Hill Country, Palo Duro Canyon, and the San Antonio River Walk all under a four-and-a-half-acre atrium. Those wanting to play golf on the adjacent eighteen-hole championship course, however, must still contend with the Texas weather.

COURTESY OF GAYLORD TEXAN RESORT & CONVENTION CENTER, GRAPEVINE.

Auntee Explains Christmas, an original production written by Rudy Eastman and scored by Joe Rogers, enchanted audiences at the Jubilee Theater during the 2003 holiday season.

COURTESY OF BUDDY MYERS AND THE JUBILEE THEATER, FORT WORTH.

Star-Telegram columnist Bob Ray Sanders and UTA professor Marvin Delaney, both prominent African Americans, declined speaking invitations, explaining their purpose "is to bring black history programs into the mainstream so the subject will be integrated into the year-round curriculum." Not everyone agreed, and Black History Month continued to be a popular outlet for increasing the general awareness off the African-American past. At the same time, the response of local school administrators indicated that in the classroom multiculturalism was the rule, rather than the exception. Indeed, times were changing.

While racial tension in Fort Worth certainly remained, it was also matched by the willingness of city leaders from every culture to meet problems head-on. Following the Los Angeles riots of 1992 black organizers invited the mayor, their U.S. congressional representatives, and others of different races to join them at the first "African-American Summit on Peace, Justice, and Equality." As black Fort Worthians aired out their concerns over matters such as representation, education, and the media, the establishment listened. Deputy Police Chief Sam Hill, responding to a proposal for a citizen board to review officers' actions, affirmed his faith in the department's internal investigations branch. Still, he responded positively: "I personally don't see a need for a citizens' review board…but if citizens of Fort Worth want a citizens' review board, that's what we are going to have." State District Judge Maryellen Hicks, the county's first elected African-American judge, called the meeting historic. "There's a new day in Tarrant County, and I'm very excited and very enthused about that."

The Hispanic community, which comprised twenty percent of Tarrant County's population in 2000, also asserted itself. North of the river, the symbiotic development of the Stockyards and the "Hispanic North Side" generated some grumbling among old-time residents. "The Stockyards in every direction is bordered by the Hispanic community, yet it's just simply Cowboy," complained Danny Zapata Johnson. "I grew up in that area and we have no representation in the Stockyards." His remedy came swiftly. Together with business partner Tony Sanchez, Johnson opened Zapata's Tejano Club Y Sports Bar across the street from Billy Bob's Texas in the spring of 1997.

A more ambitious project, the Mercado de Fort Worth, targeted several blocks

The Mercado awaits finishing touches before opening to an expectant public.

COURTESY OF THE CITY OF FORT WORTH.

Fiesta! Fort Worth, organized by the League of United Latin American Citizens of Tarrant County, has quickly grown into a "Fun Calendar" highlight.

COURTESY OF MAIN EVENTS INTERNATIONAL, WWW.MEIFESTIVALS.COM.

between the Stockyards and downtown for redevelopment. Enthusiastic backers—Anglo as well as Hispanic—in the mid-Nineties envisioned the Mexican market as a boon to the growing tourist trade. With both the city and the federal governments involved, however, the development grew long on planning and short on action. Finally, in November 2002, officials broke ground to construct a three-story, $3.8 million building. The project promised to fulfill the dream of many North-Siders who longed to add a Southwestern flair to the tourist district.

Certainly, by the turn of the new century, the ascending influence of tejano culture had made an indelible mark. "Fiesta! Fort Worth," organized by the League of United Latin American Citizens of Tarrant County, became the Hispanic community's third yearly celebration, joining Cinco de Mayo and Diez y Siez de Septiembre on the events calendar. From its inception the downtown festival drew a crowd of thousands that browsed dozens of vendor booths and listened to the music of such tejano bands as the ever-popular David Lee Garza y Los Musicales. Other performers bedecked in Aztec dress and brightly colored traditional costumes provided exhibitions of dance. Like the other two celebrations, "Fiesta," said one participant, "belongs to everyone, not just Hispanics."

Still, it was Cinco de Mayo that drew the most eclectic crowd. So much, in fact, that competition with Mayfest led the Hispanic organizers to move their date up to April to accommodate others who would have otherwise attended the larger festival on the banks of the Trinity River. What began as a source of friction ended up reaping benefits for Cinco de Mayo as event officials realized they would be able to attract the kinds of acts that were already booked on May 5 for places like Los Angeles and San Antonio.

In 1995, however, the fifth of May would be remembered not as a typical Cinco de Mayo, but as a day of tragedy at Mayfest. The hot, muggy afternoon ended when a violent supercell formed over the festival, catching about ten thousand people in the open. Suddenly hail began falling, in places propelled by winds that reached eighty miles per hour, throwing the crowd into a panic. Everywhere, people ran pell-mell for shelter; others huddled close together, while parents lay across their children. The sound of loud praying competed with the roar of fist-sized stones careening off everything exposed to the sky and the cracking limbs of giant oaks.

✧

The Bank One Tower after the tornado. Soon, workers would replace the remaining window glass with plywood.

COURTESY OF JOHN T. ROBERTS, FORT WORTH, WWW.FORTWORTHARCHITECTURE.COM.

Many of those who made it to their cars were showered by broken glass. It was a miracle no one was killed by the hail, although close to a hundred injured people ended up in the hospital with giant welts and cuts.

The hailstorm passed quickly, but one of the heaviest rains in memory followed. Flash flooding from one end of the Metroplex to the other left a dozen drowning victims. Insurance adjusters eventually paid out close to a billion dollars, making the storm one of the state's costliest disasters on record.

Five years later Fort Worth ran out of luck again. It was thought to be the only major American city without a recorded tornado death. Then, on March 28, 2000, a Gulf breeze had turned the otherwise humid weather into a salubrious springtime day marked by clear skies and sunshine. Chief meteorologist Skip Ely of the National Weather Service, however, was growing more wary as the afternoon unfolded. To the west, a warm dry front was converging with an approaching cold front from the north. "It reminded me of Mayfest, another gorgeous day," he said. "The sky had that same look late in the day, a hazy thing off to the west, sort of dark and fuzzy and just a little early for sunset."

Downtown, the rush-hour traffic was ebbing and office workers who remained were either working late or had retired to shops and eateries by the time the skies began to take on the hue of a deep, green bruise that signaled hail—or worse. At the KXAS-TV studio of Channel 5 News, meteorologists monitoring the storm could only gape in silence as they watched it intensify, wrapping almost completely around the top and left sides of their screen. "Oh, my God!" Ely finally gasped.

The storm became a killer even before it spawned the first of two tornadoes. At Lake Worth, a softball-sized hailstone split the skull of a nineteen-year-old man as he ran into the parking lot at CiCi's Pizza to move his pickup truck. The dark wall gathered strength as it began its rotation just north of downtown. At

✧

An automobile shows the damage from an airborne chair that found its way there from the Bank One Tower.

COURTESY OF JOHN T. ROBERTS, FORT WORTH, WWW.FORTWORTHARCHITECTURE.COM.

✧

The Cash America building sustained heavy damage, but miraculously no fatalities.

COURTESY OF JOHN T. ROBERTS, FORT WORTH, WWW.FORTWORTHARCHITECTURE.COM.

River Oaks it snapped power lines, uprooted hundred-year-old oaks, and ripped the roof from a building at Castleberry High School, where drama students and the softball team had taken cover.

Between the arts district and downtown, the first tornado cut a violent path along West Seventh Street. Douglas Thornton, a shuttle driver, stopped at Montgomery Ward to spread the alert. "He was warning people to get down, get down, but the tornado caught up with him and he never made it," said a maintenance worker.

Crossing the Trinity River into the heart of the business district, the swirling mass of debris battered everything in its path. From their vantages in office buildings, awestruck men and women stood riveted in place; just as many made a mad scramble for the safety of stairwells on first sight. At the Reata Restaurant atop the thirty-seven-story Team Bank Tower (originally the Fort Worth National), over a hundred diners watched the tornado barrel down on them from the floor-to-ceiling windows. Most of them ignored the sirens. Not until three windowpanes shattered did the stampede for cover begin in earnest. Diner Chris Batch, bringing up the rear, witnessed the tornado hit the building. "As we started to run, we could tell the windows were starting to blow out." In all, the storm shattered or damaged 3,200 of the 3,540 panes covering the building.

After sweeping through downtown Fort Worth the tornado dissipated, but another formed as the system moved toward Arlington. There, it concentrated its fury on neighborhoods south of I-20. On its west-to-east course through the Metroplex, the storm destroyed 171 homes—including a west side house where JFK assassin Lee Harvey Oswald had once lived—and damaged ten times that number in addition to hundreds of businesses, schools, and churches. It would be among the costliest storms in the state's history. Both Governor Bush and President Clinton declared Tarrant County a disaster area, which helped scores of uninsured victims recover from their losses.

Although five people lost their lives to the storm, its timing spared countless others. An hour earlier, and it would have caught the city in the middle of rush hour. It would be unthinkable to imagine the scale of tragedy at the Calvary Cathedral, where parents picked up about five hundred children at the church's daycare and school just before the storm hit.

The most visible and long-lasting reminder of the great tornado was the Team Bank Tower. While a succession of owners and the city debated about what to do with it, the darkened monolith became a public embarrassment. The first proposal to redevelop it revealed that the costs would exceed the value of the building. Then, plans to demolish it had to be aborted because of asbestos removal and insurance concerns.

Almost three years after the storm, the city council finally approved economic incentives for yet another redevelopment plan. This one succeeded. As 2004 segued into 2005, the former bank building—rechristened The Tower—was beginning to look like the architect's rendering posted on the plywood wall that blocked off the construction site. Then, at last it was finished.

Among those who attended The Tower's ribbon cutting were men and women who had done business there during the 1970s. Never would they have envisioned the building's fate. Even among the most optimistic, few would have predicted the economic course that resurrected the downtown surrounding it.

✧

The ill-fated former Fort Worth National Bank—variously known afterward as the Bank One Tower, Team Bank Tower, and Block 82 Tower—blighted Fort Worth's skyline for over three-and-a-half years, while a series of owners and city officials tried to figure out what to do with it. TLC Realty Advisors finally took charge and remodeled it as a high-rise residential building. Rechristened "The Tower," it opened in 2005 with over three-hundred units. Along with the new façade, TLC added a sixty-thousand-square-foot base with the intention of attracting a grocery, restaurants, and a variety of shops. The ambitious plans also included an outdoor plaza and at least one swimming pool. TLC's efforts earned the consortium a CLIDE award for development excellence.

COURTESY OF JOHN T. ROBERTS, FORT WORTH, WWW.FORTWORTHARCHITECTURE.COM.

✧

RadioShack.

COURTESY OF JOHN T. ROBERTS, FORT WORTH, WWW.FORTWORTHARCHITECTURE.COM.

Every decade during the last century imparted unique surprises, and the city "Where the West Begins" will most likely look different than the one that sits on drawing boards today. If planners have their way, however, the Fort Worth of the future will see changes as breathtaking as any that citizens today have experienced. City officials predict that a light rail system to be developed over the next three decades will one day connect every corner of the greater metropolitan area. It might have to. Demographers foresee that suburban growth will continue to mushroom, and that new waves of residents will be drawn to the central business district.

At the top of the city's wish list is a vision that would transform the Trinity River into a bustling waterfront with a town lake. Dreamers predict that condominium towers, restaurants, and retail businesses will someday arise on the water's edge along several miles of lake and river frontage. If that happens, the twenty-story Pier 1 Place, a breathtaking glass and gray granite building that opened in 2004, will enjoy a commanding view. So will the corporate offices of its ultra-modern neighbor, RadioShack, whose thirty-eight acre campus straddles the bluff where Major Ripley Arnold founded the military post in 1849.

In twenty years, insiders say that downtown Fort Worth could be twice as large as it was at the beginning of the new century. Seventh Street, between the edge of the bluff and the arts district, seems particularly poised for development, as does Lancaster Boulevard, where foot traffic would be within walking distance to the Trinity Railway Express. Taken together, downtown projects already started or planned by 2003 involved an investment of almost three-and-a-half billion dollars.

In Tarrant and seventeen other counties, the recent discovery of an estimated twenty-seven trillion cubic feet of natural gas in the Barnett Shale formation may well take all of North Texas in a direction no one ever envisioned. As energy companies swing deals with suburban communities for the rights to punch holes through golf courses, ball fields, and other municipal lands, the possibilities are open-ended. The likelihood of gas wells producing individual fortunes seems certain. Perhaps the philanthropic successors of the men and their heirs who helped shape the area's unique history and culture are one big strike away from realizing the same kinds of dreams.

Standing on the threshold of the new millennium, Tom Vandergriff, Arlington's "Boy Mayor" of the 1950s, was asked to reflect on the growth Fort Worth and Tarrant County had enjoyed over roughly the past half-century, a phenomenon of which he had played a significant part. Characteristically, he chose to look at the possibilities in the area's future, rather than taking a long, satisfying look backward. What he conveyed in one brief comment will someday fill the books of men and women whose passion is precisely what Vandergriff avoided—embracing that reflective journey. Flashing a furtive smile, he said: "We probably haven't seen anything yet." If the past provides any indication, the "ride," so to speak, may not always be smooth, but it will certainly be worth remembering. ***Fort Worth!***

✧

COURTESY OF AND COPYRIGHT BY ST. CLAIR NEWBERN III, WWW.STCLAIRPHOTO.COM.

Endnotes

All references are cited in block paragraph form. An excerpt from each leading sentence in the documented paragraph precedes the citations used. Abbreviations and short titles in notes:

CF	Clippings File
DMN	*Dallas Morning News*
FWD	*Fort Worth Democrat*
FWM	*Fort Worth Magazine* (Fort Worth Chamber of Commerce)
FWMR	*Fort Worth Morning Register*
FWP	*Fort Worth Press*
FWPL	Fort Worth Public Library
FWNT	*Fort Worth News-Tribune*
FWR	*Fort Worth Record*
FWS&T	*Fort Worth Star & Telegram*
FWST	*Fort Worth Star-Telegram* (morn. ed. when morn. and eve. ed. printed)
NHT	*New Handbook of Texas* (Texas State Historical Association)
RD	Federal Writers' Project, *Research Data: Fort Worth & Tarrant County, Texas*, Works Progress Administration, 1941
TCHC	Tarrant County Historical Commission, Fort Worth
TSLAC	Archives and Information Services Division, Texas State Library and Archives Commission, Austin, Texas
ms	Manuscript
UTA-SC	University of Texas at Arlington, Special Collections Library

Introduction

Note to Introduction: No era in Fort Worth's history has been covered so thoroughly—or so uncritically—as the "old frontier." In the author's effort to address some of the most common misperceptions and errors of fact, he felt it necessary to provide explanatory notes and documentation out of proportion to those in the chapter text.

Page 8

- *Just as surely as the frontier story of the pioneers…* Few would argue that the best single-volume survey of the area's history is Oliver Knight's *Fort Worth: Outpost on the Trinity* (1953, reprint, Fort Worth: TCU Press, 1990). As a journalist writing at a time when scholarship in western history was undemanding, he produced a delightfully enduring narrative, but it also came to represent a fountain of apocrypha that many writers over the years casually tapped. More exacting scholars have certainly built upon his work, revising and expanding a basic story that still resides at the core of Knight's monograph. Originally published in 1953, it naturally magnifies the era of formative development. Nevertheless, long-time *Fort Worth Star-Telegram* columnist Cissy Stewart Lale composed a perceptive essay that ably extends the history forward to 1990. Her "Suggested Readings and Other Sources for Fort Worth History" includes an annotated bibliography of the area's broad survey works as well as a discussion of local history and photographic collections.

Page 10

- *Amon Carter Museum.* (caption) Bryan Woolley, *The Edge of the West and Other Texas Stories* (El Paso: Texas Western Press, 1990), 44.

Page 11

- *The first inhabitants, of course, are lost to history… FWST*, "Indian campground may be excavated," Nov. 8, 2004, 1B.
- *Other native groups attracted…* George Green, *Hurst, Euless, and Bedford: Heart of the Metroplex, An Illustrated History* (Austin: Eakin Press, 1995), 1-3.
- *It was an ignominious beginning…* A. B. Benthuysen, Houston, to M. B. Lamar, No. 633, Dec. 8, 1837, in Charles Adams Gulick, Jr., ed. *The Papers of Mirabeau Buonaparte Lamar, 1798-1859* (Austin: A. C. Baldwin, 1922-27) vol. 1, 592-5. Perhaps the most ably and exhaustibly researched volume on Fort Worth's early years can be found in Clay Perkins' *The Fort in Fort Worth* (Keller, Texas: Cross-Timbers Heritage Publishing Company, 2001). It includes an outstanding account of this episode and the larger context in which it unfolded (pp. 8-10).
- *White men returned in greater numbers…* J. W. Wilbarger, "Fannin's First Campaign," in *Indian Depredations in Texas* (1889, reprint, Austin: Eakin Press, 1985), 426-8.
- *Anthropologists believe the earliest inhabitants…* (caption) Renee Tucker, Asst. Curator of History, Fort Worth Museum of Science & History, correspondence with author, Sept. 2, 2005.

Page 12

- *Another foray in September 1838…* William B. Stout, "Statement of the Indian Wars on the Red River border…from 1836 up to 1838," to Lamar, c. 1850, No. 2465, vol. 4, 273-5; Adj. Gen. Hugh McLeod, Red River County. Below Clarksville 60 miles, to Lamar, Jan. 9, 1839, No. 997, vol. 2, 406 (both quotations); and, McLeod, Nacogdoches, to Lamar, Jan. 18, 1839, No. 1024, vol. 2, 423, in *Papers of Lamar*.
- *Such reports excited the imaginations…* Maj. Jonathan Bird, letter of petition to the Republic of Texas, Nov. 2, 1842, TSLAC, cited in Dee Barker, "The City of Fort Worth: How It Relates to the Settlement of Tarrant County and to the Establishment of the Military Fort and Fort Worth Growth by Decades," ms, TCHC, 1993, 1. Dee Barker, long-time director of the commission's archives, compiled this useful manuscript in the course of county-related research. She stated in her preface: "It became evident…that many newspaper articles and books relating the [early] city and county history were interesting and informative, but not always consistent with facts." While brief—the text is only twelve single-spaced pages—it nevertheless employs reliable primary sources from local, state, and federal archives, the bulk of which is now reproduced and organized in the TCHC Collection. This manuscript thus corrects many of the most common inaccuracies repeated in the body of early history regarding Fort Worth and Tarrant County.
- *Arriving in a land unbroken by plows…* General Edward Tarrant, "Official Report of Village Creek Battle," Texas Sentinel (Austin), July 8, 1841, TSLAC. Tarrant chose an auspicious time for the attack. Most of the men were hunting bison far to the west, leaving the complex of villages inhabited mostly by women, children, the elderly, and the infirm. Many of them, unarmed, were shot in the back as they fled before the charging horsemen. As many as ten-thousand people—Caddos, Wichitas, Cherokees, Shawnees, and Kickapoos—lived in the community of several towns, one which included a blacksmith shop. In each place the residents possessed an array of farm implements and goods acquired through trading. Plundering, perhaps even more so the eventual resistance of Indian warriors, impelled Tarrant to order the retreat. When they returned to Northeast Texas, the men pushed before them a column of captured horses and mules burdened with such goods as axes, metal hoes, buffalo robes, and firearms. See Gary C. Anderson, *The Conquest of Texas: Ethnic Cleansing in the Promised Land, 1820-1875* (Norman: University of Oklahoma Press, 2005).
- *The auspicious circumstances…* Charles De Morse, Editorial Correspondence, *The Standard* (Clarksville, Texas), June 4, 1853 (microfilm), UTA-SC; Barker, 2.
- *As these unlucky émigrés from Fannin County learned…* Copies of selected documents from Peters Colony Papers, Texas State Library, Austin; and, Maps of the Peters Colony land grants in Tarrant County, General Land Office, cited in Barker, 2.
- *First-comers from these sections…* Charles H. Young, "Grapevine, Texas," in Ron Tyler, ed. in chief, NHT (Austin: Texas State Historical Association, 1996), vol. 3, 285-6; see also Maps of the Peters Colony; and, H. P. N. Gammel, ed., *The Laws of Texas, 1822-1897* (Austin, The Gammel Book Co., 1898), vol. III, chaps. XVII, X, LI, CXX, cited in Barker, 5; I. C. Spence, Robertson County, to Thomas G. Western, Supt. of Indian Affairs, No. 314, Sept. 9, 1845, in Dorman H. Winfrey and James M. Day, *The Indian Papers of Texas and the Southwest, 1825-1916* (Texas State Historical Association, 1995), vol. II, 356-7.

Page 13

- *As these developments unfolded…* Gen. W. J. Worth, Head. Qrs. 8th & 9th Military Depts., San Antonio, Texas, to Gov. George T. Wood, Austin, Texas, Feb. 15, 1849, in Winfrey and Day, vol. V, 36-7; Perkins, 26-7, quotation, 26.
- *Hardly had the inspection party returned…* Simon Bowden Farrar to Judge C. C. Cummings, Tarrant County, correspondence, Sept. 23, 1893 (copy), TCHC (first quotation); Barker, 3; Perkins, 30-1. The commonly accepted date of the locating party's arrival is May 8, 1849. Perkins clearly establishes through official Army returns that Arnold could not have reached the site any earlier than May 16. See pp. 30, and 247 (endnote 44). There is no firm consensus, however, whether the ultimate site of the fort was its only location. Knight, and most recently, Perkins, contend the post was actually founded on Live Oak Point, near the spot where the locating party first camped. Barker believes that the Live Oak Point site was merely a convenient base where the garrison cut wood and obtained material to build the fort. It would have made sense for the soldiers to camp in the protected spot where they were working, and the fact that a report four months after the post's founding situates it atop the bluff seems to support the idea that the bluff site was the only true location of the fort. Lt. Samuel Starr, whose remarks Knight used to document the Live Oak Point site, did not arrive until Dec. 25, 1849, a full half-year after the post's founding. Knight, 244. See also "Colonel Abraham Harris," *Fort Worth Mail Telegram*, Nov. 17, 1901, Harris file, Series IV, Box 2, Mary Daggett Lake Papers, FWPL; Perkins, 30-1, 61, 79; Barker, 3; second phrase set off by quotation marks is author's emphasis.

Page 14

- *Anticipating the boon to civilian settlement…* Knight, 19-21; Julia Kathryn Garrett, *Fort Worth: A Frontier Triumph* (Austin: Encino Press, 1972), 108-9. It should be noted that scarcely a month after the Army founded the post, Edward Tarrant, in the words of Indian Agent Robert Simpson Neighbors, determined to take up to one-hundred and fifty men on an expedition to the Wichita Mountains in Indian Territory to "attack any Indian villages he may fall in with, destroy their cornfields, and capture their horses, etc." Even for one who so zealously embraced the spirit of Lamar's Indian policy of expulsion or extermination, the intent to cross the state's border was stunningly irresponsible. To his credit, Major Arnold cleverly "persuaded General Tarrant out of his trip" by informing him that "if [the settlers] intend to protect themselves…the regulars may be withdrawn for other service…" R. S. Neighbors to F. Hamilton, June 23, 1849, and R. A. Arnold to G. Deas, July 13, 1849, Letters Sent, Headquarters Western Division, Record Group 393, National Archives, Wash., D.C., cited in Perkins, 31-2.
- *For troops stationed at Fort Worth…* Garrett, 70-4, 80 (quotation, 74); Perkins, 217-32; Samuel Starr to Eliza [Starr], Jan. 6, 1850, Samuel Henry Starr Papers, Center for American History, University of Texas at Austin.
- *About the only native peoples the troops… Ibid.*, 78-9; Howard Peak, *A Ranger of Commerce or 52 Years on the Road* (San Antonio: Naylor Printing Co., 1929), 163-9; Knight, 3-5; *Fort Worth Register*, June 1, 1902; Perkins, 113-8, see also p. 258, endnotes 7, 9, 12, 15.
- *Even if the troops never engaged…* Perkins, 177-8, 183-5, 187; Garrett, 81-2; Knight, 19-21.
- *Other than seeding the civilian settlement…* Garrett, 122; Knight, 23-4.

Page 15

- *Then, in November 1856, the forward-looking little community…* Charles J. Swasey and W. M. Melton, *Directory of the City of Fort Worth: For the Year 1877* (Fort Worth: Office of the *Daily Democrat*, 1877), 9, cited in Barker, 5; see also Knight, 23-39ff.
- *Among the procession of pioneers…* "Diary of Jonathan Hamilton Baker," ms, private holding, various entries, May-Sept., 1858.
- *Certainly, the Fort Worth he described… Ibid.*

Page 16

- *Beneath the veneer of those serene observations…* Knight, 36-7; Garrett, 144-5.
- *Added to the editors' enmity…* Garrett, 181-2; for a general outline and brief bibliography, see Donald E. Reynolds, "Texas Troubles," *NHT*, vol. 6, 439.
- *By then, war was imminent.* Knight, 56; Leonard Sanders, *How Fort Worth became the Texasmost city, 1849-1920* (Fort Worth: TCU Press, 1986), 35.
- *When the war ended…* K. M. Van Zandt, with Sandra L. Myres, *Force without Fanfare: The Autobiography of K. M. Van Zandt* (Fort Worth: TCU Press, 1968), 113; I. C. Terry, ms (copy), TCHC.
- *It did not all happen at once…* Garrett, 258-9.

Page 17

- *Then, in 1867 and 1868…* Ty Cashion, *A Texas Frontier: The Clear Fork Country and Fort Griffin, 1849-1887* (Norman: University of Oklahoma Press, 1996), 291.
- *By 1868 the meager population doubled…* Sanders, 40.
- *Serving the prosperous community by 1873…* For conflicting surveys of general conditions during this period, see Knight, 51-76ff, and Terry ms, cited in Barker, 6. See also, Patricia L. Duncan, "Enterprise: B. B. Paddock and Fort Worth—A Case Study of Late Nineteenth Century American Boosterism," M.A. thesis, University of Texas at Arlington, 1982.; Ruby Schmidt, ed., *Fort Worth and Tarrant County: A Historical Guide* (Fort Worth: TCU Press, 1984).
- *Eighteen seventy-three also marked another…* *FWD*, Feb. 15, 1873.
- *Certainly, by 1873 Fort Worth possessed all the features…* Knight, 76.
- *The ensuing Panic of 1873…* Sanders, 46.

Page 18

- *Yet, while the country in general continued to flounder…* Cashion, 115-6; 168-9.
- *In the meantime, community leaders had not given up…* Terry ms; Swasey and Melton, cited in Barker, 7; Knight, 74-5 (quotation, 75).
- *The new era began immediately…* Swasey and Melton, cited in Barker, 7; Knight, 84; Cashion, 174.
- *Otherwise a welter of activity…* *FWD*, Apr. 10, 1878, Jan. 1, 1887.

Page 19

- *The blocks centered on Twelfth Street and Rusk…* *FWD*, April 18 (first and second quotations), June 15 (third quotation), 1879.
- *Soon enough, however, the sight of bawling cattle…* Department of the Interior, *Population of the United States in 1880: the Tenth Census* (Washington, D.C.: Government Printing Office, 1881); Department of the Interior, *Population of the United States in 1890: the Eleventh Census* (Washington, D.C.: Government Printing Office, 1891); Department of the Interior, *Population of the United States in 1900: the Twelfth Census* (Washington, D.C.: Government Printing Office, 1901).
- *The railroad, just as its original boosters had promised…* *Fort Worth City Directory*, 1883-1884, 1885-1886, 1886-1887, 1888-1889; Barker 8; Knight, 112, 114-5.
- *As a key transportation center that employed legions of railroad workers…* Robert K. DeArment, *Jim Courtright of Fort Worth: His Life and Legend*·(Fort Worth: TCU Press, 2004), 195-7. This biography represents the most recent scholarship on Courtright and takes previous works into consideration, correcting some inaccuracies and filling out a larger context in which the errant lawman's final days unfolded.

Page 20

- *Much of the acrimony…* *Ibid.*, 198-202.
- *Then, on the evening of February 8, 1887…* *Ibid.*, 217-8, 223-6.
- *The widely reported "shootout"…* *Fort Worth Gazette*, May 25, 1887 (quotation); Minutes of the Fort Worth City Council, Vol. E, 331, in Barker, 8; *FWD*, May 31, 1877; City Directory, 1888-1889; Fairmount addition, Fort Worth, Texas, National Park Service, National Register of Historical Places, U.S. Dept. of the Interior, Wash., D.C.; Van Zandt and Myres, 171; Barker, 10-11.
- *Full of pride and confidence…* Barbara Knox and Rita Martin, Fort Worth, posted a well-researched piece for the State of Texas's GenWeb project that included details not previously published. See www.rootsweb.com/~txtarran/places/springpalace.htm.

Page 22

- *William Fife Somervell built a comfortable home…* (photo caption) Scott Barker, Fort Worth, correspondence with author, Aug. 21, 2005, based on forensic investigation of the photograph by Barker, Ron Tyler (former executive director of the Texas State Historical Association), Susie Pritchett (archivist, TCHC), local collectors Morris Matson and Dalton Hoffman, and Fort Worth photo historian Jack White; Ruby Schmidt, Granbury, telephone interview with author, Aug. 2, 2006, based on correspondence between Schmidt and Mayra McGregor (Somerville's granddaughter), Inverness-shire, Scotland.
- *As the old century waned …* *City Directory*, 1894; *Fort Worth Register* Aug. 11, Sept. 27, 1897; Barker, 10-11; Van Zandt and Myres, 163; Knight, 125.
- There remained a final chapter… The Wild Bunch's rendezvous and experience in Fort Worth is discussed in a number of books. See particularly Rick Selcer, *Hell's Half Acre: Life and Legend in a Red-light District* (Fort Worth: TCU Press, 1991).

Chapter 1

Page 24

- *The people of Fort Worth counted down…* *FWMR*, Dec. 17, 1899.
- *Four years later the grand terminal…* Sanders, 161.
- *With a new century upon them…* *Twelfth U.S. Census* (1900).
- *Everywhere signs pointed to a greater destiny…* *FWMR*, July 3, 1900

Page 25

- *Fort Worth also possessed the kinds of services…* Knight, 152.
- *The 1900s would also begin with Fort Worth…* *DMN*, Jan. 4, 1900.
- *Over four thousand stockmen…* *Ibid.*

Page 26

- *That evening the Knights staged a ball…* *Ibid.*, Jan. 9, 1900.
- *No less than the governor of Texas…* *Ibid.*, Jan. 11, 13, 1900.
- *Awash in success, president Springer predicted…* *Ibid.*, Jan. 13, 1900.
- *Clearly, Fort Worth was enjoying the progress…* *Ibid.*, Oct. 10, 1900.
- *Buffalo Bill Cody himself, who had last visited…* *Ibid.*, Oct. 11, 1900.
- *If the Fort Worth of 1900 had impressed Cody…* Knight, 155-6.

Page 27

- *When the century began, a single block…* *DMN*, Jan. 6, 1900.
- *The pressure for contractors to rush their jobs…* *FWR*, July 3, 1903 (quotation), Oct. 28, 1907.
- *Increasingly, horses and wagons yielded…* Knight, 160.
- *In 1904 a municipal code began regulating…* *FWST*, June 1, 1909.

Page 28

- *Once outside of town, the condition of the roads…* *Ibid.*
- *Despite its limitations, the automobile was here to stay…* *Ibid.*, Jan. 8, 1909.
- *Throughout the decade promoters came…* *Ibid.*, Jan. 3, 8, 1909.
- *In every part of the city, new businesses…* *FWR.*, Oct. 20, 1907.

Page 29

- *All manner of commercial and institutional structures…* Knight, 182.
- *Building permits reflected Fort Worth's growth…* *FWST*, March 7, 1909.

Page 30

- *The building boom that had the greatest effect…* *DMN*, Jan. 4, 1900 (quotation); J'Nell Pate, *North of the River: A brief history of North Fort Worth* (Fort Worth: TCU Press, 1994), 27. (All subsequent references to Pate refer to *North of the River* unless otherwise stated.)
- *After the National Livestock Association meeting…* Pate, 23; "For Big Packery," *Texas Stock Journal*, June 12, 1901, 1.
- *The transformation was total…* *FWST*, March 17, 1909; Pate, 27-33.

Page 31

- *Soon, North Side, composed of Rosen Heights…* Pate, 40-1.
- *If the professional men of North Side…* *FWR*, Oct. 20, 1907.
- *In other parts of town, the social drums…* *Ibid.*
- *The Garden of Eden, across the Trinity…* *Ibid.*

Page 32

- *Similarly, African-American neighborhoods…* *Ibid.*
- *One African American in particular…* William O. Bundy, *Biography of Honorable William Madison McDonald* (Fort Worth: Bunker Printing & Book Co., 1925), 113.
- *As the people of Fort Worth worked, so, too, did they play…* Knight, 133, 169; Pate, 104-5.
- *America's favorite pastime was also Fort Worth's…* *FWST*, Jan. 10, March 1 (quotation), 6, 7, 1909.

Page 33

- *Academic events, too, commanded a place…* *Ibid.*, June 17, 1909.
- *Families also looked forward each year…* *FWR* Oct. 6, 1907
- *On a clear, crisp April morning, the president arrived…* For a detailed account of TR's visit, see *FWR*, April 9, 1905.

Page 34

- *Finished in another instant…* *Ibid.*, Oct. 8 (quotation), 14, 1907.

Page 35

- *When the momentous day arrived…* *Ibid.*, Oct. 14, 1907.
- *Then…BOOM!…* *Ibid.*
- *In Fort Worth, as in the rest of the country…* Irvin Farman, *The Fort Worth Club: A Centennial Story* (Fort Worth: The Fort Worth Club, 1985), 34.
- *While the men cultivated business…* *FWST*, April 17, 1909.

Page 36

- *The Federation also embraced the consummately progressive slogan…* *Ibid.*, April 17, 1909.
- *Then, there was always the bothersome Hell's Half Acre…* Selcer, 269.
- *While the popular crusader was mourned…* *Ibid.*, 230.
- *The new century began with great hope…* *DMN*, Jan. 1, 1900.
- *The attitude that engendered racism…* *FWST*, April 5, 1909.
- *On the other hand, the rapacious fire did not discriminate…* *Ibid.*, April 5, 1909.

Page 37

- *Progress could also be measured…* *Ibid.*, March 7, 1909.
- *The welcoming speech for the event…* *Ibid.*, March 16, 1909.

Chapter 2

Page 38

- *Fort Worth, as a popular phrase of the times put it…* *FWR*, Sept. 23, 1910 (quotation); RD, 7745.
- *Few vestiges of the old frontier survived these years…* *FWR*, March 8, 1917 (quotation); Tarrant County Historical Commission Timeline, ID 526; RD, 2206.
- *A grisly reminder of bygone days…FWR.*, Jan. 2, 1910, *RD*, 2208, 7562; *FWST*, May 15, 1917.
- *Yet some people feared the world…* *FWST*, May 8 (quotation), 13, 15, 16, 1910.
- *When the "mortal threat" was finally over…* *Ibid.*, May 19, 1910.
- *The very next day…* *Ibid.*, May 20, 1910.

Page 40

- *Even though Nation got the cold shoulder…* *FWR*, Nov. 18, 19 (quotation), 1915; *RD*, 8346-49.
- *Several times aerial shows commanded crowds…* *FWST*, Jan. 13, 1911.
- *Teddy Roosevelt also returned…* *Ibid.*, Oct. 30, 1949, 100th Anniversary Edition.
- *By the time of Roosevelt's second visit…FWR*, March 14, 16 (quotation), 1910; RD, 7661-7.
- *Elsewhere, citizens enjoyed the amenities…* *FWNT*, Mack Williams, "In Old Fort Worth," 34.

Page 41

- *Shortly after the completion of Lake Worth…* *RD*, 16467, 22349-50.
- *On the baseball diamond…* Jeff Guinn, *When Panthers Roared: The Fort Worth Cats and Minor League Baseball* (Fort Worth: TCU Press, 1999), 37.
- *Free weekend concerts…* *FWR*, June 2, 1910, April 18, 1915, July 3, 1916; *RD*, 7707-8, 8134, 8562-3.

- *Most of the crowd arrived…* Madeline Williams, "60 Years Ago You Paid Cash for a Car," *FWNT*, 21; *RD*, 2516.
- *Even so, women, too, began showing an interest…* *RD*, 516; Williams, "60 Years Ago," 21.

Page 43
- *Increasingly, the automobile was becoming…* *FWST*, Jan. 2, 1910, Aug. 5, 1917; *RD*, 2995.
- *The growing traffic put pressure on the city…* *FWR*, Aug 22, 1910 (quotation), Sept 9, 1911; *RD*, 7763.
- *City departments themselves became motorized…* *FWR*, July 25, 1910, Sept. 9, 1911 (quotation); *RD*, 7732.
- *Despite the network of all-weather roads…* *FWR*, Jan. 31, 1915.
- *Passengers arriving in Fort Worth…* *Ibid.*, Jan 17, 19, Feb. 10, May 16, 1915; *RD*, 8059, 8064, 8077-8, 8151-3.
- *Likewise, the 1910s saw motion pictures…* *FWST*, Oct. 30, 1949, "Community Life," 29; *FWR*, Aug 20, 1911; *RD*, 7762.

Page 44
- *The last of the holdouts…* *FWR*, Feb. 11, 24, 1910; *RD*, 7630, 7635, 9560; *FWST*, Oct. 12, 1934.
- *The passing of Fort Worth University…* *FWR*, April 2, 10, 1910; *RD*, 1108, 7716.
- *Even as TCU trustees were arranging…* Jerome A. Moore, *Texas Christian University: A Hundred Years of History* (TCU Press, 1974), 66-69; see also Colby D. Hall, *History of Texas Christian University: A College of the Cattle Frontier* (Fort Worth: TCU Press, 1947).
- *TCU actually traced its origins to Fort Worth…* Moore, 66-69.
- *During the 1910-1911 school year…* *Ibid.*

Page 45
- *The Christian enlightenment represented in TCU…* *FWR*, Jan. 22, April 8, 1910; *RD*, 7604-5 (quotation).
- *Nobody, however, could galvanize a congregation…* Mack Williams, "The Trials of J. Frank Norris," in *FWNT*, "In Old Fort Worth," 33 (quotation); Barry Hankins, *God's Rascal: J. Frank Norris & the Beginnings of Southern Fundamentalism* (Lexington: University of Kentucky Press, 1996, 12-17.
- *Norris could have settled into the comfortable life…* Hankins, 14.
- *Then, in the early hours of February…* *FWR*, March 29, 1912.

Page 46
- *At the trial, a milkman…* Williams, "Trials of Norris," 33.
- *Certainly, Norris had not cornered the market…* *FWR*, Dec. 2, 1918 (quotation), Jan. 6, 1919; *RD*, 8951, 8960.
- *More quietly, several congregations…* Carol Roark, *Fort Worth's Legendary Landmarks* (Fort Worth: TCU Press, 1995), 84, 94, 98; *FWR*, Feb. 17, 1914; 7839; Pate, 62-3, 145.

Page 47
- *On January 13, 1913, Amarillo rancher…* (caption) Mack Williams, "Murder at the Metropolitan," *FWNT*, "In Old Fort Worth," 22.
- *During the 1910s a significant foreign enclave…* Pate, 59; *RD*, 18429.

Page 48
- *Many European immigrants saved their money…* Laurene Sharp, comp. and ed., *100 Years of the Black Man in Fort Worth* (Fort Worth: L. Sharp & Co. Publishers, 1973).
- *During these years, barrios also emerged…* Carlos E. Cuéllar, *Stories from the Barrios: A History of Mexican Fort Worth* (Fort Worth: TCU Press, 2003), 7-12; Jamie McIlvain, "History of Hispanic Fort Worth," M.A. Thesis, Texas Christian University, 1993, 64-65, 96.
- *Although Hispanic Fort Worth can claim…* *FWR.*, March 29, (1st quotation), April 25, 1914 (2nd quotation); RD, 7873-6.

Page 49
- *A brief preoccupation with the revolutions…* Mack Williams, "When Arlington Heights was an Army Camp," *FWNT*, in "In Old Fort Worth," 22.

Page 50
- *The enthusiastic pitch brought Army brass…* *Ibid.*
- *To sweeten the pot…* *Ibid.*
- *At the same time, Keith was vying…* Robert Hays, "Military Aviation in Texas," *Texas Military History 3* (Spring 1963).
- *The training facilities meant boom times…* *FWR*, Dec. 19, 1917 (quotation); *RD*, 8837-8840.

Page 51
- *Before the war was over…* *FWR*, March 18, 1918 (quotation); *RD*, 8873-4.
- *The city had been a good host to the soldiers…* *FWR*, April 11, 1918.
- *While the Allies were prosecuting an end…* *Ibid.*, Oct. 18 (quotation), Nov. 4, 1918, Jan. 19, 1919.

Page 52
- *At the same time another, more welcome, event…* *FWST*, Oct. 30, 1949, "Oil and Gas," 2; Mack Williams, *FWNT*, "When the Oil Stock Bubble Burst," in "In Old Fort Worth," 26.
- *By the end of the next year…* *FWR*, May 26, Dec. 9, 1918, Jan. 30, Feb. 14, 1919; *RD*, 8908, 9894-5, 8970, 8966-69.
- *After all the confetti from the Armistice Day…* Bernice B. Maxfield, *Camp Bowie, Fort Worth, 1917-1918: An Illustrated History of the 36th Infantry Division in World War I* (Fort Worth, Tex. : B. B. Maxfield Foundation, 1975); *FWST*, Oct. 30, 1949, "Transportation," 6 (quotation).
- *During the last days of the decade…* *FWR*, July 20, 1919 (quotation); RD, 9023.

Page 53
- *In an age when barnstorming…* (caption) J'Nell Pate, "Ormer Leslie Locklear: The 'Epoch of Flying' Has Arrived," in Ty Cashion & Jesus F. de la Teja, eds., *The Human Tradition in Texas* (Wilmington, Del.: Scholarly Resources, 2001), 145-60; see also Art Ronnie, Locklear: The Man Who Walked on Wings (South Brunswick, UK: A.S. Barnes and Company, 1973).

Chapter 3

Page 54
- *Standing tall in the center of all the action…* Jerry Flemmons, *Amon: The Texan Who Played Cowboy for America* (Lubbock: Texas Tech University Press, 1998), xx (quotation), 27.
- *Bowie native Amon Carter…* *Ibid.*, 13-14, 46-7 (quotation 46), 58-9.

Page 55
- *It was West Texas that boosted…* *Ibid.*, 23, 226-31 (quotation, 229).
- *Amon Carter cultivated his contacts…* *RD*, 18621; Flemmons, 110-14 (first quotation, 110, second quotation, 111).
- *To Carter it was all about boostering…* Flemmons, xx, 149, 292 (quotation); *FWST*, Sept. 2, July 7, 1925, Oct. 30, 1949, "Transportation," 22; RD, 5970-1, 6019-20; "From Wire Crate to B-36 Fort Worth Has Been Center for Aviation," *Fort Worth Press*, July 13, 1949.

Page 56
- *Fort Worth for awhile…* (caption) *FWST*, Oct. 30, 1949, "Aircraft Industry."
- *Carter represented modernity…* *RD*, 2517, 5871-2 (quotation); *FWST*, May 2, 1925, April 23, 1931, Oct. 30, 1949, "Automotive," 14; *FWR*, Sept. 7, 1919.

Page 57
- *Change also engendered a sense of history…* *RD*, 2263-4 (quotation 2263), 2266, 5632, 5671; *FWST*, Sept. 10, 24, 30, 1923; *FWP*, Oct. 29, 1923.
- *As the date of the celebration approached…* *FWST*, Nov. 11-16, 1923; *RD*, 2267-74 (quotation 2267), 5696-8; *FWP*, Nov. 14, 1923.
- *The crowning touch of the Diamond Jubilee…* *RD*, 5615-17; FWP, Oct. 24, 1923.
- *Meanwhile, the big oil strikes…* Williams, "Oil Stock Bubble," 26-7.

Page 59
- *Most of the victims were shamed into silence…* Mack Williams, "How Norfleet Captured the Master Swindler," 114-15, in "In Old Fort Worth" (quotation); *FWST*, Oct. 23, 1923.
- *Into the early years of the 1920s Norfleet…* Williams, "Norfleet."
- *For other swindlers the bubble burst…* *FWST*, Oct. 30, 1949, "Oil and Gas," 26; Williams, "Oil Stock Bubble," 26 (quotation).

Page 60
- *Another oil company found guilty…* Williams, "Norfleet," 115.
- *The notoriety of the protracted oil fraud trials…* *FWST*, Oct. 30, 1949, "Oil and Gas," 17 (quotation); Roark, 109-115, 130.
- *Still other structures added to the skyline…* *RD*, 3075-6, 5909, 9035-6; *FWP*, May 23, 1925; *FWST*, Jan. 18, 1920; Roark, 150; *FWR*, Aug. 31, 1919.
- *Where there was building…* Knight, 199-200; *RD*, 5855-6 (quotation), 6160-6; *FWP*, April 24, 1925, Feb. 23, 1926.
- *Early in the decade a series of strikes…* *RD*, 3088 (quotations); *FWST*, April 4, 1920.
- *Railroad workers during the summer of 1922…* *RD*, 4341-3, 4366-69; *FWP*, July 4, 22, 1922.

Page 61
- *Despite their violent tactics…* *FWP*, July 15, Sept. 1922 (quotations)
- *The most serious strike...* *Ibid.*, Nov. 28, Dec. 2, 1921, *RD*, 4122-61.
- *Then, the situation grew ugly…* *FWP*, Dec. 7, 1921; *FWST*, Dec. 12, 1921.
- *Rouse was carried to the City-County hospital…* *FWP*, Dec. 12, 13, 1921; *FWST*, Dec. 12, 23, 1921.

Page 62
- *Meanwhile, the strike ran its course…* *RD*, 4181-2, 4194-5; *FWP*, Jan. 23, Feb. 1, 1922 (quotation).
- *Soon a back-to-business attitude prevailed…* Victoria and Walter Buenger, *Texas Merchant: Marvin Leonard & Fort Worth* (College Station, 1998), 6, 32-3.
- *Consumers also developed an appetite…* *RD*, 5852-3, 5903, 6304-6, 6312; *FWP*, April 18, May 21, 1925, July 5, 6, 1926 (quotation).
- *As elsewhere, Fort Worth during the Roaring Twenties…* Mack Williams, "1925 Police: Thrills, Spills, and $90 a Month," *FWNT*, in "In Old Fort Worth," 35 (quotations); *FWP*, June 12, 1924.

Page 63
- *However reluctant, the law responded…* *RD*, 6299, 4201; *FWP*, Feb. 16, July 2, 1926.
- *In the normal course of affairs…* *RD*, 5827, 6002; *FWP*, March 9, Aug. 11, 17 (quotation), 1925.
- *Perhaps the greatest attendance records…* *FWST*, Oct. 30, 1949, "Community Life," 29 (quotation); Richardson, et. al., *Texas: The Lone Star State*, 8th ed. (Upper Saddle River, NJ: Prentice-Hall, 2001), 374.

Page 64
- *Among the brightest stars in Hollywood…* *RD*, 5423-4; *FWP*, March 26, 1923 (quotation).
- *Of course, the 1920s was the "Golden Era of Sports,"…* Guinn, 35, 41-45.
- *So successful were the Cats…* *Ibid.*, 24.
- *The Cats' answer to Babe Ruth was Clarence…* *Ibid.*, 42-4.

Page 65
- *For some men and women who associated change…* *RD*, 9061-3; *FWR*, Feb 23, 1920 (quotation).
- *The harshest face of resistance to change…* Charles C. Alexander, *The Ku Klux Klan in the Southwest* (Norman: University of Oklahoma Press, 1965), 41.
- *In February 1922 about eighteen hundred Klansmen…* *RD*, 4204-6; *FWP*, Feb. 17, 1922.
- *As elsewhere, a vocal bloc of Fort Worthians…* *RD*, 4241-2, 4251-56; *FWP*, April 4 (second quotation), 21, 22 (first quotation), 24, 1922.

Page 66
- *In the early summer of 1923, downtown traffic…* *RD*, 5502-4; *FWP*, June 9, 1923.
- *The next evening the Ku Klux Klan…* *RD*, 5204; *FWP*, June 9, 27, 1923.
- *Then, seemingly overnight, the Klan's prestige…* *RD*, 5989, 5992-3; *FWP*, Aug. 1 (quotation), 3, 1925.
- *The nightmarish episode of white hoods…* *FWST*, Oct. 24-26, 1929.

Page 67
- *The stock market that crashed so resoundingly…* *Ibid.*, Oct. 24, 1929.

Chapter 4

Page 68
- *To casual observers…* Roark, 173; Sister Mary Ailbe Keaveney, "The Depression Era in Fort Worth, Texas, 1929-1934," MA Thesis, University of Texas at Austin, 1974, 47-8.
- *Despite all the construction dollars…* Keaveney, 34-8 (second quotation), 43 (first quotation).
- *Yet already, undercurrents of the business collapse…* *FWST*, Jan. 30, 1930.

Page 69
- *The first pitiful cases…* Keaveney, 41-2.
- *All too soon such heartrending scenes…* *Ibid.*, 90.
- *With so many men and women on the dole…* *Ibid.*, 86.

Page 70
- *Some of the jobs the bureau was finding…* Cuéllar, 48-9.
- *By the spring of 1932 it became clear…* Keaveny, 105-9.
- *To its credit, the Panther City responded…* *Ibid.*, 51-2, 88 (quotation), 118; *FWST*, Oct. 30, 1949, "Automotive," 7.

Page 71
- *Of course, the list of religious charities…* Keaveny 124.
- *Yet, while many gave, others took…* *RD*, 9255; *FWST*, March 22, 1931 (quotation); Keaveny, 45-6.
- *One of Fort Worth's most spectacular crimes…* *FWP*, July 13, 1933 (quotation); *FWST*, March 8, 1982.
- *A few days following his return…* *FWP*, July 13, 1933.
- *After stripping the dead men…* *Ibid.*

Page 72
- *Following a series of trials…* *Ibid.*; *FWST*, March 8, 1982.
- *The story did not end there…* *FWP*, July 13, 1933; *FWST*, March 8, 1982.
- *Every bit as malicious were several outlaws…* Mack Williams, "The Day They Captured Machine Gun Kelly," *FWNT*, in "In Old Fort Worth," 124-5.
- *Bonnie and Clyde were also occasional Cowtown visitors…* Pate, 87-88; Flemmons, 251 (quotation).
- *Although none of the era's most notorious outlaws…* Keaveny, 65-6: *FWST*, Aug. 9, 1930 (quotation); *FWP*, Feb. 25, 1973; Pate, 88.
- *In the second attempt, a gang…* Pate, 89.

Page 73
- *On the last day of January 1930…* Keaveney, 53-4.
- *However repentant they were, the bankers got little sympathy…* *Ibid.*, 56-7.
- *Even more tragic was the story of Louis B. Ward…* *Ibid.*, 56-7.

Page 74
- *The failure of the Texas National inspired rumors…* *Ibid.* (first quotation), 63-4; *RD*, 9233 (third quotation), 9308-9 (fourth quotation), 9566 (second quotation).
- *After overcoming one last crisis early in 1931…* Flemmons, 168.
- *With the distressed crowd threatening to get unruly…* *Ibid.*, 168-170.
- *Hesitant applause turned to light cheering…* *Ibid.*, 170.

Page 75
- *By the time newly inaugurated president…* Keaveney, 70-2.
- *At Texas Women's College…* *FWST*, April, 6, 1935; UTA-SC, CF, *FWST*, Dec. 14, 1942.
- *Miraculously, the good reverend led his flock…* *RD*, 9555 (quotation); *FWST*, Sept. 21, 1934, June 23, 1936, Nov. 9, 1938.
- *Although hard times lingered…* *FWP*, March 11, 1933.
- *What America also needed about that time…* Mack Williams, "The 'Noble Experiment' That Failed," *FWNT*, in "In Old Fort Worth," 30-1.
- *Within an hour after the stroke of twelve…* *Ibid.*

Page 76
- *The same irreverent spirit…* Jan Jones, *Billy Rose Presents…Casa Mañana* (Fort Worth: TCU Press, 1998),1-9.
- *The unsuspecting coup…* *Ibid.*, xii
- *The Frontier Centennial opened a month late…* *Ibid.*, 77.
- *As it shaped up, the Frontier Centennial…* *Ibid.*, 32-3, 67-8, 88-89.

Page 77
- *The provocative Rand…* *Ibid.*, 64-6, 90-1.
- *As titillating as the flesh shows were…* *Ibid.*, 33-35, 75 (quotation).
- *Despite losing almost a hundred thousand dollars…* *Ibid.*, 1-9, 93-4, 103 (quotation).

Page 78
- *Ironically the Will Rogers Memorial Center…* Flemmons, 172-3.
- *The PWA also provided funds…* Roark, 210.

Page 79
- *If New Deal spending and the Frontier Centennial…* Ty Cashion, *Pigskin Pulpit: A Social History of Texas High School Football Coaches* (Austin: Texas State Historical Association, 1998), 105-9.
- *During a four-season stretch…* *Ibid.*
- *Other Fort Worth schools…* Roark, 204, 214-15.

Page 80
- *During the spring of 1939…* (photo caption) www.genealogyimagesofhistory.com.
- *TCU likewise broke ground…* *RD*, 9095, *FWST*, Jan. 8, 1930; Flemmons., 212-19 (quotation, 214).
- *It was on the arm of "Slingin' Sammy" Baugh…* Dan Jenkins and Francis J. Fitzgerald, eds., *Greatest Moments in TCU Football* (Louisville, KY: AdCraft Sports Marketing, 1996, 52.
- *With seven minutes left to play…* *Ibid.*, 52-72.
- *As good as Baugh was, it was his understudy…* *Ibid.*, 73-83; Flemmons, 217-8.
- *Riding the wave of gridiron success…* *FWST*, Nov. 27, 1937, March 21, 26, May 31, 1938 (first quotation), Oct. 30, 1949, "Historical," 22 (second quotation);

Page 81
- *In the material culture, motor use…* *Ibid.*, Oct. 30, 1949, "Historical," 22.
- *Finally, on New Year's Day 1939…* UTA-SC, CF, *FWST*, "City Bids Adieu to Street Cars," Jan. 1, 1939.
- *In 1925 a newspaper report…* *FWP*, Jan. 4, 1925 (quotation), April 14, 1938.
- *Aboard that final trip…* UTA-SC, CF, *FWST*, "Rider on First Trolley Also Will be on Last Trolley," Dec. 30, 1939.

Chapter 5

Page 82
- *In the fall of 1940 almost every edition…* *FWST*, Sept. 19, 1940, 3.
- *Organizers whipped up enthusiasm…* *Ibid.*, 1, 3.
- *As hundreds of spectators crammed office buildings…* *Ibid.*, 1.
- *The parade ended at the Will Rogers Coliseum…* *Ibid.*, 3.
- *If Gary Cooper took Fort Worthians minds…* Philip Atlee, *The Inheritors* (New York: Dial Press, 1940), 259.

Page 83
- *The early 1940s also saw the Jim Hotel…* FWPL, CF, Christopher Evans, "The Hot Spot," *FWST*, June 30, 1991, F, 1.
- *The white owners of those nightclubs…* *Ibid.*

Page 84
- *Record crowds also packed the once-cavernous coliseum…* Clay Reynolds, *A Hundred Years of Heroes: A History of the Southwestern Exposition and Livestock Show* (Fort Worth: TCU Press, 1995), 207-9.
- *Despite the emotional display…* *Ibid.*, 210-11.
- *Efforts to rebuild the heart of the North Side…* Chamber of Commerce, "This Month in Fort Worth," March 1943.
- *By that time, of course, Fort Worth and America…* Richard Schroeder, *Texas Signs On: The Early Days of Radio and Television* (College Station: Texas A&M Press, 1998), 119.
- *Amon Carter sent his own cable…* Flemmons, 260.

Page 85
- *Carter's diatribe was not the idle talk of a rabble-rouser…* Stanley Gunn, "AAF Training Command Controls Nationwide Flying Schools," *FWST*, Feb. 20, 1944, Section 2, 1.
- *On the outskirts of the city…* Knight, 212.
- *Next door, at the Tarrant Field Airdrome…* Art Leatherwood, "Carswell Airforce Base," *NHT*, Vol. 1, 997.
- *Among the accomplishments that won…* *DMN*, Feb. 12, 1946.

Page 86
- *The war effort in Fort Worth…* *FWP*, Oct. 3, 1971.
- *In the summer of 1942…* FWPL, CF, *FWST*, "Crowds Here Greet Heroes," July 3, 1942.
- *As legions of young Fort Worth men…* Pate, 138-44.

Page 87
- *At the beginning of the decade…*

Page 88
- *On the other hand, the headline…* FWPL, CF, *FWST*, "2 New Bus Conductors Never Shave!" Sept. 28, 1943.
- *No doubt a recent near-catastrophe…* *Ibid.*
- *Yet, with bus fares doubling…* *Ibid.*
- *White-collar jobs also went begging…* *FWP*, Oct. 3, 1971; Flemmons, 266.

Page 89
- *It was a more somber office…* Flemmons, 272-85.
- *Then, after two agonizing months…* *Ibid.*

Page 90
- *As the war wound to its conclusion…* Flemmons, 283 (quotation); FWPL, CF, *FWP*, Aug. 14, 1945.
- *Those who returned found a different Fort Worth…* FWPL, CF, Hugh Williamson, "Fort Worth Still Cowtown but Yankees and Airplanes Move In," *FWST*, Feb. 24, 1946.
- *The effect of such sudden growth…* Williamson, "Fort Worth Still Cowtown."
- *Guffaws and merrymaking also radiated…* See Ann Arnold, *Gamblers & Gangsters: Fort Worth's Jacksboro Highway in the 1940s & 1950s* (Austin: Eakin Press, 1998).
- *At such high-tone venues as the 2222 Club…* *Ibid.*
- *B. M. Kudlaty, a wrecker driver…* *Ibid.*, 13.

Page 91
- *It was a new kind of Cowtown to be sure…* Williamson, "Fort Worth Still Cowtown."
- *The ending of the war did little to slow production…* Bruce D. Callander, "Lucky Lady II," *Air Force Magazine Online*, 82 (March 1999).
- *A fear of communist Russia made the bomber necessary…* FWPL, CF, "Airfield Here 'Bars' Its Gates for Security Reasons," *FWST*, Sept. 17, 1947.
- *Nothing led ordinary citizens to wonder…* *FWST*, July 9, 1947.

Page 92
- *Everyday life would never quite be the same…* Reynolds, 215, 219.
- *A few months later, along those same downtown streets…* FWPL, CF, *FWST*, "Negroes Plan Parade Here for June 19," June 18, 1946.
- *Quietly, African American leaders pressed the city…* FWPL, CF, "City Won't Hire Negro Policemen, Council Decides," *FWST*, Dec. 12, 1949.
- *Seemingly, the only constant…* Curt Sampson, *Hogan* (New York: Broadway Books, 1996), 21, 91, 112.

Page 93
- *Then, in February 1949, the Hawk suffered…* *Ibid.*, 115-7.

- *Television, the medium that would one day popularize...* Schroeder, 118; "Fort Worth Firsts," *FWM*, June 1977, 8.
- *Earlier, in June, the station had previewed... Ibid.*, 139-40.
- *Suddenly a frantic, red-faced crewman... Ibid.*

Page 94
- *By the end of the year WBAP-TV-Channel 5... FWP*, Oct. 3, 1971.
- *The decade ended with the commemoration...* UTA-SC, CF, "Imprints of Frontier Adventure From Which City Grew Being Lost," *FWST*, June 6, 1948.
- *The newspaperman-author admonished that Fort Worth... Ibid.*

Page 95
- *The Fiesta-cade, another of Fort Worth's... FWM*, Aug. 1949.
- *Margaret Woodruff, a great-great-granddaughter...* UTA-SC, CF, "Traditional Legend Comes to Life For Worth's Great-Granddaughter," *FWST*, July 17, 1949.
- *She also registered some amusement... Ibid.*
- *The year 1949, however, would not be... FWP*, May 18-9, 1949; *FWST*, May 18, 1949.
- *On a night that also brought tornadoes... FWST*, May 18, 1949.
- *Yet just as city officials saw the great fire...* UTA-SC, CF, "Fort Worth, General, Prior to 1960."

Chapter 6

Page 96
- *During the 1950s the population...* Green, 64.
- *The failed Gruen Plan...*, "A Dream Realized," *FWST*, March 6, 1956.

Page 97
- *Fort Worth was far from dead...* FWPL, CF, Nedra Jenkins, "Groundbreakers' Ball Offers Prelude To Coming Art Museum Ceremonies," *FWST*, May 24, 1957.
- *Even as the art museum was breaking ground...* Reuben Strickland, "They Flock by Thousands to Youth Museum," *FWM*, Nov. 1951.
- *In the weeks before the opening...* FWPL, CF, "4,000 Attend Open House For Children's Museum," *FWST*, Nov. 2, 1953.
- *The Fifties was an exciting time to be a child...* FWPL, CF, "Zoo Will Open Acquarium Named for Editor Nov. 14, *FWST*, Nov. 3, 1954; FWPL, CF, Mabel Gouldy, "Rare Birds Being Bought for House Opening Soon at Forest Park Zoo," *FWST*, Feb. 24, 1957; FWPL, CF, "Zoo's Additions To Attract Both Children, Adults," *FWP*, March 9, 1960.
- *For a brief, shining moment Queen Tut...* FWPL, CF, Frank X. Tolbert, "Why Queen Tut is Brown's Favorite," *FWST*, March 15, 1956.

Page 98
- *Running a close second...* FWPL, CF, Jack Gordon, "10,500 Shove To Ride New Park Trains," *FWP*, June 15, 1959.

Page 99
- *At the time, the Tiny T&P...*, "Tiny T&P," *FWP*, Sept. 11, 1960, supplement, "Texas."
- *Perhaps nothing in the emerging cultural district...* FWPL, CF, John Ohendalski, "New Casa Manana [sic] Projected," *FWP*, Nov. 13, 1957, 3.
- *Upon its completion in 1958, Casa Mañana...* FWPL, CF, Jack Gordon, "97,000 Saw Five Summer Casa Shows," *FWP*, Sept. 7, 1958, 33.
- *Of all the shows that summer...* FWPL, CF, Jack Gordon, "97,000 Saw Five Summer Casa Shows," *FWP*, Sept. 7, 1958.
- *Billy Rose, no doubt, would have loved it...* FWPL, CF, *FWST*, July 28, 1986.
- *For old-times sake... Ibid.*

Page 100
- *The march of time also trod past... FWST*, June 23, 1955, A1.
- *From across the country, an outpouring of calls...* Flemmons, 312.
- *To help promote the 1951 world premier... (caption)* FWPL, CF, Grace Halsell, "More Than 200 Greet Randy Scott Here for Premier of 'Fort Worth,'" *FWST*, n.d.; FWPL, CF, Irvin Farman, "World Records Topple At Opening of 'Fort Worth,'" *FWST*, June 14, 1951.
- *Even before Carter's passing...* Jim Wright, "An open letter to Mr. Amon G. Carter and the *Fort Worth Star-Telegram*," *FWST*, July 23, 1954. For a recent, detailed account of this episode, see Dave Montgomery, "Amon Carter vs. the 'boy mayor,'" *FWST*, July 24, 2004, 1A, 17A.

Page 101
- *The very next day, the inspired challenger...* Wright, "Open letter."
- *The next day the people spoke with their ballots... Ibid.*, Montgomery, "Carter vs. 'boy mayor.'"
- *Like death, change, of course, was inevitable...* FWPL, CF, John Ohendalski, "Fort Worth Being Bottled Up By Land-Grabbing Little Cities," *FWP*, Sept. 2, 1956.
- *Within the corporate limits of the Panther City...* "Edwards Ranch To Be Developed," *FWM*, Nov. 1955, 8.
- *At Arlington the familiar sight of the well house...* Jimmy Browder, "Rich Mineral Water Lies Unused Below Arlington Streets," *Arlington Citizen*, Oct. 21, 1954.
- *As Arlington grew into a bedroom community...* FWPL, CF, "Arlington Plans for Fort Worth and Dallas," *FWP*, Feb. 16, 1950.

Page 102
- *Shortly afterwards, at the former Arlington Downs...* FWPL, CF, E. D. Alexander, "Wrecking Crew Starts Dismantling Big Arlington Downs Grandstand," *FWST*, July 13, 1957.
- *Orchestrating most of the action...* FWPL, CF, Bud Shrake, "Vandergriff, Once Boy Mayor, Now Veteran as Arlington Grows," FWP, Aug. 18, 1957.
- *He quickly proved them wrong... Ibid.*
- *Land prices in Arlington during the 1950s skyrocketed...* FWPL, CF, Tony Slaughter, "Industries Credited In Arlington Growth," *FWST*, Sept. 6, 1955.
- *At local schools, growing faculties... Ibid.*
- *Anticipating the rural growth...* Green, 51.

Page 103
- *Nevertheless, the dusty lanes that fed into 183... Ibid.*
- *All of that was about to change...* Green, 63.

- *The announcement by company president...* FWPL, CF, Bill Morrison, "Helicopter Plant Near Hurst Will Cost $3 Million," *FWP*, March 27, 1951 (quotation); FWPL, CF, Ira Cain, "Bell Helicopter Plant to Be Built at Hurst," *FWST*, March 27, 1951.
- *Sure enough, Bell during the 1950s...* FWPL, CF, Blair Justice, "Bell Aircraft 'Promoted,' Gets New Name and Full Corporation Status," *FWST*, Dec. 28, 1956.
- *As Bell churned out its turbine-powered...* FWPL, CF, John Troan, "Convair, Bell May Aid On 17,500-MPH Plane," *FWP*, June 17, 1959; FWPL, CF, "Convertiplane Passes Tests in Wind Tunnel," *FWST*, Nov. 14, 1957; FWPL, CF, Jack Moseley, "Bell Bares Plans For Atom 'Copter,'" *FWP*, June 17, 1959.

Page 104
- *The same year that Bell opened its factory...* "Dedication Day Brings Praise to Carter Field," *FWM*, May 1953; FWPL, CF, "'Mandate' for Adequate Carter Service Asked," *FWST*, Jan. 23, 1957.
- *Briefly it looked as if Fort Worth had pulled...* "Dedication Day"; "Greater Fort Worth Airport To Open Officially Saturday," *FWST*, April 19, 1953.
- *In many respects, the grand opening...* FWPL, CF, Bob Sellers, "New Airport's Wings Won't Spread for Year," *FWP*, April 11, 1957; "Mandate Asked."

Page 105
- *The next year the Star-Telegram took a shot...* FWPL, CF, "Future is Bright for Carter Field," *FWST* , July 7, 1957.
- *Giving the airport another boost... Ibid.*
- *Civilian uses for helicopters... (caption)* FWPL, CF, Frank X. Tolbert, "Fort Worth Out Front In Building Heliports," *DMN*, Sept. 12, 1954.
- *At a speech delivered at Carter Field...* FWPL, CF, Bill Hitch, "Rayburn Dedicates Airlines College," *FWST*, Nov. 21, 1957; FWPL, CF, "Stewardess Class of 51 Graduated," *FWST*, Dec. 11, 1957.

Page 106
- *The breathtaking pace of suburban growth...* See "Roads and Freeways" in CF, FWPL.

Page 107
- *On the turnpike's opening day...* FWPL, CF, "Business Good On Toll Road," *FWST*, Aug. 27, 1957 (first quotation); FWPL, CF, "Load of Pigs on Toll Road Gives Officials First Big Headache," *FWST*, Aug. 27, 1957 (second quotation).
- *The experience that changed the face of Fort Worth...* For a probing sociological study of this phenomenon as it relates to one Fort Worth community, see Scott Cummings, *Left behind in Rosedale: Race Relations and the Collapse of Community Institutions* (Boulder, Col.: Westview Press, 1998).
- *To African Americans, it seemed as if...* FWPL, CF, John Ohendalski, "Keep Pools Open, Says Spurlock," *FWP*, May 11, 1956 (first quotation); FWPL, CFs, Ann Jones, "Large Share of Money Going to Negro Schools, *FWST*, Sept. 6, 1956 (second quotation); FWPL, CF, "Says Board Ruling is Violation," *FWST*, Aug. 9, 1956 (third quotation).
- *For the time being, however, it was a hollow threat...* For the most detailed work regarding this affair, see Robyn Duff Ladino, *Desegregating Texas schools : Eisenhower, Shivers, and the crisis at Mansfield High* (Austin: University of Texas Press, 1996).

Page 108
- *Other manifestations of white resistance...* FWPL, CF, "Negro Rental Project Stirs League Again," *FWST*, Nov. 7, 1950.
- *Things turned even uglier...* FWPL, CF, Dave Brown, "'Hanging' Provokes Rifle Shot," *FWST*, Sept. 3, 1956; FWPL, CF, "Riverside Woman Says Property to Lose Value After Negroes' Entry," *FWST*, Sept. 3, 1956.
- *There was another side of white Fort Worth...* FWPL, CF, "Group Named On Human Relations," *FWST*, May 20, 1950; FWPL, CF, "Negro Living, Working Conditions Improved by Efforts of Urban League," *FWST*, Sept. 9, 1955; FWPL, CF, Urban League Seeks to Help Negro Solve Living Problems," *FWST*, July 2, 1956; FWPL, CF, "Large Share of Money Going to Negro Schools," *FWST*, Sept. 6, 1956.

Page 109
- *Fort Worthians marked progress in other ways...* FWPL, CF, "City Play Areas Won't Remove All Color Bars," *FWP*, Nov. 11, 1955 (first quotation); FWPL, CF, "Negroes, Whites Play Ball Game," *FWST*, Aug. 13, 1955 (second and third quotations).
- *One visitor to the Fort Worth Public Library...* FWPL, CF, B. T. Gallant, "Trojan Horse?" *FWST*, May 1, 1958.
- *Given the Cold War rhetoric of the day...* Hitch, "Rayburn Dedicates College."
- *Then, there was the problem of Jacksboro Highway...* Arnold, 23.

Page 110
- *Little more than a month later... Ibid.*, 26-7.
- *It would be the first of several...* FWPL, CF, Carl Freund, "'Party Girls,' Gambling Bring in FBI and State Undercover Men," *FWP*, Dec. 6, 1953.

Page 111
- *In the world of college football, TCU also enjoyed...* "Frog Heaven," *FWST*, June 27, 1999, supplement, "The Century in Sports."
- *It was a happier ending for Ben Hogan...* FWPL, CF, Grace Halsell, "400 Attend Reception Honoring Ben Hogans," *FWST*, April 24, 1951.
- *His story soon attracted Hollywood...* FWPL, CF, Jack Gordon, "Valerie Hogan Admits Tears at Screening of Follow the Sun," March 12, 1951; FWPL, CF, Jack Gordon, "Hogan Plays to Biggest Gallery," *FWP*, March 24, 1951.

Chapter 7

Page 112
- *Materially, Fort Worth gave up on a number...* Fort Worth Convention and Visitors Bureau, *Fort Worth in the 1960s: A Dramatic Decade of Change*, n.d.; FWPL, CF, "Coming Down," *FWST*, Aug. 11, 1960.
- *With the passing of so many landmarks...* FWPL, CF, Bob Trimble, "Death of a Giant...What Killed Armour's in Fort Worth?" *FWP*, March 14, 1962.

Page 113
- *Structural changes in the petroleum industry...* FWPL, CF, "Walkout Hits Bell; 1700 Stay Off Jobs," *FWP*, June 9, 1960.

- *Despite the dire outlook, Fort Worth businessmen*… FWPL CF, Al Altwegg, *DMN*, "Texas Economy at Mid-Year: Fort Worth Adapts," Aug. 12, 1962.
- *The power vacuum left by Amon*… FWPL, CF, Jim Vachule, "Citizens Take Step for Progress," *FWST*, June 28, 1963.
- *Two thousand men and women*… *Ibid.*
- *Like the old North Side Coliseum*… "…From the Nation's Best," *FWM*, Nov. 1968, 34.

Page 114
- *The fourteen-block site*… FWPL, CF, *FWST*, Roger Summers, "Convention Center Site Has Promise of Riches-Salvage," Feb. 5, 1966.
- *On the eve of the demolition*… FWPL, CF, Ed Johnson, "Tumbling Walls To Start Center," *FWST*, June 29, 1965.
- *Then, there was the old Majestic Theater*… FWPL, CF, *FWP*, Jack Gordon, "Famous Stage Door Sheds a Majestic Tear," Sept. 1, 1966.
- *Four years later the Tarrant County Convention Center*… FWPL, CF, "Dream Big, Connally Urges City," *FWST*, May 18, 1965; "It Happened Like This," *FWM*, May 1965.

Page 115
- *After a weeklong siege of hard spring rain*… "Sunshine Bolsters Hope For All-America City Celebration," *FWST*, May 17, 1965.
- *Among dozens of floats was a model*… FWPL, CF, "All-America Parade Kicked Off in Fast Style," *FWST*, May 18, 1965.
- *As in times recently past*… "Dream Big."
- *Even before the governor took the dais*… FWPL, CF, "Youth, 9, Shows Courage, Poise; Gets Ringside Seat," *FWST*, May 18, 1965.

Page 116
- *At the Children's Museum*… FWPL, CF, Mabel Gouldy, "Center Added By Gift," *FWST*, Dec. 15, 1963.

Page 117
- *Beyond the Arts District, other museums*… FWPL, CF, "Link to Past Opens Tommorrow," *FWST*, June 10, 1966; FWPL, CF, "Udall Visits, Likes Our Heritage Hall," *FWST*, June 13, 1966.
- *More enduring was the Pate Museum*… FWPL, CF, Nancy Kemplin, "Love of transportation seed for museum," *FWP*, July 13, 1969 (quotation); FWPL, CF, "Astronaut's Widow Opens Museum of Transportation," *FWST*, Aug. 3, 1969.
- *So she did in July 1969*… Kemplin.

Page 118
- *Across University Drive*… FWPL, CF, "Exhibit Result Of Vision By Texas-Spirited Group," *FWST*, April 10, 1966.
- *Yet, as piles of weathered and rotted logs*… Terry G. Jordan, *Log Cabin Village: A History and Guide* (Austin: Texas State Historical Association, 1980), viii.
- *Along with the two-story Harold Foster cabin*… Docia Schultz Williams, *Phantoms of the Plains: Tales of West Texas Ghosts* (Plano: Republic of Texas Press, 1996), 119-21.
- *If the ghost of the Log Cabin Village*… FWPL, CF, Jim Marrs, "Police, Residents Observe But Can't Identify 'Monster,'" *FWST*, July 11, 1969.
- *The only shooting, however, came from the camera*… *Ibid.*

Page 119
- *"Earlier there were some sheriffs deputies there"*… *Ibid.*
- *Such frivolity stood in stark contrast*… Dwight Cumming, "JFK's Last Meal," *FWM*, Nov. 1975, 16.
- *As the president waded through well-wishers*… *Ibid.*
- *The next morning the president flipped*… Dwight Cumming, "JFK's Last Meal," *Ibid.*, Nov. 1975, 17-18, 34-5.

Page 120
- *In matters of race, the mixed bag*… FWPL, CF, John Moulder, "Backlash? Not Much Seen Here," *FWP*, Sept. 10, 1964.
- *Yet, in the Panther City and elsewhere*… FWPL, CF, Delbert Willis, "Quiet, Behind-the-Scenes Revolution: FW Integration…A Progress Report," *FWP*, June 23, 1963.
- *Indeed, whether in church groups*… FWPL, CF, Jean Wysatta, "Journey to Understanding," *FWP*, June 28, 1964; Willis, "FW Integration."
- *Arguably, the zenith of the movement*… FWPL, Jerry Flemmons, "Bomb Threat Comes But Police Prepared," *FWST*, March 15, 1965; FWPL, CF, "Civil Rights Marchers Stage Orderly Protest," *FWST*, March 15, 1965 (quotation).
- *Nowhere, of course, had segregation*… FWPL, CF, Caroline Hamilton, "Stair-Step Integration Expected to Be Orderly," *FWP*, Feb. 10, 1963; FWPL, CF, Sandi Major, "Dr. Busby Defends Integration Policy," *FWP*, Sept. 6, 1966.
- *Already most suburban schools*… FWPL, CF, "Birdville Approves Mixing," *FWST*, Feb. 5, 1965; FWPL, CF, Pat Reed, "Nine Years Later, Mansfield Integration Quiet, Uneventful," *FWP*, Aug. 26, 1965 (quotation).
- *In the Hispanic community, men and women*… "Minority in Quest of Leader," *FWST*, July 26, 1970, G2.
- *The "crux of the problem"*… *Ibid.*

Page 121
- *Blatant racism in Fort Worth did not disappear*… FWPL, CF, John Tackett, Defendant Gets Life In Slaying of Negro," *FWST*, May 21, 1966.
- *Far from the massive protests*… "State Responds; Mail Floods Marines," *FWST*, April 7, 1966, A1.
- *The stories of local heroes also boosted the cause*… FWPL, CF, "FW Hero of Battle With Cong Ship Given Medal," *FWP*, Oct. 14, 1966.
- *Just as Amon Carter had sent* Star-Telegram *reporters*… FWPL, CF, "S-T Staffer to Cover Viet Nam," *FWST*, Dec. 12, 1965; FWPL, CF, "S-T's Man in Viet Brings Back Praise for Soldiers," *FWST*, April 13, 1966.

Page 122
- *During his four-month tour*… FWPL, CF, "Sergeant Recalls Air Base Disaster," *FWST*, Jan. 10, 1966.
- *So tough had the Fort Worth native been*… FWPL, CF, Bob Schieffer, "Point Proven By Sergeant," *FWST*, March 30, 1966.
- *The war, of course, unfolded alongside happier times*… FWPL, CF, Elston Brooks, "Rare Hands Given 'Rare Breed' Star," *FWST*, Feb. 3, 1966.

Page 123
- *As first announced by the Star-Telegram in 1957*… FWPL, CF, "Sports Center Planned," *FWST*, Nov. 9, 1957; *FWM*, Aug. 1961, 10.

Page 124
- *The park-minus the giant retail center*… "'Six Flags' Opens With A Bang!" *FWM*, Aug. 1961, 10, 58.
- *Befitting the theme of the six flags*… FWPL, CF, "Jerry Flemmons, "Six Flags Still a Winner," *FSWT*, Aug. 4, 1968.
- *Each season brought new attractions*… FWPL, CF, "Excitement Sparks Confederacy Section," *FWST*, Aug. 4, 1961.

Page 125
- *Six Flags immediately became the most popular*… FWPL, CF, Frank Friauf, "Six Flags Brings Business Boom," *FWST*, March 3, 1963.
- *There was no question that Wynne's park*… FWPL, CF, "Six Flags Turnstiles To Stop at 1,264,000," *FWST*, Nov. 25, 1962; FWPL, CF, Jim W. Jones, "Six Flags Tops Alamo as Lure," *FWST*, Nov. 19, 1964.
- *Seeking a complement to Six Flags*… FWPL, CF, Walter Robinson, "Bi-County Stadium Off the Drawing Board," *DMN*, Aug. 21, 1960.
- *In the end Houston got the dome*… FWPL, CF, Bill Van Fleet, "Stadium To Open At 6 P.M.," *FWST*, April 23, 1965.

Chapter 8

Page 126
- *In 1971 all of North Texas at last celebrated*… *FWST*, "New Heroes Due at Turnpike," Sept. 22, 1971, C1 (quotation); Roy Hall, "Big League Baseball…Ranger Style," *FWM*, April 1972, 1313-16.

Page 127
- *After the disastrous debut, Ted Williams called it quits*… *FWM*, Nov. 1973, 12.
- *Other issues and episodes with roots*… FWPL, CF, Martha Hand, "Carswell POWs Home in Texas," *FWST*, n.d.

Page 128
- *Sally Rand, from an even earlier era*… TCHC, CF, *FWP*, Jack Gordon, "The naked truth about Sally Rand," n.d.
- *Backstage, columnist Jack Gordon passed on the remark*… *Ibid.*
- *Nothing, however, marked the passing of time*… Fred Blalock, "Boiling Flames Gut Old Armour Plant," *FWST*, May 12, 1971, A1.

Page 129
- *Another, more salacious, drama unfolded*… Gary Cartwright, *Blood Will Tell: The Murder Trials of T. Cullen Davis* (New York: Harcourt, Brace, Jovanovich, 1979); Skip Hollandsworth, "Blood Will Sell," *Texas Monthly*, March 2000, 117-21, 130-3 (quotation, 118).
- *According to Priscilla, Cullen waited*… Hollandsworth.
- *Enter Houston trial attorney Richard "Racehorse" Haynes*… *Ibid.*
- *Nine months later T. Cullen Davis was back*… *Ibid.*
- *The realization that together Fort Worth and Dallas*… Jerry Richmond, "FW/D and the SMSA, or, A Tale of Two Supercities," *FWM*, Feb. 1970, 21-4; The North Texas Commission, "NTC History," http://www.ntc-dfw.org/ntchistory.html

Page 130
- *Joining forces formally was an idea*… "Fort Worth-Dallas Regional Airport: An Open Door to Opportunity," *FWM*, May 1970, 24-6; Richmond, "FW/D."
- *Just after midnight on January 13, 1974, the first*… *Ibid.*, cover, February 18-19, 1974.

Page 131
- *The windfall that brought American Airlines to Fort Worth*… Edward Hanley, "American to announce move to D/FW," *FWST*, Nov. 15, 1978, A1.

Page 132
- *Over in Hurst, boys like Buddy Hamm*… Hugh Winston Hamm, Jr., Fort Worth, conversation with author, March 15, 2004.
- *The same scene repeated itself at Ridgmar Mall*… "Ridgmar opened 1 year ago," *FWST*, Oct. 19, 1977, 2g; Steven Tillman, "Shopping Centers; Name for Convenience," *FWM*, Nov. 1971, 7-9, 40-1.
- *In the city itself, specifically at Amon Carter Square*… FWPL, CF, *FWP*, John Ohendalski, "Kimbell Art Museum on Carter Square Given 'Go,'" Nov. 9, 1964.
- *The building itself was designed*… FWPL, CF, *FWP*, John Ohendalski, "Kimbell to Be Friendly Home, Says Kahn," May 4, 1969.
- *Kimbell's gift capped*… *Dallas Herald*, April 14, 1964.

Page 133
- *If Cowtown seemed an unlikely seat*… Nancy Maples Madsen, "The Theatre Smorgasbord," *FWM*, July 1978, 35-43.
- *They also enjoyed ballet and the symphony*… *Ibid.*, Rose Tulecke, n.t., Feb. 1974.
- *Yet Fort Worth would not be Cowtown*… FWPL, CF, [n.a., partial title] "…you can find people," *FWST*, Aug. 15, 1978, B1.

Page 134
- *When WBAP 820 acquired a clear channel*… "Fort Worth's Western Culture," *FWM*, Nov. 1971, 34-6, 45.
- *At the same time, a new "progressive" country sound*… *Ibid.*, Larry Fitzgerald, "Panther Hall," Nov. 1975, 29-31.
- *As the Baby Boom generation began to reach maturity*… "Mayfest Scheduled on Banks of Trinity," *FWST*, Apr. 8, 1973, H1.
- *Mayfest, as the event came to be called*… "Mayfest Scheduled on Banks of Trinity," *FWST*, Apr. 8, 1973, H1; Gloria Record, "Festival on the Trinity," *FWM*, April 1975, 15.
- *A product of that first festival*… Barbara Geddie, "Mayfest '79," *FWM*, April 1979.

Page 135
- *Even before Mayfest became such a hit*… Nancy Maples Madsen, "Oktoberfest," *FWM*, Oct. 1978, 17-19.

- *Fort Worth was coming of age…* *Ibid.*, "Jubilee!", Feb. 1971, 13-15; FWPL, CF, Raymond Teague, "Engine 610 to pull Bicentennial Freedom Train," *FWST*, Feb. 17, 1975; FWPL, CF, Dave Tipton, "Freedom Train led to FW berth by 610," *FWST*, Feb. 26, 1976.
- *When the Fourth of July rolled around…* "Fort Worth Firsts," 8.
- *Unexpectedly, a fierce but brief thunderstorm…* "Fort Worth's party dampened by rains," *FWST*, July 5, 1976, A1.

Page 136
- *Also enjoying larger-than-expected crowds…* Nancy Maples Madsen, "The Most Outstanding Arena in America," *FWM*, March 1975, 49.
- *Performance magazine, the insiders' rag for the rock world…* *Ibid.*
- *For officials and staff, some who had worked…* *Ibid.*

Page 137
- *Other than The Keg, a popular restaurant…* TCHC, CF, Paul Goldenberger, no title, *FWST*, Jan. 5, 1975 (first quotation); TCHC, CF, *FWST*, Randy Nordhem, "Ceremony opens Water Garden," Oct. 20, 1974 (second quotation).
- *The mind's eye of movie director Michael Anderson…* FWPL, CF, Elston Brooks, "FW's Water Garden land role in MGM film" *FWST*, May 16, 1975; FWPL, CF, Elston Brooks, "Water Garden 'destroyed' for film's final scene," *FWST*, May 22, 1975.
- *Downtown was beginning to come alive…* Janice Williams, "Downtown's Big Building Boom," *FWM*, Aug. 1971, 15-17; *FWST* archives, *FWST*, "Glass-Sheathing Job One For Mechanical Octopus," Apr. 21, 1974 (quotation).
- On hand to help open the giant padlock… FWPL, CF, "Gala Opening Will Start Off Business Day," *FWST*, Apr. 21, 1974; FWPL, CF, "Bank Also Home For New Gallery," *FWST*, Apr. 21, 1974.

Page 139
- *Equally impressive was the construction…* "City Center," *FWM*, Nov. 1971, 10-11.
- *By the 1970s, Charles D. Tandy had parlayed…* *Ibid.*, Jerry Richmond, "Tandy: Baby Booties to Super Sales," Nov. 1971, 22-4.
- *Just when it looked as if he might begin…* "Charles Tandy dies at 60," *FWST*, Nov. 5, 1978, A1.
- *At mid-afternoon a maid…* *Ibid.*
- *Led by far-sighted developers…* "Downtown vs. Shopping Centers," *FWM*, Nov. 1972.

Chapter 9

Page 140
- *In the waning days of 1979…* Janice Wiliams, "'Blast' marks hotel groundbreaking," *FWST*, Aug. 9, 1979, 1, 2C.
- *At the other end of downtown, facing the Convention Center…* Mary Sumner, "The New Fort Worth," *FWM*, June 1983, 13-24, 82.

Page 141
- *In the wee hours of Sunday morning…* Thomas Koresec, "Downtown FW explosion packs force of earthquake," *FWST*, Dec. 8, 1986, 1A; Korosec, "Worthington's loss estimated at $1 million," *FWST*, Dec. 8, 1986, 7A.
- *Miraculously, the explosion claimed no lives…* Earnest L. Perry, "UT professor cut by flying glass," *FWST*, Dec. 8, 1986, 8A.
- *A deep roar, followed by a numbing concussion…* Koresec, "Downtown FW explosion," 6A.

Page 142
- *Before the decade began…* FWPL, CF, "Sundance Sensation," *FWST*, June 2, 2000.
- *The Bass Brothers Development Corporation wasted no time…* Sumner, "New Fort Worth."
- *Sundance Square earned Sid Bass rich praise…* Joe Nick Patoski and Bill Crawford, "The Long, Strange Trip of Ed Bass," *Texas Monthly*, June 1989, 102-4, 123-7.
- *One reviewer likened the Caravan's effect…* Mike Ritchey, "Caravan: oasis of art or mirage?" *FWST* eve., Sept. 30, 1983, 1-1.
- *Dominating Sundance Square…* Sumner, "New Fort Worth."
- *Unfortunately, several downtown icons surrendered…* For a well-captioned graphic survey of current and historical architecture, see John T. Roberts, "Architecture in Downtown Fort Worth," http://www.fortwortharchitecture.com/arch.htm.

Page 143
- *Democratic Congressman Jim Wright…* (caption) Memo on Jim Wright's Accomplishments, Sept. 4, 1985, in "Accomplishments 1985," RC Box 18/5, Jim Wright Papers, Special Collections, Mary Couts Burnett Library, Texas Christian University, Fort Worth, Texas; Tom Curtis, "On the Defensive," *Texas Monthly*, July 1989, 82, 121-4.
- *Downtown property owners who wanted to cash in…* "Art for fun's sake," *FWM*, April 1989, n.p.

Page 144
- *To the rescue came Judge Mike Moncrief…* *Ibid.*, Paul Cozby, n.t., Jan. 1984, 21-23, 46.
- *As long as the seemingly Soviet-inspired Tarrant…* Rich Heiland, "What you see is…," *FWST*, June 25, 1988, 1A.
- *The problem, in the end, turned out to be as illusory as the solution…* FWPL, CF, Andrew Marton, "Fort Worth's big cover up," *FWST*, July 14, 2002.
- *So successful was his Texas-sized optical illusion…* *Ibid.*
- *Not everybody hailed trompe l'oeil, however…* *Ibid.*
- *Building a unique modern culture…* *FWM*, Sept. 1981, 74.

Page 145
- *Backers of the Cowtown Marathon…* Judy Macbain, "What Makes Cowtown Marathoners Run?" *FWM*, Feb. 1989, 25-6.
- *As the event began attracting runners…* *Ibid.*
- *As the crowd waited to hear updates…* *Ibid.*
- *All along the route…* *Ibid.*, Yale Youngblood, "Are we nearly there yet?", Feb. 1989, 29-32..
- *While most local people perceived "Cowtown" as largely symbolic…* Daryl Wagoner, "Contemporary Cowtown," *FWM*, March 1984, 10-13.

Page 146
- *Perhaps the most storied group was the Texas and Southwest…* *Ibid.*
- *Nothing, however, said Cowtown quite like Billy Bob's Texas…* *Ibid.*, Rose Tulecke, "Billy Bob's Texas," May 1981, 33-5.
- *On opening night, in April 1981…* *Ibid.*
- *Back at Billy Bob's, none of that mattered…* *Ibid.*
- *What emerged from the gutted shell…* *Ibid.*
- *Billy Bob's Texas was certainly the most prominent…* *Ibid.*, Judy Alter, "Cowboy Murrin Favors the 3R's…Rodeo, Restoration, and Rebirth," Sept. 1981, 13-16, 72-5.
- *With Amonesque enthusiasm…* *Ibid.* (quotation); Judy Alter, "Go Cattle Baron Baroque," *FWM*, Sept. 1984, 16-22.

Page 147
- *Van Cliburn also did his ambassador's duty…* *Ibid.*, Cissy Stewart, "Van Cliburn: He Makes It Easy to Sell This City He Calls Home," Aug. 1989, 19-25, 36-7; Yale Youngblood, "A Magical Night in a Magical Life," Feb. 1988, 6-8.
- *Back in Fort Worth a new sound assaulted the airwaves…* King Coffey, Hugh Beaumont Experience and Butthole Surfers, Austin, correspondence with author, Sept. 19, 20, 2005.
- *The growth of North Side's Mexican Independence…* FWPL, CF, Frank Trejo, "Hispanic fiesta to be big, colorful," *FWST*, Sept. 7, 1980.

Page 148
- *It came as no surprise then…* Janice Williams, "Tarrant S&Ls not on the list, executive says," FWST, June 13, 1981, 2B.
- Greene was speaking for the little man… Ibid.
- *Then, all at once, in January 1986, a meteoric plunge…* Julius Karash, "$22 million loss in quarter listed by banking firm," *FWST*, April 16, 1986, B1; Steve Zuckerman, "$135 million second-quarter loss largest ever for Texas American," *FWST*, July 27, 1988, Sec. 1, 1.
- *For a while it looked as if the bank would fare better…* Dan Piller, "Awaiting a rescue," *FWST*, May 3, 1986, Sec. 2, 3; Kristen Moulton, "Reaction to merger generally favorable," *FWST*, July 21, 1988, 1-10 (quotation).
- *For customers, the industry shakeup…* Jack Z. Smith, "What's in a name? Confusion for bank customers," *FWST*, Aug. 2, 1988, Sec. 1, 2; Mike Nichols, "Names you can bank on," *FWST*, Dec. 6, 1984, D1.

Page 149
- *Measured in human terms the financial catastrophe claimed…* Kirk Spitzer, "Billy Bob Barnett files for bankruptcy," *FWST*, Aug. 2, 1988, Sec. 1, 1.
- *No one, however, illustrated the fall…* Cissy Stewart, "Old Glory, New Visions," *FWM*, April, 1988, 29-33.
- *But it was radio that gave Chiles a public platform…* *Ibid.*
- *Yet all too suddenly the downward spiral…* Stephen Rassenfoss, "Eddie Chiles no longer mad as he bows out," *FWST*, May 3, 1988, Sec. 2, 1; Rassenfoss, "Western shareholders to lose most of holdings," *FWST*, May 3, 1988, Sec. 2, 1.
- *Just before the oil and thrift fiasco…* "Disaster at D/FW," *FWST*, Aug. 4, 1985, 21-8A"; "A storm blows up and Delta 191 crashes," *FWST*, Oct. 27, 1985, A14 (quotation).

Page 150
- *At 6:03, as 191's captain Edward Connors…* "Storm blows up."
- *Amid the sounds of the driving rain…* *Ibid.*
- *Of 165 passengers, only two walked away…* "Who was on Flight 191, Survivors," *FWST*, Aug. 4, 1985, 23A.
- *Although Fort Worth certainly lost its balance…* Cissy Stewart, "Robert Bass & the Friendly Hospital," *FWM*, May 1989, 21, 24-27.

Chapter 10

Page 152
- *Backing up its bold proclamation as the state's…* "It's Lockheed! Fort Worth plant wins historic fighter contract decision to secure thousands of jobs," *FWST*, Oct. 27, 2001, 1A.
- *Fort Worth no doubt would have survived…* FWPL, CF, Ron Hutcheson, "Carswell base backers making last-ditch try to save facility," *FWST*, June 23, 1991; FWPL, CF, Thomas Korosec, "Carswell marking end of era," *FWST*, June 1, 1992 (quotation).
- *All sorts of speculation…* FWPL, CF, Mike Menichini, "Tonkawa Indians trying to acquire Carswell property," *FWST*, June 6, 1994; FWPL, CF, Jennifer Packer, "New era will begin for Carswell with hand-over this week," *FWST*, Sept. 29, 1994.
- *In an earlier time the threat of losing …* Douglas Harman, "Travel and Tourism, Yesterday and Today: Challenges of Texas Heritage Tourism," paper presented at Texas State Historical Association Annual Meeting, El Paso, Texas, March 7, 2003.

Page 153
- *Certainly Harman enjoyed a head start…* *Ibid.*
- *To commemorate the city's 150th Anniversary…* "Chisholm Trail heads downtown this year," *FWST*, Jan. 29, 1999, A1.

Page 154
- *No attraction, however, could outdo…* FWPL, CF, Christopher Evans, "Area offers more family-friendly enterprise," *FWST*, Sept. 18, 1992.
- *During the first month of 1992…* FWPL, CF, Stefani Gammage, "Starting today, Tarantula gives public local motion," *FWST*, Jan. 18, 1992.
- *Four years later the Tarantula Train…* FWPL, CF, Darrin Scheid, "Iron Horse Steams into Grapevine," *FWST*, Aug. 30, 1996.

Page 155
- *The same kind of personal commitment to the city's welfare…* Andrew Martin, "The wait is over: A new dawn," *FWST*, Oct. 14, 2001, D2 (first quotation); "Modern Magic," *DMN*, C1, Dec. 8, 2002.
- *Joining the arts district in 2002…* "Wild West Women Saddle up to enjoy tributes, style and history at the National Cowgirl Museum and Hall of Fame," *FWST*, June 2, 2002, 1C.

- *Despite all the attention focused on Amon Carter Square...* Joe Nick Patoski, "Wowtown!" *Texas Monthly*, April 1988, 122.
- *Unlike most other kindred venues... Ibid.*, 125.
- *Always near the top of the Bass's priority lists... Ibid.*, 122.

Page 156
- *For a "city center that had been left for dead... Ibid.*
- *Among the other notable triumphs of reinventing downtown...* FWPL, CF, Chris Vaughn, "A Barrier Tumbles," *FWST*, Aug. 17, 2001.
- *The occasion brought together key city leaders...* FWPL, CF, Paul Bourgeois, "A Festive Send-Off: Fort Worth marks end of overhead freeway," *FWST*, Aug. 18, 2001.
- *West Lancaster, I-CARE proponents crowed... Ibid.*
- *The great hall that had seemed so modern...* Jack Z. Smith and Neil Strassman, "Fort Worth buys convention center," *FWST*, Oct. 29, 1997, A1.

Page 157
- *Passing ownership from the county to the city...* FWPL, CF, Anna M. Tinsley, "Revamped center opens," *FWST*, April 9, 2002; FWPL, CF, Anna M. Tinsley, "Star Attraction," *FWST*, March 31, 2002 (quotation).
- *All of the positive changes...* FWPL, CF, "Newspaper to take part in town hall meeting," *FWST*, Feb. 22, 1994.
- *Cowtown was among thirty finalist cities...* FWPL, CF, Jeri Clausing, "Fort Worth named All-America City," *FWST*, May 23, 1993.
- *The next year Mayor Kay Granger headed a committee...* FWPL, CF, Roland S. Martin, "Fort Worth Open House begins today," *FWST*, June 24, 1994.
- *It was a new concept in transportation... Ibid.*

Page 158
- *The project far exceeded the expectations...* D'Ann Mabray Shippy, "Gamble on Alliance area pays off," *FWST*, Dec. 12, 1999, A1.
- *Perot and his Hillwood Development Corporation... Ibid.*
- *Other successes could be tracked by the announcements...* FWPL, CF, Stefani Gammage, "Currency plant opens to dollar days, praise," *FWST*, April 27, 1991; FWPL, CF, Barbara Powell, "$3 million grant awarded for Alliance," *FWST*, April 14, 1995; FWPL, CF, Steve Brown, "Hub of Activity: Alliance development draws range of industries," *FWST*, July 29, 1995; FWPL, CF, Bill W. Hornaday, "Shipping News: Alliance Airport's prodigious rate of growth puts it among 25 biggest cargo depots in U.S., reports say," *FWST*, Sept. 9, 2000.
- *With over one hundred and fifty thousand seats...* "Blue sky, green flag More than 100,000 at speedway's debut," *FWST*, April 6, 1997, 1A; "Speedway making its mark as economic engine," *FWST*, March 21, 1999, 1A; "Club shifts into gear in high style," *FWST*, March 31, 1999, B8.
- *At one point, according to the Texas Workforce Commission...* Shippy, "Gamble on Alliance"; Monica S. Skaggs, "Keller's atmosphere attracting more residents," *FWST*, June 2, 1996, AA21.

Page 159
- *What happened to the Fechtel Farm...* FWPL, CF, Leslie Hueholt, "A harvest of memories: Southlake farm yielding to Town Square," *FWST*, April 6, 1997.
- *The farm that son Charles described... Ibid.* (first quotation); FWPL, CF, Kathryn Hopper, "Raising the bar: Developer's dream realized as Southlake's new-fangled, old-fashioned downtown debuts," *FWST*, n.d.
- *Areas that had developed in earlier decades...* FWPL, CF, Lila LaHood, "A New Look," *FWST*, July 21, 2000; FWPL, CF, Lila LaHood," Mall of Fame," *FWST*, Oct. 1, 1999 (quotation).
- *In its plans to help the Simon Property Group...* FWPL, CF, Melissa Williams, "Hurst can force owners to sell houses near mall," *FWST*, Aug. 26, 1995.
- *Fort Worth itself annexed vast tracks of land...* Valerie Fields, "Annexation dragon breathes fire into Fort Worth growth," *FWST*, June 8, 1991, A1 (quotation); FWPL, CF, Ginger D. Richardson, "Annexation opponents rally," *FWST*, June 28, 2002; FWPL, CF, Ginger D. Richardson, "City looking at big annexation," *FWST*, Feb. 20, 2002.

Page 160
- *Tarrant County itself added two hundred thousand people...* FWPL, CF, Mike Lee, "Tarrant 3rd-fastest in growth in Texas," *FWST*, Sept. 15, 1999.
- *Fort Worth's African-American community...* FWPL, CF, Jerome Weeks, "Downtown Jubilee," *DMN*, Nov. 9, 1992; FWPL, CF, Steven Vonder Haar, "Fort Worth persistence finally bags the big one," *FWST*, June 16, 1992; FWPL, CF, Ruth M. Bond, "A Cry from the heart, an answer in art," *FWST*, April 6, 1995; FWPL, CF, Veronica Puente, "Black history archives expected to move to library," *FWST*, June 15, 1996.
- *Earlier, in 1993, the black community invited members...* FWPL, CF, Christopher Evans, "a Juneteenth for everyone: This year, all are invited to celebrate the emancipation of African-Americans," *FWST*, June 15, 1993.
- *While many did, the overwhelmingly black crowds...* FWPL, CF, Valerie Fields, "Black history boycotts: African-American speakers plan to avoid 'belittling' programs," *FWST*, Feb. 17, 1992.

Page 161
- *Star-Telegram columnist Bob Ray Sanders... Ibid.*
- *While racial tension in Fort Worth certainly remained...* FWPL, CF, John Yearwood, "African-American summit draws more than 300 in FW," *FWST*, May 31, 1992.
- *The Hispanic community...* FWPL, CF, Bechetta Jackson, "The changing face of Tarrant County," *FWST*, March 14, 2001; FWPL, CF, Rosanna Ruiz, "Going Tejano: Proprietors hope to breathe new life into former bar across from Billy Bob's in the Stockyards," *FWST*, Feb. 26, 1997 (quotation).
- *A more ambitious project, the Mercado de Fort Worth...* FWPL, CF, Rosanna Ruiz, "North Main Mercado approved," *FWST*, Jan. 3, 1997.

Page 162
- *Certainly, by the turn of the new century...* FWPL, CF, Victor Inzunza, "A moveable fiesta," *FWST*, May 26, 1991 (quotation); FWPL, CF, Matt Brunworth, "Diez y seis," *FWST*, July 15, 1991.
- *Still, it was Cinco de Mayo that drew the most...* FWPL, CF, Indira A. R. Lakshmanan, "Hispanic leaders cite conflict between Cinco de Mayo, Mayfest," *FWST*, April 23, 1993.
- *In 1995, however, the fifth of May would be remembered...* Tim Marshall, "The Fort Worth, Texas, Hailstorm," Storm Track, www.stormtrack.org/library/1995/hail.htm.
- *The hailstorm passed quickly... Ibid.*
- *Five years later Fort Worth ran out of luck again...* Mike Cochran, *Shattered: The Tarrant Tornadoes* (Fort Worth: *Fort Worth Star-Telegram*, 2000), 5, 7.
- *Downtown, the rush-hour traffic was ebbing... Ibid.*, 19
- *The storm became a killer... Ibid.*, 25, 30.

Page 163
- *Between the arts district and downtown... Ibid.*, 33, 36, 42, 46 (quotation).
- *Crossing the Trinity River into the heart... Ibid.*, 71, 75, 79 (quotation), 83.
- *After sweeping through downtown Fort Worth...* FWPL, CF, Kristin Sullivan, "Four tornado-damaged houses bulldozed," *FWST*, June 28, 2000.
- *Although five people lost their lives...* Cochran, *Shattered*, 61, 107.
- *The most visible and long-lasting reminder...* Dan Malone, "Bank One Fallout: On the trail of the $80 million insurance settlement," *Fort Worth Weekly*, May 30-June 5, 2002, 6-7; Laurie Fox, "FW deal may restore tower," *DMN*, 19A.
- *Almost three years after the storm...* See Roberts, "Architecture in Downtown Fort Worth."

Page 164
- *Every decade during the last century...* FWPL, CF, Jack Z. Smith, "The Locomotion," *FWST*, June 2002; Jack Z. Smith, "How now, Cowtown?" *FWST*, May 25, 2003, E1.
- *At the top of the city's wish list...* Ginger D. Richardson, "Plan calls for bustling waterfront," *FWST*, Oct. 30, 2002, B1; "Grand Visions," *FWST*, June 12, 2005, 21A.
- *In twenty years, insiders say that downtown...* Scott Farwell, "N. Texas poised for growth spurt," *DMN*, April 25, 2003; Sandra Baker, "Building from Square one," *FWST*, June 3, 2002, Tarrant Business (supplement), 3.
- *In Tarrant and fifteen other counties...* "Big play gets bigger Federal agency boosts estimate of Barnett Shale gas reserves to 26.2 trillion cubic feet," *FWST*, March 25, 2004, 1C; "Barnett Shale output jumps," *FWST*, Feb. 22, 2005, 1C; "Lots of work in Barnett play, With prices hovering near record highs, the natural gas in the Barnett Shale field is providing jobs for many people," *FWST*, June 27, 2005, C1.
- *Standing on the threshold of the new millennium...* Lee, "Tarrant 3rd-fastest in growth."

INDEX

#

150 Years of Fort Worth Museum, 142
2222 Club, 90

A

Adams, Mrs. Ira, 95
Add-Ran Male and Female College, 44
Adelphi Theater, 18
African-American Summit on Peace, Justice, and Equality, 161
Akopova, Lilian, 155
Aldrich, Ki, 80
Allen Chapel A.M.E., 47
Allred, James, 76
Alston, James W., 130
Alter, Joel, 145
Ambrose, George Ann, 105
American Airlines, 56, 81, 85, 104-06, 131, 142-143, 158
American Airlines Stewardess College, 105, 109-110
American Can Company, 102
American Freedom Train Foundation, 135
Americana Hotel, 140
Amon Carter Field, 105
Amon Carter Foundation, 137
Amon Carter Museum of Western Art, 10, 42, 116-117, 145
Amon Carter Square, 117, 132, 140, 155
Anderson, Michael, 137
Anderson, Neil P., 54, 60
Ando, Tadao, 155
Annie Richardson Bass Building, 134
Arlington, 10-12, 29, 101-103, 123-126, 132, 149, 163-164
Arlington Downs, 79, 102, 125
Arlington Heights, 40, 47-48, 50, 60, 101, 116
Arlington Independent School District, 102
Arlington Savings, 148
Armour and Company, 26, 30-31, 48, 61-62, 113, 128-129
Armour, Phillip D., 26
Army Air Force Training Command, 85
Arnold, Ripley A., 13-14, 48, 94, 164
Arnst, Amy, 133
Atchison, Topeka, and Santa Fe Railroad, 24, 27
Atz, Jake, 127
Austin, Bill, 102-103
Austin, Lloyd G., 108
Aviation Building, 142
Azle, 101

B

Baird, Ninnie L., 43
Baker, Jonathan Hamilton, 15
Ballpark in Arlington, The, 152
Bank One, 148, 162
Bank One Tower, 163
Baptist Standard, 45
Barnett, Billy Bob, 146, 149
Barron Field (Taliaferro Field 3), 49-50, 53
Barrow, Clyde, 72
Bass Brothers Development Corporation, 142
Bass Brothers Enterprises, 141
Bass, Beverly, 129
Bass, Ed, 141-142
Bass, Lee, 141
Bass, Nancy, 141
Bass, Perry, 134, 141
Bass, Robert, 141, 151
Bass, Sid, 140-142, 155
Batch, Chris, 163
Battle of Village Creek, 12
Baugh, Sammy, 80, 83, 111
Bean, Alan, 125
Bedford, 131
Bedwell, Robert, 122
Bell Aircraft Corporation, 103
Bell Helicopter Corporation, 103-105, 113, 121, 129, 143
Bell, Lawrence D., 103
Bell, N. T., 45
Benbrook, 101
Benbrook Field (Taliaferro Field 2/Carruthers Field), 49-50
Benbrook Village, 90
Benton, Vanecka, 133
Bewley Mills, 60
Bewley, Anthony, 16
Bewley, Murray P., 39
Big Train Crash, The, 33, 36
Bijou Theater, 44
Billy Bob's Texas, 145-146, 149, 151, 153, 161
Bird, Jonathan, 12
Bird's Fort, 12
Birdville, 15, 16, 31, 57
Blackburn, David, 125
Blackstone Hotel, 59-60, 72, 112, 118, 156, 180
Block 82 Tower, 163
Bloodworth, L. P., 67
Blue Bonnet Packing Company, 71
Bodine, C. C., 103
Boecker, Bill, 144
Bogard, Ward, 144
Bolen, Bob, 151
Bomar, D. T., 40
Bonham, 11
Bowen Bus Station, 88
Bowie, 54
Bowie Theater, 50
Boyce, A. G., 47
Brabham, T. W., 75
Bragan, Bobby, 65
Bragg, George, 114
Braniff Airlines, 104
Brant, Harry C., 85
Breckenridge, 52
Bronstad, Betty, 137
Brooker, Bob, 36
Brooklyn Heights, 31
Brown Derby, 146
Brown, Jim, 98
Brown, Richard F., 133
Brown, Wilbur, 57
Buck, Raymond, 117
Buckholtz, Charley, 40
Buffalo Bill Wild West Show, 26, 76
Burkburnett, 52
Burlington, Northern, Santa Fe Railway, 158
Burnett Park, 54, 69, 127, 147
Burnett Plaza, 138, 143
Burnett, Anne, 84
Burnett, Burk, 31, 33
Burns, Henry, 18
Burrus Mill and Elevator Company, 60
Busby, Eldon, 120
Busby, T. O., 109
Bush, George W., 149, 163
Butcher Workmen's Union, 61
Buttermilk Switch, 19
Butthole Surfers, 147

C

C. W. Connery Drug Store, 35
Cabell, Earle, 124
Caddo, The, 11-12, 14, 102
Calder, Alexander, 139
Calloway, Hiram, 16
Calvary Cathedral, 163
Camfield, Bill (Icky Twerp), 122
Camp Bowie, 18, 49-50, 52, 57, 60
Camp Cooper, 15
Campbell, Mrs. H. H., 22
Campbell, Tom, 38
Capitol Theater, 57
Caravan of Dreams, 141-142
Carlson, D. W., 75
Carnegie Library, 21, 29, 31, 34, 38, 81
Carr, O. E., 66
Carswell Air Force Base, 85-86, 91-92, 115, 119, 127, 152
Carswell Redevelopment Authority, 152
Carswell, Horace S., Jr., 85-86
Carswell, Virginia, 86
Carter, Amon Giles, Sr., 10, 17, 54-56, 64, 72, 74, 76, 78, 80, 82-85, 88-89, 93, 94, 100-101, 104, 113, 116, 121, 131, 139, 142, 180, 209
Carter, Amon Giles, Jr., 89-90
Carter+Burgess Plaza, 142
Carver, William, 23
Casa del Sol, 128
Casa Mañana, 76-77, 95, 99-100, 115, 133, 137
Casey, Albert, 143
Casey, Albert V., 131
Cash America International, Inc., 163
Casino Ballroom, 90
Cassidy, Butch, 22, 23, 26, 140
Castle, Irene, 49, 80
Castle, Vernon, 49-50, 80
Castleberry High School, 163
Cattleman, The, 146
Cattleman's Steakhouse, 146
Cecil, Lorene, 135
Central Fire Hall, 26
Central High School, 63
Charles D. Tandy Center, 139-140
Cherokee, The, 11
Chickasha, The, 33
Chiles, Eddie, 149, 158
Chipps, D. E., 67
Chisholm Trail, 17
Chisholm Trail Roundup, 153
Choctaw, The, 11
Circle-T Ranch, 158
City Center Towers, 142
City Federation of Women's Clubs of Fort Worth, 35-36
City of Hurst, 159
Civil War, 14, 19, 95
Civilian Conservation Corps, 70
Clark, Addison, 44
Clark, Alan D., 91
Clark, Randolph, 44
Clarksville, 12
Cleburne, 43
Cliburn, Van, 98, 146-147, 155
Clinton, Bill, 163
Clyde, David, 127
Cockrell, Dura Louis, 56
Cockrell, E. R., 57
Coconut Grove Pub, 90
Cody, Buffalo Bill, 26, 33
Coffey, King, 147
Cogdell, James, 29
Cohen, Judith, 144
Colonial Country Club, 92, 118
Color Tile, 139
Comanche, The, 11-12, 14, 16, 18
Community Theater, 133
Company F, Second Dragoons, 13, 94
Compton, Orra, 120
Concho Wagon Yard, 57
Connally, Joe, 115
Connors, Edward, 150
Consolidated-Vultee Aircraft Corporation (Convair), 56, 85, 87, 91, 103-104, 113, 152
Continental National Bank, 60, 97, 149, 156
Cook, Frederick A., 59
Cook-Fort Worth Children's Medical Center, 151
Cooper, Bob, 83, 84
Cooper, Gary, 82, 83, 112
Cooper, Levi, 83
Cooper, Oscar, 83
Cotten, Fred, 118
Cotton Belt Depot, 8, 9, 154
Courtright, Timothy "Longhair Jim", 19-20, 38, 95
Courtyard Hotel by Marriott, 156
Cowart, Robert E., 18
Cowtown Marathon, 145
Cresson, 117
Cromer, H. R., 27
Crook, Sebastian C., 48
Cross Timbers Energy, 156
Crow, Albert, 80

D

D/FW Airport, 25, 143
Dacus, Melvin, 99
Daggett, Charles Biggers, 16
Daggett, E. B., 18
Dallas, 9, 12, 16,-18, 25, 28-29, 41-44, 50, 56, 59, 62, 65, 67, 74, 76-77, 88, 101, 103-104, 109, 115, 119, 123-126, 129-131, 136, 142, 151-153, 156, 157
Dallas Black Hawks, 136
Dallas Cowboys, 137
Dallas Independent School District, 141
Dallas Morning News, 109, 113, 119
Dallas/Fort Worth Airport, 130-131
Dallas-Fort Worth Spurs, 125
Dallas-Fort Worth Turnpike, 106-107
Dalworthington Gardens, 90
Darnell, N. H., 18
Davis, Bill, 45, 154
Davis, Clifford, 107
Davis, John B., 84
Davis, Priscilla, 129
Davis, T. Cullen, 129
DDD Stock Farm, 123
De Zavala School, 97
Dean, Earnest, 131
Decatur, 29
Delaney, Marvin, 161
Delaware, The, 11
Delta Airlines, 104
Delta Airlines Flight 191, 149-150
Denton, 43, 99, 114, 129
Denton, John B., 12
Desdemona, 52
Deutscher Verein, 32
Diamond Hill, 31, 87
Dodger, 159
Douglas Thornton, Douglas, 163
Downtown Fort Worth Association, 117
Downtown Fort Worth, Inc., 143
Dreamland Dance Hall, 60
Drug Enforcement Administration, 158
Duarte, G. L., 120
Dugan, Gregg, 141
Dysart, R. E., 92

E

Eagle Mountain Yacht Club, 90
Eagles Nest Resort, 105
Edwards, Cass II, 101
Egypt Theater, 44
Eighth Air Force, 86
Eighth Military Department, 13
Eighty-fourth Canadian Training Squadron, Royal Flying Corps, 49-50

Eisenhower, Dwight D., 108
El Sol de Texas, 120
Electra, 52
Elks Hall, 26, 59
Elliott, "Skeets", 53
Ely, Skip, 162
Emma's Café, 103
English, Roy, 144
Estes, Nolan, 141
Euless, 11-12, 116, 131
Evans, W. T., 71
Everman, 53, 90

F

Fair Building, 69
Fairmount Addition, 20
Fairmount Land Company, 44
Farley, James, 78
Farmers and Mechanics Bank, 60
Farr, Stan, 129
Farrar, Simon B., 13
Farrington Field, 79, 94
Farrington, Ervin Stanley, 79
Feathertail, 14
Fechtel, Alicia, 159
Fechtel, Charles, 159
Fechtel, Hazel, 159
Fechtel, Joseph, 159
Federal Building, 27, 31, 38
Ferguson, Miriam Amanda Wall "Ma", 66
Fields, Valerie, 159
Fiesta! Fort Worth, 161-162
Finley, Bob, 80
Fire Station No. 1, 142
First Baptist Church, 45, 67, 100
First Christian Church, 16
First National Bank, 30, 38, 60, 74, 75, 149
First RepublicBank, 149
First United Tower, 142
Flatiron Building, 21, 30, 31, 38
Flemmings, G. D., 107
Flower Parade and Festival, 33
Flying X Ranch Boys, 93
Forest Hill, 90
Forest Park, 36, 41, 57
Forest Park Civic League, 108
Forest Park Zoo, 97, 118
Fort Belknap, 15
Fort Donelson, 16
Fort Graham, 14
Fort Griffin, 17, 18
Fort Inglish, 11
Fort Phantom Hill, 15
Fort Richardson, 17
Fort Sam Houston, 50
Fort Worth, 9-12, 14-20, 22-35, 36, 38-45, 48,-50, 52-54, 56-88, 90-98, 100-101, 103-105, 107-110, 112-115, 117, 119-133, 135-137, 139-140, 142-150, 152-153, 155-164
Fort Worth & Denver City Railroad, 23, 40
Fort Worth Aerial Transportation Company, 52
Fort Worth Alliance Airport, 151-153, 157-158
Fort Worth Art Center, 117
Fort Worth Art Museum, 97, 119, 133
Fort Worth Board of Trade, 38, 46, 59
Fort Worth Board of Trade Building, 21, 24, 38
Fort Worth Botanical Gardens, 78, 79, 95
Fort Worth Cats, 18, 32, 33, 64, 95, 127, 159
Fort Worth Chamber of Commerce, 49, 68, 70, 76, 84, 103, 117, 139, 157
Fort Worth Children's Museum, 97, 116, 133
Fort Worth Club, 35, 54-55, 59, 60, 76, 86, 111, 113, 142, 147
Fort Worth Coliseum, 30, 32, 40, 42, 46
Fort Worth Colored High School, 66
Fort Worth Daily Gazette, 19-20
Fort Worth Democrat, 17
Fort Worth Fair, 33-34, 36
Fort Worth Federal Center, 143
Fort Worth Grain and Cotton Exchange, 69
Fort Worth Heavyweights, 33
Fort Worth Herd, 153
Fort Worth High School, 37
Fort Worth Hispanic Chamber of Commerce, 147
Fort Worth Independent School District, 79, 94, 120
Fort Worth Industrial & Mechanical College, 48
Fort Worth Livestock Exchange, 32
Fort Worth Men's Advertising Club, 43
Fort Worth Mexican American Chamber of Commerce, 128
Fort Worth Museum of Modern Art, 154, 155
Fort Worth Museum of Science & History, 11, 117, 133, 212
Fort Worth National Bank, 16, 60, 137, 148-149, 163
Fort Worth Opera House, 22, 23
Fort Worth Press, 61, 66, 71, 90, 99, 113, 120-121
Fort Worth Public Library, 109, 148
Fort Worth Public Market, 69
Fort Worth Record, 27, 29, 34, 36, 40, 43, 46, 48, 50, 52
Fort Worth Register, 36
Fort Worth Sokol, 48
Fort Worth Star-Telegram, 10, 17, 31, 33, 37-38, 54-56, 58, 60, 67, 68, 74-75, 81-82, 85-86, 88, 90, 94, 100-101, 103, 114, 121-123, 126-127, 134, 137, 146, 161
Fort Worth Star-Telegram Building, 58, 86
Fort Worth Stock Yards Company, 30
Fort Worth Stockyards, 8-9, 16, 30, 32, 53, 75, 84-85, 90-91, 93, 129, 140, 143-146, 149, 151, 153-154, 161-162
Fort Worth Strangers, 127
Fort Worth Traction Company, 42
Fort Worth Transit Company, 81
Fort Worth University, 25, 30, 32-33, 36, 44
Fort Worth Urban League, 108, 109
Fort Worth Visitors & Conventions Bureau, 152
Fort Worth Wings, 136
Fort Worth Zoo, 63
Fort Worth/Tarrant County Convention Center, 156-157
Foster, Harold, 118
Foulois, Benjamin D., 50
Four-Sixes Ranch, 31
Fox, Will, 52
Frank Kent Cadillac, 8
Fraternal Bank & Trust Company, 32, 33, 74
Freedom Train, 88, 134-135
Freeman, William G., 15
Frenchman's Well, 93-94
Frontier Centennial, 75-79, 81, 95, 99, 104, 128
Furey, Joe, 59

G

Galaxy Aerospace, 158
Garcia, Joe T., 100
Garden of Eden, 31-32
Garros, Roland, 40
Gavrel, Bubba, 129
Gayety Theater, 44
Gaylord Texan Resort & Convention Center, 160
Gem Theater, 44
General Dynamics Corporation, 113, 115, 121, 143
General Motors, 102, 129
Gibson, F. P., 36
Giordano, John, 155
Glen Garden Country Club, 41, 92
Glenwood, 31, 45
"Golden Goddess," The, 52-53
Gorbachev, Mikhail, 147
Gorbachev, Raisa, 147
Gordon, Jack, 99, 114, 128
Gossman, Jenelle, 159
Gould, Harry, 63
Gould, Jay, 19
Graham, 146
Granbury, 44
Grand Prairie, 124
Granger, Kay, 157
Grapevine, 8-9, 12, 154
Grapevine Convention and Visitors Bureau, 154
Grapevine Mills, 159
Grapevine Vintage Railroad, 9, 154, 156
Great Air Robbery, The, 53
Great Depression, 68, 70, 73-74, 77, 79, 80-81, 87, 114, 156
Great Southwest Corporation, 102, 116, 129
Great Southwest Strike of 1886, 19
Greater Fort Worth International Airport, 104-105, 143
Greater Southwest Airport, 130-131
Greeley, Horace, 37
Green Oaks Inn, 116
Green, H. R., 32
Greene, Richard, 148
Greenwall's Opera House, 29, 57
Greer Island, 118
Gribble, Lewis, 114
Gruen Plan, 96-97, 113, 132
Gruen, Victor, 96
Guinn, Edward, 128

H

Haas, Richard, 144
Hale, I. B., 80
Haltom City, 90, 101
Haltom Theater, 85
Hames, Bill, 98-99
Hamm, Buddy, 132
Handley, 43, 71, 108
Harman, Douglas, 152-153, 156
Harney, W. S., 13
Harris, Jack, 118-119
Harris, Nelson, 110
Harrison, Hastings, 81
Hawks, Frank, 180
Hayne, Alfred S., 21
Haynes, Jerry (Mr. Peppermint), 123
Haynes, Richard "Racehorse", 129
Hell's Half Acre, 8, 19-20, 23, 24, 36, 38, 44, 45, 51, 68, 90, 114
Hellman, Stewart, 109
Henry, Ed R., 43
Heritage Hall, 117-118
Heritage Park, 135
Hermann Park, 32
Herzog, Whitey, 127
Hicks Field (Taliaferro Field 1), 49-50
Hicks, Maryellen, 161
Higgins, J. M., 81
Hight, Grady, 121
Hildreth, V. O., 8
Hill, Sam, 161
Hillard, Charlie, 148
Hillbilly Flour Company, 73
Hillwood Development Corporation, 158
Hip Pocket Theater, 133
Hippodrome Theater, 44, 57, 209
Historical Preservation Council of Tarrant County, 143
Hite, Morris, 130
Hogan, Ben, 92-93, 111
Hogan, Valerie, 93
Holland, Nancy, 133
Hollywood Theater, 112
Honea, Bert, 41
Hood, John Bell, 14
Hopkins, Henry, 133
Horwitz, I. E., 81
Hotel Texas, 54, 70, 74, 75, 82, 93, 114, 119, 140-141
Houston, 55, 76, 125, 127, 149
Houston, Sam, 11-12
Howard, Frank, 127
Howard, M. D., 71-72
Howard, M. T., 71-72
Hudak, Paul, 122
Hudson, A. J., 118
Hudson, Edward, Jr., 133
Hugh Beaumont Experience, 147
Hume, Michael, 133
Hurst, 96, 103-104, 131-132
Hurst Lake, 32
Hurstview Addition, 104
Hyatt Regency/Fort Worth, 140, 141

I

I. M. Terrell High School, 107, 120, 128
I-30 Citizen Advocates for Responsible Expansion, 156
Ickes, Harold, 78
Iglesia de San Jose, 47
Indian Territory, 12, 16, 30
Ingram Flats, 45, 46
Inheritors, The, 82-83
InterFirst, 149
International and Great Northern Railroad, 31
Ireland, John, 19
Irving, 124
Irwin, Joe, 115, 117
Isis Theater, 44

J

Jacksboro, 15
Jacksboro Highway, 90, 109, 112
Jett Building, 144
Jim Hotel, 83, 84, 112
Johnson Station, 13, 16
Johnson, Danny Zapata, 161
Johnson, Kate, 137
Johnson, Lyndon B., 73, 100
Johnson, Middleton Tate, 13
Johnson, Ruth Carter, 119
Johnston, Albert Sidney, 14
Jones, Albert S., 101
Jones, Jesse, 78
Jonsson, Erik, 130
Jordan, Betty, 137
Jubilee Theater, 160, 161
Junior League of Fort Worth, 143
Justin Boot Company, 60
Justin, John, 124

K

K. M. Van Zandt Land Company, 16
Kahn, Louis, 132
Keg, The, 137
Keith, Ben E., 49-50, 76, 86
Keller, 71, 158
Kelly, George, 72
Kemble, Watt, Jr., 128
Kennedale, 90
Kennedy, John F., 119, 163
Kent, Frank, 8
KFJZ, 67, 84, 122, 147
KFQB, 67
Kickapoo, The, 12
Kid Curry, 23
Killits, John M., 59
Kilpatrick, Ben, 23
Kimbell Art Museum, 132-133, 155
Kimbell Foundation, 132
Kimbell, Kay, 119, 132
Kimbell, Velma, 119
King, John, 41
King, Marion, 137
Kiowa, The, 16, 18
Knight, Oliver, 14, 18, 94
Knights of Labor, 19
Kraft, Clarence "Big Boy", 64, 126
Kress Building, 117
KTVT, 113, 115, 122
Ku Klux Klan, 65-67, 81
Kudlaty, B. M., 90
KXAS-TV, 162
KXOL, 145

L

LaGrave Field, 65, 79, 94-95, 159
LaGrave, Paul, 127
Lake Arlington, 102
Lake Arlington Golf Course, 11
Lake Benbrook, 95
Lake Bridgeport, 69, 95
Lake Como, 32, 34, 48
Lake Eagle Mountain, 69, 95, 105
Lake Erie, 32, 43, 57
Lake Grapevine, 95, 109, 159-160
Lake Worth, 41, 50, 55, 57, 62-63, 70, 85-86, 95, 110, 119, 162
Lake Worth Monster, 118-119
Lake Worth Village, 90
Lamar, Maribeau B., 11-12
Land Title Building, 139
Landmark Bank, 149
Lane, Rodney, 99
Larimer, Wilbur, 41
Lawson, Mehl, 11
League of United Latin American Citizens of Tarrant County, 161-162
Lee, Opal, 160
Lee, Robert E., 14
Lena Pope Home, 71
Leonard Brothers Department Store, 62, 75, 87, 139
Leonard, Marvin, 62, 75, 111
Leonard, Obie, 62, 75
Lewis Garage, 37
Liberty Theater, 98
Lightfoot, R. P., 33
Livestock Exchange Building, 30, 84, 153
Lockhart, 16
Lockheed Martin, 152
Locklear, Ormer, 53
Log Cabin Village, 118
Logan, Harvey, 23
Logan's Run, 137
Lone Star Chili Parlor, 146
Long Branch Saloon, 133
Longbaugh, Harry, 22-23
Love Field, 104-105
Lowe, Jim, 22-23
Lower Calhoun, 48
Lucas, Wingate, 100-101
Lusk, John P., 95
Lyric Theater, 29, 57

M

Mack, Bill, 134
MacLean, Christina, 8
Maclin, Tom, 61
Maclin, Tracey, 61
Maddox Flats, 23
Madsen, Nancy, 136
Main Street Art Festival, 155
Main Street Arts Festival, 143
Majestic Theater, 29, 38, 44-45, 112, 114
Mallick Tower, 113
Malone, Gene, 121
Malone, John, 61
Mansfield, 29, 107-108, 120
Mansfield High School, 108
Marcel, Jesse A., 92
Margowski, William, 81
Marine, 30
Marine Park, 147
Marion, Anne Windfohr, 139
Marrow Bone Springs, 12-13
Martin, M. C., 80
Martin, Nathan, 72
Masonic Home, 79
Matador Land & Cattle Company, 22
Matador Ranch, 22
May, Ernest, 81
May, W. D., 71-72
Mayberry, William, 150
Mayer, Roland G., 56
Mayfest, 134-135
MBank, 149
McCann, Tom, 118
McDonald, William Madison, 32-32, 74, 83, 100
McElyea, R. G., 110
McGoodwin, "Little Sid", 121
McLain, Denny, 127
McLean, Jefferson, 36
McLeod, Hugh, 12
McMahan, Howard, 128
Meacham Field, 56, 104, 131
Medical Arts Building, 54, 69, 138, 142
Menasco Manufacturing Company, 102
Méndez, Anthony, 48
Mercado de Fort Worth, 161
Metropolitan Black Chamber of Commerce, 128
Metropolitan Hotel, 41, 47, 112
Mézières, Athanase de, 11
Military Road Act, 12
Miller, Edward, 119
Miller, H. C., 102
Mills, Frank, 93
Mills, Gray, 122
Milner, Hal, 140
Mineral Wells, 43, 80
Moncrief, Mike, 144
Monnig, William, 74, 76, 78
Morton, Charles G., 50
Moslah Shrine Temple, 209
Mount Gilead Baptist Church, 47
Mr. Peppermint Show, 122
Mt. Gilead Baptist Church, 48
Murrin, Steve, 144, 146
Myers, J. J., 16
Mystic Knights of Bovinia, 25-26

N

Nancy Lee and Perry R. Bass Performance Hall, 155
National Breeders and Feeders Show, 30
National Cowgirl Museum and Hall of Fame, 11, 155
National Cutting Horse Association, 146
National Livestock Association, 25, 30
National Municipal League, 114
Naugle, Dave, 84
Naval Air Station Fort Worth Joint Reserve Base, 152
Ned, Jim, 14
New Liberty Theater, 71
Niles, Louville V., 30
Nisbet, Fairfax, 77
Nolan, Philip, 11
Norfleet, Frank, 59
Norris, J. Frank, 45-46, 67, 100
North Fort Worth, 30, 37
North Fort Worth State Bank, 88
North Mistletoe Heights, 108
North Side Coliseum, 110, 113
North Texas Commission, 130
North Texas Traction Company, 42
North, Phil R., 140
Northeast Mall, 131, 132, 159
Northern Texas Traction Company, 25, 144
Northside Coliseum, 111
Nowlin, Clark, 139

O

O'Brien, Davey, 79, 80, 111
O'Daniel, Wilbert Lee "Pappy", 73
Oakhurst, 81
Oakwood Cemetery, 22
Ohendalski, John, 99
Olson, Douglas, 113
Onassis, Jackie Kennedy, 119
Oswald, Lee Harvey, 119-120, 163
Oswald, R. L., 120

P

Pace, J. C., 130
Paddock Viaduct, 26
Paddock, B. B., 17, 19-20, 36, 37
Palace Theater, 57, 63, 112, 122
Palo Pinto, 14-15
Panic of 1873, 17-18
Panic of 1893, 21-22
Pantego, 90
Panther Hall, 115, 134
Paradise, 72
Parker, Bonnie, 72
Parker, Donna, 157
Parmer, Hugh, 139
Paschal, R. L., 63
Pate Museum of Transportation, 29, 117
Pate, A. M., Sr., 117
Pate, Marie, 117
Patoski, Joe Nick, 155, 156
Pawnee Bill, 33
Peak, Carroll M., 8, 15
Peak, Florence, 8
Pearson, Drew, 88
Pearson, Russell H., 52
Pelton, Fred, 72
Perkins, Clay, 14
Perot, H. Ross, Jr., 151, 158
Pershing, John J., 52
Petroleum Building, 58, 156
Petroleum Club, 53, 142, 147
Phillips, James Young (Philip Atlee), 82
Pickens, Slim, 117
Pickin' Parlor, 146
Pier 1 Place, 164
Pier 1 Imports, 139
Pier, W. L., 72
Pigg, Willie, 120
Pillsbury, Edmund, 133
Pinkerton Detective Agency, 19, 23
Pioneer Palace, 77, 99
Place, Etta, 23
Polytechnic College, 25, 75
Polytechnic Heights, 32
Pool, Roger, 133
Pottawatomie, The, 33
Prairie Chapel, 32
Presley, Elvis, 110-111, 137
Price, Rudy, 149-150
Princess Theater, 44
Prohibition, 75-76
Public Works Administration, 76, 78-79
Pulliam, W. A., 71
Purina Mills, 48

Q

Quality Hill, 31-32
Queen Tut, 63-64, 97, 98, 112

O

Radcliffe & Sons, 44
RadioShack, 13, 139, 164
Radisson Plaza Hotel, 140
Ramey, Roger, 86
Rand, Sally, 77, 99, 128
Randle, Eve, 88
Ranger, 52
Rayburn, Sam, 105, 109-110
Reata Restaurant, 163
Reconstruction Finance Corporation, 78
Record, Jim, 88
Red River Campaign, 18
Regester, Betty, 118
Reid Auto Company, 37
Renfro Drug Company, 29
Renteria, Rudy, 147
Republic of Texas, 11-12
Reynolds, George, 31
Rialto Theater, 44
Rice, Grantland, 80
Richardson, Sid, 142
Richland Hills, 97, 101-102
Richland Plaza, 132
Ridglea Country Club, 139
Ridgmar Mall, 132, 159
Ripley Arnold Housing Center, 13
River Crest Country Club, 40, 209
River Oaks, 90, 149, 163
Riverside, 108
Rogers, Virginia "Ginger", 80
Rogers, Will, 180
Roosevelt, Elliott, 76
Roosevelt, Franklin Delano, 75-76, 78, 84
Roosevelt, Theodore, 26, 33-35, 38, 40
Rose, Billy, 76-77, 99-100, 112
Rosen Heights, 31
Rosen, Sam, 34
Rouse, Fred, 61
Rusk, Thomas, 12
Russell, Allen, 125
Rutherford, High, 71
Rutherford, Shorty, 71

S

Saginaw, 73, 90
Samuels, B. B., 73
San Antonio, 13, 50, 76, 99, 153, 160, 162
Sanchez, Tony, 161
Sanders, Bob Ray, 148, 161
Sansom Park, 90
Saunders, Bacon, 30
Sayers, Joseph D., 26
Schieffer, Bob, 121-122
Schmid, Mickey, 118
Schwarz, David, 159
Scoreboard Lounge, 91
Scott, Thomas, 17
Second Ward School, 22
Security State Bank, 149
Seminary South Mall, 132
Sendera Ranch, 160
Seventh Bombardment Wing, U.S. Air Force, 86, 152
Shady Oak Farm, 55
Shakespeare in the Park, 133
Shawnee, The, 11
Shenandoah, 56
Sheraton Fort Worth, 141
Shivers, Allen, 108
Short, Luke, 20, 38
Sid Richardson Foundation, 144
Simon Property Group, 159
Simons, Johnny, 119
Simpson, Greenlief W., 30
Sinclair Building, 69
Six Flags Over Texas, 122-125, 129
Skyliner Ballroom, 112
Skywayman, The, 53
Slack, Tom, 94
Slam Bang Theater, 122
Slaughter, Kirk, 157
Slaughter, Mrs. John B., 26
Smith, C. R., 85, 105
Smith, John Peter, 15, 19, 22, 24
Smith, Mrs. Tennessee, 48
Sneed, Beal, 47
Snowden, J. H., 99
Sojourner Truth Players, 133
Somerville, Alfred, 22
Somerville, Harold, 22
Somerville, Mary, 22

Somerville, William Fife, 22
Southern Air Transport, 56, 142
Southern Christian Leadership Conference, 120
Southern Methodist University, 80
Southlake, 159
Southlake Town Square, 159
Southwestern Baptist Theological Seminary, 44
Southwestern Exposition, Fat Stock Show and Rodeo, 30, 33, 40, 42, 57, 63, 74-75, 78, 84, 85, 92, 114, 135-136, 145-146, 212
Springer, John H., 25, 26
St. Andrew's Episcopal Church, 47
St. Joseph's Hospital, 119
St. Patrick's Catholic Church, 21, 30, 38
Standard Theater, 44
Stebbins, Brian, 159
Steele's Tavern, 15
Stevens, O. D., 71, 72
Stevenson, Coke, 86
Stevenson, Ruth Carter, 116
Stockyards Hotel, 72, 146
Stockyards National Bank, 72
Stockyards Station, 154
Stone & Webster, Inc., 42
Stovall, Sharkey, 128, 132
Strategic Air Command, 91
Stripling, W. K., 127
Striplings Department Store, 87
Sturdivant, Jack, 71
Summers, Roger, 114
Sundance Kid, 22-23, 26, 140
Sundance Square, 8-9, 142, 144, 152, 159-160
Sundance West, 153
Sunday, Billy, 46, 48
Super Frog, 134
Swartz View Company, 23
Swift & Company, 26, 30-31, 48, 61-62, 113, 128
Swink, Jim, 111
Symphony League of Fort Worth, 135
Szafranski, Richard, 152

T

Tandy Computers, 139
Tandy, Anne, 139
Tandy, Charles D., 139, 142
Tandycrafts, 139
Tarantula Map, 19
Tarantula Train, 9, 154
Tarrant County Black Historical and Genealogical Society, 160
Tarrant County Civil Courts Building, 144
Tarrant County Community College, 116
Tarrant County Convention Center, 114-115, 136
Tarrant County Courthouse, 13, 23-24, 38, 140, 143
Tarrant County Historical Society, 95
Tarrant Field Airdrome, 85
Tarrant, Edward H., 12, 14, 102
Tate, William D., 154
Taylor, Dorothy, 116
Taylor, Jennifer, 133
Taylor, Spencer, 146
Team Bank Tower, 163
Terrell, Edward S., 95
Terrell, I. M., 36, 66
Terrell, John L., 36
Texan Immigration & Land Company, 12
Texana, 98
Texas & Pacific Railroad, 17-19, 24-25, 30, 37, 57, 60, 65, 71-72, 134-135, 156, 180
Texas & Pacific Railroad Building, 85, 157
Texas Air Transport, 56, 131
Texas Airways, 131
Texas American Bancshares, 148-149
Texas American Bank-Fort Worth, 148
Texas and Southwestern Cattle Raisers Association, 146
Texas Boys Choir, 114
Texas Brewing Company, 22
Texas Cattle Raisers' Association, 37
Texas Christian University, 27, 44-46, 54-55, 77, 79-80, 83, 85, 101-111, 121-122, 129, 134-135
Texas College of Osteopathic Medicine, 145, 152
Texas Cowboy Hall of Fame, 153
Texas Electric Service Company, 96, 115
Texas Grain Dealers Association, 60
Texas Lodge of the Knights of Pythias, 29
Texas Midland Railroad, 32
Texas Motor Car Association, 57
Texas Motor Speedway, 152, 158
Texas National Bank, 73-74
Texas Playboys, 73
Texas Progressive Youth Cup, 107
Texas Rangers, 127, 149
Texas Refinery Corporation, 117
Texas Spring Palace, 20-22
Texas Wesleyan College, 75
Texas Wesleyan University, 25, 57, 152
Texas Women's College, 57, 75
The Western Company of North America, 149
Theater Comique, 19
Theo's Saddle and Sirloin, 146
Thirty-sixth Division (Panther division), 18, 50-51
Thomas, J. B., 96
Thorp Spring, 44
Tiny T&P, 98, 99
TLC Realty Advisors, 163
Tolbert, Frank X., 98
Tonkawa, The, 11, 102
Trans American Life Insurance, 142
Travis Avenue Baptist Church, 32
Travis, Will, 57
Triangle Park, 41
Trimble Tech High School, 32
Trinity Park, 41, 61, 79
Trinity Railway Express, 25, 156, 164
Trinity River Festival, 134
Trinity State Bank, 60
Turney, W. W., 37
Turnpike Stadium, 123, 125
Twenty-first Amendment, 75
Two Tandy Tower, 140

U

U.S. Army Air Corps, 52
Udall, Stewart, 117
Union Bank and Trust Company, 60
Union Gospel Mission, 69, 71
Union Station, 24, 33
Universal Mills, 60
University of Texas at Arlington, 121
Usher, Caroline, 8

V

Van Cliburn International Piano Competition, 155
Van Zandt, Khleber M., 16, 80, 137
Vandergriff, Hooker, 102
Vandergriff, Tom, 102-103, 124-125, 164
Vendome Theater, 29
Vial, Pierre, 11
Vietnam War, 112, 121, 127

W

W. T. Waggoner Building, 54, 59-60, 156
Waco, 33, 44
Waggoner, Tom, 33
Waggoner, W. T. "Pappy", 31-32, 55-56, 74, 142, 180
Walker Sanitarium, 37
Walkup, Jimmy, 64
Wallace, Dorothy, 103
Wallace, John Hughes, 121
Walsh Ranch, 160
Ward, Louis B., 73
Washington Heights, 31
Water Gardens, 126, 133, 136-137, 156
Watering Trough, 133
WBAP, 58, 80, 93-94, 113, 115, 134
Weatherford, 15, 100, 118
Weems, Ted, 97
Werst, Harry, 130
Westbrook Hotel, 40-41, 48, 52-53, 59, 65, 75, 112, 137
Western Company, 158
Western Hills High School, 135
Western Trail, 18
Westerner, The, 82
Westlake, 158
Westworth Village, 90
WFAA, 122
Wheat Building, 24, 30, 38, 54
White City, 31, 32, 34
White Elephant Saloon, 20, 38, 146
White Settlement, 85, 88, 90
Whiteman, Paul, 77, 83, 100
Wichita, The, 11, 12
Wiggins, Jack, 63
Wilborn, Andrea, 129
Wild Bunch, 22, 23, 73
Will Rogers Coliseum, Auditorium, and Memorial Tower, 78, 82, 83, 85, 92, 97, 113, 115, 117
Will Rogers Memorial Center, 78, 79
Williams, Ted, 127
Williamson, Hugh, 90, 91
Willis, Delbert, 120
Wills, Bob, 73
Wilson, Bobby, 80
Wilson, Frank, 104
Windmill Dinner Theater, 133
Women's Federation Clubs of Fort Worth, 26
Wood & Wood Carriage Repository, 28
Wood, George T., 14
Woodbine Corporation, 142
Woodruff, Margaret, 95
Woody, Sam, 15
World War I, 18, 144
World War II, 9, 29, 56, 60, 85, 96, 104, 119, 121, 145
Worth Hotel, 137
Worth Theater, 112
Worth, William Jenkins, 13, 56-57, 95
Wortham, Louis J., 49
Worthington Hotel, 140-141
Wright, Jack, 121
Wright, Jim, 101, 119, 143
Wynne, Angus G., Jr., 122, 124-125

Y

Yellow Cab Company, 63
York, John B., 16
Youngblood, Yale, 145
Yount, Barton K., 85

Z

Zapata's Tejano Club Y Sports Bar, 161
Zero's New Wave Lounge, 147
Ziegler, Sam, 27

Sharing the Heritage

Historic profiles of businesses, organizations, and families that have contributed to the development and economic base of Tarrant County

The Marketplace 180

Quality of Life 210

Building a Greater Tarrant County 238

Special Thanks to

Bistro Louise

Family 1st of Texas Federal Credit Union

Fort Worth Stockyards Business Association

Grapevine Convention & Visitors Bureau

Harris Methodist Hospitals

LandAmerica Commonwealth Title of Fort Worth, Inc.

✧

Guests at the Blackstone often luxuriated at this rooftop court on the fifteenth floor; for one forlorn guest, however, it simply provided a prominent spot from which to leap to his death.

COURTESY OF THE *FORT WORTH STAR-TELEGRAM* PHOTOGRAPH COLLECTION, SPECIAL COLLECTIONS, UNIVERSITY OF TEXAS AT ARLINGTON LIBRARIES, ARLINGTON, TEXAS, AR 406 1-31-2A.

✧

Fort Worth entertained a number of celebrities during the 1930s. Humorist Will Rogers (third from left) was a frequent visitor of his close friend, Amon Carter (right). Oilman "Pappy" Waggoner (next to Rogers) and pilot Frank Hawks (left), who made the first transcontinental glider flight in 1930, share the moment.

COURTESY OF THE *FORT WORTH STAR-TELEGRAM* PHOTOGRAPH COLLECTION, SPECIAL COLLECTIONS, UNIVERSITY OF TEXAS AT ARLINGTON LIBRARIES, ARLINGTON, TEXAS, AR 406 2-19-14.

✧

The razing of Texas & Pacific passenger station.

COURTESY OF THE *FORT WORTH STAR-TELEGRAM* PHOTOGRAPH COLLECTION, SPECIAL COLLECTIONS, UNIVERSITY OF TEXAS AT ARLINGTON LIBRARIES, ARLINGTON, TEXAS, 6-3, AR 406 6-108-1.

The Marketplace

Tarrant County's financial institutions, service industries, and retail and commercial establishments provide the economic foundation of the county

The Ashton Hotel and The Ashton Depot 206
The Bombay Company 205
Brants Realtors 207
Classic Chevrolet 186
Courtyard by Marriott 190
Crescent Real Estate Equities Company 201
EECU 182
Fort Worth Convention & Visitors Bureau 200
Hilton Hotel Fort Worth 198
Marshal Utley Carpets 192
Metro Golf Cars 204
National Farm Life Insurance Company 194
Pier 1 Imports 196
Sam Pack's Five Star Ford 202
Southside Trim & Glass 208
Texas Land and Country, LLC 203

EECU

✧

CEO/President Jerry A. Deering (left) and Chairman of the Board Lee H. Tannahill, Jr; c. 1971.

With humble beginnings of $50 in assets and ten members, EECU has grown over the past seventy years from a small credit union for a handful of teachers to a significant Fort Worth area financial institution serving thousands of local citizens.

On December 4, 1934, ten Fort Worth educators and administrators met with the Dallas Teachers Credit Union president to discuss forming a credit union for area teachers. By the end of the evening, J. F. Bateman, Clyde L. Brown, T. R. Carleton, K. W. Dunkelberg, E. E. Dyess, G. N. Fisher, Glenn M. Holden, F. F. Tarleton, C. A. Thompson, and Nat M. Wilson had all signed the charter and deposited $5 each for a share in the newly formed Fort Worth Teachers Credit Union.

Three months later, with the approval of a fifty-year charter by the banking commissioner of Texas, FWTCU opened its doors in an office in the Fort Worth Independent School District administration building, which was managed on a part time basis by members. In the charter was a carefully worded statement of purpose, which read, "To promote thrift among its member and to enable them, when in need, to obtain for productive and provident purposes moderate loans at reasonable rates of interest; to receive the savings of its members; to invest the funds accumulated..."

By the end of 1935, FWTCU had relocated to a desk on the mezzanine level of the Westbrook Hotel, which had generously donated the space. The credit union now boasted a total of 188 members, had given out seventy-five loans for a total of $8,560, and had $9,563 on deposit.

A basement classroom at John Peter Smith Elementary School became FWTCU's new home in 1949 and was later expanded with the addition of two other rooms. As membership increased, the first full time employee was hired and by 1954 there were five employees, with Jerry A. Deering heading up the team. He says "Situated in that basement classroom...our staff of five took in savings and loaned out money."

That same year FWTCU's membership count went over 2,500 and the credit union reached another milestone—assets over $1 million. The credit union began to departmentalize and services were expanded to include real estate loans, loan protection insurance, and life savings insurance.

In the 1950s credit unions were flourishing, with 759 operating in Texas, with 151 in Fort Worth alone. Across the nation 18,000 of these financial institutions represented nearly $1.5 billion in assets. The surging popularity of credit unions was due to the fact that they are cooperative financial organizations, owned and controlled by the members who use its services. Since the members, in effect, own each credit union, there are extra benefits for them, including more favorable rates on deposits and loans and better service.

"Since its early inception, EECU has been perceived as the 'Members' credit union. We are member owned, and member operated for the sole purpose of helping members reach their financial goals. That's the 'American Dream.' To have access to low-cost financial services through which people of modest means are able to become financially sufficient. In its infancy EECU epitomized the concept of people helping people. That's still our hallmark today. We have always been committed to serving this community in the past, we are positioned to serve effectively tomorrow and our long-range plans show EECU to be a prominent player in the future," says George Thompson, chairman of the FWTCU Board of Directors.

Twenty-five years after the ten founders invested $50 to get the FWTCU up and running, the credit union's assets had grown to $2.6 million for a membership numbering 4,729. In 1965, ground was broken for a new home office, an 8,500-square-foot building at 1000 Summit Street and in 1966 the credit union moved to its new facilities. That year Johnson County educators were invited to join the credit union and its name was changed to Fort Worth-Tarrant Teachers Credit Union to better reflect the full membership, which had increased to over 9,000, with assets surpassing $7 million. A surge of expansion accompanied the new spacious facilities and the next five years brought a wave of growth, as the credit union opened offices in Arlington, Hurst, and Burleson, and Parker County educators were invited to join the FWTTCU fold.

Change and growth continued, and in 1974, the board of directors adopted a new name, Educational Employees Credit Union. All educational employees in an eight county area were now offered membership, as were the employees of the Baptist Radio and Television Commission. A Weatherford branch was opened to serve the west and northwest areas, the Arlington and Hurst offices moved to larger facilities, and drive-up window services were added in Fort Worth. Over the next several years,

EECU is located at 1617 West Seventh Street in Fort Worth, Texas.

branches were opened in Stephenville and Arlington and the Weatherford, Hurst, and Burleson offices expanded their facilities.

To accommodate its rapidly expanding membership, in 1980 EECU moved into its present home office at 1617 West Seventh Street. This four-story, 37,000 square-foot building offers a six-lane drive-thru and the credit union's first safe deposit boxes. The growing list of services now included private new car sales, a direct loan service line open from 8 a.m. to 8 p.m., credit card programs, and certificates of deposit; and membership was now available for retired educators and parents of primary members, regardless of residence.

Less restrictive national guidelines opened EECU's membership to municipal employees in 1982, and by December 1984, fifty years after opening its doors; assets totaled over $75 million, with 35,167 members served. EECU's loans totaled over $49 million , and within a year's time services included Individual Retirement Accounts; money market deposit accounts; a checking account line of credit; Master Card and Visa Card program; discount brokerage services; the Buckaroo Club, a youth savings account for members age 7 to 13; and the Gold Star account for members fifty-five years of age and older. The Weatherford Public Employees Federal Credit Union merged with EECU, and by the end of the year, entire families, not just parents, were eligible for membership.

The next year access to ATM networks was made available and the board of directors approved another expansion to allow membership to include government and medical groups in a ten county area. In 1986 the Weatherford office moved to a new expanded facility and the credit union began offering home financing, in cooperation with Fort Worth Mortgage Corporation. A major milestone was reached on November 30 of that year, when assets exceeded $100 million.

In 1990, EECU merged with the Dealership Employees Credit Union and the Fort Worth Area Central Credit Union. This opened up the credit union's field of membership to auto dealer employees and organizations with 500 or fewer employees in an eight-county area. Ground was broken for a new Burleson office and the credit unions services now also included Advantage Checking; an audio response system called Service on the Spot (S.O.S.), which gave members twenty-four hour access to their accounts; and EECU was also offering a scholarship program for youths entering the education field.

Fee-free ATMs were opened a year later, and in 1994 a new Hulen office was opened and ground was broken for a larger Hurst office. The next year the Medical Professionals Federal Credit Union merged with EECU, and after serving for forty-one years as president, Jerry A. Deering retired. Former Texas Credit Union Department Commissioner, Robert W. Rogers, succeeded him.

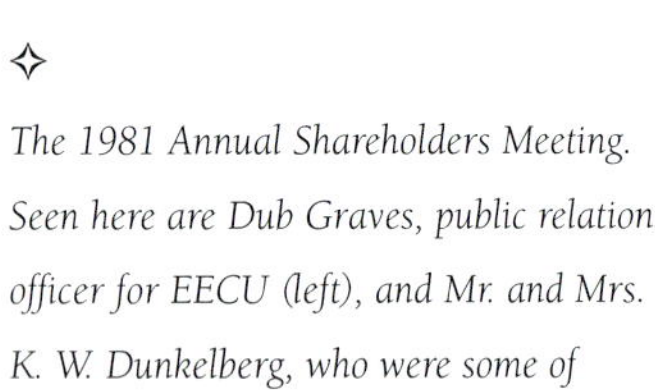

The 1981 Annual Shareholders Meeting. Seen here are Dub Graves, public relations officer for EECU (left), and Mr. and Mrs. K. W. Dunkelberg, who were some of the original founding members of the credit union.

✧

John Peter Smith Elementry.

In March 1997, EECU became a Community Chartered Credit Union, which opened up membership to almost all Burleson, Tarrant, and Parker County residents and their families. A year later, EECU entered the computer age when its web page was introduced at www.eecu.org.

EECU was challenged, when a tornado roared through Fort Worth in March 2000 heavily damaging its corporate offices. A temporary building was placed on the Seventh Street parking lot for member assistance until the building could be repaired and renovated.

In December the official name of the credit union changed from Educational Employees Credit Union to EECU, and four months later, the Montgomery Ward Credit Union merged with EECU, bringing fifteen hundred new members with it. Subsequently the Dixie Bell Credit Union and the Santa Fe Railroad Credit Union also merged with EECU, bringing a total of seven thousand more members on board.

The Grand Reopening of the Fort Worth branch was celebrated on July 29, 2002, after all the tornado damage to the building had been repaired. In October, EECU opened its first in-store branch in the Albertson's grocery store in South Arlington and its eighth traditional branch opened its doors in North Fort Worth in June 2003.

Today EECU is viewed as the community credit union, where members shop and transact their business in their neighborhoods with ease and comfort. The credit union's modern facilities are emblazoned with bold colors, attractive signage, equipped with state-of-the-art technology and staffed by cheerful employees who know the importance of serving members well. As members use our facilities, employees work to provide exciting, enjoyable experiences so that our members look forward to return visits.

EECU is here to do business and is thoroughly committed to helping this community with its financial needs.

EECU continues to grow and develop its services for an expanding member base. Its primary focus continues to be on individual members, and its "people helping their neighbors" philosophy is what has made it a vibrant and strong financial organization, that will continue to play an important role in the community for many years to come.

Classic Chevrolet

There was no grand design early in life that led Tom Durant to become one of the top four General Motors dealers in the nation, nor one of the most well-known names in thoroughbred horseracing. It was, to a far greater degree, a combination of good-natured sibling rivalry, honesty beyond reproach and a fierce competitiveness that belies Tom's laid-back personality. Some know Tom Durant as a man with a keen sense of vision, others simply know him as man who has a knack of making the right decisions at the right time and sticking with them.

Above: Tom Durant purchased the old Century Chevrolet in downtown Fort Worth on West Seventh Street in 1988 and renamed it Classic Chevrolet/Geo.

Below: Tom Durant looked to downtown Fort Worth for the original location of Classic Chevrolet/Geo.

The story of the Durants' beginnings in Tarrant County is a humble one. Shortly after the Civil War had ended, a feisty young man by the name of Durant left the State of South Carolina one step ahead of the law and headed for the Wild West. His son, Alfred, later settled in Mitchell's Bend in the lower part of Hood County on the Brazos River. There, he married and started his family, which eventually grew to nine children. The family was poor and the country was in a grave depression. While out fishing in icy waters of the Brazos, Alfred fell in and later died of pneumonia. Eight-year-old Julian, the eldest of the nine children, was called upon to provide for the family of ten, forcing an abrupt end to his formal education at only the third grade.

The hardships of rural life in the early part of the twentieth century and mounting responsibilities for this young man contributed to a lifelong work ethic for Julian. Not surprisingly, that same work ethic has been passed along for generations.

After serving in World War II, Julian married Opel Maples and they had two small sons, Tom and Jerry. The Durant's provided for them by laboring on the construction of pipeline through Louisiana, Mississippi and Missouri. They instilled a powerful resolve in their boys, holding steadfast to their primary goal of providing stability and a permanent home for the family. Opel encouraged her sons to compete with one another and actively urged them to develop their own creative and spirited individuality.

In 1951 the family moved back to Texas and settled in the agricultural town of Granbury, where Julian founded the Durant Construction Company. In an effort to make ends meet, the Durants also opened a wrecking yard behind the family home. From

that wrecking yard, Julian, a man with a third-grade education founded the Durant Automobile business.

In 1960, Julian sought to expand his automobile business. He approached the local Chevrolet dealer, Mr. Durham and proposed buying the dealership. Durham, who was recovering from a recent heart attack, was ready to sell. Julian bought the business, the building and everything in it. Two months later, officials from Chevrolet showed up. Julian introduced himself as the new owner. The gentlemen from Chevrolet disagreed. "No you're not," they told Julian, "you have not been approved by General Motors to own a franchise." Durant was not a man to be easily rebuked. In a matter of a few months, Julian was approved.

After graduating from Texas Tech in 1972, Julian's son, Tom, bought Durant Chevrolet from his father. Sixteen years later, he expanded the business when he purchased a Chevrolet dealership in downtown Fort Worth, a space formerly occupied by Century Chevrolet. Tom installed a manager to run the dealership and renamed it Classic Chevrolet.

In 1969, Tom's brother, Jerry, was also approved by Chevrolet to own his own Chevy dealership in Weatherford, becoming one of the youngest ever to be approved for a Chevrolet franchise.

The two brothers have always been competitive. "I basically got into the car business so I could outrun my brother," Tom dryly admits. According to Tom's brother, he was constantly trying to beat Jerry's numbers, "and I was trying to beat his," says Jerry.

In 1992, Tom looked to Grapevine as a new location for Classic Chevrolet/Geo. "No one was out here except Payton-Wright Ford," explains Tom. But the visionary instinct that has led to much of Tom's success told him to move the dealership to Grapevine. "Chevrolet told me I could build a 2.9-acre, 20,000-square-foot facility. Instead, I built a 45,000-square-foot facility on 11 acres." By 2004, Tom had expanded six times to 160,000 square feet and more than forty acres of real estate. "Grapevine

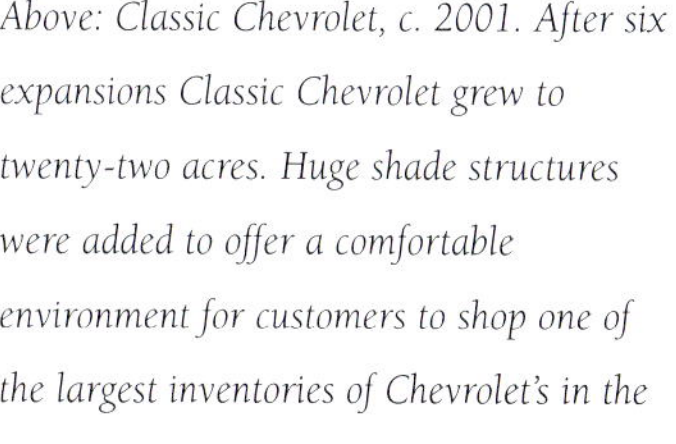

✧

Above: Classic Chevrolet, c. 2001. After six expansions Classic Chevrolet grew to twenty-two acres. Huge shade structures were added to offer a comfortable environment for customers to shop one of the largest inventories of Chevrolet's in the country. Over 1,700 vehicles are kept under 22 acres of shade.

gives us a lot of credit for opening up this side of the highway," says Tom. "It wasn't easy; it was at the end of the first Iraq war and economic times were tough."

The mayor of Grapevine could not agree more. Says Mayor William D. Tate, "Classic has created a strong presence in our community, becoming a leader not only in the sale of vehicles but also becoming a major supporter of community activities. The City of Grapevine is very fortunate to have a businessman like Tom Durant simultaneously rise to become one of the top Chevrolet dealers in the nation and still set the tone as a gracious community leader and staunch supporter of local interests, ideals and moral values. As mayor of Grapevine, I think I can speak for everyone when I say we are proud to call Tom Durant and Classic Chevrolet one of our own."

Almost immediately after moving Classic Chevrolet to Grapevine, Tom began beating his brother Jerry in sales figures. "He instantly began beating me at Classic," Jerry said. "He started faxing me his numbers daily, as he still does today." Tom beat more than his brother's sales figures. Under Tom's leadership, Classic Chevrolet has risen to be the top volume Chevrolet dealership in Dallas-Fort Worth, beating out forty-five other Chevrolet dealers in the region. With the addition of a state-of-the-art Hummer dealership in 2003, Classic is the fourth largest GM dealer in the country. Larry Hice, regional manager of Chevrolet, has nothing but praise for Tom Durant. "Tom Durant is much more than just a great car dealer. He is exactly the kind of person you would want as your next-door neighbor. He tells you exactly what he thinks with no guile or subterfuge. He is a wonderful family man and he never sacrifices his personal integrity just to 'make a deal.' If there was ever anyone that embodied the 'Golden Rule,' it is Tom Durant."

Tom's passion for the car business is equally matched by his passion for horseracing. While Jerry was heavily involved in cutting horses, Tom decided to get into the racing part of the horse business. When Jerry started competing in cutting, Tom went to a few of the competitions, "but it was just too slow for me," he says laughing. "I told Jerry that I would rather stand at the finish line to watch which horse would win than wait for a judge to tell me."

Tom's foray into horseracing began when a customer enticed him to purchase a thoroughbred mare that was bred to a quarter horse for $100,000. "The mare had a filly by her side out of Pie in the Sky. Six months later, I sold that filly for $125,000. I thought this horse business was too easy."

Tom soon discovered that the horseracing business wasn't easy, but quickly made a name for himself in the quarter horse racing society. "In '92, I had a horse named Texas Heartbeat

Classic Hummer Grand Opening ceremony, c. 2003.

that I raised from a foal in Granbury. He ran second in the All American," Durant says, "and I won $306,000 for that race. Of all the quarter horses I have ever raised or raced, Texas Heartbeat was my all time favorite. He was quite a horse."

After ten years of success on the quarter horse side, Tom was ready for a new challenge. He moved to thoroughbred racing in 1997 and currently owns Classic Racing Stables just outside of Granbury. Susan, his wife since 1978, also takes an active part in the business.

While Tom is immersed in the actual racing of his horses, Susan takes care of business on the farm, delivering and raising foals, administering medication and overseeing the day-to-day operations of the farm. Tom and Susan have four children; Hagen, Bently, Garner and Stormy. Hagen and Bently have already followed in their father's footsteps, taking active roles in the car dealerships, "and I imagine all of my kids will eventually take part in the business," predicts Tom.

Susan is a lay minister who is actively involved in the Granbury community. She has a master's degree in practical ministry and she specializes in emotional healing.

By 2004, Tom had expanded his car dealerships to include Classic Chevrolet, Classic Pre-Owned and Classic Hummer in Grapevine, Classic Lincoln Mercury Mazda Isuzu in Denton; and Durant Chevrolet, Durant Autoplex and Mike Brown Ford and Mike Brown Dodge Chrysler Jeep in Granbury.

In addition to his horseracing and car businesses, Tom has served as president of the Texas Quarter Horse Association and has been on the board since the early 1990s. From 1994-1998 he also served as president and has been on the board of the Texas Horsemen's Benevolence Protective Association, representing horsemen at all the racetracks in Texas. During those years, he helped write the original contracts for all the Class One tracks in Texas. He also is on the board of the association for the thoroughbred side.

A family man, devout Christian, car dealer and horseman, Tom finds time for all his passions in life. The key is trust. "Tom finds the time to do everything so well because he empowers his managers and his employees," explains long-time friend and employee Donna Lawlis. "He trusts us to do our jobs. It starts there. He can then go to the racing side and not worry because he has enough faith to let us do our jobs. Horseracing is his hobby as well as his business. Tom is very competitive and always wants to be Number one, whether it's in the car business or the horse business."

Durant says he intends to be number one, as both the number one Chevrolet dealer in the nation and the first Texas winner of the coveted Breeders Cup World Championship trophy. He has the elusive key ingredient—people who believe in him and will do whatever it takes to win his trust. In fact, many consider working at Classic Chevrolet the ideal job in the car business. The atmosphere at the dealership is relaxed and without a hint of pressure. The employees wear shorts from Memorial Day to Labor Day and enjoy most of the major holidays off, while competing dealerships remain open. "The customers like the atmosphere here," explains Tom, "because the employees feel at home here. People don't shop with a building or a company. They shop with other people."

Tom Durant is man who has surrounded himself with the best of the best and it shows in everything he does. Six hundred employees are empowered to do their job to the very best of their ability and everyone works toward a common goal—the winner's circle.

✧

Two generations of Durants stand in front of the dramatic Classic Hummer building, c. 2004 (from left to right): Bently, Tom, and Hagen Durant.

Courtyard by Marriott

Located on Main Street in the heart of downtown Fort Worth, The Courtyard by Marriott offers modern accommodations combined with the charming atmosphere of the 1920s art deco building it occupies. The hotel's 203 spacious guest-rooms are equipped with amenities designed for the comfort and convenience of both business and leisure guests and on-site food service; recreational facilities and business accouterments provided by the hotel are designed to make every visit rewarding.

The Courtyard occupies the historic building once known as the Blackstone Hotel. Built in 1929, the building was designed by Mauran, Russell and Crowell of St. Louis and built by Bellow and Maclay. Opening shortly before the stock market crash that preceded the Great Depression of the 1930s, the three-hundred-room hotel was billed as "Fort Worth's finest." The Blackstone, with its ornate exterior, stone carvings, elegant lobby and luxurious ballroom, hosted presidents, movie stars and other dignitaries and celebrities of the time. The building's 23 stories rise 268 feet and its unique stepped and spired cap is a prominent feature of the Fort Worth skyline.

From 1952 until 1962, the hotel was part of the Hilton chain. Hilton made extensive renovations to the interior and base of the building and constructed a five-story annex to the south. During the 1960s and 1970s, the hotel changed ownership many times and the building began to decline along with the rest of downtown Fort Worth. The hotel sat abandoned in 1982 and the grand old building remained largely ignored.

It was not until 1995 that serious efforts to reclaim the once elegant hotel began as part of the general revitalization of downtown Fort Worth. During the National Trust for Historic Preservation Conference in Fort Worth, representatives of Historic Restoration, Inc., (HRI) of New Orleans expressed an interest in renovating the building. With the support of Fort Worth's historic preservation organization (Historic Fort Worth, HFW), the project was soon under way. The city, county and hospital districts provided property tax incentives to offset some of the cost of the renovation and work on the $26-million project began in 1997. In 1999 the Blackstone reopened as the Courtyard by Marriott-Downtown Blackstone. The Courtyard by Marriott chain includes hundreds of hotels throughout the United States and in twelve other countries and is known for its appeal to business travelers.

While current guests are likely to be ordinary people rather than high-profile celebrities, the building itself retains much of the character of the 1920s. The brick and stone facade remains unchanged. The lobby was designed to reflect the art deco style of the 1920s, with marble and granite floors and special carpet created by a local designer. To enhance the deco design, portions of the hotel's facade were cast and plaster replicas of those decorations were added

Original Blackstone Hotel built in 1929.

audiovisual services may be reserved. Guests may enjoy the pool, spa and exercise room on the fifth floor or watch television on a big-screen set in the cozy lounge.

Nearby restaurants offer a variety of meal choices. Bennigan's Bar & Grill (American), Chili's (American), Riscky's BBQ, and Mi Cocina (Mexican) are open for lunch and dinner. Del Friscos Double Eagle Steakhouse is another option for dinner. The Corner Bakery Café, located in the hotel, serves breakfast, lunch and dinner.

For those interested in the fine arts, many galleries and museums are within a few blocks of the Courtyard, as is the Bass Performance Hall. The celebrated Kimbell Art Museum and Amon Carter Museum are located within driving distance as is the Fort Worth Zoo. For shopping and entertainment, Sundance Square, with two movie theaters and a variety of shops, is only a short walk away.

to lobby pillars. The setbacks on the building were redesigned as rooftop terraces and an outdoor pool built atop the annex.

The 1920s are left behind when it comes to the hotel's rooms, however. The spacious rooms feature king-size beds, comfortable sitting areas and generous work desks with no-glare lighting and ergonomic chairs. Free high-speed Internet access, two phones with data ports and voice mail, cable television, hair dryers, coffeemakers, irons and ironing boards are provided in every room. Room and valet services and in-room movies are available and the hotel furnishes complimentary newspapers and in-room coffee and tea.

The hotel provides on-site laundry facilities, a gift shop, newsstand, coffee shop and cocktail lounge. Restaurants provide a hot breakfast buffet and cooked-to-order selections. For the business traveler, fax machines, printers and copiers are available at the front desk and small meeting rooms with

For the sports enthusiast, tennis and squash courts, along with four 18-hole golf courses, are available nearby. Recreational facilities for sailing, water-skiing, jet skiing, fly-fishing and mountain biking are located within a fifteen-mile range of the hotel. The Texas Rangers baseball stadium and Six Flags over Texas in Arlington are also convenient for hotel guests.

For more than seventy years, the Blackstone Hotel building symbolized the sophistication and elegance of a bygone era. The restoration of the hotel structure and its rebirth as the Courtyard by Marriott heralded a new beginning for downtown Fort Worth. Hotel management and staff, who are dedicated to providing patrons with all the practical conveniences of the modern chain while retaining much of the grandeur of the past, enhance the success of the operation. Future success is likely to stem from this attractive combination that rewards travelers to Fort Worth with thoroughly enjoyable visits.

✧

Courtyard by Marriott is located at 601 Main Street in downtown Fort Worth.

MARSHAL UTLEY CARPETS

Marshal Utley Carpets traces its roots to 1953 when Marshal Utley and his brother, John, opened Utley Carpets in Dallas. The two ran the business, expanding to as many as four stores, before Marshall Utley decided to open his own store in Fort Worth.

The store did well in its first year, grossing more than $1 million in 1954. Marshal, a Medal of Honor recipient for his heroics in World War II, worked hard to make the business a success, expanding the first store and eventually opening two others.

He worked at Convair, now known as Lockheed, until opening his first location at 1561 Berry Street. The company incorporated in 1965, and in 1978, Marshal opened a second location in Hurst at 1313 Norwood. He moved the store to Bedford sometime after that and then to Grapevine, where it stands today.

Marshal Utley.

Marshal moved the original store to its 2209 Eighth Avenue location in 1972. The stores carried a wide range of carpeting from some of the best manufacturers in the country. In the 1970s, shag carpeting made up eighty percent of their business, a trend that eventually gave way to more natural and muted styles.

The Eighth Avenue location was praised in one industry publication as the "fanciest floor covering shops this "Cowtown"—or any other town for that matter—has ever seen." Marshal reported that the new store had been visited by retailers from as far away as Chicago and New York City, who came to view the store and borrow a few ideas for displaying carpeting at their stores.

The 60-by-70-foot store was equally divided between the showroom and the warehouse, where the company stored its inventory of 100 to 200 rolls. The showroom was reserved for displaying the more than two thousand carpet samples, and the company took what was then the innovative step of displaying large patches of samples on the floor so people could actually walk on them.

The Eighth Avenue location was chosen because it was located on a major traffic artery and had ample parking (thirty-three spaces) for customers. Marshal set a good example for his staff by working hard and continually looking for ways to grow and improve the business.

"I'm here at this store every day, the first to arrive in the morning and the last to leave at night," he said in an interview with *The Southwest Floor Covering News*. "You have to be good at your job because these days the customer is more familiar with what she is looking for in floor covering. People are willing to buy better carpet, but they must be sold carpet."

Ray Utley, Marshal's son, began working at the store at age eighteen upon graduating from high school. He eventually graduated from Texas Wesleyan University with a degree in business and accounting, and worked his way up through the ranks to the position of vice president.

His daughter, Kimberly Utley-Brooks, joined the business in June 2004. She purchased it from her grandmother in April

2005 after her grandfather passed away. She took over as president after her father's failing health forced him to retire.

Today, Marshal Utley Carpets carries hardwood laminates, ceramics, carpeting and all sorts of floor coverings in its residential and commercial departments at its two stores. The company plans to continue the tradition of providing customers with quality products and top-notch service first introduced by the company's founder more than a half century ago.

For more information about what Marshal Utley Carpets has to offer you, please visit www.marshalutleycarpets.com.

Top: Marshal Utley Carpets' original store in Fort Worth on Berry Street.

Middle: The Marshal Utley Carpets' second location at 1313 Norwood.

Bottom: Marshal Utley Carpets at 2209 Eighth Avenue.

National Farm Life Insurance Company

Left: Ron G. Downing, president and director of National Farm Life Insurance Company.

Right: J. D. "Chip" Davis, Jr., senior vice president and chief operating officer of National Farm Life Insurance Company.

National Farm Life Insurance Company of Fort Worth provides life insurance and annuities to the people of Texas. It is the largest Texas based life insurance company to restrict its market to residents within the state. At National Farm Life, the tradition of providing high quality insurance coverage at the lowest possible cost continues today.

William C. "Brigham" Young founded the company in 1946 to provide life insurance to professional agriculture workers. Before entering the insurance business as a salesman, Young earned a degree in agriculture at what is now Texas Tech University and taught vocational agriculture. During World War II, he gained valuable experience by serving in the insurance division of the Air Force. While in the military, he also obtained a degree in business administration through correspondence courses at Texas Tech.

From its beginning, National Farm Life was unique among life insurance companies in the way shareholders' dividends were structured. Annual stockholder dividends are limited to ten percent of the original stock purchase price or a maximum of $14,000. All other earnings are used to pay policyholder dividends or retained for the financial security of policyholders.

National Farm Life expanded in the 1950s to include all Texas residents. Until 1968 the company's home office was located next to the Fort Worth stockyards. In 1968 the company moved its headquarters to the east side of Fort Worth on a twenty-acre tract near the interstate highway that links Dallas and Fort Worth.

The company sells life insurance policies with other coverage, such as accidental death and disability, mortgage cancellation and family protection provided as riders. In the early 1990s, 800 independent agents represented the company throughout the state and the company reached more than $1 billion of insurance in force.

Today National Farm Life offers a range of life insurance options to fit the needs of policyholders. In addition to traditional whole life insurance, the company offers a blended policy that combines whole life with decreasing term insurance. The whole life portion of the policy has a guaranteed cash value and death benefit, while the term portion provides additional protection while reducing overall premiums. The company also offers a twenty-year term life insurance policy with a level death benefit. This policy is renewable to age seventy with no evidence of insurability required and may be converted to whole life insurance. The company's flex term life policy is renewable to age one hundred and convertible to whole life prior to the expiration date of the policy. The company also offers a fixed rate annuity with minimum interest rate guarantees.

Because National Farm Life is committed to standards of excellence in its business operations, the company qualified for the

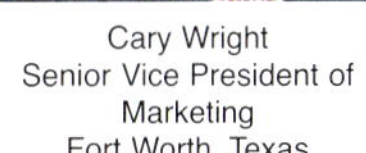

Cary Wright
Senior Vice President of Marketing
Fort Worth, Texas

Monte Roach
Recruiting Director
Lubbock, Texas

Scott Anderson
Area Coordinator
Hubbard, Texas

Glen Baecker, CLU
Area Coordinator
Goliad, Texas

Coy Worden
Area Coordinator
Kaufman, Texas

Insurance Marketplace Standards Association (IMSA) in 1998. IMSA promotes ethical market conduct in the life insurance industry. Membership in IMSA requires the insurance company abide by a specific set of market conduct standards. The company must perform a rigorous self-assessment to ensure that its policies and practices promote honesty, fairness and integrity in the sales process. The company must also demonstrate to an independent assessor that its established policies and programs meet consumer needs for individual life insurance and annuities. As a member of IMSA, National Farm Life agrees to conduct business with honesty and fairness while providing competent, customer-focused sales and services. The company agrees to engage in fair competition and to provide advertising and sales materials that are clear, truthful and equitable. The company must handle customer complaints and disputes in a timely manner and maintain an ongoing review of its compliance with IMSA standards.

National Farm Life has grown from its modest beginning in 1946 to a position of prominence in the insurance industry. In 2003 the company set new records in sales, agent recruitment, policyholder dividends and net earnings. That year, the company issued more than 5,000 new policies, a thirty-eight percent increase over the prior year. Sales increased 8.3 percent from 2002 to 2003. With the addition of 190 new agents, recruitment also reached a record high. The company paid policyholder dividends of $3,782,408 and stockholders received the maximum return of $14,000. Total assets grew to $206,346,544 and the company finished the year with a net gain of $790,782.

In 2000, National Farm Life formed American Farm Life Insurance Company, which is currently licensed in Texas, Oklahoma and New Mexico.

For more than fifty years, National Farm Life has served the insurance needs of Texas residents with integrity, efficiency and economy. Future success will stem from commitment to the same basic principles that have guided the company's performance in the past.

✧

Above: Some of the agents who represent National Farm Life Insurance Company across the state of Texas.

Below: The headquarters of National Farm Life Insurance Company.

Pier 1 Imports

Pier 1 Imports is North America's largest specialty retailer of imported decorative home furnishings and gifts. The company acquires merchandise from more than fifty countries and offers it in more than 1,200 stores throughout the United States, Canada, Mexico, Puerto Rico, and the United Kingdom—making it one of the world's largest import retailers.

Now based in Fort Worth, Texas, Pier 1 Imports started in 1962 as a single store in San Mateo, California, with an initial customer base of post-World War II baby boomers. The flower children of the 1960s wanted beanbags, love beads and incense. By 1965, Pier 1 had sixteen locations offering these and other novelty items, and in 1966, the company's headquarters were officially established in Fort Worth. By 1970 the company had grown to forty-two stores, including its first Canadian store, and was listed on the American Stock Exchange. A listing on the New York Stock Exchange followed in 1972, and in 1979, a store in Royal Oak, Michigan, was the first Pier 1 to post $1 million in annual sales.

As the baby boomer generation evolved into the largest and most affluent segment of the American population, its tastes changed. Instead of novelties, customers wanted high-quality, distinctive home furnishings and decorative accessories that offered good value. In 1985, Pier 1 began to reshape the company's image to reflect these changes. There were 265 stores in operation by the end of the year, with plans to have 500 stores by 1990. In 1987, stores in Framingham, Massachusetts and Los Angeles, California each reached a record $2 million in sales. The company reached its 500-store goal by 1989.

The 1990s were a time of continued growth and expansion into markets outside the U.S. Pier 1 celebrated its thirtieth-year anniversary in 1992 with record earnings of $26.3 million. In 1993 the company opened its first store in Puerto Rico, entered into a partnership with The Pier, a chain of retail import stores in the United Kingdom and opened "boutiques" in Sears de Mexico stores.

✧

Pier 1's new 460,000-square-foot corporate headquarters, Pier 1 Place, sits on the banks of the Trinity River and houses almost 1,000 associates.

The first Pier 1 stores in Hawaii opened in December 1998. In 1999, a 750,000-square-foot distribution center opened in Ontario, California, as did stores in Alaska and western Canada. And for the first time, sales reached $1 billion in fiscal year 1999 with a net income increase of forty-three percent above the prior year.

Pier 1 ushered in the new century by launching its online store in 2000. In 2001 the company acquired Cargokids, an eighteen-store chain based in Fort Worth, to be developed into the first national, value-oriented retailer of children's furnishings and accessories. Pier 1 celebrated forty years as

America's leading retailer of imported home furnishings in 2002 with the mantra, "From Hippie to Hip." Pier 1 also unveiled plans for a twenty story, $90-million headquarters to be built along the banks of the Trinity River in Fort Worth. In 2003 the retailer opened its thousandth North American store, the largest yet, in Summerlin, Nevada outside Las Vegas.

Today, Pier 1 Imports offers high-quality, distinctive home furnishings at a good value. The ever-changing collections are displayed in a sensory environment that encourages customers to enjoy the sights, scents, sounds, colors and textures unique to the Pier 1 shopping experience. Since sixty-five percent of the stores' merchandise changes throughout the year, shoppers discover something new with each visit.

Pier 1 is a socially conscious company that conducts business with personal and professional integrity, employing committed, caring associates whose first priority is responding to the needs of customers. Associates, vendors and agents are expected to uphold a high standard of business ethics, in compliance with applicable laws and with regard to human rights and fair labor practices.

In addition, the company is committed to giving back to communities where customers, associates, shareholders and vendors live, work and play. Over the years, Pier 1 has contributed more than $30 million to hundreds of worthy causes at the local, national and international levels. It is the world's largest retailer of UNICEF greeting cards, donating a hundred percent of proceeds to provide life-saving medicines, vaccines, food, primary education, clean water, sanitation, and emergency relief to people across the globe. Nationally, Pier 1 raises money for the Susan G. Komen Breast Cancer Foundation through the sale of the Komen Candle and contributes to hundreds of local "Race for the Cure" events. On the local level, it ranks tenth in the top one hundred companies contributing to the United Way of Tarrant County, where Pier 1 is based.

Currently, Pier 1 employs more than eighteen thousand people worldwide. In the fall of 2004, Peir 1 moved into its new corporate headquarters on the banks of the Trinity River. And in 2005, the company plans to open one hundred stores in single-store markets and in growing areas of major metropolitan areas. This strategy creates new jobs and provides customers with the convenience and pleasure of shopping at a Pier 1 store in growing retail communities. Pier 1 has come a long way since opening its first store in San Mateo, California and today continues its commitment to giving customers a sensory shopping experience that offers home furnishings and gifts they won't find elsewhere.

✧

Pier 1 currently has over twelve hundred locations nationwide.

Hilton Hotel Fort Worth

The historic Hilton Fort Worth is ideally situated in the heart of downtown near the city's major points of interest and easily accessible to Fort Worth/Dallas's major tourist attractions, airports and train stations.

The Hilton Fort Worth is a full-service hotel with 294 guestrooms and one presidential suite with over 2,200 square feet. The hotel features more than 60,000 square feet of flexible banquet and meeting space and Fort Worth's largest hotel ballroom, a facility that can accommodate as many as 1,600 people. Between 1995 and 1996, a $11-million renovation was completed, renovating all of the guestrooms and adding a twenty-four hour, self-serve business center, and two executive floors with an executive lounge.

Amenities at the Hilton Fort Worth include room service, express checkout and valet parking. Other amenities include valet dry cleaning and laundry service, express room service, and wheelchair-accessible guestrooms. In-room amenities include wireless and hardwired internet access, large desks, voice mail, in-room coffee and tea service, hair dryer, iron and full-size ironing board, and deluxe granite bathrooms. Select guestrooms also feature wet bars and refrigerators.

The Hilton Hotel Fort Worth features the Café Texas restaurant, which serves traditional fare for breakfast, lunch, and dinner seven days a week, and Biscotti's Coffee Bar, which offers an array of Biscotti's and rich coffees.

Guests at the Hilton Fort Worth can choose from 108 rooms with two double beds, 185 rooms with king-size beds, or one presidential suite.

The hotel's dedicated Convention Services and Banquet Staff is flexible, creative and committed to providing each group with the finest experience possible. Each event is handled with the utmost care and every detail is carefully managed and executed to make each event as flawless as possible.

Take advantage of the hotel's on-site audio/visual and banquet equipment as well as special services and a twenty-four-hour business center.

The Hilton Forth Worth is located one block north of the Fort Worth Convention Center and steps away from Sundance Square Entertainment District, a popular enter-tainment venue packed with a wide array of restaurants, bars and nightclubs. No matter what your taste in food, drink or music, you'll find something at the Sundance Square Entertainment District that is to your liking. Other area attractions include the Fort Worth Stockyards National Historic District, Bass Performance Hall, Amon Carter Museum, Kimbell Art Museum, Modern Art Museum and the Fort Worth Zoo. Other attractions include Six Flags Over Texas, Six Flags Hurricane Harbor, Texas Motor Speedway, Fort Worth Brahmas Ice Hockey and Fort Worth Cats Baseball.

The Hilton Fort Worth is twenty-five minutes from Dallas/Fort Worth International Airport and forty minutes from Dallas Love Field. It is also close to major thoroughfares such as I-35, I-30, and the Airport Freeway. The Trinity Railway Express, a few blocks away, provides quick and easy transportation to downtown Dallas.

Other quick and affordable transportation services include the T Bus Service offered by the Fort Worth Transportation Authority through-out the city. In the downtown area, riders can enjoy the red, white and blue buses at no charge. Shuttle service is provided to and from Dallas/Fort Worth Airport, and Fort Worth is the hub of the south-central corridor for Amtrak's Texas Eagle, linking San Antonio, Austin, Fort Worth and Little Rock, Arkansas. High-speed rail service also links Tulsa, Oklahoma City, St. Louis and Chicago. The Fort Worth hub is two blocks from the Hilton Fort Worth.

The Hilton Fort Worth's proximity to local corporations and the Fort Worth Convention Center make it an excellent choice for business travelers and convention attendees. Popular tourist attractions like Billy Bob's Texas, The Ballpark at Arlington (home to the Texas Rangers baseball team) and the Fort Worth Cultural District are within a five-mile radius, making the Hilton an equally great choice for leisure-time travelers.

The Hilton Hotel Fort Worth is located at 815 Main Street. For more information, please call 817-870-2100.

Fort Worth Convention & Visitors Bureau

In Fort Worth, history and tourism are forever intertwined. After all, some of the very first out-of-town visitors to Fort Worth were cowboys who drove enormous herds of cattle up the Chisholm Trail. As the city grew, it attracted all kinds of interesting characters—from outlaws Butch Cassidy and the Sundance Kid to lawman Wyatt Earp.

Fort Worth's status as the place "Where the West begins" is a major reason why so many people visit the city today. But that's by no means the sole reason: Fort Worth is one of the most diverse cities in America, with an amazing collection of art museums, world-class sporting venues, and wonderful family attractions.

It's the job of the Fort Worth Convention & Visitors Bureau (FWCVB), founded in 1965, to promote the city to a variety of audiences nationally and internationally.

"No other city in America is like Fort Worth," said Douglas Harman, president and CEO. "There are so many different aspects to the city, from Western heritage to the museums and culture. Everybody on our staff loves Fort Worth, and feels so fortunate that we have such a unique destination to show the world."

In spreading the message about Fort Worth, the FWCVB reaches out to three major audiences: professional meeting planners, leisure travelers, and the media. To meeting planners, the FWCVB stresses the city's central U.S. location, remodeled convention center and other meeting facilities, vibrant downtown, and popular attractions. To persuade leisure travelers to spend vacation dollars in Fort Worth, the FWCVB uses a wide variety of communication vehicles, from conventional advertising to online promotions. The staff regularly conducts city tours for print and broadcast journalists, resulting in feature placement in some of the most respected publications and networks in America. The FWCVB also plans innovative events like the "Big Drive of 2005," held in Manhattan's Times Square. This highly successful promotion featuring the Fort Worth Herd and Texas Motor Speedway was picked up by media from coast to coast.

"We rarely follow conventional thinking when we're promoting Fort Worth," said Harman. "We use a multi-dimensional approach in order to get the most exposure for our marketing initiatives."

All of these diverse efforts of the FWCVB add up to millions of dollars in economic impact to Fort Worth each year.

"People may not readily relate the importance of the convention and tourism industry to the economic health of Fort Worth," said Harman. "It affects everyone in the city by providing thousands of jobs, making local businesses more profitable, and increasing the revenue available to improve the city's infrastructure."

As Fort Worth continues to grow and improve, the Fort Worth Convention & Visitors Bureau will be there, working tirelessly to promote this remarkable city. For additional information on Fort Worth and the wonderful sites and sounds of the city, visit www.fortworth.com on the Internet.

CRESCENT REAL ESTATE EQUITIES COMPANY

Economic downturn is too gentle a word to describe what happened in Texas in the 1980s. Catastrophe might be a better word. It began when the oil prices that had fueled the economic boom plummeted, growth stopped and the economy began a nosedive that would take years to come to an end.

Then came the decline in the real estate market as businesses either closed their doors or moved away. Texas suddenly had a glut of office space and banks and savings and loans began to foreclose. They, in turn, began to fail as projected income from real estate loans became liabilities that gobbled away capital.

Friends and colleagues told John Goff and Richard Rainwater they were crazy to start a business amid this economic climate, especially in the real estate business where they were almost guaranteed, their friends said, to lose everything.

But Goff and Rainwater spotted opportunity where others saw only gloom and doom. Experienced investors know that booms are usually followed by busts and that busts, in turn, are usually followed by recoveries. So why not take advantage of the real estate glut by purchasing foreclosed properties at bargain prices from lenders desperate to unload them?

Working on a yellow legal pad, Goff sketched out the strategy for what eventually became Crescent Real Estate Equities Company. From 1990 to 1994, Goff engineered six partnerships to purchase specific properties with a total area of 3.2 million square feet. The partnerships purchased such buildings as The Crescent in Dallas, MacArthur I & II and Caltex House in Las Colinas, Carter Burgess Plaza in Fort Worth, and The Citadel in Denver.

All the deals were complex, especially The Crescent, which had 8 lenders and took 18 months to complete, coming to a conclusion shortly before the company went public on May 4, 1994.

Goff rang the opening bell at the New York Stock Exchange that day. The event signaled the arrival of a new player in the real estate industry and what would eventually become one of the most successful real estate investment firms in the nation.

Beginning with eleven employees, and ten properties, Crescent Real Estate Equities Company has grown to employ more than 200 people in its Fort Worth office and owns and manages more than 75 premier office buildings in markets such as Dallas, Houston, Austin, Denver, Miami, and Las Vegas. Its initial valuation of slightly more than $500 million has grown since 1994 to approximately $5 billion today.

Crescent understands that success doesn't occur without support from the communities in which it operates, so the company founded its signature community partnership program, FACES of Change in 1997. Through FACES of Change, Crescent employees, customers and business partners form three-year partnerships with local elementary schools, which have limited resources. The innovative program has generated more than $1.25 million in funding, services and supplies for more than 61 schools across the country, and its volunteers have donated more than 35,000 hours. In 2004, Crescent properties were partnered with twenty-eight schools.

Crescent Real Estate Equities Company is located at 777 Main Street, Suite 2100 in Fort Worth, Texas, and on the Internet at www.crescent.com.

✧

Above: Carter Burgess Plaza.

Below: FACES of Change was founded and is supported by Crescent Real Estate to help and support future generations of their Tarrant County Community.

Sam Pack's Five Star Ford

No one could have imagined back in 1991 that Sam Pack Ford would one day be Tarrant County's leading car dealership. After purchasing the assets of Sam Lingard Ford in the summer of 1991, the dealership sold only 460 units. Compare that with the 10,784 cars sold just ten years later. How did they do it? By making a commitment to customer satisfaction, professionalism, and exceptional service.

The dealership ranks in Ford's top one hundred dealerships in the nation for new vehicle retail sales and achieved Blue Oval certification with near perfect scores. As representatives of Ford Motor Company, Sam Pack's employees' motto is: "We will provide the best possible service and atmosphere of professionalism to all our customers. We will treat everyone, as we would like to be treated." Ford has acknowledged this attitude by awarding the dealership the "President's Award" for both customer satisfaction and market leadership. Customer satisfaction scores, which reflect the "voice of the customer," are at their highest levels ever. Pack, named *Time Magazine*'s "Quality Dealer of the Year for his exceptionally high customer satisfaction standards, also earned Ford's "Distinguished Achievement Award," which is the highest Ford Division honor. Pack's outlet has been listed by *Auto Age* magazine as one of the leading dealerships in the United States by virtue of its numerous listings in the Top 100 Club of the nation's 4,600 Ford dealerships. From 1980 to 1999, Sam Pack's Lee Jarmon Ford was in the Top Twenty Club, as well as being named a "Top 500 Dealer" by *Ward's Dealer Business* magazine. More recently, Pack was honored with the highest honor for customer satisfaction and owner loyalty at Ford Mother Company, the NACE award, for the third year in a row.

But Pack also gives back to the community that has contributed to his success. The dealership, which now covers 16 acres, provides employment to 200 area residents, and his commitment to the community shows in the numerous awards he has received over the years. Northwood University recognized him with the Automotive Marketing Dealer Education Award, which honors individuals in the industry who have made noteworthy contributions to education. He is also known for supporting Brookhaven College's "Asset" program that prepares young adults for entry and employment in the auto industry. The Metrocrest Chamber of Commerce also recognized Pack as "Citizen of the Year," based on his community involvement and service.

Sam Pack's Five Star Ford, located at I-35E and Crosby Road in Carrolton, continues to grow at record levels, and is sure to keep giving customers and the community the very best of service and satisfaction.

TEXAS LAND AND COUNTRY, LLC

In recent years, enjoying rural property has become an ever-increasing priority for folks from all walks of life. For some individuals who were raised in the country and moved away to pursue careers, it is the quest to regain and relive the great memories of childhood or pass on the value of the rural outdoors to children and grandchildren. For others, rural property offers the serenity and diversion to help balance the hectic lifestyle of living in a metropolitan area. Rural property represents a good investment whether the end use of the property may be recreational, ranching or for development. For whatever reason, owning and enjoying rural property has become an ever-increasing priority for current lifestyles.

James Thompson spent thirty years as an executive in the corporate world. During that time, he and his wife Cissy learned the value and benefit of owning rural properties. With a background in sales and marketing management, James knows the importance of monitoring changes in lifestyles from a business perspective. As populations become more urban, careers become more demanding and lifestyles become more chaotic, James believes that owning rural property is one way many people will choose to "balance" their lifestyle in the future. Although people have owned rural property forever for any number of reasons, James believes significantly more people will be in the market to purchase rural property in the coming years.

As a past resident of Dallas and a newcomer to Fort Worth, James wanted the involvement of someone from Fort Worth for a Fort Worth based business. A mutual friend set up a meeting between James, Sam Day and Darrell Lester. Sam and Darrell had graduated from TCU, were long time residents of Fort Worth and were involved in the business community. After a few discussions, James, Sam and Darrell decided a business endeavor to market rural properties had opportunities for the future. In 1999, Texas Land And Country, LLC was formed with James as president, Sam and Darrell as vice presidents. "Although Sam and Darrell have their own business endeavors, they have been invaluable particularly because I was new to Fort Worth when the business was established" said James.

The past and current focus of TLC is marketing medium to large rural properties (on thousand acres and larger) approximately within a four-hour drive of the Dallas-Fort Worth metroplex. This priority may be expanded in the future. The primary client profiles are business executives, professional people, investors and ranchers. Whether a client is a seller or a buyer, the firm works very hard to make the experience of marketing a ranch property a pleasant experience. Its professional approach is the primary reason the firm experiences the high number of client "repeats" and referrals.

Fort Worth is the ideal city with the perfect heritage, location and mindset for any business, but particularly if you are involved in marketing ranches. Frequently when James is asked about his background and how he became a ranch real estate broker, his response is "if I only knew then what I know now, I would have moved to Fort Worth and started a ranch real estate business twenty-five years ago." Thanks Fort Worth for your heritage, your way of life and for being such a great place to be from!!!

✧

Texas Land and Country's business office is located at 2561 Highview Terrace in Fort Worth and on the Internet at www.txlandandcountry.com. You may contact them by calling (817)921-9332 or by e-mail at jamesttlc@aol.com.

Metro Golf Cars

Above: H. Wayne King, his wife Beverly, and their children, c. 1984.

Below: Beverly King and children, August 2004.

An initial investment of $2,000 has grown into a multimillion-dollar business through the past three decades thanks to the vision and hard work of company founder H. Wayne King, his wife Beverly, and their eight children.

Metro Golf Cars began in 1974 when Wayne purchased the Westinghouse golf car dealership from an engineer at Bell Helicopter. It began as a partnership between Wayne and his brother, Dale, and has survived despite a change in location, a devastating fire and Wayne's death.

The company took off after Wayne and Dale moved it to its current location at 4063 South Freeway in Fort Worth. People began to use golf cars for commercial and industrial purposes and farmers and ranchers found them and other small utility vehicles useful.

As the business grew, notable customers included Roger Penskie and Willie Nelson as well as large businesses like American Airlines, Lockheed Martin, Radio Shack and Texas Christian University. The company also designed and built the first electric personnel carrier inside Dallas-Fort Worth International Airport to move passengers and luggage between the terminal and the Amfac Hotel.

After the fire, Dale moved to Granbury to start Lake Country Golf Cars, while Wayne, with help from suppliers, employees and friends, managed to bring Metro Golf Cars back on its feet. New business opportunities appeared in the 1980s. Metro pioneered the use of golf cars in the apartment and multi-housing industry in Texas and captured business in golf car rentals for special events and replacement of full-size vehicles on college campuses.

On September 21, 1990, Wayne died suddenly from a heart attack at the age of fifty-five. His wife, now Beverly Werner, took controlling interest in the business and Nelson King, one of their eight children, became president. Another son, Curtis, left another family business to support Metro in the early 1990s.

Eventually, everyone in the family would lend a hand making Metro Golf Cars into a success story, including sons-in-law Jerry McWhorter and Manuel Cabrera, and daughters Kathryn, Virginia and Laura. By the late 1990s, Beverly became president with sons Ed, Ben, Joel, Curtis and Nelson playing supporting managerial roles.

Today, Metro's future is bright. The company has around forty-five employees and is researching the possibility of new locations. Former Dallas Cowboy Jay Novacek, an avid outdoorsman, endorses the company.

It is Beverly's intention to support and strategically grow the business. Metro Golf Cars and its supporting cast wants to be the best it can be and will use sound business principles mixed with family values to guide its growth for decades to come.

Metro Golf Cars is located on the Internet at www.metrogolfcars.com.

The Bombay Company

The Bombay Company started in New Orleans, Louisiana, in 1978 when Brad Harper came up with the idea of selling inexpensive reproductions of traditional eighteenth- and nineteenth-century English furniture. Through the years, Bombay evolved from Harper's mail-order business selling furniture that customers assembled themselves to a multifaceted, publicly owned company with retail stores across the United States and Canada. Today, The Bombay Company consists of approximately 500 stores, with more than 5,000 employees. Bombay calls Fort Worth home, with its headquarters located in the renowned Fort Worth Arts District.

In 1983 the company began designing and sourcing its own proprietary home furnishings, resulting in a unique, fashion-focused product line. With this transition, Bombay became a leader in self-assembled furniture, especially small accent tables. This new style and tone reflected a more sophisticated look, featuring designs inspired by various cultures from around the world, along with coordinating accents and wall décor.

In the early 1990s, Bombay converted most of its 1,500-square-foot mall stores into 4,000-square-foot stores, which provided an excellent showcase for its larger furniture pieces and complete furniture collections. This allowed customers to see various room designs fully decorated for the entire home—from bedding ensembles paired with a furniture collection, area rug and wall art to the fully furnished home office with stately desk, coordinated storage units and executive desk accessories.

As Internet accessibility grew, Bombay made its presence known, becoming one of the first online home-furnishing retailers. After leading in this area, Bombay led the retail trend of building stores in off-mall lifestyle centers. By 2004-2005 more than fifty percent of Bombay stores had relocated to off-mall sites. At the same time Bombay began moving its store locations, the company launched BombayKIDS as an online retail outlet only. It was such a tremendous success that the company opened a physical store in Dallas in 2002. It, too, was received with a positive and overwhelming response. At present, there are more than fifty BombayKIDS retail stores.

Bombay works to anticipate its customers' home decorating desires. Today's consumers are asking for efficient, functional pieces that are comfortable and complement today's fast-paced, technology-based lifestyle. Its customers want quality merchandise, fashionably styled, with a mix of classic designs, transitional colors and sumptuous fabrics gathered from across the globe. Its stores are merchandised to inspire the shopper and give her decorating ideas, allowing her to create a space in which she and her family truly feel comfortable. Even if she has not traveled the world in search of fine collectibles, Bombay affords her the luxury of decorating her home as if she had.

The Ashton Hotel and The Ashton Depot

The Ashton Hotel and the Ashton Depot (formerly known as the Santa Fe Depot) are two of the finest examples of historic Texas buildings in downtown Fort Worth. The Ashton Hotel occupies the former Fort Worth Club Building and the Winfree Building at 610 Main Street. The Ashton Depot is located near the Fort Worth Convention Center and both the hotel and depot are listed on the *National Register of Historic Places.*

The Ashton Hotel is a small luxury hotel with thirty-nine rooms on six floors offering exemplary service in an elegant setting. With an excellent restaurant, ballroom and executive meeting facilities, the Ashton Hotel blends the best of historic ambience and modern convenience. Rich fabrics and warm woods combine with a collection of original art to offer guests intimate, inviting spaces in which to enjoy their visits to Fort Worth.

The Ashton Hotel is the result of owners Shirlee J. and Taylor Gandy's decision to restore the Fort Worth Club Building, built in 1915, and the adjacent Winfree Building, built in 1890, to their original architectural styles and convert them into a luxury hotel. Wrought-iron balconies, decorative brick patterns and cast stone demonstrate the Italianate style of the Fort Worth Club Building, the only building of its style in Fort Worth. The restoration of the Winfree Building to its original Victorian facade makes it one of the few surviving commercial examples of pre-1900 architecture in Fort Worth.

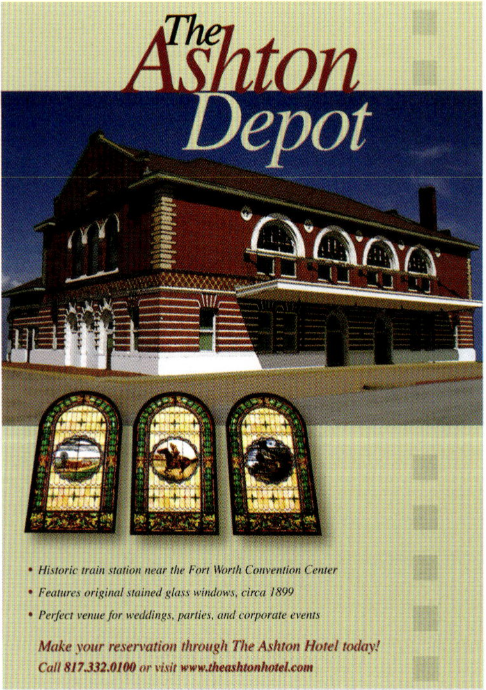

The Ashton Depot has undergone a number of changes and restorations since first constructed in 1899. The building is an example of Beaux-Arts style, which originally included stained glass windows depicting the evolution of transportation. The stained glass, painted by an anonymous artist, depicts the prairie schooner (covered wagon), the pony express, and the iron horse, better known as the steam engine. The windows were removed in 1969 and donated to the Pate Museum of Transportation, where they remained in storage until 2001. At that time, the owner's requested that Smith Studios of Fort Worth restore them and they were reinstalled in 2003 after a thirty-four year absence.

The Ashton Depot was scheduled for demolition in 1963 in favor of a parking lot and operations were to be moved to the Texas & Pacific Passenger Station. An agreement was never reached, however, and it remained open. Amtrak took over operations in 1971. In 1999 the depot marked 100 years of operations and remained in service until 2002, the only passenger train station in Texas in continuous service for more than 100 years.

The Ashton Depot was renovated in 2005 and put into service as a site for wedding receptions, corporate events and other catering opportunities. It boasts a full commercial kitchen and will be an additional catering venue for The Ashton Hotel.

The Ashton Hotel and The Ashton Depot exemplify Fort Worth's respect for the past and its dedication to the future.

Brants Realtors

Brants Realtors has been a fixture in the Fort Worth landscape since 1926, when Harry E. Brants formed an insurance mortgage and real estate partnership. Finding homes for clients was initially an accommodation for the company's insurance clientele, a benefit for friends and neighbors; a role that expanded as the years went by.

In the 1930s, The Brants Company, as it was called in those days, represented one of the first fine homes for sale in a new "incorporated village" in Fort Worth called Westover Manor in Westover Hills—now a landmark neighborhood and home to many leading citizens.

A decade later, the company provided many loans for wartime housing through Burdette Brants, one of five Brants brothers, who arranged development and mortgage financing for A.C. Luther's Ridglea and Ridglea Hills subdivisions. Later successful subdivisions developed by Clayton Brants, Jr. included Highland Park, Bryce Avenue Town Homes, Harbour Point, Dosier Cove, Glen Eagles and Mony Street Business Park.

In 1950, Doug McKenzie joined the firm to focus on commercial and residential real estate brokerage. The company opened its first independent brokerage office in 1962, and ten years later Brants Realtors emerged as a separate partnership from the parent company. The company incorporated in 1978 to become Brants Realtors, Inc.

Through the years, the company has remained true to its philosophy and vision while incorporating cutting-edge technology and forward-thinking strategy into today's challenging and complex real estate environment.

As clients' needs have changed, Brants Realtors, Inc., has added resources and expanded its presence to reach beyond the borders of Fort Worth. A branch office of W. R. Starkey Mortgage Company provides an array of mortgage financing options. As a proud member of RELO Leading Real Estate Companies of the World since 1990, the firm provide its clients with access to a network of more than 120,000 sales associates nationally and internationally. Brants Realtors, Inc., also maintains its exclusive affiliation with Christie's Great Estates and is a charter member of the Board of Regents for Who's Who in Luxury Real Estate, creating international exposure for clients. Other services include move management, destination services, and RELO National Home Search.

Knowledge, Integrity, Professionalism—these three words describe Brants Realtors, its partners and its employees. Year after year, generation after generation, thousands of clients honor the company in a most unique manner, they entrust the professionals of Brants Realtors to guide them in their most intimate business transactions. The agents of Brants are active ambassadors for the entire Fort Worth community through an array of civic and cultural involvements. The company finds itself fortunate to be able to showcase to friends and visitors what makes Fort Worth unique.

Brants Realtors, Inc., enjoys a solid reputation for sterling service since 1926, and thus has adopted the motto of "Opening Doors and More, since 1926." The company is open and honest with its clients at all times. Brants Realtors prides itself on maintaining diversity among its agents and putting forth a team effort to better serve its clients. In the future, you can count on Brants Realtors to keep abreast of the latest developments in an ever-changing real estate market, while remaining true to the firm's heritage, philosophy and vision.

Visit Brants Realtors on the Internet at www.brantsrealtors.com.

✧

Above: The Brants Family, c. 1926. Back row (from left to right): Harry Brants, Howard Brants, Juanita Brants, Burdette Brants, Lucy Brants Costello, D. T. (Bill) Costello (Doc), and H. H. Brants. Front row (from left to right): Gretchen Brants, May (Gramma) Brants, Fred (Grampa) Brants, Cynthia Brants, and (Bud) Hebert Brants.

Below: 8 Westover Road. Westover Hills, Texas.

Southside Trim & Glass

✧

Above: Southside Trim & Glass, 1949.

Below: Southside Trim & Glass, 1964.

Southside Trim & Glass is an automotive aftermarket business with locations in Dallas and Fort Worth. The two shops work with car dealerships to add leather interiors, sunroofs, video equipment, top packages and custom interiors on approximately 13,000 automobiles per year.

Fort Worth native, H.L. Stanley, Jr., started what would become Southside Trim & Glass in 1949 when he opened a used car dealership at 415 Hemphill Street in Fort Worth. He had saved enough money for a down payment while working at a gas station on Berry Street, a job he took after completing his military service.

His pick struck gold in the 1950s when he began working with insurance companies installing glass in damaged vehicles. Insurance companies sent cars involved in accidents or receiving weather-related damage to Stanley for repair. He capitalized on this opportunity before the automotive glass chains began to flourish. He did so well, in fact, that he began buying up the block where Southside Motors was located. His purchases included an automotive trim shop on the corner and Southside Motors became Southside Trim & Glass.

He worked exclusively from the shop on Hemphill until 1978 when he expanded to 755 West Broadway. His daughter, Carol Walsh, began buying the company in 1981 while learning the ins and outs of the business to prepare her for taking the reins from her father. She now serves as president.

Stanley died in 2003 and a short time before his passing the business had moved all its operations to the 10,000-square-foot Broadway location. The company owns the Hemphill Street location and leases it out to another business. A second location in the Dallas area opened in June 2005, providing Southside Trim & Glass with more opportunities for growth. The two locations employ forty people.

The twenty-thousand-square-foot Dallas-area location can be found at 1725 Hurd Street in Las Colinas. Southside Trim has served dealerships in places like Abilene, Waco, Wichita Falls and San Antonio for a long time. Although ten percent of its business comes from retail customers, Southside Trim will continue to concentrate on serving dealerships in North Texas.

In 2005, Carol's husband, Terry, and their son, Bryan, joined her at Southside Trim to help grow the family business. Bryan will follow in the footsteps of his grandfather and mother, hoping to continue building the business that has been growing since 1949.

✧

Members of the Moslah Shrine Temple on the way to their parade contend with a stubborn cow. The parade promoted the temple's circus held annually to benefit disabled children.

COURTESY OF THE FORT WORTH PUBLIC LIBRARY.

✧

A poster advertises Orphan of War, *a 1913 silent featurette that played at the Hippodrome.*

COURTESY OF SPECIAL COLLECTIONS, UNIVERSITY OF TEXAS AT ARLINGTON LIBRARIES, ARLINGTON, TEXAS.

✧

Amon Carter, booster extrordinaire.

COURTESY OF SPECIAL COLLECTIONS, UNIVERSITY OF TEXAS AT ARLINGTON LIBRARIES, ARLINGTON, TEXAS, AR 1-21-47.

Fort Worth Stock Show participants queue up at the chow line.

COURTESY OF SPECIAL COLLECTIONS, UNIVERSITY OF TEXAS AT ARLINGTON LIBRARIES, ARLINGTON, TEXAS, AR 368 126.

✧

A group of children gather in the rotunda of the Fort Worth Museum of Science and History for a "hands-on" nature lesson.

COURTESY OF SPECIAL COLLECTIONS, UNIVERSITY OF TEXAS AT ARLINGTON LIBRARIES, ARLINGTON, TEXAS, AR 1-31-29.

✧

A parade in early Fort Worth.

COURTESY OF THE *FORT WORTH STAR-TELEGRAM* PHOTOGRAPH COLLECTION, SPECIAL COLLECTIONS, UNIVERSITY OF TEXAS AT ARLINGTON LIBRARIES, ARLINGTON, TEXAS, AR 406 5-18-20.

Quality of Life

Healthcare providers, school districts, and universities, and other institutions that contribute to the quality of life in Tarrant County

Baylor All Saints Medical Centers 216
DFW Urology Consultants 231
Fort Worth Police Department 228
Harris Methodist Fort Worth Hospital 222
Kenneth Copeland Ministries
Eagle Mountain International Church, Incorporated 220
Lena Pope Home 229
Medical Center of Arlington
North Hills Hospital
Plaza Medical Center of Fort Worth 212
Moncrief Cancer Center 226
The Murrin Family 237
Radiology Associates of Tarrant County 233
River Legacy Foundation 235
Tarrant County Historical Society 236
Tarrant Regional Water District 224
Texas Christian University 230
The University of Texas at Arlington 234
YMCA of Metropolitan Fort Worth 232

Medical Center of Arlington

North Hills Hospital

Plaza Medical Center of Fort Worth

HCA is one of the nation's leading providers of healthcare services with almost 200 hospitals and more than eighty outpatient surgery centers in twenty-three states, England and Switzerland. Founded in Nashville, Tennessee in the 1960s, the company's North Texas division, known as Lone Star Health and headquartered in Las Colinas, includes thirteen hospitals, including three in Tarrant County: North Hills Hospital, Medical Center of Arlington and Plaza Medical Center of Fort Worth.

Like all HCA hospitals, those in Lone Star Health are committed to the care and improvement of human life. In recognition of this commitment, HCA strives to deliver high quality, cost-effective healthcare in the communities it serves.

In pursuit of its mission, HCA believes the following value statements are essential and timeless. It recognizes and affirms the unique and intrinsic worth of each individual; it treats all those it serves with compassion and kindness; it acts with absolute honesty, integrity and fairness in the way it conducts its business and the way its employees live their lives; and HCA trusts its colleagues as valuable members of its healthcare team and pledge to treat one another with loyalty, respect and dignity.

The oldest of the three Lone Star Health hospitals is North Hills Hospital in North Richland Hills. Seven physicians founded the hospital in 1961, combining their expertise with a dream of improving healthcare in Northeast Tarrant County.

They put up $500 to pay a developer to find funding for the hospital, which began on Glenview Drive before moving to its current location on Booth Calloway Road in 1983. But before the hospital opened, the founders had to scramble to find furniture. They had run out of money and faced the prospect of opening an empty hospital until they convinced a hospital supply company to loan them the money to buy furnishings.

Major developments in the hospital's history include the opening of an inpatient rehabilitation unit in 1989, its first cardiac catheterization lab in 1990 and the addition of open-heart surgery in 1992. North Hills also added additional cardiac catheterization labs in 2003 and 2004.

North Hills Hospital opened a primary care clinic at Alliance Airport in 1992 and from 1997 to 1999 expanded its emergency room, outpatient department, surgery, and gastrointestinal/endoscopy lab. It also constructed a second professional building and completed construction of the Texas Pediatric Surgery Center, the state's first children's outpatient surgery center.

North Hills Hospital performed its first bariatric surgery in 2003 and operates the emergency room clinic at the Texas Motor Speedway on race days. The hospital that began with seven physicians now has 450 associated with it as well as 650 employees. Together, they handle 750 deliveries, 13,000 surgeries, 36,000 outpatient visits and 39,000 emergency room visits.

North Hills began construction on a cardiac intensive care unit in 2005.

The hospital is accredited by the Joint Commission of Accrediting Healthcare Organizations and has received three commendations in its last three surveys. The College of American Pathologists certifies the lab and the Texas Pediatric Surgery Center is accredited by the Accreditation Association of Ambulatory Healthcare. North Hills Hospital is a member of the Texas Hospital Association and the American Hospital Association as well as the Dallas/Fort Worth Hospital Council.

The Senior Health Center is a service of North Hills Hospital. It's committed to superb primary medical care and is designed and dedicated to men and women sixty-five years of age and older. Specially trained healthcare professionals, who can assess, coordinate and monitor all aspects of treatment and progress, staff it. The Senior Health Center offers the same personal involvement and quality care services you would expect from a traditional family physician and more.

Medical Center of Arlington was founded in 1968 as a fifty bed hospital owned by physicians of the City of Arlington. HCA purchased the hospital in 1969 and renamed it Arlington Medical Center. The hospital staff is committed to the care and improvement of human life and strives to deliver high-quality,

✧

North Hills Hospital.

cost-effective healthcare in the communities it serves.

MCA focuses on being a hospital that provides high-quality patient care at a good value, is customer-oriented, technically proficient and known as a system that meets the needs of patients, physicians, employees and payors.

MCA is an acute care general hospital with a complete range of healthcare that includes emergency, diagnostic, therapeutic and surgical services. MCA offers comprehensive care including women's services, cardiology and rehabilitation services, neurological services, advanced technology and an emergency department with around-the-clock care serving patients twenty-four hours a day.

Medical Center of Arlington is growing with the community with the recent completion of a $70 million expansion dedicated almost exclusively to clinical enhancements. Serious critical care and ongoing health services are all available in the neighborhood.

MCA's staff provides multidisciplinary, compassionate team treatment and uses cutting-edge technology. They extend both a personal touch and advanced capabilities and offer a dedicated guest services VIP program. A hospital director is on call twenty-four hours a day, seven days a week to do whatever it takes to make sure patients receive the care they need.

Medical Center of Arlington has nearly 500 board-certified or board-eligible physicians representing more than forty specialties. In May 2002, Medical Center of Arlington increased its services in Mansfield with completion of a new diagnostic clinic. The satellite facility allows convenient access to basic imaging and lab services for residents in the Mansfield area who currently use facilities in Arlington.

The diagnostic capabilities were incorporated in MCA's existing Mansfield medical office. In addition to housing primary care and specialty physicians, the location provides Mansfield a single location where patients can also access a laboratory drawing station and imaging services for chest, head, neck, leg, arm and wrist X-rays.

Medical Center of Arlington's latest extension streamlines the treatment process for patients, eliminating drive time by housing physician and diagnostic services in one Mansfield location. MCA specializes in

✧

Plaza Medical Center of Fort Worth.

providing a complete range of healthcare services. Residents in Arlington and surrounding cities gain peace of mind knowing they don't have to look far for state-of-the-art medical treatment.

Plaza Medical Center, a 320-bed medical facility in the heart of the Fort Worth medical district, specializes in tertiary care, teaching and research. Founded in 1974, Plaza Medical Center is recognized regionally for its neuroscience and orthopedic programs and has been recognized twice nationally as one of the top one hundred heart hospitals in the United States.

The hospital's five major product lines are cardiac care, oncology, orthopedics, general and specialty surgery and neurosciences. In July 2000, Plaza began offering post-graduate training for physicians. These residencies have now grown to five accredited programs: traditional internship, family practice, internal medicine, general surgery and a cardiology fellowship.

In 2003, Plaza added four state-of-the-art open-heart surgery suites and a second cardiovascular intensive care unit. It also doubled the number of cardiac catheterization labs and expanded the emergency room.

Cardiovascular thoracic surgery and rheumatology will be added in 2005.

Plaza remains a leader in cardiac care offering a full line of cardiovascular services and cardiac rehabilitation. It is the only adult facility in Fort Worth to offer patent foramen ovales (PFOs). A PFO results from incomplete development of the heart shortly after birth, and frequently goes undiagnosed until it causes a stroke or other loss of consciousness later in life.

Once properly diagnosed through advanced methods of heart imaging such as esophageal echocardiography, they are relatively simple to repair using a non-invasive alternative to traditional open-heart surgery.

Plaza is now updating its facility through an $85 million project that will refurbish the entire hospital. Plaza has an on-site Institutional Review Board and annually conducts more than thirty clinical trials. New medicines and devices are utilized in cancer and cardiac care as well as orthopedics.

Plaza Medical Center had the first American College of Radiology accredited MRI in Fort Worth. It also enjoys full accreditation with full standards compliance from the Joint Commission Accreditation of Healthcare Organizations in 2002 and accreditation with commendation in 1999.

The hospital's outpatient self-managed education program was recognized by the American Diabetes Association and is accredited by the American Association of Blood Banks. The College of American Pathologists awarded Plaza with accreditation with distinction and the hospital has received Accreditation for Medical Rehabilitation and National Accreditation for Cardiac Rehab.

HCA had assets of more than $18.7 billion in 2002 and revenues of $19.7 billion. HCA and its affiliates employ around 190,000 people and, building on the foundation of its mission and value statement, follow the following strategy:

- The company puts patients first and works constantly to improve the care it give its patients, implementing measures that support its caregivers, help ensure patient safety, and provides the highest possible care.
- HCA also believes in investing in its communities and plans to invest more than $1 billion per year to keep hospitals modern and up to date technologically. The company plans to expand and add services to its hospitals and selectively acquire new facilities to better serve the community.
- Focusing on leading hospitals in core communities is part of HCA's strategy. HCA focuses on communities where the company is a leading healthcare provider. The company also employs industry leading measures to enhance the performance of the company's local facilities, including organized group purchasing, efficient supply acquisition and distribution, shared administration and business services, and other initiatives that allow its hospitals and their communities to benefit from economies of scale.
- A final part of HCA's strategy is to build strong physician relationships. The company values its relationships with local physicians, working to provide them with a wide array of services and modern facilities in order to help them deliver the best possible care.

For more information on Medical Center of Arlington, North Hills Hospital and Plaza Medical Center of Fort Worth, please visit the website at www.lonestarhealth.com.

✧

The Medical Center of Arlington, Plaza, North Hills Hospital, Medical Center are all members of the HCA family.

Baylor All Saints Medical Centers

By the late 1800s, Fort Worth was a thriving town on the west Texas frontier and a premier cattle trading and packing center. A small group of civic-minded women decided it was time to build an institution to care for the sick.

Calling themselves the "Comfort Band," the women rallied the citizens of Fort Worth to raise the funds needed for a hospital. Fort Worth's Episcopal Church soon joined their cause, and by 1906, All Saints Episcopal Hospital, with twenty-four beds and an affiliated nursing school, was ready to serve the community.

The hospital flourished during Fort Worth's oil boom of the 1920s, and a brand-new three-story facility accommodated the growing population. But unfortunately, that prosperity was short-lived and only the generosity of local businessman Dr. T. C. Terrell kept the hospital's doors from closing during the depression years.

Fortunately, by the end of World War II, a new period of affluence boosted Fort Worth's economy, and benefited All Saints. In 1959, All Saints opened a new nine-story, 365 bed hospital to meet the demand for healthcare.

In the decades that followed, the hospital expanded services, establishing the Moncrief Cancer Center with a $2.5-million donation from Mr. and Mrs. W. A. Moncrief in honor of

Baylor All Saints Medical Center at Fort Worth has provided quality healthcare to citizens of Fort Worth since 1906. In order to meet future needs of the community, an additional three floors are being added to this building built in 1995. These floors will house dedicated transplant, cardiac and oncology patient care areas.

their sixty-first wedding anniversary. Later, the Moncrief Ambulatory Care Center opened and the Carter Rehabilitation and Fitness Center began offering cardiac, pulmonary and orthopedic-related rehabilitation, along with a fitness center featuring an indoor heated pool, spa, track, aerobics room and resistance training equipment. Then in 1987, All Saints expanded its reach again by building a second full-service hospital in the growing area of southwest Fort Worth, All Saints Hospital Cityview (now known as Baylor Medical Center at Southwest Fort Worth).

By 2001, neurology and neurosurgery were at the forefront with the opening of the Laura Leonard Hallum Neuroscience Center. Today, the center offers expertise in spinal services, stroke, neurosurgery and minimally invasive procedures, along with advanced technology such as deep brain stimulation for treatment of Parkinson's disease, essential tremor and dystonia, and the Gamma Knife* program, which uses gamma radiation and advanced imaging to treat previously inoperable or untreatable conditions in the brain.

A major milestone took place in 2002 when the All Saints Hospitals joined the Baylor Health Care System, an extensive network of private, not-for-profit hospitals in North Texas. The new affiliation would change the hospitals name to Baylor All Saints Medical Centers and give them access to the resources and expertise of Baylor Health Care System, including the Baylor Regional Transplant Institute.

By the summer of 2002, Baylor All Saints Medical Center at Fort Worth was performing Tarrant County's first liver transplant, and by the fall of 2003, the hospital became the only hospital in the county to perform pancreas transplants. Since then, over two hundred patients in Tarrant County have benefited from Baylor All Saints' growing transplantation program, which also includes kidney transplantation.

Today, Baylor All Saints' reputation for full-service acute care continues to grow, not only in cancer, transplantation and neurosciences, but other areas as well. The George Kemble Rehabilitation Center, named in honor of the late George Kemble, M.D., medical director of

✧

Baylor Medical Center at Southwest Fort Worth (formerly Baylor All Saints Medical Center at Cityview) has experienced a revival over the last few years through the addition of numerous specialty physicians to its medical staff and through the development of new programs such as the Weight Management and Surgical Program.

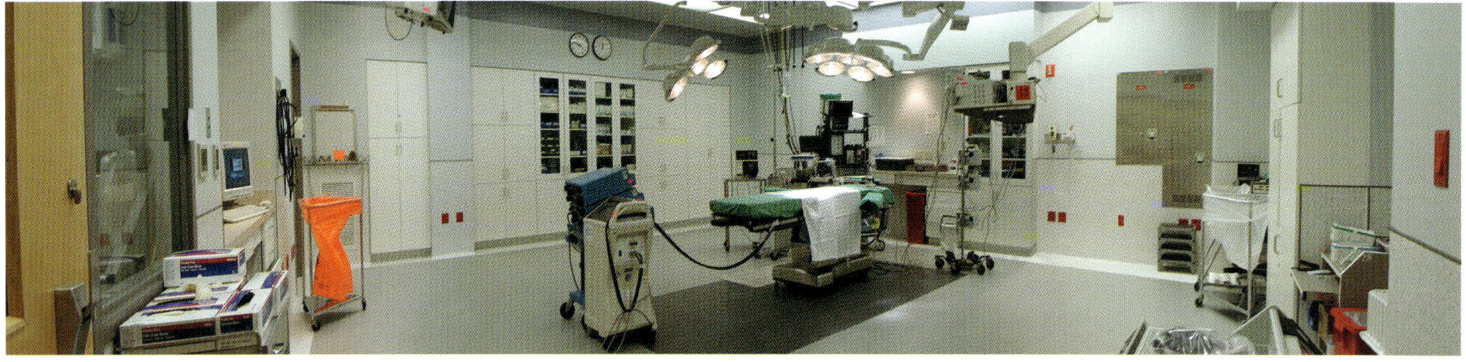

The Transplant Surgical Suite at Baylor All Saints Medical Center was custom designed to meet the needs of its patients and the surgeons, nurses and other healthcare professionals who perform the life-changing transplants. Baylor All Saints Medical Center performs kidney transplants and is Tarrant County's only provider of liver and pancreas transplantation services.

rehabilitation services from 1983 until 2000, was dedicated in January 2003. The center houses Baylor All Saints' comprehensive inpatient rehabilitation services.

In 2004 the Baylor All Saints Regional Heart Center added two new heart therapies to its comprehensive cardiovascular program—cryoablation, which freezes and kills diseased heart tissue, and alcohol ablation, which uses medically prescribed alcohol to kill and shrink excess heart muscle tissue. These procedures complement the heart center's expertise in advanced diagnostic, surgical and noninvasive cardiac techniques, as well as cardiac rehabilitation programs to help heart patients make healthy lifestyle changes.

Women's services are an important focus for both hospitals. In 2004 more than nineteen hundred babies were born in the family-centered childbirth programs at Baylor All Saints and at Baylor Southwest. Specialists at Baylor All Saints also offer prenatal diagnosis and services, high-risk pregnancy care and newborn intensive care. Rounding out the services offered to women are diagnostic screenings like breast imaging and mammography, bone density for osteoporosis,

and medical and surgical treatment for gynecological conditions.

In 2005, Baylor All Saints was the first hospital in Texas and the third in the country to offer patients the new floor-mounted, flat panel interventional radiology suite. The suite allows doctors to perform minimally invasive surgery using high-tech imaging technology. Both Baylor All Saints and Baylor Southwest also have a full range of diagnostic imaging services, including CT scanning, magnetic resonance imaging, ultrasound, and diagnostic radiology.

Also in 2005, the Nicholas and Louella Martin Center for Chronic Pain Management opened to offer patients and their families an interdisciplinary resource to turn to for coping with chronic pain. The center offers medical and surgical treatment, medication management, nutrition, vocational and psychological counseling, rehab therapy and education.

In late 2005, Baylor All Saints benefactors Judy and Paul Andrews, Jr., donated $10 million to the All Saints Health Foundation and laid the groundwork for a $75-million, 170,000-square-foot, four-story Women's Hospital on the campus of Baylor All Saints Medical Center at Fort Worth. The planned 92-bed hospital, will offer comprehensive specialty services such as reproductive medicine, gynecological surgery, pelvic medicine, obstetrical services, a level III intensive care unit for premature and low-birth weight infants. In addition to the traditional women's health services, Baylor All Saints plans to offer a comprehensive breast center, genetic testing services, an aesthetic center, urinary incontinence treatment center, and a sexual dysfunction clinic.

As Baylor All Saints Medical Centers begins its second century of service, the hospitals continue to move forward in order to provide quality healthcare services that make a difference in the lives of residents in the greater Fort Worth community.

**Gamma Knife is owned by and leased from an affiliate of HEALTHSOUTH and is a service of Baylor All Saints Medical Center. The Gamma Knife is not a joint venture of HEALTHSOUTH and Baylor All Saints Medical Center. The physicians providing Gamma Knife services are independent physicians.*

✧

An artist's rendering of the planned Baylor All Saints Medical Center Women's Hospital.

KENNETH COPELAND MINISTRIES

EAGLE MOUNTAIN INTERNATIONAL CHURCH, INCORPORATED

The international headquarters of Kenneth Copeland Ministries (KCM) and Eagle Mountain International Church (EMIC) is located on Eagle Mountain Lake in Fort Worth, Texas. The ministry has offices in Australia, Canada, the United Kingdom, South Africa and Ukraine.

From its inception it has been the mission of KCM, at the time known as Kenneth Copeland Evangelistic Association, to preach the good news of Jesus Christ around the world using every available voice, proclaiming the truth of God's Word and His unconditional love.

Kenneth and Gloria Copeland began the ministry in 1968 with home Bible studies after Kenneth attended Oral Roberts University in Tulsa, Oklahoma. While a student, Copeland had served as a pilot for and participated in the healing crusades conducted by Evangelist Oral Roberts. While traveling, attending classes, and listening to teaching tapes by Kenneth E. Hagin, Copeland gained a wealth of knowledge. It was during that time that he recognized God's call on his life to preach the gospel to the nations.

The Copeland's local home Bible studies eventually grew into revivals that subsequently led to meetings held in convention centers across America. In 1981 they launched an international ministry with meetings in the Philippines.

During the early days of his ministry, Copeland established principles that he believed were critical to the future of the ministry. He determined that the ministry would never ask for a place to preach, never ask people for money in order to get by, and never preach anywhere based on financial considerations. Copeland was surprised to learn after the first meeting that people had ordered ninety-eight tapes of the services. He reports that for several days he was up until almost 4 a.m. making copies—one reel at a time. To reach a wider audience, Copeland started giving the tapes to other Christian ministries for duplication and distribution.

✧

Kenneth Copeland.

Since 1984, KCM has designated the first ten percent of its income to help other ministries, local and worldwide. In this way, KCM touches the lives of people the ministry normally would not reach. Both Kenneth and Gloria Copeland have ministered in prisons throughout Texas, and in 1995, KCM provided funds for the installation of satellite systems in eighty-seven Texas prisons, as well as in Arkansas and Oklahoma prisons, so that inmates would be able to watch special Christian broadcasts by KCM and other ministries.

KCM also reaches out to the community and the world through its prayer department, week long conventions (one of which is held annually in downtown Fort Worth), three-day campaigns, the *Believer's Voice of Victory* television broadcast and magazine, the children's magazine *Shout!* and on the Internet. The ministry also offers product that includes audio and videotapes, CDs, DVDs and books.

Eagle Mountain International Church (EMIC) is an integral part of Kenneth Copeland Ministries. George and Terri Pearsons have been church pastors since 1993. Membership is a blend of brand-new believers and established, mature Christians worshiping together. Services are held Sunday mornings at 8:30 and 11 a.m. and on Wednesday evenings at 7:15 p.m. Childcare and services for children and youth from birth through the teenage years are provided, and special services and classes are held each week.

EMIC offers many opportunities for its members to become involved in educational programs, volunteer activities and outreach endeavors. The Believer's Institute, for example, holds classes with topics of interest for all teens and adults. For young adults, College & Career classes provide fellowship, support and fun. Eagle Home Educators offer parents help with home schooling. Life groups are small groups devoted to building relationships from neighborhood groups to common-interest groups. The Overcomers Class offers love and support for individuals dealing with more challenging life issues. In addition, a number of prayer groups meet every week.

For those who wish to volunteer, there are opportunities to help by providing audio, working in the bookstore, driving a shuttle bus, working the teleprompter at church services or directing traffic in the parking lot. Members act as greeters, hostesses and ushers, may serve on the television crew, at the information station, or in welcoming newcomers. Members may participate in artistic expressions of the ministry through drama, instrumental music and voice. Outreach programs include the altar prayer ministry, hospital and nursing home ministry, prison ministry, prayer groups to include Operation Troops 91 which ministers to military families, Angel Food Ministry and evangelism teams.

In the future, as at present, KCM and EMIC will continue to fulfill a multi-faceted mission which, in part, is: to teach Christians worldwide who they are in Jesus Christ and how to live victoriously; to teach others the biblical principles of faith, love, healing, prosperity, redemption and righteousness; to assist believers in becoming grounded in the Word of God by giving God's Word first place in their lives; to reveal the mysteries and victorious revelations of God's Word that have been hidden throughout the ages; to build an army of mature believers, training them to become skillful in the word of righteousness, and to stand firm in the spiritual warfare against the kingdom of darkness; to proclaim that "Jesus Is Lord" around the world, through the local church and the use of television, campaigns, conventions, books, tapes, magazines, recordings and personal correspondence, as well as through the financial support of other ministries of like purpose.

✧

Above and Bottom, left: Kenneth and Gloria Copeland.

Harris Methodist Fort Worth Hospital

✧

Above: Dora Lucile Estell, Ed.D., the first baby born at Harris Methodist Fort Worth Hospital.

Top, right : Dr. Charles H. Harris.

Bottom, right: Postcard depicting the main entrance, c. 1930.

Below: A new family is born.

In 1919, World War I officially ended, prohibition began, Jack Dempsey knocked out champion Jess Willard for the Heavyweight crown and Dr. Charles H. Harris proposed that the Methodist Church build a hospital in Fort Worth. And so began what has become a Fort Worth icon: Harris Methodist Fort Worth Hospital.

Dr. Harris was so committed to the project he even offered to give the church his private, fifty-bed hospital, including land, located at Fifth Avenue and West Rosedale Streets valued at $100,000.

In 1920 a campaign to raise funds for the construction of the new hospital in the amount of $1 million was agreed upon. The City of Fort Worth was to raise half of the funds and the other half was to be raised by the Central

Texas Conference of the United Methodist Church outside of Fort Worth.

In 1923 the City of Fort Worth had pledged its part of the funds and the Conference had pledged $260,000. Construction began on the building in 1924. After several stops and starts due to lack of funds, Methodist Hospital opened for patients on March 3, 1930 with 146 beds and two floors for patients. Mrs. Hugh Estell had the honor of being the first patient, giving birth to the first baby, Dora Lucile Estell.

By 1932, Methodist Hospital had a medical staff of 200 physicians and 1,200 patients. The hospital performed 600 surgeries and gave $10,000 in charity care that year.

Today, more than 900 physicians are affiliated with the hospital and more than 600 beds are available for patients.

Since 1930, several firsts in Fort Worth have occurred at the hospital, including the first open-heart surgery, first intensive care unit, first heart catheterization and first kidney transplant, just to name a few.

Another first will be the new $62 million, 150,000-square-foot Heart Center being built on the campus. The new Harris Methodist Heart Center, home to the Doris and Robert Klabzuba Tower, will offer 100 cardiac beds, four large interventional procedure labs, four surgery suites solely dedicated to cardiac procedures and an expanded rehabilitation program.

It has been said, success breeds success. With the success of Harris Methodist Fort Worth Hospital has come the success of six other facilities under the same umbrella organization of Texas Health Resources: Harris Methodist Erath County Hospital, Harris Methodist H•E•B Hospital, Harris Methodist Northwest Hospital, Harris Methodist Southwest Hospital, Harris Methodist Walls Regional Hospital and Harris Methodist Continued Care Hospital.

At Harris Methodist Fort Worth Hospital, the staff could not be more proud of its heritage in Fort Worth and are looking forward to another seventy-five years of caring for this community.

For more information about Harris Methodist Fort Worth Hospital or other Texas Health Resources facilities, call 1-888-4-HARRIS or visit www.HarrisMethodistHospitals.org. Harris Methodist Fort Worth Hospital is the choice of a lifetime.

✧

Above: The new Harris Methodist Heart Center opening in 2006.

Below: Over seventy-five years of healing hands and caring hearts.

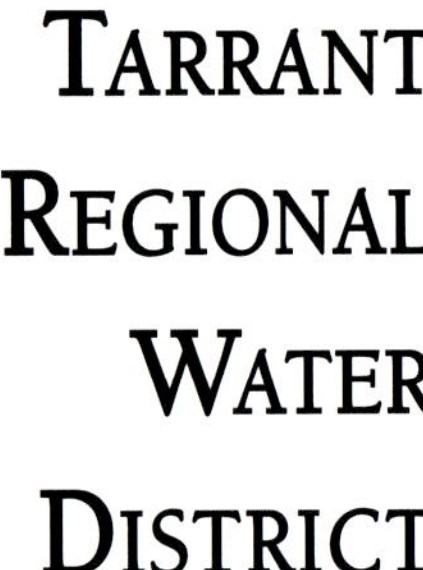

TARRANT REGIONAL WATER DISTRICT

For more than eighty years, the Tarrant Regional Water District has provided quality water to its customers, implemented vital flood control measures and created recreational opportunities for Tarrant County residents and their communities.

Led by a publicly elected five-member board, the Water District owns and operates four major reservoirs in the area, including Lake Bridgeport, Eagle Mountain Lake, Cedar Creek and Richland-Chambers Reservoirs. It also has constructed more than 150 miles of water pipelines, twenty-seven miles of floodway levees, more than forty miles of Trinity River Trails and a 260-acre wetland water reuse project aimed at increasing future water supplies for the area.

After a flood in 1922 claimed the lives of eleven people in Tarrant County and caused massive destruction along the Trinity River, residents took action and prompted civic leaders to create a water control board. Although it would later be changed to its current name in 1996, the Tarrant County Water Improvement District Number One was established in 1924, and took on the challenge of protecting residents from future flooding events and creating a safe water supply for a growing population.

In 1927, voters approved a $6.5 million bond to fund construction of Eagle Mountain Lake, located in Tarrant and Wise Counties, and Lake Bridgeport, located in Wise and Jack Counties. Lake Bridgeport Dam was completed in 1931, and Eagle Mountain Dam was completed in 1932.

After another damaging flood in 1949, the Water District and the U.S. Army Corps of Engineers assumed control of the city's floodway system. The two worked together to make extensive improvements to the river's levees and channels in hopes of preventing future flood events. However, more improvements were needed after another flood in 1957, and by 1968, most of the river's current floodway configuration was in place.

Following a severe drought in the 1950's and a continued rise in the area's population, the Water District later built two additional reservoirs. Cedar Creek Reservoir, located in Kaufman and Henderson Counties, and a pipeline needed to transport water back to Tarrant County were completed in 1964 and 1973, respectively. Richland-Chambers Reservoir, located in Navarro and Freestone Counties, and its pipeline were built during the 1980's. An additional pipeline used to send water to Lake Benbrook for storage and distribution was built during the 1990's.

Today the Water District is one of the largest raw water suppliers in the State of Texas, providing water to more than 1.6 million people in the North Central Texas area. Some of its wholesale customers include the cities of Fort Worth, Arlington, Mansfield and the Trinity River Authority. Operations span a ten-county area that reaches from Jack County to Freestone County, and includes

Above: Water District crews replace a pipe segment that has degraded in strength. It is part of an ongoing testing and maintenance program, in which potentially damaged or corroded pipeline segments are targeted for replacement before they rupture.

Below: A view from Main Street, just north of the courthouse, shows the Trinity River overflowing a levee to flood low-lying areas just north of downtown. The flood of April 25, 1922 in Fort Worth caused loss of life and massive destruction.

maintaining dams at the Water District's four reservoirs and the more than 150 miles of pipeline used for water transport.

Another of the Water District's primary functions is to manage an extensive flood control system in Tarrant County. Featuring more than twenty-seven miles of floodway levees designed by the U.S. Army Corps of Engineers, the system provides vital flood protection to area residents along the West and Clear Forks of the Trinity River. During a heavy rainfall event, a team of Water District engineers uses a network of stream gauges to monitor and analyze river and stream flows. The team's experience and expertise in such situations can help minimize the impact of heavy rainfall on the river and surrounding areas. They also work closely with other organizations, such as the National Weather Service, to gather data and provide information to the public during emergency situations.

Although water supply and flood control remain the Water District's top priorities, lakes and floodway levees provide excellent recreational opportunities for residents and visitors to the area. The floodway's Trinity River Trails stretch more than forty miles through Tarrant County and offer users a safe and scenic venue to enjoy activities such as walking, running, cycling and horseback riding.

Because the population in its service area is expected to reach 2.6 million by 2050, the Water District is already planning for the future. While building additional reservoirs to meet increasing water demands remains a possibility, the Water District has taken a proactive approach to water conservation. It has constructed the first stage of a wetlands water reuse project near Richland-Chambers Reservoir in Navarro County. The goal of the fifteen-year project is to create an environmentally safe alternative to conserving and reusing existing water supplies while enhancing wildlife habitats throughout the wetlands area. Additional stages of the water reuse project are currently in the planning process.

In addition, the Water District will construct another pipeline from Lake Benbrook to Eagle Mountain Lake that will enhance its ability to move and store additional water resources. Construction of the pipeline is expected to be complete by 2008.

As it faces a new set of challenges in a new century, the Tarrant Regional Water District will continue to use its knowledge of the past to help it plan for the future.

✧

Above: River water pumped into wetlands adjacent to Richland-Chambers Reservoir gently flows through a series of cells to remove sediment and nutrients (phosphorous and nitrogen). In approximately seven days, the cleansed water is pumped back into the reservoir to supplement water supplies.

Below: Recently added whitewater chutes at Trinity Park near downtown Fort Worth offer an opportunity for canoeist and kayakers to brush up on their paddling techniques.

Moncrief Cancer Center

Some people never do anything to make their dreams come true. Others, like those who founded Moncrief Cancer Center in 1958, understand that a dream becomes a goal the moment you take action.

The genesis for what is now one of the premier cancer treatment facilities in the nation occurred in the 1950s when Dr. Thomas Burke Bond and several colleagues dreamed of opening a radiation center. They applied for help to the Donnor Foundation of Philadelphia, which granted them a $75,000 Van de Graaff super-voltage X-ray generator, one of twelve given away that year and the only one given to a private group.

Fort Worth's leading citizens then raised funds to build and equip a 5,000-square-foot center near downtown next to All Saints Hospital, a brand new hospital that welcomed its new neighbor, referred to at that time as The Radiation Center. Two prominent residents, William A. "Monty" Moncrief, Sr. and Marvin Leonard, were the center's primary supporters.

Moncrief, a successful oilman, and his wife, Elizabeth, have been such strong supporters of the center that in 1980 it was renamed to honor them following a $2.5 million gift by the couple. Two years later they proved that actions speak louder than words when, during a speech promoting philanthropy before more than 100 healthcare workers and guests, Moncrief pledged to donate another $1 million to the center.

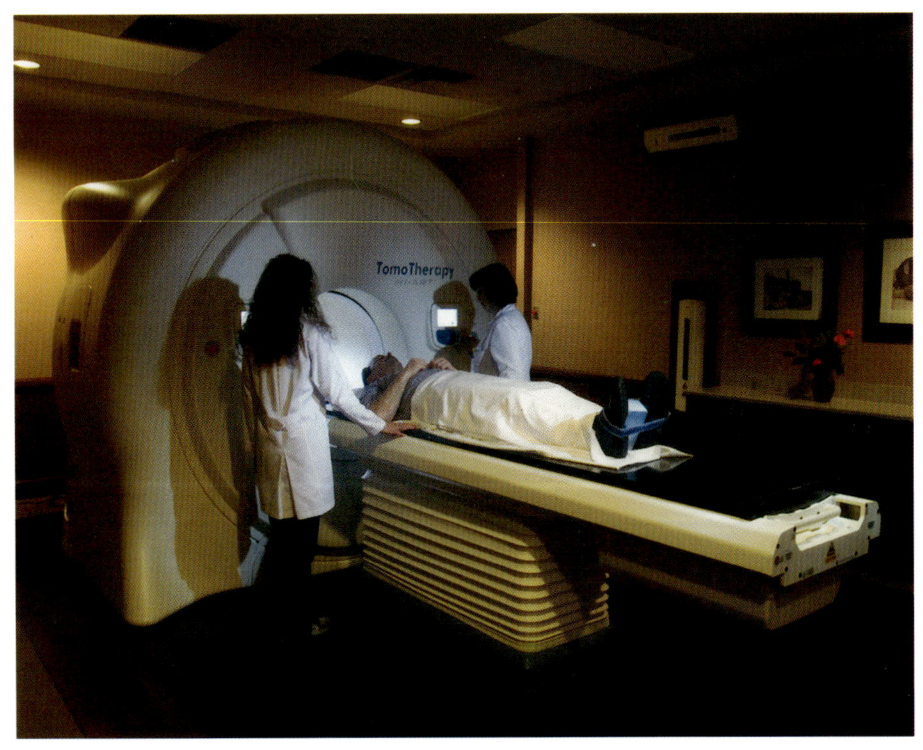

The Radiation Center, operated by the nonprofit Medical and Research Foundation of the Southwest, quickly became both successful and acclaimed as a role model for community radiation centers nationwide. The center treated all patients regardless of their ability to pay and served as a training facility for doctors and technicians.

Through the years, Moncrief Cancer Center has added facilities in southwest Fort Worth, south Tarrant County and Weatherford. Moncrief's experts have been caring for cancer patients and their loved ones through state-of-the-art cancer prevention, treatment and support services for more than four decades.

Today, it continues to offer an array of cancer services, including therapeutic, nutritional and social services. The facilities and equipment are cutting-edge and the medical and support staff is trained at leading medical institutions in Texas and across the nation.

Seeking affiliation with a more comprehensive institution, in 1999 the cancer center's board transferred the center to UT Southwestern Medical Center in Dallas, representing the largest single philanthropic addition to a Texas university or medical center. At the time, Moncrief's physical plant was valued at $20.8 million and its foundation endowment stood at $46.5 million.

The endowment had tripled in value in the previous decade under the leadership of W.A. "Tex" Moncrief, Jr., the Fort Worth oilman and son of Monty Moncrief. Though radiation remains at the core of its mission, the center began expanding its care-giving services when UT Southwestern took control.

The center more vigorously embraced a multidisciplinary approach to patient care that utilizes new and innovative treatment options. With its relationship with UT Southwestern, the center has access to the latest clinical trials and research at one of the premier medical research facilities in the world.

Becoming one of the world's outstanding cancer care centers is the Moncrief Cancer Center's primary goal. The Moncrief Diagnostic Center, which opened in 2000, is a 7,000-square-foot facility adjacent to the Moncrief Center in the south wing of All Saints Hospital. This and a $1 million expansion and renovation at the main Moncrief building are proof that the center is well on its way to becoming one of the best in the world.

The more than 1,500 patients treated yearly at Moncrief find the latest in radiation treatment technology. In 2001, Moncrief put two CAT scanners in its outlying centers at Weatherford and Tarrant County's Huguley Hospital. The center also has added two Varian linear accelerators to complement its comprehensive array of radiation equipment and treatment capabilities. The center offers intensity-modulated radiation therapy and TomoTherapy, the only such system in North Texas.

Patient care enhancements in recent years include further development of social and nutritional services, genetic counseling and risk management, consultations and second opinions, access to clinical trials and research and surgical, gynecologic and orthopedic oncology.

Technology, highly trained oncologists and other healthcare professionals are among the reasons patients value Moncrief Cancer Center. But it is the atmosphere and the attitude that sets the center apart from other healthcare facilities.

The center's carpeted halls are among the reasons patients find the center far from cold and clinical. But it is really the personal touch from the entire staff that makes the center such a pleasant place to be. Staff members greet patients by name and treat them like beloved friends rather than "patient counts."

Fresh-cut flowers, a pot of coffee and the morning newspaper also make the center feel more like home than a cancer center. Or perhaps it is more apt to describe the atmosphere, as one patient did, as that of a five-star resort.

But don't let the friendly, comfortable atmosphere fool you. The staff at Moncrief Cancer Center is serious when it comes to patient care and, like the visionary leaders who founded The Radiation Center all those years ago, those leading the center into the future know that action is the key to turning dreams into reality.

FORT WORTH POLICE DEPARTMENT

Chief Ralph Mendoza.

The Fort Worth Police Department began in 1873 with town marshal Ed Terrell and four deputies. A fifth officer, an African-American named Hague Tucker, joined the force a short time later to police other African-American citizens.

Although three of the four were soon laid off because of the sluggish economy, new officers had to be hired for the duration of the cattle season when the cowboys proved to be too much for the marshal and two deputies.

Through the nineteenth century, the marshal doubled as police chief, an arrangement that would continue until the city adopted the city commission form of government. The city appointed L.J. Polk as police chief on April 14, 1909.

The police force grew with the city and for many years policemen supplemented their salaries with a percentage of fees and fines collected by the city. This system, unfortunately, encouraged rampant corruption. In 1889, Marshal Sam Farmer introduced the first written policies and procedures for the department.

In the late nineteenth century, officers walked their beats or rode horseback. A six-gun and billy club were standard equipment and the officers themselves had to supply them. Officers kept in touch with the station house through telephone call boxes placed throughout town.

Early in the twentieth century, the department moved from horses to motorcycles and bikes. In 1909, Henry Lewis became the first officer to patrol on a motorcycle, a 5-horsepower "Indian" bike. Lewis immediately put his motorcycle to work catching speeders.

Five years later, the department put fifteen patrolmen on bicycles, an experiment that ended in 1917. The department added its first patrol car in 1914. The mounted police force did not come to an end, however, until 1924 when the last horse retired and the last mounted officer, Thomas Bounds, was reassigned to the animal pound.

The next significant innovation came in the 1930s. On Halloween night in 1933, headquarters dispatched a police car by radio to 3454 Lovell to investigate a report of pranksters. In a few years, every patrol car had been equipped with a two-way radio.

Over the next seven decades, steady growth in the size of the department has been accompanied by new technologies, evolving policies and growing diversity in the makeup of the force.

The four-man force has grown into a modern, professional department of more than 1,300 uniformed officers and detectives. Officers now have computers in their patrol cars and use the latest in weapons and forensic technology. As the city expands into the twenty-first century, the department will expand with it, continuing to provide a safe community for everyone.

LENA POPE HOME

Lena Pope looked at her terminally ill son one day in the early part of the twentieth century and wondered aloud what she would do without him. Conrad, her first-born child, pulled a hammer from the beloved tool set he had received for Christmas. "I see a big mansion out beyond the blue," said Conrad, who had always found mansions fascinating. "You and my Daddy must fill it with children."

Conrad eventually succumbed to diphtheria, but the dream that was born that day endured as his mother worked tirelessly to make her son's final wish come true.

With help from the Martha Sunday School Class at Broadway Baptist Church, Pope established Lena Pope Home in 1930 to meet the needs of orphaned children and struggling families. Together, they built several homes and, eventually, a "mansion" on a hill in west Fort Worth, filling each home with children who needed help.

Pope and those who worked with her provided a positive, caring environment to children whose short lives had been filled with tragedy and neglect. She set high expectations for her children and instilled within them a value system as well as a sense of personal responsibility.

Though faced with the ever-changing needs of the community, that philosophy has endured at Lena Pope Home where the ultimate goal is developing young people to their full potential as conscientious citizens. The Home now meets the needs of more than 20,000 adults, children and families each year.

Lena Pope Home Inc. offers alternative education opportunities as well as consultative and therapeutic services in collaboration with the Fort Worth Independent School District and the Crowley Independent School District. These programs focus on teaching students appropriate classroom behavior while maintaining and enhancing academic skills.

Therapeutic foster care is provided to children in homes throughout Tarrant and surrounding counties. The goal is to help children who have been abused, neglected, and abandoned find safe, loving homes where their physical and emotional wounds can heal. Many times an adoptive placement is the appropriate answer for a child, and every resource is devoted to helping match the child with their "forever family."

As a United Way agency, Lena Pope Home offers counseling services to Tarrant County residents through four Family Matters Counseling Centers. Family Matters programs also provide counseling, home-based crisis intervention and stabilization services to adults, children and families twenty-four hours a day. In addition, short-term, family focused intensive services are provided to families with youth that are at risk of abuse, neglect, truancy, running away or involuntary removal from their home and community.

Conrad Pope's dream of a mansion filled with children has grown beyond the dream shared by him, his mother and the Martha Sunday School Class. Lena Pope Home, Inc. is the name given to a wide range of behavioral healthcare services provided by staff and volunteers who are devoted to creating a future of hope for Fort Worth-area children and families.

The Marty Leonard Community Chapel was opened in 1990, and named for long-time board member, Marty Leonard. The interfaith Chapel provides an uplifting environment that inspires people to think their highest and best thoughts. It is a place for worship, inspiration, prayer, guidance, celebration, joy, meditation, hope, relaxation, research, education, music and spiritual and cultural enrichment. Lena Pope Home, Inc. is located at 3131 Sanguinet Street and on the Internet at www.lenapopehome.org.

✧

Below: Marty Leonard Community Chapel.

Bottom: Lena Pope greets her children.

Texas Christian University

Texas Christian University grew from the vision of two brothers, Addison and Randolph Clark, in the tumultuous period after the Civil War. Their dream was to bring education and culture to the rugged Southwestern frontier and to educate leaders who could help to rebuild the shattered nation.

In 1873 the Clarks established TCU's forerunner, AddRan Male & Female College, in Thorp Spring, Texas. Classes began on the first Monday of September with thirteen pupils. It was a radical experiment, for AddRan was among the first post-Civil War schools to teach young men and women co-educationally.

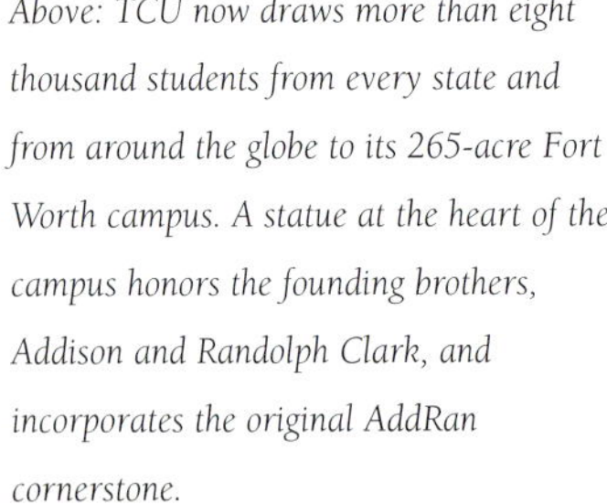

Above: TCU now draws more than eight thousand students from every state and from around the globe to its 265-acre Fort Worth campus. A statue at the heart of the campus honors the founding brothers, Addison and Randolph Clark, and incorporates the original AddRan cornerstone.

Below: TCU's forerunner, AddRan Male & Female College located in Thorp Spring, Texas, c. 1890. The college opened on the first Monday of September 1873 with thirteen pupils. AddRan was one of the nation's first post-Civil War colleges to teach young men and women together.

AddRan relocated to Waco in 1895 when offered the campus of the former Waco Female College. In 1889 the Clarks turned the young school over to the Brotherhood of the Christian Church and the new charter changed the name to AddRan Christian University. The name was again changed in 1902 to Texas Christian University.

The main building of the Waco campus was ravaged by fire in 1910. School trustees accepted an offer of fifty acres for a campus in Fort Worth. After a year of operation in the city's downtown, TCU moved to its present site in 1911.

In the century and a third since its founding, tiny AddRan College has fulfilled the dream of its founders. It has flourished to become one of the top 100 national universities, drawing more than 8,000 students each year from across the country and from around the world. The original three-building campus has expanded to 265 acres and TCU has invested more than $190 million in new and renovated facilities in the last half-decade.

TCU provides students with the benefits of a major university: nearly 100 undergraduate majors, professors who are leaders in their fields, rigorous academic programs, some 200 student organizations and big-time college athletics. The university is known for innovative offerings such as entrepreneurship and nurse anesthesia. TCU makes international education a priority, and about one-third of its students study abroad.

With a fifteen to one student-faculty ratio and a teacher-scholar model that results in close, mentoring relationships, the university also offers many of the advantages of smaller liberal arts colleges. Consequently, a TCU education is not just the sum of semester hours, but an entire experience that grows from its mission: "to educate individuals to think and act as ethical leaders and responsible citizens in the global community."

The university remains related to the Christian Church (Disciples of Christ), a denomination that encourages a reasoned faith and understanding among the world's religions.

DFW Urology Consultants

DFW Urology Consultants began in 1980 with a single Fort Worth office under the direction of its founder, Dr. Wayne A. Hey, D.O., a Philadelphia native and graduate of the Philadelphia College of Osteopathic Medicine.

Dr. Hey, who received his training at the Detroit Osteopathic Hospital Corporation, worked hard to build his business by providing the most complete and modern care possible to both adults and children.

Today, DFW Urology Consultants has grown to include four physicians, twenty-five staff members and satellite offices in Aledo, Arlington, Bedford, Granbury, Grand Prairie, Mansfield, Southlake, Weatherford and West Fort Worth.

Dr. Robert Stroud, D.O., began his residency with Dr. Hey in 1987 and in 1991, joined Dr. Hey in his practice. Dr. David Rittenhouse, D.O., and Dr. Todd Young, D.O., both joined the group in 2001. They treat between 12,000 and 15,000 patients a year.

The four physicians and their staff provide specialty services for adults, including treatments for kidney stones, bladder infections, urinary leakage, and cancer of all the urinary organs. They also treat male impotence and prostrate problems and urological problems in children, namely urinary tract infections, bed-wetting and birth defects.

DFW Urology Consultants uses the latest equipment in treating patients. That includes equipment needed for stone blasting, microwave treatments for the prostrate, laser treatments for surgery and stones and laparoscopic surgery to remove cancer and organs without incisions. They emphasize outpatient, quick-recovery technologies.

The group is affiliated with the University of North Texas Health Science Center, which had the only osteopathic urology residency program in the history of the state. Dr. Hey founded the program. Through this affiliation, the four physicians are constantly updating and teaching the latest surgical techniques and new technologies in urology to present and future physicians.

Dr. Hey opened his first office at Arch Adams and Camp Bowie Boulevard in 1980. Two years later, he opened his first satellite offices in Bedford and Grand Prairie. In 1984, his main office moved to 655 South Great Southwest Parkway. At this same address, Dr. Hey opened the first freestanding MRI facility to operate in the State of Texas. In 1989, DFW Urology Consultants moved its main office to 3821 Camp Bowie Boulevard in Fort Worth. The main office moved to its present location at 1101 University Drive in Fort Worth in 2001. The group has opened other satellite offices through the years as needed.

DFW Urology Consultants is the only group of board-certified osteopathic urologists in Texas and Dr. Hey was the first urologist in Texas to be named a Fellow by the American College of Osteopathic Surgeons. He also received the "Physician of the Year" Award in 2003 from the Physicians Advisory Council in Washington, D.C., and the National Republican Congressional Committee in Washington, D.C has named him "Businessman of the Year" twice, "Entrepreneur of the Year," and "Republican of the Year."

✧

Dr. Hey opens a new office at 1101 University Drive, Fort Worth TX 76107. Shown in this photograph are (from left to right) Ron Hey, Dr. Wayne Hey, and Johnann Davis.

Dr. Hey and the rest of the group owe much of their success to their staff, especially two longtime employees. Johnann Davis has served as head secretary for more than twenty years and Ron Hey, Dr. Hey's brother, who left a teaching career in Minneapolis in 1982 to work as his office manager and business administrator.

DFW Urology Consultants plans to continue offering personalized, state-of-the-art service to patients and plans to add more physicians and open additional satellite offices to serve more North Texas residents. Dr. Hey emphasizes compassionate care from a Christian perspective.

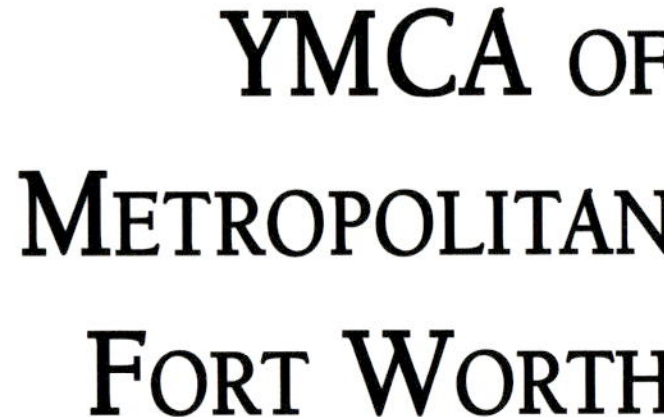

YMCA of Metropolitan Fort Worth

The YMCA of Metropolitan Fort Worth is part of a worldwide organization dedicated to putting Christian principles into practice through programs that build healthy spirit, mind and body for all. The YMCA is a nonprofit entity that offers a variety of services to its members, including fitness classes, sports and aquatic programs, camping, childcare programs and health center memberships.

Founded in 1844 in London, the YMCA was established in Fort Worth in 1890 when Fort Worth was still a frontier settlement. A "Gospel Wagon" was used to transport young men from the streets to rented YMCA facilities at Fourth and Houston Streets, where their physical and spiritual needs were addressed. In 1903, the Negro YMCA branch was established as an independent association. It became a branch of the Fort Worth YMCA in 1919. Bill "Gooseneck" McDonald, a noted African-American leader, was an important contributor in the early days, donating a building to the Negro YMCA. The building was later renamed the McDonald YMCA in recognition of his service to the organization.

Amon Carter, Sr., and his son, Amon Carter, Jr., were instrumental in building the YMCA during the twentieth century. Amon, Sr., served on the YMCA board in the early years, while Amon, Jr., was active in the organization in the post-World War II era. Amon, Sr., laid the cornerstone for the Downtown YMCA building in 1924. After the death of Amon, Jr., the central YMCA building was renamed the Amon Carter, Jr., Downtown YMCA in honor of Carter's service as board chair. In 1948 the Carter family donated land and established the Camp Carter YMCA.

It was during World War II that Amon, Jr., was inspired to become involved in service to the Fort Worth YMCA. When he was a prisoner of war in Poland, Carter befriended a YMCA worker who assisted in prisoner of war camps. Carter later reported that the young worker provided him with comfort and hope at a dark time in his life, and this experience resulted in his lifelong bond with the YMCA.

Through the years, a number of additional branch YMCAs have been opened in Fort Worth, including the Poly YMCA (1937), which later became the Eastside YMCA, the Northwest YMCA, which began as the Northside YMCA in 1946, the Westside YMCA (1948), originally called the Arlington Heights YMCA, the E. R. Van Zandt Southwest YMCA (1952), which began as the TCU-Southside branch, the Airport YMCA (1985), the Southeast YMCA (1991), the Clark Nowlin YMCA (1991), the Ryan Family YMCA (1994) and Benbrook Community Center/YMCA (2000). Together, the various YMCA branches and community centers serve the Fort Worth and surrounding areas, continuing the organization's mission of building strong kids, strong families, and strong communities.

For more information on the YMCA of Metropolitan Fort Worth, please visit www.ymcafw.org .

Above: Amon Carter, Sr. (standing) addresses a crowd as the cornerstone is laid for the Downtown YMCA building in 1924.

Below: The YMCA Gospel wagon used in its early years.

Radiology Associates of Tarrant County

Radiology Associates of Tarrant County is the largest radiology practice in Texas with facilities in Fort Worth, Arlington, Southlake, and Weatherford. Radiology Associates provides high-quality, value-oriented diagnostic services to patients, referring physicians, and payers in the North Texas medical community. The mission of Radiology Associates is to enhance the quality of life of those they serve through continuous improvement in the provision of medical services.

The group began in 1937 when Dr. Tom Bond established the Bond Radiology Group; Bond was the son of Dr. George Bond of Hillsboro, one of the first radiologists in North Texas. Through the years, the group grew to its current size of sixty-one board-certified members. The size and reputation of Radiology Associates have attracted physicians from the best training programs in the country to provide a diverse group with expertise in all areas of radiology.

Radiology Associates has been at the forefront of advances in medical technology over the years, most recently introducing Positron Emission Tomography (P.E.T.) to Tarrant County in 1998 and P.E.T./CT in 2002. There are currently seven Radiology Associates outpatient sites; three in Fort Worth, two in Arlington, and one each in Southlake and Weatherford.

Procedures performed at Radiology Associates include: open and high-field MRI, computed tomography/spiral CT (CT Scanning), P.E.T., nuclear medicine scanning, bone mineral density (DEXA), diagnostic ultrasound, and color Doppler vascular imaging. Also available is ACR accredited mammography, including breast sonography, breast localization, and routine radiology, arthrography, fluoroscopy intravenous pyelography, hysterosalpingography, and sialography are also offered.

Radiology Associates' commitment to serving the community goes beyond its provision of medical services, every year donating funds to benefit Tarrant County residents in need. Recent recipients of donations from the fund include: The Warm Place, AIDS Outreach Center, The Gladney Fund, The Women's Center of Fort Worth, and Tarrant County, and the Women's Shelter of Arlington, Union Gospel Mission, the Presbyterian Night Shelter of Tarrant County, Camp El Tesoro De La Vida, The Boys and Girls Club, Cancer Care Services, Ronald McDonald House of Fort Worth, and the Hill School of Fort Worth.

At each of Radiology Associates' location, the goal is to provide the highest quality of care while making each patient feel special through individualized service. Members of the group believe that both patients and their referring physicians deserve to receive prompt, high-quality service, provided courteously, efficiently and at reasonable cost. All reports are available within twenty-four hours and telephone reports are available upon request. In the future, Radiology Associates plan to continue providing excellent patient care at convenient locations throughout Tarrant County.

✧

Above: Hulen Imaging Center is located at 2911 Oak Park Circle in Fort Worth, Texas.

Below: Southlake Imaging Center is located at 525 East Southlake Boulevard in Southlake, Texas.

The University of Texas at Arlington

✧

Above: The UT Arlington campus offers a wide variety of activities and opportunities for students to be involved and engaged.

Below: The Lady Mavs earned their first NCAA Tournament bid by capturing the Southland Conference Championship in 2005.

The University of Texas at Arlington is located in the heart of the Dallas/Fort Worth Metroplex, one of the fastest growing areas in the nation. UT Arlington is a Carnegie doctoral-extensive teaching, research, and public service university, offering 92 undergraduate and 111 graduate degrees.

Founded in 1895 as Arlington College, a private liberal arts institution, UT Arlington has undergone a succession of names, ownerships, and missions. Its final name change came in 1967, when it became The University of Texas at Arlington.

The student body, more than 25,000 strong, is diverse, representing nearly every state and more than 100 countries. The University's academic programs include architecture, business administration, education, engineering, liberal arts, nursing, science, social work, and urban and public affairs. Additionally, UT Arlington offers one of only six Honors Colleges in the state of Texas.

In response to societal needs, UT Arlington has evolved into a renowned university within the state and is emerging nationally and internationally. The University's history of academic achievement can be attributed to its outstanding faculty, a strong student body, and a record of successful graduates in their chosen fields. UT Arlington's reputation for training its students to hit the ground running from day one makes its graduates more attractive to some of the nation's most prestigious firms.

UT Arlington is leading the way in developing technological innovation and research centers across academic departments. In addition, its partnerships with the business community, including the Arlington Chamber of Commerce, are long-standing and have resulted in the establishment of the Arlington Technology Incubator. Through the Incubator, UT Arlington's research capabilities are linked with the business community to benefit the University, the marketplace, and the local economy in fields such as biodegradable medical devices, computer hardware and software development, and data-protection systems, as well as continuing education and business services.

Research work being conducted in the University's Nanotechnology Research & Teaching Facility, one of only a handful in the nation, involves the study and fabrication of extremely small devices that may well revolutionize the twenty-first century.

UT Arlington students enjoy rigorous academics and access to scholarly research, but also the traditional college experience, including national sororities and fraternities and NCAA Division I athletics. Thousands of students live on campus in new residence halls and apartments with state-of-the-art facilities. Several residence halls also include living and learning centers for students to immerse themselves in their interests.

The University of Texas at Arlington, with a history of academic excellence that is both affordable and accessible, has served more than one hundred thousand alumni.

For more information about UT Arlington, please visit www.uta.edu.

River Legacy Foundation

Situated on the banks of the West Fork of the Trinity River in Arlington, River Legacy Parks encompasses an area graced by huge hardwood trees and native plants and inhabited by countless birds, fish and mammals. It is a place that offers serenity and the solace of nature to urban residents of the Metroplex as well as an unparalleled learning experience for children and adults alike. This haven for plants, animals and people opened as a city park in 1990 as a result of a partnership between private citizens and the City of Arlington known as River Legacy Foundation.

The land for the original park was donated to the city in 1976 by relatives of Arlington pioneer James Gibbins and its 204 acres were called Rose Brown May Park. As the population of Arlington grew, community leaders approached the Parks and Recreation Department (PARD) about expanding and improving the park for greater public use. As a result, another 171 acres were donated to the city and $100,000 in seed money raised. As the scope of the project became clear, PARD officials and citizens joined forces and established the nonprofit River Legacy Foundation. The Foundation acts in concert with the North Central Texas Council of Governments' master plan for Trinity Trails, a greenbelt that, when completed, will reach from Dallas to Fort Worth.

The first phase of River Legacy parkland opened to the public in 1990, with visitors exploring trails and river overlooks and enjoying picnic areas and playgrounds. Phase II of the park was completed the following year with the inclusion of a new picnic pavilion, trail enhancement, and the planting of additional trees.

From the beginning, Foundation board members agreed that education should be an intrinsic part of the River Legacy experience, but a home was needed for this endeavor. In keeping with the goal of environmental protection and enhancement, architect Eddie Jones designed the Living Science Center to appear as an integral part of the surrounding forest. At a cost of $5 million, the 12,000-square-foot Center houses classrooms, interactive exhibits, a gift shop and offices.

During the school year, nature classes are offered to children from three to five years old. Programs for older children include studies in seasonal ecology, animal behavior and aquatic ecology. People of all ages enjoy nature walks, hiking, bird watching and the ponds where water lilies grow.

River Legacy Parks resulted from the hard work of dedicated people who over many years made it into a prized asset for the Arlington area. The city will soon complete its segment of Trinity Trails, with River Legacy Parks the crown jewel of the entire system. The Foundation is committed to preserving the Trinity River habitat and enriching the parkland for the benefit of generations to come.

TARRANT COUNTY HISTORICAL SOCIETY

The mission of the Tarrant County Historical Society is to preserve history, enhance education, and encourage interest in learning and promoting the history of Tarrant County. The Society meets on the third Thursday of the month at various locations.

Old Settlers and Historical Society was first founded in Fort Worth in 1897 with a membership of one hundred people. One meeting was held annually until 1924 when the group ceased to exist. Following Fort Worth's Diamond Jubilee, the group was reorganized in 1926 as the Fort Worth Historical Society. This group lasted until it became inactive during the years of World War II.

On a recommendation by the Fort Worth Library Board, the Historical Society was reorganized and R. L. Paschal, a principal in the Fort Worth school system, was elected president. The Society began in 1980 and remained active for eight years. In April 1948, fifty-seven members met and reorganized the group as the Tarrant County Historical Society. Frank Kent became the first president. The Society has met continuously since this reorganization.

From 1948 until the mid-1960s, the Society took on many special projects. Among those projects were the mounting of seven bronze markers identifying Fort Worth's earliest buildings. The sites included the first church, school, bank, hotel, railroad terminal, trading post, and grist mill.

With the permission of the Fort Worth City Council and with a site set aside by the City of Fort Worth's Parks Department, the Society collected and restored numerous buildings for the Log Cabin Village. The Society continues to maintain Log Cabin Village, though the Village is owned and operated by the City of Fort Worth. Another project in which the Society was involved was the publication of the *Guide to Historic Sites in Fort Worth and Tarrant County*. The first edition of the guide was publised in 1963. It was revised in 1975 and then again in 1985. Texas Christian University Press published book with funding from the Society. The publication is still available.

In 1999 the Society took part in the City's 150-year celebration by publishing a brochure of the "Fort Worth's Firsts" markers. These brochures were available to tourists and citizens. The Society underwrote Judith Cohen's book *Cowtown Modern: Art Deco Architecture in Fort Worth*, which was published in 1988. The Society sponsored the placement of paintings by a local artist, Sweetie Ladd, in the Fort Worth Central Library. In 2000 a microfilm reader was funded for the public library and began an annual discretionary fund that would allow the archivist to purchase incidental items. In 2006 the Society has underwritten awards to students in the Regional History Fair for projects concerning the history of Tarrant County. A recent cash grant to the Friends of the Van Zandt Cottage will further the goal of preserving and restoring this early Tarrant County home.

Donald Sutton, president of the Tarrant County Historical Society, 2005-2006.

THE MURRIN FAMILY

To get to an appreciation for the River Ranch in the Fort Worth Stockyards or the West Fork Ranch located west of Fort Worth on Marys Creek, one needs to return to 1885 when Stephen Murrin (1855-1911) arrived in Fort Worth. Murrin left his home at Killeybegs, County Donegal, Ireland in 1879. Son of James and Susan (McNelis) Murrin, he was the sixth son in a family of nine children, a position that guaranteed he would have no chance of owning any of the land his father had accumulated. Armed with optimism and a dedication to hard work, he opened a saloon with his brother John on Front Street across from the train depot. The next year, with a new partner, he owned the Grand Hotel Bar at 108 East Weatherford, across from the county courthouse. By 1900, he was the sole owner.

Stephen Murrin became an upright member of the community. Married to Mary Hegarty, he fathered five children: Susan, John, Joseph, Stephen, and Frances. He supported the building of the new church, St. Patrick's, and participated in the fundraiser which provided the incentive to attract both Swift and Armour packing houses to the stockyards. He was prosperous enough to be able to travel back to Ireland on several occasions to visit his parents. A home for the family at 101 Elm had a large barn behind to hold the family horses, a carriage, and a rig he liked to use for harness racing below Samuels Avenue.

His son Stephen (1893-1973) inherited his father's penchant and respect for hard work. He sold newspapers and the *Saturday Evening Post* downtown as a boy, and delivered packages on his bicycle to Washer Brothers customers on Quality Hill at $8 a week. He first became involved with the Fort Worth Stockyards as a cowboy for cattle traders Edger Kerr and T. B. Saunders & Co, then progressed to a level of responsibility of making trades, and delivering cattle to ranches north and west of Fort Worth or to Kansas and Chicago.

The cattle business in postwar days was depressed from the exercise of the "Armistice Clause." The clause cancelled all supply contracts at the end of WWI, and cattle prices plummeted. Stephen had done a little trail cooking and opened a "stand up-only "chili parlor, between the F&M and First National Banks facing West Seventh. His "Steve's" proved a real success for the lunch crowd during the '20s boom that followed the discovery of oil in West Texas. In 1927 he purchased a pie shaped lot at the end of the trolley line at 4700 Camp Bowie Boulevard and opened a new "Steve's" that had plenty of room for diners and even featured "curbservice" for the automobile trade. In 1935, he bought the ranch west of Fort Worth, married Caroline Cuilty and generally fulfilled his life long dream. A home was built in 1940, high on a hill where he could look out with joy and pride over the land he called Donegal Hills. Here his three children—Caroline, Steve, and Susan—were raised and the area instilled in them a love for the land as deep as his own.

His son, Steve, Jr, grew up at his father's side, working cattle, going with him to sell them at the Stockyards, and listening to all the cattle talk at home, at the Stock Show, and at sales. After embarking on a career in real estate, Steve, Jr., along with others, could see that the Stockyards that had been such a prosperous part of the city was in trouble. Much of the cattle business had left, leaving few related businesses that had to compete with an aging and deteriorating district. There were proposals to demolish the cattle/packing house facilities in order to take advantage of heavy industry zoning that would permit the area to take advantage of the new market for industrial parks. Murrin, along with others, began to accumulate real estate in the area, but his real goal was to change the perception of the Stockyards as a "down-and-out" area. It was a struggle, but joined by a variety of like-minded enthusiasts, the battle to return the original home of indoor rodeo to its proper use was won, and in 1975, the rodeo returned. The Cowtown Rodeo remains the world's only yearround weekly rodeo.

For a while, the city fathers were blind to the possibilities in the Stockyards and the North Side, but by the 1980s, things were changing. An economic force—tourism—that had nothing to do with aviation, the military, computers, or any of the other businesses in town, became an asset that the city began to foster. Today, visitors from around the world visit Fort Worth to enjoy its world-class museums, lively downtown, but especially to see what Cowtown is made of.

✧

Steve Murrin, Jr.

COURTESY OF JEREMY ENLOW, *FORT WORTH, TEXAS MAGAZINE.*

Main Street, Fort Worth, 1889.

COURTESY OF THE JACK WHITE PHOTOGRAPH COLLECTION, SPECIAL COLLECTIONS, UNIVERSITY OF TEXAS AT ARLINGTON LIBRARIES, ARLINGTON, TEXAS, AR 407 1-9-3.

The arrival of the railroad heralded a period of spectacular growth. The crops brought to town on this market day late in the 1870s would directly be loaded onto freight cars bound for distant mills. Surely some of the farmers' profits ended up in the hands of merchants along this busy row of business houses, further stimulating local commerce.

COURTESY OF THE JACK WHITE PHOTOGRAPH COLLECTION, SPECIAL COLLECTIONS, UNIVERSITY OF TEXAS AT ARLINGTON LIBRARIES, ARLINGTON, TEXAS.

The clubhouse and course at River Crest, completed in 1911, provided a fashionable anchor for the upscale suburb, just east of Arlington Heights. Its developers, however, had to ring the links with a fence to keep out livestock.

COURTESY OF SOUTHWESTERN MECHANICAL COMPANY COLLECTION, SPECIAL COLLECTIONS, UNIVERSITY OF TEXAS AT ARLINGTON LIBRARIES, ARLINGTON, TEXAS, 98-97-50.

Building a Greater Tarrant County

Tarrant County's utilities, construction companies, and manufacturing industries shape the county's future and provide fuel for the state

A. E. Petsche 254
Acme Brick 256
AMSCO Steel 260
Coca-Cola Enterprises, Incorporated 250
DFW Movers & Erectors, Inc. 252
Eberle Engineering Company, Ltd. 262
General Electrodynamics Corporation 265
General Motors Arlington Assembly 248
Harbison-Fischer Manufacturing Company 266
Justin Brands 264
Kenneth William Davis 240
Onis Stone, Inc. 258
Reeder Distributors, Inc. 247
Sand Trap Service Co., Inc. 267
Schrickel, Rollins and Associates, Inc. 268
SkiHi Enterprises Incorporated 269
Thomas S. Byrne, Ltd. 270
Williamson-Dickie Manufacturing Company 244

Kenneth William Davis

by William S. Davis

Kenneth William Davis of Fort Worth was a thoroughly modern man. His vision and innovation brought into being one of the most astonishing arrays of diverse industrial companies ever forged by one man in a single lifetime. Their manufacturing and services extended around the earth.

Davis was born on November 25, 1895, in Morrellville, Pennsylvania. In this obscure town he hawked newspapers and sold baseball score cards for money, and later played semi-professional baseball. When World War I began, he applied for pilot training in the fledgling U.S. Army Air Corps, traveling to Fort Worth for his first assignment. At Fort Worth's Barron Field he was promoted to lieutenant and flight instructor after a brief period of flight training; there he remained till the war's end. During this period, he met and eventually married his lifetime partner, Alice Mae Bound, whose grandfather had moved to Fort Worth in 1876, where he made and repaired boots for the cowboys coming through town on the trail drives.

✧

Above: Lieutenant Ken Davis, U.S. Army Air Corps, shown here in the flight togs he wore when he first came to Fort Worth and was stationed as a flight instructor at Barron Field.

Below: Ken and Alice Mae Bound were married in 1921.

Davis and his new bride moved to El Dorado, Arkansas. Davis recalled how he and Alice first arrived at El Dorado on horseback. As they entered town, they passed the fire station, which was hurriedly mobilizing its horse drawn wagon to respond to a nearby house fire. Davis arrived at the fire minutes before the firemen and in a moment of inspiration, he located the owner from among the onlookers and immediately purchased the house. The fire quenched, he eventually turned all the burned boards around so that only the good sides showed, partitioned the house into two parts, rented one part to a tenant, and lived in the other. He proclaimed himself to be the only person ever to buy a house while it was on fire.

After briefly working for an oilfield supply company in El Dorado, Ken and Alice moved to Orange, Texas, where he sold supplies in the budding oil boom. In 1929 he moved back to Fort Worth, and joined Mid-Continent Supply, a struggling pipe and fittings business. The depression was under way, and oil was selling for just ten cents per barrel. But in 1930, Davis optimistically assembled $5,000 and purchased Mid-Continent.

Despite the depression, huge oil fields were coming into play in Texas, Louisiana, and Arkansas. Fort Worth had become the geographical center of rail transportation access to the nascent industry. Davis combined market timing with quick reaction and began opening boomtown stores. At

✧

Left: The Mid-Continent Supply headquarters building located at the corner of Sixth and Main Street, Fort Worth, Texas.

Right: The world's deepest well. Loffland Brothers Company Rig 32 towering into the air as high as a seventeen-story building on an Oklahoma farm land location, drilled deeper into the earth than man has ever drilled before—31,441 feet in 504 days.

the end of the '30s, Mid-Continent owned thirty strategic locations. Davis was the first to install radio communication between all field sales, vehicles and stores for quick response delivery of supplies and services from Mid-Continent's local stores to regional rigs. Mid-Continent leaped to the forefront in oilfield service and the profits it stimulated for the company quickly elevated its financial base.

From his permanent Fort Worth office at Sixth and Main Street, Davis established his reputation and fame as a world leader in product service and innovation. Over the years, Davis bought Unit Rig & Equipment Company, a maker of drilling rig drawworks in Tulsa, Oklahoma. He started Livermore and Company in Midland, Texas, a drilling contractor later renamed Great Western Drilling Company. He formed Dorris Ballew Company, a Natchez partnership for oil exploration in Mississippi. Later came the acquisition of Tulsa's Loffland Brothers Company, soon thereafter to become the world's largest drilling company with 150 rigs operating worldwide. The company drilled discovery wells and developed many of the world's major oil deposits. Stratoflex Incorporated of Fort Worth was a fledgling entry into development of the futuristic use of the innovative, flexible, high-pressure rubber, wire braided hose and fittings to replace metal tubing. Stratoflex soon became a major component supplier to the automotive, aircraft, marine, and defense industries. Harrisburg, Inc., a Houston based small oilfield specialty company, was organized and grew to become a major specialty supplier to drilling rigs. Fort Worth's Cummins Sales & Service purveyed the Cummins diesel engine in its exclusive territory encompassing Texas, New Mexico, Oklahoma, Louisiana, and Kansas. Davis founded Diesel International in Arlington, Texas and fleshed it out with distribution rights for a wide variety of European sourced small-size diesel engines for every application in its southwest distribution area. He opened the doors of Kendavis Industrial Supply to furnish a complete line of industrial goods in Texas and Oklahoma and to the defense industry. Fort Worth's newly formed Sierra International grew to supply publication and publicity services to diverse companies. Mid-Continent Pipeline Equipment Company of Houston was organized to develop, build, sell and service heavy equipment to the pipeline construction industry. Under his banner of Kendavis Industries International, Inc., more than forty diverse stars sprinkled the Davis constellation of companies that operated in thirty countries on six continents.

Under Davis' leadership, his astounding conglomerate led the world in many areas. His Unit Rig & Equipment Company furnished many of the tow tractors for the

Right: The seventy-five-foot Golden Driller statue, presented by Ken W. Davis as the symbol of the 1966 International Petroleum Exposition in Tulsa, Oklahoma.

Below: The Chapel of the Intercession, First Presbyterian Church, given by Alice and Kenneth W. Davis in 1957. "This chapel is Given to the Glory of God and that People who Here Assemble May Worship the Father In Spirit and in Truth."

world's airports to position the new generation Boeing 747 commercial aircraft. U.S. Army battle tanks carried Unit Rig bridges on-board to span river channels for troop movements. The company's new electric wheel drive trucks revolutionized open pit mining, capturing three quarters of the free world's open pit mining truck market.

Davis' superb marketing skill was evidenced by his creation of a unique corporate icon for Sratoflex, "Zing Zong." Leaders from all aspects of American industry were engaged to give support to the return of Zing Zong "back to his home on the moon." The promotion culminated when an image of Stratoflex's "spokes creature" became the first commercial icon to be placed on the moon's surface.

Davis' Loffland Brothers Company drilled alternate energy source, geothermal wells in California; he oversaw the drilling of large diameter atomic test holes for the Atomic Energy Commission in Nevada. A ten-foot-diameter hole drilled to 5,000 feet achieved the record for the largest diameter hole ever drilled. In Oklahoma, Loffland held the world record for drilling the deepest hole, bottoming out at 31,441 feet. The company's ocean jack-up platforms, designed to rest on the ocean floor and operate in three hundred feet of water, were the world's largest. The company also led the way in inland waterway barge drilling techniques in Louisiana. Davis' rigs operated extensively in Colombia, Chile, Argentina, Venezuela, and Bolivia, as well as throughout Africa and the Middle East, Indonesia, the North Sea, and Canada.

Cummins Sales & Service, a company he formed in 1934, became the predominant service organization for highway trucks in the Southwest. By the 1960's Davis' Cummins engines were powering over seventy percent of cross-country, heavy duty freight trucks, and his engines were heavily represented in the oil well drilling rig and marine industries.

Great Western Drilling Company expanded from contract drilling to wildcatting and eventually participated in the development of oil and gas production from hundreds of wells on thousands of acres of leased properties. On a train trip one day, during which he shared a coach compartment with strangers, one of the passengers revealed himself as an oil operator who annoyingly and endlessly bragged about the five oil wells he owned. When finished, he asked his fellow passengers what they did, and Davis responded that he, too, had some oil wells. When asked how many, Davis replied, "Well, I don't know exactly, but I have five on fire right now."

Davis' innovations changed oil drilling technology and power applications. His turnkey waterflood oil recovery installations led the industry, and Mid-Continent Supply became the largest world supplier of gas turbine power packages to oil and engineering companies. The company's massive, one-of-a-kind depot in Houston provided oilfield related components, equipment, and off-the-shelf power packages of every kind for American and international users. Davis oversaw the invention and application of the Desert Master, the largest rig moving equipment on earth, designed to move a complete, 500-ton rig through open country from one location to the next, ready to drill. Mid-Continent's patented Rock Over Trailer revolutionized desert rig transportation. Davis also patented his "Any Engine" swinging compound, which enabled a driller to switch to any combination of engines on his rig during uninterrupted operations; the "AE" swinging compound became an invaluable standard on drilling rigs worldwide.

During a significant cycle of expansion, Davis contracted out his Loffland Brothers Company to complete a huge Pan American Petroleum Corporation oil development project in the forbidding Patagonia region of Argentina. Davis successfully rallied his organization to meet a thirty day deadline to place on outward bound ships at the Port of Houston a fleet of ten, new, complete Mid-Continent drilling rigs and support equipment, a historic and yet unequaled "first" in the petroleum industry.

Davis sponsored a promotion to make the Trinity River navigable for shipping from Fort Worth to the Gulf of Mexico. Although Fort Worth failed to become an inland seaport, the project lit the fuse for the construction of the many lakes along the Trinity. To dramatize the seaport possibility, Davis had freight shipped up the Trinity waterway from the Gulf of Mexico to Gateway Park, in Fort Worth, Texas the first ever commercial use of the putative "Port of Fort Worth."

To symbolize Davis' prestige and popularity in the halls of world industry, the International Petroleum Exposition commissioned him to erect his commercial icon, "The Golden Driller" as the I.P.E.'s grand symbol of the worldwide petroleum industry. This seventy-five foot statue guards Tulsa's exposition hall to this day.

Ken and Alice were leaders in Fort Worth's religious, cultural, educational, and medical institutions. They were instrumental in the establishment of the Gonzales Warm Springs Foundation for polio-crippled children, Fort Worth's Noble Planetarium at the Museum of Science and History, the First Presbyterian Church chapel, and a complete floor of the All Saints Episcopal Hospital, where he was a member of the Board of Directors. Davis was a director of Great Southwest Corporation, owner of the Six Flags over Texas theme park. A loving family man, a private man, he died at his home in Fort Worth on August 29, 1968.

✧

Above: Kenneth Davis' family home in Fort Worth until his death in 1968.

Below: The Davis Family mausoleum in Greenwood Cemetery, Fort Worth, Texas. The inscription "Man's greatest happiness comes from the joy he gives others. That which we create from God's bounty will be our living legacy."

WILLIAMSON-DICKIE MANUFACTURING COMPANY

Williamson-Dickie Manufacturing Company, headquartered in Fort Worth, is the largest manufacturer of work apparel in the world, with market outlets in all fifty states and across six continents. Through continuing expansion and modernization of its product line, the company now offers, in addition to work shirts and pants, garments for casual wear, women's work clothing, school uniforms, outerwear, denim jeans and a variety of accessories. The Dickies brand is known the world over for its quality workmanship and durability and has continued to appeal to consumers for generations.

The company grew from very modest beginnings to its current position as a market leader. It started in 1918 when C. N. Williamson and E. E. "Colonel" Dickie, together with a few friends, purchased the U.S. Overall Company for $12,500 in order to manufacture bib overalls for workmen. Four years later, Williamson's son C. Don Williamson joined his father and Dickie in purchasing one-third each of the company and renamed it Williamson-Dickie Manufacturing Company.

In the beginning, the company operated from a small frame building on Boaz Street where thirty-five employees, using twenty sewing machines, produced overalls and children's play suits. At that time, the clothing was made of 100 percent cotton. Within three years of its opening, the company had 400 employees working twenty-four hours a day in three eight-hour shifts and had rented a larger workspace.

Williamson-Dickie grew steadily from its early years, slowed only by the Great Depression of the 1930s. In 1937, founder C.N. Williamson died, Dickie became president and C. Don Williamson became vice-president. By 1943 the company had 2,200 employees engaged in producing nine million uniforms for soldiers fighting in World War II. After the war, Williamson established new factories, warehouses and sales territories throughout the United States, greatly expanding the company's geographical reach. In 1947 the company produced almost two million pairs of work pants. Dickie died in 1951 and C. Don Williamson became president of the company. In the late 1950s, the company expanded into the European and Middle Eastern markets.

Williamson-Dickie introduced a number of innovative improvements in the garment industry, including "Easy-Alter" waistbands and "Shape-Set," the first wrinkle-free fabric. The no-iron fabric was developed after C. Don Williamson watched his wife give herself a home permanent. Williamson wondered if the same chemical process used in permanents could be applied to fabric and hired a chemist to find out. The result was the patented "Shape-Set" that became enormously popular with consumers. Other innovations were the zipper fly to replace buttons and a vacuum cylinder pants press that lessened the labor required in the production process.

A major reason for the success of Williamson-Dickie was the vision of C. Don Williamson. Williamson believed in manufacturing what customers needed and wanted and was open to change. In the 1930s he instituted a consumer research program that predated modern market research by many years.

The company was also ahead of its time in its management style and treatment of employees. In 1944 the company established a profit-sharing retirement plan for employees and soon provided air-conditioned facilities, a cafeteria, paid vacations, life and hospitalization insurance, a library and other amenities and employee benefits that were far from standard at the time.

Throughout the 1950s and 1960s, the demand for Williamson-Dickie's garments continued to grow. Advertising on radio programs, billboards and use of the Dickie's brand in major movies boosted sales. Dickie clothing was featured in several movies in the 1950s, such as *Quicksand*, *The Returning of the 45th Division*, and the award-winning *From Here to Eternity*. In 1956 the company used thirteen million yards of cloth producing work and casual clothes primarily for men and boys. In 1960, C. Dickie Williamson, the elder son of C. Don Williamson, became vice-president and general manager of the company. The first foreign factory opened in Belize in 1961, with J. Don Williamson, younger son of the elder Williamson, as manager. When C. Don Williamson died in 1961, Dick Williamson became president and chief executive officer; Don Williamson was named executive vice-president.

In the 1970s, Williamson-Dickie attracted consumers through its sponsorship of television shows such as *NBC Evening News, The Joey Bishop Show, The Today Show and The Tonight Show*. The company reached ninety-four percent of American homes through television. Dick Williamson was named chairman and CEO in 1971; Don Williamson became the company president. Sales of the Dickie brand continued to increase.

In 1982 the company purchased the building at 319 Lipscomb Street in Fort Worth that serves as corporate headquarters. Built in 1892, the red brick building formerly housed the Stephen F. Austin Elementary School, which C. Don Williamson attended as a child. By 1989, Williamson-Dickie had twenty-one

factories in operation in eight countries. The company produced twenty-three million garments and sold eight million pairs of jeans.

During the late 1980s, Don Williamson retired from his position as president and shortly thereafter Dick Williamson died. Gail Williamson, Dick's widow, was named chairman of the company, with her son, Philip C. Williamson, as vice-president of operations. Currently, Philip Williamson is chairman, president and CEO of Williamson-Dickie and Gail Williamson Rawl, who has remarried, is vice chairman.

Dickies work and casual clothes still appear on television shows and in some of Hollywood's most celebrated movies. In 2003-2004, the Dickie brand was prominent in *Monster, Training Day, John Q, Terminator 3* and *The Stepford Wives*, among others. Williamson-Dickie also makes the clothing for Big Tex, the mascot for the State Fair of Texas and supplies uniforms for State Fair workers.

Williamson-Dickie contributes to numerous community endeavors and charities. The company is a major sponsor of the annual Fort Worth Stock Show and Rodeo, the Fort Worth Cats Baseball Team and the Texas State Fair. Williamson-Dickie also supports the Fort Worth Zoo, the Modern Art Museum, the Van Cliburn Competition, the Jewel Charity Ball, the Colonial Golf Tournament and many local charities.

In 1985, C. Dickie Williamson gave a speech to the Newcomen Society at the Fort Worth Club in which he presented the history of Williamson-Dickie and expressed his view of the company's products:

"Work clothing has always been an important product for Williamson-Dickie Manufacturing Company. From its very beginning as U.S. Overall, the company has manufactured work clothes. Even though we have made clothing that ranges from jeans to jackets, from leisure suits to jump suits, from disposable paper coveralls for atomic plant workers to fleece-lined coveralls worn by snowmobilers, the core of the product line is work clothes."

Two decades later, under the leadership of Dick's son, Philip, this theory still holds true. Work clothes are the centerpiece of the Dickies line and it is emphasized in the company's goal statement: "To be the branded choice in work apparel."

Although people of all social strata, from college students to Hollywood celebrities now wear Williamson-Dickie apparel, the company has not forgotten the workers of America. Each year, the company sponsors the American Worker of the Year Contest. Winners are chosen based on short essays and often receive national recognition and congratulatory phone calls from the White House. The annual contest continues the tradition of showing respect for customers, long a hallmark of Williamson-Dickie and a primary contributor to the company's great success. As Williamson-Dickie continues to meet the needs of customers through innovative manufacturing technologies, effective market strategies and responsible customer service, the company that began in the early twentieth century is likely to flourish well into the twenty-first.

Reeder Distributors, Inc.

Gary Reeder saw an opportunity where others saw only a crisis. The year was 1973 and the Middle East had cut off the supply of crude oil to the United States. Cars lined up at gas stations to get what little gasoline the stations had to sell.

The entire U.S. economy—not to mention the rest of the world—was in a perilous position. Most would not have had the courage to start a new business amid such a gloomy economic forecast.

But Reeder, who was working at a small independent refinery in Euless at the time, saw his chance. So he left his job and founded Reeder Distributors, Inc. in Fort Worth with plans to become a wholesale distributor of fuels and lubricants.

His actions were not based on a whim. His uncle owned the refinery where he had worked, which meant Reeder had access to fuel. He started the company with himself as the only employee and 30 years later employment topped 50 people.

Reeder had help along the way from other people and events that few could have foreseen. One critical hire was Jim Norman, senior vice president and fuel manager, who joined the company in 1975. And one critical event was the U.S. Department of Energy allocations that became important and profitable to the company in the late 1970s.

Other key events in the company's history occurred in 1985 when RDI decided to get into the bulk lube business and 1987 when the company built new offices and a terminal to allow the lubricant business to expand.

Also, the key to the success of the lubricant division was the hiring of Jim Moore as vice president of lubricants in 1990.

In 2002, RDI moved its equipment division to a new location at 821 East Loop 820 in Fort Worth. The company is now one of the largest wholesale fuel and lubricant distributors in North Texas.

The company has given back to the community by supporting Faith Christian School of Grapevine and various other charities. RDI plans to continue giving back to the community and working hard to remain both profitable and a responsible member of the North Texas business community.

✧

Reeder Distributors, Inc. offices in 1973, 1987 and 2005.

GENERAL MOTORS ARLINGTON ASSEMBLY

In June 2004, General Motors Arlington Assembly Plant celebrated its fiftieth-year anniversary with an open house attended by more than 30,000 people. The number in attendance was almost four times the entire population of Arlington when GM began production in 1954. In its fifty years of operation, GM grew along with the City of Arlington from a business with fewer than 600 employees in a town of 8,000 to one that employs 3,000 in a city of more than 350,000.

In previous years, GM Arlington produced Buick, Cadillac, Chevrolet, Oldsmobile, GMC, and Pontiac vehicles. Currently, the Chevrolet Tahoe, Chevrolet Suburban, GMC Yukon, Yukon XL and the Cadillac Escalade are assembled at GM Arlington. The plant is the sole producer of the Escalade and of SUVs using Quadrasteer technology.

Groundbreaking for the Arlington plant was held in 1952 and the plant opened in 1954. The first car off the assembly line was a black Pontiac four-door Starchief. The Starchief was purchased by publisher Amon Carter and donated to the March of Dimes for a raffle. At that time, the plant operated one shift with 366 hourly and 220 salaried employees and line operators earned $1.78 per hour. The plant produced 36,790 vehicles that year. By the following year, that number almost tripled when 106,947 vehicles were produced.

Plant Manager E. C. Klotzberg, GM President Harloe Curtice, Division Manager J.C. Collin, Division Vice President John Gordon and Publisher, (*Fort Worth Star Telegram*) Amon Carter were among those attending the groundbreaking ceremony in 1952. Mayor of Arlington, Tom Vandergriff also attended. Vandergriff is credited with convincing GM to build its facility in Arlington rather than in Dallas or Fort Worth. "I remember telling them that if they located in Fort Worth they would make Dallas mad and if they located in Dallas they would make Fort Worth mad. But if they located midway between the two major cities, everybody would be happy," he said.

Vandergriff was delighted that the facility was to be built in Arlington and with the specific site that was chosen. The street leading through the field where he used to park with his girlfriend to look at the stars, and now leading to the Body Shop, was recently named Tom Vandergriff Way in honor of his dedication to GM Arlington.

The construction of the GM plant had major effects on the city. Lake Arlington was constructed to meet the needs of GM for a million gallons of water daily and the right of way for the road that is now Highway 360 was built to accommodate the plant's needs. Contributions from GM helped establish Arlington Memorial Hospital. Over the years, the GM plant attracted other big

businesses to Arlington, contributing to the city's population growth.

The plant has been remodeled and expanded several times over the years. The original plant, located on 250 acres, had 1.3 million square feet under the roof. With the expansion of the main building and additions of a new paint shop, a tire, wheel and seat assembly building, a new body shop and a wastewater treatment facility, the plant is three times its original size with 3.75 million square feet. It houses 700 robots and approximately 18 miles of conveyer. The original plant cost $33 million to build; the conversion in 1996 to the 800 series truck cost more than $500 million. In its first year of operation, GM Arlington produced about 3,000 vehicles per month. The plant now assembles 900 vehicles per day. Altogether, GM Arlington has produced more than 7.5 million vehicles.

The people of GM Arlington are proud of the company's philanthropic contributions. Since 1995 the company has donated more than $7.5 million to various Texas charities, schools and other organizations. GM and its employees gave more than $500,000 to Toys for Kids, United Way and civic organizations in 2003. Recently the company also donated a 2004 model Yukon to Mission Arlington in honor of their longstanding commitment to the people of Arlington.

The company is very involved in supporting various programs throughout Arlington. One of many programs they are involved in is at the University of Texas Arlington (UTA). Twice a year, GM conducts special tours for students enrolled in UTA's mechanical engineering program. On many occasions, GM Arlington provides letters of support for grant applicants at UTA. Bob Murday, director of manufacturing, works closely with senior staff from UTA and with corporate GM to procure corporate research funds for the university. When the Automation and Robotics Research Institute was implemented at UTA, GM donated $40,000 per year for five years to help establish the program. The company continues to support the robotics program by donating robots from the plant for use in the classroom. Mike Glinski, plant manager, serves as chairperson of the institute. He also serves on the advisory board for the school of engineering. GM sponsors the Formula SAE Car that the school builds and races each year in the nation's largest intercollegiate racing competition. In 2003, GM donated $10,000 to the program. The company also supports the Society of Women Engineers, the College of Engineering and the George Campbell Scholarship Fund.

Recently, the neighbors of the City of Arlington bestowed its Good Neighbor Award to GM for the company's civic contributions. For the past three years, the industry has recognized the plant as setting a benchmark in the production of full-size SUVs. The Tahoe, Yukon, Yukon XL, and Suburban were *Consumer Reports'* "recommended buys" for 2003 and 2004. With the recent receipt of $160 million for expansion, GM Arlington will continue to produce world-class vehicles of superior value.

✧

Below: General Motors- Arlington Assembly Plant is located at 2525 East Abram Street in Arlingtom, Texas 76010-1346.

Coca-Cola Enterprises, Incorporated

Coca-Cola Enterprises, Inc., is the world's largest marketer, producer and distributor of the Coca-Cola Company products, which include some of the most popular beverage brands in the world. Among the entities that make it number one is the Coca-Cola Bottling Company of Fort Worth, a company that is almost as old as Coca-Cola itself.

The Coca-Cola story is one of the greatest success stories the business world has ever seen and the Coca-Cola Bottling Company of Fort Worth is proud to have played an important role in the company's success. An Atlanta pharmacist, Dr. John Pemberton, began producing Coca-Cola syrup for sale in fountain drinks in 1886. The bottling business began in 1899 when two Chattanooga, Tennessee businessmen, Benjamin F. Thomas and Joseph Whitehead, secured the rights to bottle and sell Coca-Cola for most of the United States.

Henry Bush founded the Fort Worth bottling plant in 1906 with two wagons and four mules. The original plant site, measuring 190 feet by 200 feet, began with fifty employees, including an office staff that consisted of a sales manager and two employees.

Three years after its inception, Bush sold the bottling plant to the McDaniel brothers, who, in turn, sold the plant two years later to C.A. Lupton and T.J. Brown, men who would play pivotal roles in the plant's growth. Lupton acted as president and general manager from 1911 to 1945, while Brown served as vice president. The two men led the company through many milestones, including moving to a new plant at 650 South Main Street in 1922.

The new plant had something its predecessor did not: electrically operated machines that produced 130 bottles per minute. Lupton retired in 1945 and Glen Woodson, his nephew, took over as manager. Sam Woodson, Glen's brother, assumed control after his brother's death in 1959. By 1972, 270 people worked at the bottling plant, producing 1,450 bottles per minute from three bottling lines.

A canning plant at 4920 Northeast Parkway operated two additional lines capable of producing 1,000 cans per minute. Two more warehouses in Fort Worth and Arlington stored and distributed all Coca-Cola products and the storage and maintenance warehouse at 1405 East Hattie Street brought the number of locations to five.

In 1979 an investment group known as AEA Investors, Inc. purchased the Fort Worth bottling operations in addition to several others. Sam Woodson served as president. He became board chairman of the various operating companies in 1980, assuming a less active role in daily operations. Charles R. Cummings became president of Coke

Dasani, Barq's Root Beer, Cherry Coke, Fanta, Fresca,Minute Maid Juices, Minute Maid Soft Drinks and Pibb X-tra, to name just a few.

The Coca-Cola Bottling Company of Fort Worth is more than a Coca-Cola bottler. It is also an outstanding local citizen that strives to be an integral part of the community. The Coca-Cola Bottling Company of Fort Worth donated more than $175,000 in product in one recent year and gave $1.8 million in sponsorships for charity, nonprofit and community organizations in the Fort Worth area alone.

Coca-Cola Enterprises is a young company by the standards of the Coca-Cola System. The exclusive right to produce and distribute Coca-Cola products in its territories is their most significant asset. Each franchise has a strong heritage in the traditions of Coca-Cola that is the foundation of the company.

Coca-Cola products have now been a part of three centuries, and, although competition is increasingly fierce in the beverage business, Coca-Cola Enterprises plans to continue providing consumers with some of the most popular beverages in the world. And you can rest assured that the Coca-Cola Bottling Plant of Fort Worth will continue to play a crucial role in the company's success.

Enterprises, Inc. and David Van Houten became president of the Coca-Cola Bottling Company of Fort Worth.

In 1982, John T. Lupton (JTL) Corporation purchased Coke Enterprises. The Coca-Cola bottling system continued to operate as independent, local businesses until the early 1980s, when bottling franchises began to consolidate. On May 21, 1983, Coca-Cola Bottling Company of Fort Worth moved into a new facility at 3400 Fossil Creek Boulevard on a forty-acre tract in the northeast corner of the intersection of Loop 820 and I-35 North.

In 1986, the Coca-Cola Company merged some of its company-owned operations with two large ownership groups—the JTP Corporation franchises and BCI Holdings Corporation—to form Coca-Cola Enterprises, Inc. The company offered its stock to the public on November 21, 1986, at a split-adjusted prices of $5.50 a share.

Today, Coca-Cola Enterprises employs some 74,000 people operating 454 facilities and selling approximately 4.3 billion unit cases each year. The Coca-Cola Bottling Company of Fort Worth employs 700 team members producing more than 35 million cases and serving more than 16,000 outlets. These outlets range from large retail companies selling 200,000 cases annually to small service companies selling 100 cases a year.

The unmatched brand portfolio of Coca-Cola Enterprises includes Coca-Cola Classic, Diet Coke, Sprite, Caffeine Free Diet Coke,

DFW MOVERS & ERECTORS, INC.

DFW Movers & Erectors, Inc., a company that has meant quality service and customer satisfaction since its inception in 1980, has emerged as one of the leading woman-owned rigging and millwright contractors in the industry. Joanne and Neal Ingle started this company as a two-person operation from their home. While Neal delivered equipment, installed machines, operated hydraulic tilt-bed trucks with electric mule, Joanne was acting dispatcher, job scheduler and accounting manager.

Together they worked to grow this business as a complete rigging, millwright service company, with a commitment to customer satisfaction in all areas of services provided.

Throughout the company's growth, DFW Movers found in order to be competitive, they needed to be able to move heavier equipment and machinery. The company purchased a forty-thousand-pound Kalmar forklift in 1982 along with Mack Trucks, specialized trailers and hired additional skilled employees to handle the busy schedule. This was a major transition to opening doors for new customers on a larger scale.

DFW Movers moved its facility from the Ingle's home to Arlington, then in several years moved to Dallas and in 1997 to their present location on North Sylvania Avenue in Fort Worth. Their son, Jerod Ingle moved to open the San Marcos facility in 2002 to handle the booming I-35 corridor between Austin and San Antonio. Although the company is based in the DFW Metroplex, it has become one of the leading rigging/millwright contractors in the United States. However, DFW Movers provides the highest quality professional service to customers throughout the United States, Canada and China.

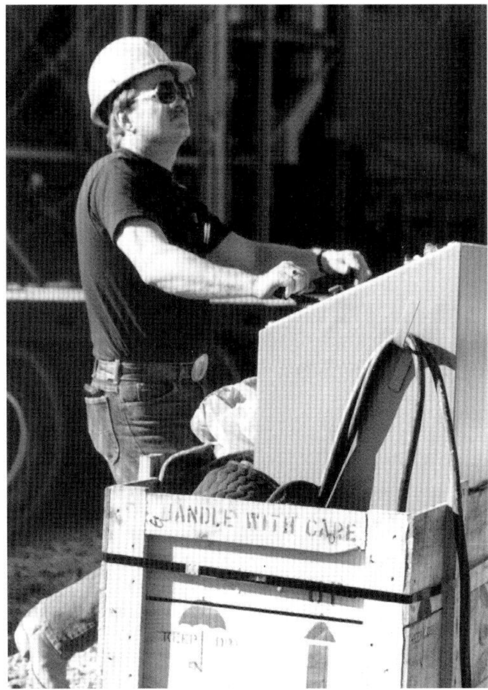

✧

Above: Neal Ingle operating 400-ton Gantry controls, c. 1987.

Below: Machine and forklift loaded for delivery, c. 1984.

Using specialized equipment, DFW Movers can provide service for many types of machinery, including optical comparators, delicate cameras, printing presses, semiconductors, clean-room services, lasers, hospital equipment/MRI, plastic injection molding machines, food processing equipment, metal stamping (punch presses, brakes and shears), metal working (lathes, mills and five-axis gantries) and even sculptures. In addition, with the company's 160,000-square-foot warehouse, machines can be received, stored until needed, and be electrically connected for testing prior to operation.

Expanding to meet the customers' needs and expectations, the Crate Master division was formed. Equipped to handle any crating specialty, the Crate Master team can fabricate containers for helicopters, industrial machines, containers for shipment overseas; crate both on-site/off-site, special art works and even antiques.

Machines require calibration and alignment after years of machining specific parts. Laser Precision is both the name and the goal of the division to perform diagnostic testing to comply with strict ISO 9002 governmental standards. Factory-trained Hamar and

Renishaw technicians use three dimensional and calibrating equipment to align machines for peak efficiency and performances.

More than just a slogan, "One machine or a complete plant," the diversity of high quality services has made DFW Movers the first choice of a wide variety of industries. DFW Movers has been a member of SC&RA (Specialized Carrier and Rigging Association) for more than twenty-three years. DFW Movers can offer the expertise to move one machine or a complete plant move (turnkey service), which includes millwright, electrical, plumbing, pipefitting and carpentry. Additional services include complete machine disassembly, reassembly and erection services, as well as machine cleaning, repairing, refurbishing and electrostatic painting. (Making used machines look like brand new).

The company is made up of many qualified, skilled, talented millwrights, riggers, electricians, carpenters, mechanics, laser technicians, painters, welders and tool room monitors. The sales team is led by Vice President/General Sales Manager G. E. (Jerry) Kopsovich, with more than twenty-three years with the company. Randy Robertson, John Martyn, and Jerry Jones have more than twenty combined years of service. Marc Cartwright is sales manager for the San Marcos location and keeps his skilled workers busy. Yvonne Knill is the sales team assistant to support each member with her organizational skills.

DFW supervisors, Steven R. Bates, Sr.; Jerry Lemke; Richard Johnson; and James Gentry offer their expertise and leadership for training DFW employees. The dispatcher team of Alan Meacham and Mark Saylor schedule the jobs in a timely manner based on labor, equipment and tools required to meet the customer's needs.

Safety is DFW Movers number one concern and Tom Moore is the safety manager/senior mechanic for all ongoing jobs. The accounting team is led by Mike Pippen, CPA/controller. Mike and Leigh Knox have a major part in making this company effective and efficient. The Crate Master division is led by Robert A. Gibb, Sr., with Rick Troglin in sales, and a staff of expert wood craftsmen. Dana Gibb is the Crate Master secretary and keeps jobs in order. CEO/President Joanne Ingle, and Vice President Neal Ingle, know that the most important asset of DFW Movers is its employees. This is what "DFW Movers & Erectors, Inc." is really all about.

DFW Movers is active in the business community through memberships with Dallas, Fort Worth, Austin, San Antonio, and U.S. Chambers of Commerce and belongs to the Better Business Bureaus in Dallas/Fort Worth. As a women-owned business, certifications with HUB (State of Texas), NCTRCA, SCTRCA, WBENC and Women Business Enterprise-Southwest are very important to acquiring business both locally and nationwide.

The Plano High School mascot on tiltbed truck, c. 1981.

Joanne is a member of the Fort Worth Business Assistance Center Advisory Board. Staying active in charitable events is a priority for DFW Movers. The company is involved in Race for the Cure, CEO's Walk the Walk-March of Dimes, Women's Haven Shelter, Smiling Women's Project, Toys for Tots, All Church Home for Children, Volunteer Christian Builders, The Salesmanship Club Youth and Family Centers along with numerous other charities. Giving back to the community is a major goal of the company.

DFW Movers has hit a landmark of twenty-five years in business and all the memories, history, mistakes, and fun times measure the blessings from God. Customers' loyalty and trust provide the same level of commitment for new customers as "we move you in the twenty-first century."

A.E. Petsche

A.E. Petsche Company is the world's largest supplier of high-performance aerospace wire, cable, connector products and related services. Based in Arlington, the company operates sales offices and distribution centers in twenty-seven locations worldwide and is recognized as a leading supplier to a broad range of customers, including commercial and military aircraft manufacturers, air carriers and medical equipment manufacturers.

Arnold E. Petsche founded the company in 1966 as a response to the aerospace industry's need for streamlined production and distribution of small parts. In the beginning, Petsche ran the business as a one-man operation with a single employee for clerical support.

His educational and business background prepared him well for running his own business. Petsche graduated from college with a degree in mechanical engineering and went on to receive electrical engineering training in the Air Force. He then worked in the private sector as an application engineer in support of field sales representatives in the aircraft industry. He later resigned his position as a regional sales manager for the East Coast to become a sales representative in Texas before starting his own business.

As the business grew, Petsche purchased a building, hired people to work in the warehouse and opened branch offices. Although the company purchased various properties through the years, Petsche eventually formed a separate company for building, developing, renting and maintaining properties, restoring old buildings and supervising the construction of facilities around the world. Petsche augmented his education by attending Harvard Business School, completing the program in 1980.

The company is based on the innovative "Just-in-Time" distribution system that reduces customers' inventory costs and shortens the procurement cycle for a wide range of products. As part of the distribution process, A.E. Petsche currently operates a Zero-Base Inventory Program for virtually every general aviation manufacturer in North America as well as military and electronics manufacturers worldwide.

An integral part of the zero-base program is the guaranteed availability of a comprehensive range of wire, cable and connector products. A sophisticated software program monitors the availability of products so that a constant inventory level is maintained. Increasingly, customers utilize electronic data interchange (EDI) links to place and monitor the status of orders. In addition, A.E. Petsche Company offers a customized "E-Serve" capability, which allows customers to manage open orders via the Internet.

Although no single wire, cable or connector product manufacturer can fulfill all the requirements of every customer, A.E. Petsche Company offers a "one-stop shopping" option that fits many customers' needs. By offering a comprehensive range of products and services related to cable assemblies, the company can reduce the number of vendors involved and thus minimize customers' costs. In addition to high-performance wire and cable, the company supplies connectors and harness management products, including shrinkable tubing, termination devices, wire identification systems and connector accessories.

Substantial value-added services are also available from the company, including complete cable assemblies, wire kits, wire and cable

marking and custom cable designs. Customers can purchase and inspect materials before storing them in one of the company's facilities through the consignment inventory program. In addition, by utilizing in-house design capabilities and engineering, A.E. Petsche Company provides design support and cost-effective solutions to its customers. The company employs rigorous controls over the quality of its products using a thirty-six-point inspection process and is certified by the industry as meeting its highest standards. The company's record of reliability is unmatched, resulting in multi-year contract renewals with many key customers.

In 2003 the U.S. Department of the Navy and the Defense Logistics Agency approved A.E. Petsche for the "Qualified Product List." This approval recognizes the company as a Category C assembler of aerospace connectors. In 2004 the Supplier Management Council of the Aerospace Industries Association (AIA) invited A.E. Petsche to become a member of AIA in recognition of the company's high ratings from aerospace suppliers and subcontractors. *Electronic Business*, an electronic component periodical, named A.E. Petsche Company one of the top twenty-five electronics' component distributors in North America in its 2004 survey. American Airlines, Northrop Grumman, Lockheed Martin and Vought Aircraft Industries have also honored the company for superior performance.

Arnold Petsche, along with Roger Studer, his general manager of twenty-five years, retired at the beginning of 2001. The new management team, headed by Glenn Davidson (CEO), posted record sales of $85 million in 2003, more than double the $41.9 million recorded in 1995. In the future, A.E. Petsche Company will remain focused on the military and aerospace markets, which are the company's primary areas of strength. The company also plans to further invest in its value-added operations (particularly connector assembly) and increase staffing in its overseas operations in order to capture a greater share of the international market. Annual sales growth is expected to range from ten percent to fifteen percent.

Currently, A.E. Petsche employs more than 150 people worldwide, including sixty who work at Arlington headquarters. With facilities in Australia, Canada, Europe, Africa and the Middle East, the company has come a long way from its beginnings as a one-man enterprise. Customers in the Dallas/Fort Worth area include internationally known firms such as Lockheed-Martin, Texas Instruments, Bell Helicopter, Associated Air Center and Boeing. Much of the company's success can be attributed to its emphasis on providing high-performance and reliable products at the lowest possible cost.

Acme Brick

Acme Brick Company, headquartered in Fort Worth, is one of the oldest manufacturers of face brick in Texas and the largest U.S.-owned brick producer in the world. In 1991, Acme celebrated the completion of a century of successful enterprise, a century marked by immense change in the industry.

In its first hundred years of existence, Acme produced and sold more than twenty billion bricks, many of which continue to grace homes, churches, schools, commercial buildings and public edifices in Texas and throughout the nation.

The Acme Brick Company began in 1891 when George Bennett founded Acme Pressed Brick near Millsap, where he operated a single kiln on Rock Creek. In the early years, Acme was primarily a Texas operation, but as the company prospered, its operations expanded to other states. Starting as one of over 100 Texas brick plants, by the end of the 1920s, Acme was the largest brick producer in Texas. By the mid-1960s, it was the largest brickmaker in the U.S., with operating facilities in six states and nationwide sales.

The 1920s were years during which the company's product expansions, plant acquisitions, and financial reorganization resulted in unprecedented prosperity. Although Acme ended the decade as a strong, modern and efficient operation, the stock market crash of 1929 and subsequent depression of the 1930s took a toll on the business.

As building construction declined nationwide, Acme's sales fell and unsold bricks stacked up in the yards. Plants and sales offices closed, employees were laid off, and company managers slashed wages and other operating expenses to survive. Total company assets declined from a high of more than $4 million in the late 1920s to just over $2 million in 1933. The company lost $120,632 in 1934, the first (and last) net loss Acme recorded on its balance sheet.

Unlike many of its competitors that went bankrupt, however, Acme weathered the crises of the 1930s and by the start of World War II was back in full production. In 1942, Acme's brick sales topped 100 million for the first time since 1929. The demand for its products created by the war effort contributed to the company's prosperity. The post-war boom in housing and other construction gave rise to another era of expansion and corporate reorganization. By the early 1950s, the company had outgrown its rented office space and began construction of a four-story, 22,800-square-foot headquarters on West Seventh Street in Fort Worth.

In 1963, Acme purchased the United Brick Division of Martin-Marietta Corporation and acquired seven plants in Missouri, Kansas and Oklahoma. In the same year, the company opened a new enlarged and modernized plant in Denton. The years from 1963 to 1968 were extremely prosperous for Acme, with net sales averaging more than $22 million a year and annual profits averaging over $1.1 million. The company's net worth increased by approximately $3.5 million during the period.

Below: Mules, steam and coal have long since given way to diesel, electricity and natural gas, but the Acme formula for quality has remained constant over the years.

During the 1960s, Acme faced increasing competition from suppliers of concrete, steel, glass and other building materials preferred by architects and builders of high-rise and other commercial buildings. Although brick facing was still used extensively in the residential housing market, Acme found it necessary to diversify in order to compete. In 1968, Acme formed the Ceramic Cooling Tower division and purchased a number of concrete block, cement, cast stone, and other building supply companies. As a reflection of diversification, Acme changed its name to First Worth Corporation and became part of a large conglomerate.

Following its incorporation, First Worth completed a merger with the Justin Companies and operated them as subsidiaries of the parent company. This move marked the company's first excursion into consumer goods since the Justin enterprise manufactured high-quality boots, belts, and other leather goods. Although the Justin companies were profitable, losses in other divisions soon led to shrinking assets and dwindling profits for First Worth. As a result of a change in leadership and structure, Acme Brick became one of three subsidiaries of First Worth Corporation. In 1972, the conglomerate was renamed Justin Industries, Inc.

More than many industries, the brickmaking business is extremely vulnerable to economic cycles and political forces. Through the ups and downs of the 1970s and the recession in the housing market of the mid-1980s, Acme Brick managed to remain profitable by adapting to changing conditions. Through innovative advances in research, product development, sales and marketing, Acme retained its position as the leading U.S. brick producer in the world throughout the 1990s.

Thousands of individuals, in management and labor, contributed to the ongoing success of Acme Brick. In more than 100 years of doing business, Acme has had ten presidents, each of whom served for an average of ten years. Each of these executives faced formidable challenges and provided strong leadership in difficult as well as prosperous times. The teamwork, diligence, and sacrifices of Acme employees also contributed significantly to the company's prosperity.

From a one-kiln Texas operation to a worldwide leader in clay products, Acme Brick has evidenced a remarkable endurance and stability in an ever-changing environment. Starting with the production of only one common brick and one face brick, the company has continued to expand its product lines. Today, Acme produces hundreds of brick styles in various shapes, colors, and textures, as well as numerous tile and concrete products, and is a leader in the development of brick sculpture and brick building technology. As the company enters its second century, prospects for the future success of Acme Brick appear bright indeed.

Acme Brick is now a part of the Berkshire Hathaway family of companies. For more information, you may visit Acme on the Internet at www.brick.com.

✧

Above: The neoclassical Burk Burnett Building, built in 1914, was Fort Worth's first skyscraper. Today it houses a fine-art gallery and anchors Fort Worth's Sundance Square district, itself a fine collection of classic Acme Brick buildings.

Below: Designed in a classical style inspired by Colonial Williamsburg, Polytechnic High School sits atop one of the highest points in Fort Worth. Multiple expansions over the years attest to this handsome building's enduring importance as a community landmark.

Onis Stone, Inc.

✧

Above: Petrified Wood Sink Bowl with Iron Oak Tree Base.

Top, right: Bob, Sheri and Alex (dog) Bennett with Travertine split face dry stack on the vertical-lay desk Front & Walls with Granite Countertop & accent pieces.

Below: Texas Star-displaying hand carved sink bowls, columns & Travertine tabletops.

Bob Bennett's decision to go into business as a wholesale supplier of stone might have seemed like a rash move to anyone who didn't know his background. Bob, who had just married his wife and eventual business partner, Sheri, announced a month after their wedding that he planned to invest their savings in a truckload of stone.

After the initial shock wore off, Sheri realized Bob's dream of owning his own business combined with his fifteen years of experience with both indoor and outdoor stone construction, as well as pool decking, kitchen countertops and more, would serve him well in this new endeavor.

So she gave him her blessing and the rest, as they say, is history.

A decade later, Onis Stone, Inc., incorporated in 1994, has seventeen employees and more than $1.5 million in gross annual sales. It offers unique, high-quality service using Mother Nature's gift of stone.

Bob and Sheri search the planet's mountains, quarries and factories to ensure the highest caliber material. They design, fabricate and install natural stone products that meet the demands of customers, employees and families. Kitchen and bath countertops, fireplaces, tabletops, pavers and columns are among the products they produce. They also produce base, chair-rail and moldings from any color stone.

Bob first came up with the idea on a trip to an Atlanta trade show for suppliers of stone. He met suppliers from a stone quarry in Mexico and spotted a good opportunity to work with them. Although Italy had been mining travertine and other stones for centuries, Mexico had only recently begun to take advantage of its natural stone resources.

So Bob bought his truckload of travertine in 1994 and sold it within hours in the Dallas-Fort Worth market. He bought more stone, sold each load, and the company grew and expanded from there. Bob handled the purchase and sale of stone while Sheri ran the business end.

Onis Stone began as a wholesale distributor of natural stone tile to large local distributors of tile flooring in the Dallas-Fort Worth area. The company expanded from there to a list of clients from Florida to New York to Nevada. The company also has sold products to customers in Arkansas, Illinois, Michigan, New Jersey, New Mexico, Oklahoma, and Louisiana.

Onis Stone's major customer base is in the Dallas-Fort Worth Metroplex. Other area communities in which the company provides service to are Weatherford, Aledo, Azle, Newark, Burleson, Cleburne, Plano, Frisco, Little Elm, Waco, Pilot Point and Wills Point.

Although the wholesale business was good, the Bennetts began to notice that buyers began to look more at price than quality when choosing a stone. So they decided to open their own showroom and sell directly to the public, offering quality stone products at competitive prices.

They opened their first showroom in a 2,300-square-foot space on Forth Worth's "tile mile" along State Highway 121. Around the same time, Bob took a trip to Germany and returned with the knowledge and inspiration to produce handcrafted fireplaces, chair rails, sinks, columns and flooring. The Germany trip inspired the idea for the "Linderhof Design Series," named for the historic castle known for its elaborate stone.

Bob and Sheri rented a location five miles from their showroom to fabricate these pieces. That made for a time-consuming, inconvenient commute between the two locations, a commute that seemed increasingly unnecessary because the showroom's location was not attracting customers.

A majority of people who came to the showroom were just searching for ideas and did not stop with the intention of buying. Therefore, beginning in 2004, the company moved its showroom to its fabrication site, a 16,000-square-foot facility on 1.5 acres near two major intersections in Fort Worth—I-30 and I-35.

Now they know that customers who walk through the door are interested in buying because they made a special trip to the store rather than just wandering by. The showroom includes door casings, bases, crown moldings and chair rails made from granite and marble, along with handcrafted fireplaces and high-end kitchens. Their products come in a wide range of prices, providing choices for everything from the $100,000 home to the $1 million-plus homes.

Onis Stone has added two installation crews to its business. Before the move, the company outsourced that part of the business, but the Bennetts felt the need to bring it in-house in order to assure quality.

Bob came up with the name Onis Stone as the company's name because he wanted the name to give the impression of Roman numerals carved in stone. He later adopted the acronym, "Our Name is Specialty" Stone, and an Internet search turned up an unexpected connection between stone and the Onis name.

An ancient city called Cangas de Onis was located in the eastern part of Spain, an area filled with beautiful materials made from natural stone. Cangas de Onis is the ancient capital of the Kingdom of Asturias on the Stella River. Cangas de Onis was the first Christian nation to be established in the Iberian Peninsula after the Islamic Moors in 711A.D conquered it.

The company's unique work has led to awards, including first place in Weatherford's 2001 Kaleidoscope of Homes and first place in the 2002 Frisco Parade of Homes as the People's Choice and All-Around Winner and 100 percent satisfied customers with Lowe's Granite Countertop Installation.

Bob's idea has proven to be more successful than anyone would have imagined. Bob and Sheri plan to continue providing customers with quality products and searching for new ideas to keep their business on the cutting edge and bringing their customers the latest in natural stone products. In April 2005 they celebrated the grand opening at the new Onis Stone Showroom and Fabrication Facility displaying all of the fifty new colors they have in stock along with their Linderhof Design Series, elegantly displayed and showcased.

Onis Stone, Inc.'s misson statement declares that they offer unique, high quality service using Mother Nature's gifts of stone. The company explores Earth's mountains, quarries and factories to insure the highest caliber of material. Through quality, honesty and integrity, Onis Stone creates an inviting and unique experience to meet the demands of its customers, employees and families.

✧

Above: The April 2005 ribbon-cutting ceremony for Onis Stone Showroom and Fabrication Facility.

Below: Glass Tile display, with Blue Dalmata Countertop and White Thassos Marble Tile on floor with Blue Lapis accent dots, along with china cabinet full of semi-precious accent tile.

AMSCO Steel

In August 1952, just six months after his son was born, John C. Sikes, Jr., started AMSCO Steel Company. His only "employee" was his wife, Leta, who answered the phones while he was out selling, purchasing or delivering. Once their daughter was born fifteen months later, he hired their first employee so that Leta could care for their baby and older son, Steve.

In the early days, Sikes wore all the hats. In the morning, he would put on his salesman's hat and make the sales calls, then come back, change clothes, load up an old truck with steel and either deliver to customers or make purchases. Back then the company also sold nails, plaster, guttering and other building supplies.

In the late 1950s, Sikes decided that by doing more processing, they could increase business. Rather than just buying the steel from the mills and reselling it, they should cut, shear and form the steel to customers' needs. So the company bought their first piece of machinery, an "alligator shear" that could do just that. Today that piece of machinery proudly stands outside the company's Fort Worth plant as a flagpole. The next equipment purchases was a shear, which cut sheet steel, and a press brake, which formed the steel into different configurations.

By 1963 it was getting difficult to store sheet steel, so the company purchased a cut to length line that allowed it to buy different gauges of coiled steel, uncoil it, flatten it, and cut it to customers' specifications. This also allowed them to better utilize their space. Another machine, bought in 1968, a slitting line, allowed them to cut specific widths and re-coil it for customers. In the late 1970s, they bought two strip mills, which can produce the strip and flat bars that used to be produced at the steel mill. This entire product is sold to their competitors in approximately fifteen states.

Through the years, the company added employees and three additional plants. The original plant in Fort Worth and in 1955 a second plant in Wichita Falls. That plant is still there, and although they no longer own it, they do business with the current owners. Fort Worth is now their corporate headquarters with seventy employees. In 1994, AMSCO expanded into Mexico with a joint venture in Queretaro. They bought Pyndus Steel and Aluminum in San Antonio in 1998 and added yet another plant in 2005 by purchasing Fisher Iron and Metal in Marble Falls, Texas.

In 1974, Sikes died, leaving his son, Steve, who was a senior in college, to take over and work full-time at the business. Since then, the business has grown ten to twelve times in size. Steve, who preceded the birth of the company by six months, has been around or actively employed in the business for fifty-two years. He is now in partnership with his mother, Leta Davis. Steve's son, John C. Sikes, III, the third generation Sikes in the business, is the vice president of AMSCO Steel Transportation, a separate corporation with eighteen tractor-trailers. The transportation company has been in business for five years and is the logistics and delivery arm of the company. AMSCO Steel Transportation presently hauls for Lowes, Home Depot, various steel mills and AMSCO customers in thirteen states.

The construction and housing industry was one of the first to use AMSCO Steel products, particularly for foundations. Today, the construction industry is still a valued source of business. Through the years, the company has diversified to provide steel to the stamping industry, which stamps out products for automobiles, computers, the oil and gas industry and the heating, ventilation and air conditioning industry. Its steel is also used for electrical transformers, guardrails, rail cars and steel roofs.

AMSCO Steel has always been customer-driven and provides customers with the best in service and quality. The company's goal is not to be the biggest, but to be the best. It does this by building relationships with customers and employees. Many employees have been with the company for thirty-five years.

The challenges are many in the ever-changing steel industry. It is no longer domestic. They buy steel worldwide, which means the international market affects their business here. Additional challenges present themselves through shortages, pricing and overnight changes. Finding appropriate sources and prices is crucial. By selling to a diversified market, they do not rely on any one industry to make up most of their business. In fact, no industry provides more than ten percent of the company's business. Building relationships with new customers is another goal. The company has well-developed relationships with domestic and offshore mills, and employees recognize that everyone is involved in selling the company's product, not just the sales people. The company strives to be proactive and sell itself to suppliers, vendors and customers.

One customer, a multinational oil service company, named AMSCO Steel the 2003 "Supplier of the Year." The company strives to remain true to its mission and vision statements, part of which is to create solid customer relationships and become the industry's supplier of choice. Presently it ships seventy thousand tons of steel annually. In the future, company officials are considering acquisitions to expand out of state. Steve Sikes likens the company growth to an oak tree, which has strength, beauty, and stability, yet grows slowly.

AMSCO Steel has a stated vision of meeting and exceeding customers' expectations through creative problem solving, outstanding customer service, excellence, and exactness in quality and timing of products, processing and delivery. The company has come a long way from Sikes selling and loading up an old truck for deliveries, yet AMSCO Steel has stayed true to its founder's original business philosophy.

For more information about AMSCO Steel, please visit www.amscosteel.com

EBERLE ENGINEERING COMPANY, INC.

Eberle Engineering Company, Inc., which manufactures automated assembly machinery for battery factories, is one of the most successful businesses of its type in the world. Based in Euless, the company is owned and operated by its chief executive officer, the late William J. "Bill" Eberle, and his family. The company serves customers throughout Europe, Asia, Australia, Canada, Mexico, and the United States. A prolific inventor with almost three hundred domestic and foreign patents, Eberle also headed Eberle Energy Enterprises, Inc., which promotes his patented invention called "Motion-of-the-Ocean," or "MOTO," a machine for the generation of electricity, hydrogen and potable water.

After working as a master plumber and in various other endeavors, Eberle entered the battery business in 1959. He later worked for a number of years at General Battery Corporation in Reading, Pennsylvania, where he designed and built numerous devices that enhanced the productivity of the company and the battery industry as a whole. In 1980, he returned to Dallas with a dream of owning a business where he could invent, design, build, sell and service machines people needed for battery production. With his savings of $100,000 and a line of credit for an equal amount from a local bank, Eberle founded Eberle Engineering Company, Inc.

Bill and June Eberle.

As the company grew, it operated from several increasingly larger locations. The first building rented had three thousand square feet with a reception area and one private office. Within three years, the business needed more space, so the company leased a ten-thousand-square-foot building with added office space and an engineering room. By 1996 the company conducted business in thirty-two countries with a backlog of orders and again required a larger space. The company bought land near the Dallas-Fort Worth International Airport and Eberle designed a building specifically suited to the company's work. The building has 20,000 square feet, including 5,000 square feet of office space, as well as a shop and engineering area.

The first product produced at Eberle Engineering was the Model 85-A-19-plate group stacker. This automated device enabled one worker to do the work formerly performed by six and was in great demand. Aware that there is a saturation point for sales of any one machine, however, Eberle designed a new type of terminal post builder, a quality control shear tester and a very popular air test machine to test for battery leaks. An acid filling machine, a machine to check for electrical shorts and a production shear test machine were also added to the product line. Many other innovative and effective inventions that contributed to the manufacture of batteries followed.

In 1980, Eberle invented the MOTO machine and was issued a patent. MOTO is designed to harness the power in waves, tides and ocean swells to produce low-cost electrical power, hydrogen gas and fresh water for agricultural use or for human consumption. MOTO produces these vital products without polluting the atmosphere, depleting oil reserves or producing hazardous wastes. Costs for a MOTO installation are estimated at $5 to $10 million, in contrast to the $5 to $10 billion required for a nuclear power plant. In addition, the offshore installation of MOTO acts as an effective breakwater, reducing coastal soil erosion and the associated costs of restoration.

Unlike Eberle's other inventions, MOTO requires outside financing, since installation costs are prohibitive for one investor. Since in 1980 funding was not forthcoming, the project was abandoned. In 1990, with the company

operating smoothly, Eberle again turned his attention to the MOTO project. He made improvements to the basic structure of the machine and identified ways the same device could be used to make not only electricity, but also fresh water as well as hydrogen and oxygen gases. In 1992, Eberle received a second patent for the machine and formed Eberle Energy Enterprises, Inc. He succeeded in obtaining outside funding to build and test a model of MOTO. Stevens Institute in Hoboken, New Jersey, where many military devices used in the ocean are tested, did testing in a wave tank. Tests indicated the design was sound, the device seaworthy, and the system commercially viable. Eberle is hopeful that MOTO installations are a reality in the near future.

Through the years, Eberle Engineering Company gained a worldwide reputation as a reliable source of low-maintenance, high-quality production equipment. In 1992, Inc. Magazine, Ernst & Young and Merrill Lynch nominated Bill Eberle for "Entrepreneur of the Year." In 1993 the Independent Battery Manufacturers Association honored the company with its "Quality and Excellence Award." This award is given each year to a business or an individual who has made noteworthy contributions to the industry. In 1996 the company was a finalist in a contest held by *The Business Press* for most innovative new product.

Five of Bill's sons and a daughter, as well as various other relatives, work for Eberle Engineering, making it truly a family enterprise. Bill also has three children from a previous marriage—son Mike, who took after his father and is very successful, and daughters Barbara Carter and Joan Hennley. The future appears to hold great promise for the continued success of the Eberle family and Eberle Engineering.

Bill Eberle passed away in September 2004. It was his wish to be published in this book as a legacy for his wife, children and grandchildren. His wife of fifty years, June L. Eberle was not surprised Bill would want to share his life with others as he was proud of all the accomplishments he and his children have made. Bill will be sorely missed.

Above: William J. "Bill" Eberle.

Below: The Eberle Engineering family (from left to right): Tracy, Terry, Camille, Kip, June, Kelly, Bill, and Guy Eberle.

Justin Brands

H. J. Justin began crafting boots 125 years ago in Spanish Fort, Texas, selling his handmade footwear to cowboys passing through town on the Chisholm Trail. From the start he believed in only making top quality products, and said "No boot shall ever bear the Justin brand unless it is the very best that can be produced...."

A decade after starting his business, H. J. moved his family to Nocona, Texas to take advantage of the better business opportunities afforded by a newly built railroad. Here his wife Annie developed a "fit kit" containing a tape measure and instructions for taking measurements for custom fit boots. Cowboys carried the kits with them on their travels and became Justin's first mobile sales force.

The company was renamed H. J. Justin and Sons when John and Earl Justin came to work for their father in 1908. Two years later the firm was able to double its production using new technology, selling boots for $11 a pair in twenty-six states as well as Canada, Mexico and Cuba. In 1918 when H. J. passed away, his sons took over the business and eventually moved it to Fort Worth in order to be part of the city's growing business community.

In 1948, H. J.'s grandson, John Justin, Jr., purchased controlling interest in the business and began to aggressively market Justin Boots. Despite a very busy schedule, he still found the time to successfully run for the Fort Worth City Council and for mayor in 1961.

An alliance was formed in 1968 with another pioneer of the Fort Worth business community, Acme Brick. The two companies resided under the umbrella of Justin Industries. In 1981 the Nocona Boot Company joined the fold, when John Jr. purchased controlling shares of the company from his aunt, Enid Justin. Three years later Chippewa Shoe Company was added to the Justin family of brands, bringing about the addition of a new line of rugged, specialty outdoor footwear. In 1990, after years of rivalry, Justin Industries purchased competitor Tony Lama Boots.

Following a long and successful tenure, John Justin, Jr. stepped down from his role as chairman of board of Justin Industries in April 1999. The next year, under his direction as chairman emeritus, along with Chairman of the Board John Roach and President and CEO J. T. Dickenson, the Justin Industries Board of Directors approved the sale of the company to Warren Buffett and Berkshire-Hathaway. At that time the company was split into Justin Brands, with Randy Watson as president and CEO and Acme Building Brands run by President and CEO Harold Melton.

While the company has grown by leaps and bounds since the nineteenth century, Justin Brands is still renowned today for crafting top quality products, just as founder H. J. Justin promised in 1879. To learn more about Justin Brands, visit their website at www.justinbrands.com.

General Electrodynamics Corporation

Once located in Garland, Texas, with little more than engineers, scientists, shareholders and ideas, General Electrodynamics Corporation (GEC) has evolved by developing innovative concepts, products and services. From 1955 and three orange diamonds, to 1996 and red wings, from publicly traded to privately owned, GEC has innovated concepts, products and services for over 50 years.

On July 14, 1965, after a 228-day journey through space, *Mariner IV* looked at Mars through a vidicon television camera tube developed and manufactured by General Electrodynamics Corporation. That mission stands as GEC's testimonial to the vision and competence of the thousands of scientists and engineers that made a profound mark on our country's space program. In the 1960s, the vidicon tube market and technology began to diminish with the evolution of solid-state-electronics. With corporate revenues declining, GEC's camera division and tube division were acquired, leaving behind assets, resources, facilities and a fully self-sustaining scale division. With engineering and technology resources in abundance, GEC patented, designed, and introduced the first heavy-duty portable wheel-load weigher (MD300 portable truck scale).

As GEC's staff became experts with very rugged, harsh and abusive truck-weighing applications, the mission continued to improve GEC's R&D efforts with another patented device, the MD500. There is no other wheel-load weigher in the world today meeting the salient performance characteristics of the MD400/500 series. As GEC continued its forward vision into new market opportunities, it quickly identified industry concerns associated with aircraft weight and balance. In conjunction with Navy requirements in 1979, GEC patented the first man-portable, thirty-thousand-pound capacity aircraft platform weighing system with one-half percent accuracy. GEC is the only manufacture that has a 60,000-pound aircraft platform weighing system that has been first article tested and approved by the United States Air Force.

Since 1995, GEC's FAA repair station license requires the firm to have certified weight and balance experts on staff meeting very stringent academic and field experience standards. GEC goes to its customers' facility and provides a fully executed weight, balance and aircraft CG allowing customers to return their aircraft to airworthiness condition.

GEC's U.S. military test equipment expertise is indicative of a solid technological base and breadth of related experience. Its recent span of programs covers aircraft training panels for L3 Communications, Fatigue Monitors for the F-18, Portable Field Calibration Test Set, AFCS Aircraft Panels and a variety of other specialized test sets.

Today, GEC continues to engineer with precision accuracies for a worldwide niche market. It is very specialized and focused on its core business objectives. GEC embraces technology and remain the only manufacturer that engineers, designs, tests, and strives to service the end user directly.

GEC's customer service is integrated into its growth strategy. General Electrodynamics Corporation is dynamically driven and founded on technological expertise and product advancements in several niche markets. Its leadership is unmatched and its products are far superior to the competition. Employees are GEC's greatest assets and their contributions to society reflect the organization's commitment to quality, customer satisfaction and product performance. GEC continues to push upward, leaving its mark on history and adding more satisfied customers.

✧

Above: A wireless aircraft weighing kit.

Below: A portable wheel-weigher.

Harbison-Fischer Manufacturing Company

◆

Above: Co-founder Dixon Thomas (Dick) Harbison (1898-1976).

Below: Co-founder Charles Anthony Fischer (1891-1983).

Harbison-Fischer Manufacturing Company, the world's largest maker of sub-surface oil well pumps, came into existence in 1933 when fate brought together two men seeking opportunities in the oil patch.

Dixon T. Harbison and Charles A. Fischer met during a sales call Fischer made on Harbison. The two men developed an appreciation for one another's talents and knowledge and quickly recognized their partnership potential.

Harbison and Fischer pooled their knowledge of the oil tool and steel industries to manufacture and sell oil well pumping equipment. They founded Harbison-Fischer in March 1933 with a furnace, belt-drive machines and a Cadillac motor to turn the lathes.

In the years that followed, Harbison-Fischer developed, expanded upon and improved its products to the point where a complete line of H-F pumps, pump parts and accessories is now shipped to all parts of the oil-producing world. The words "BEST PUMPS IN THE OIL PATCH"® stamped on all H-F products is more than a slogan: it's a statement of commitment.

Harbison-Fischer is headquartered in a state-of-the-art facility in Crowley, a suburb south of Fort Worth. The company continues to be owned by the Fischer family, which purchased the Harbison family's interest in 1972.

Through the years, the company has made acquisitions and established subsidiaries to expand its reach as well as the products and services it provides customers. In 1985 the company purchased Challenger Process Systems and began operating it as a wholly owned subsidiary. Challenger manufactures and markets process and environmental systems, ASME Code pressure vessels (including oil/water separators) and API/AWWA shop tanks. Harbison-Fischer formed a Canadian joint venture in 1985 that became a wholly owned subsidiary in 1995. Harbison-Fischer Canada Ltd. is headquartered in Calgary, Alberta.

Martin rubber-guide cages, pressure-actuated plungers and polished rod clamps as well as the Johnson-Fagg product line of stuffing boxes, polished rod clamps and pumping tees came into the H-F product line in 1999 with the acquisition of John N. Martin Manufacturer. The purchase of Martin, a well-respected company with philosophies and manufacturing objectives that mirrored H-F's, was a logical step in expanding the company's product offerings.

In June 2003 the purchase of H-F's longtime California distributor (Production Services) expanded the company's abilities to support this highly concentrated, high-volume market. The commitment that the company's founders possessed is carried on today through subsequent generations of the Fischer family as well as its talented, dedicated employees, many of whom have committed a large portion of their lives to service to Harbison-Fischer.

Their hard work and commitment to manufacturing the highest quality products is one of the most important factors in the company's success. That commitment to hard work and quality products will continue to be the cornerstones of Harbison-Fischer's success. So, too, will the company's reputation for industry knowledge and exacting quality standards and its dedication to the industry it serves.

Harbison-Fischer is located at 901 North Crowley Road in Crowley, Texas and on the Internet at www.hfpumps.com.

SkiHi Enterprises Incorporated

Richard Skipper and Tommy Hicks founded SkiHi Enterprises, Inc., in 1981 after learning the mechanical contracting business while working for industry leader Broyles and Broyles. They combined the first few letters of their last names to form the name SkiHi.

They started with no employees and, to keep from overextending their capital, grew at a steady, controlled pace. Today, a quarter of a century later, SkiHi is one of the most successful mechanical contractors in the state, with design-build capabilities, maintenance programs, energy management systems, more than 200 employees and offices in Fort Worth and Lubbock.

SkiHi owes its success to several factors. The reputation of the company's founders and the professional relationships they had developed with others in the industry were among the most important. The company also committed itself to low overhead and hired new employees only when available capital ensured their continued employment.

The company planned its growth and followed the plan carefully. SkiHi's revenues reached $1 million in its first year, $4 million in its second and, as of 2004, had reached $45 million. Renovation of the Tarrant County Courthouse proved instrumental in the company's growth. Its work on this high-profile project led to work for other Fort Worth clients.

SkiHi was also chosen to renovate the air conditioning in the sanctuary for an organ donated by Van Cliburn to Broadway Baptist Church. Other notable projects on which it has worked include the Burlington Northern Santa Fe-Fossil Creek corporate headquarters, Fort Worth Convention Center, Amon Carter Museum and the Cowgirl Hall of Fame.

The company has expanded the area in which it works from Fort Worth to the entire State of Texas and even areas of Oklahoma. In September of 1999, the company opened a branch in Lubbock, Texas to capitalize on local opportunities. Projects handled by the Lubbock office include mechanical work on The Experimental Science Building on the Texas Tech University campus and the Southwest Cancer Center Expansion at Lubbock County University Medical Center.

✧

Above: The Cowgirl Hall of Fame.

Closer to home, SkiHi worked with Thomas S. Byrne, Ltd., and Bombardier Transportation to install the de-icing system on the people-moving system at Dallas-Fort Worth International Airport. The project won the national "Excellence in Construction Award" presented by Associated Builders and Contractors in 2005.

That's just one of many national and local awards for which SkiHi has been nominated and awarded. The same year, the Fort Worth Chamber of Commerce named the company one of three finalists for "Small Business of the Year."

The chamber, like those in the contracting industry, recognizes SkiHi's skills and its history of excellence delivered under budget and on time. That's a reputation that SkiHi intends to guard every time it takes on a project and that, in turn, should assure the company's continued success.

Sand Trap Service Co, Inc.

Sand Trap Service Co., Inc., traces it's beginning to World War II when company founder, Joe Raines, who served in the Navy, learned about bilge pumps and noticed service station operators digging out sand traps.

He thought there must be a better way to remove the sand and started a business in Wichita Falls to do just that. At the same time, Eldon Beavers was working a route in Fort Worth and in 1952 bought it. Beavers and Raines eventually joined forces and through the years the business has grown to employ twenty-three people—mostly family—at both its trucking company and disposal plant, which opened in 1983.

Today, the company provides pumping, transporting and disposal of non-hazardous liquid waste from grease traps at food processing facilities and restaurants, grit traps or sand traps from car washes, trucking companies, equipment washing and non-hazardous industrial waste. The material is then taken to the company's disposal plant for processing. Sand Trap Service's trucks are permitted for transporting by the Texas Commission on Environmental Quality and are also permitted in every North Central Texas area city. The company services a 150-mile area around the Dallas/Fort Worth metroplex.

Its truck and pump operators have an average of twenty years experience with Sand Trap. Sand Trap Service does its best to bring its clients dependable and efficient service in cleaning traps and drains. It has the right equipment to service your needs whether the job is easy access or hard to reach. Pressure washer/jetter machines are available to clean drain lines as well.

Sand Trap Service Co. is located at 1300 Cold Springs Road in Fort Worth, doubled its business in 1956 when the company established a second route run by Eldon Beavers' brother-in law, Robert Marshall, who worked the route and is still active in the business today.

The company added two more trucks in the 1960s and now has a total of twelve. They have also expanded and improved the disposal plant throughout the years. The City of Fort Worth has recognized the processing facility as being in regulatory compliance for the past eight years.

Through the years, more routes were added and additional trucks purchased. In 1989, Beavers' wife, Grace, died and their children, Sherry, Gary and Terry became partners. In 1993, Beavers gave his children his half of the business and remains active in the business today. Terry Galloway, who joined the company in 1994, also plays an integral role in the company.

Gary is now president, Sherry is vice president and Terry is secretary/treasurer. The company's plans for the future are to continue to serve customers through good, reliable service at a fair price.

The company's motto since 1949 has been "Ask Those We Serve." The customers that it services can attest to the quality of service that the company strives to give and it looks forward to meeting your needs in pumping or drain line maintenance.

Sand Trap Service may be found on the Internet at www.sandtrapservice.com.

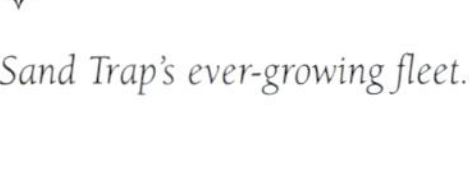

Sand Trap's ever-growing fleet.

SCHRICKEL, ROLLINS AND ASSOCIATES, INC.

Schrickel, Rollins and Associates, Inc., has played an important role in the development of Tarrant County. This landscape architecture, civil engineering, and planning firm has been responsible for creating many landmarks in the Dallas-Fort Worth Metroplex, and the firm's impact has been felt in other parts of the state as well.

Among SRA's early high-profile projects were The University of Texas at Arlington's campus and stadium, Tarrant County Convention Center, the Turnpike Stadium parking facilities and site development, three state parks, and the UTA Trading House Creek landscape. More recently, the design of The Parks at Texas Star in Euless, the Hurst Athletic Complex, several Grand Prairie parks, the Richland Tennis Center, Arlington's M.L. King Jr. Athletic Complex, and the master plan of Tierra Verde Golf Club have shown the company to be a leader in municipal athletic park design.

The company began in 1955 when Arlingtonite Gene Schrickel teamed with engineer Frank Smith to form Schrickel and Smith. A year later the company became Gene Schrickel and Associates. Schrickel, the thirty-eighth registered landscape architect in Texas, was a pioneer of the profession within the state. He was also an early Fellow of the American Society of Landscape Architects, earning the group's highest designation. In the beginning, work for landscape architects was scarce and few even knew the profession existed. Schrickel spent many hours speaking to garden clubs and civic organizations explaining the profession. These contacts provided Schrickel with most of his early work, with members' requests to design the landscapes of their homes, churches and hospitals. Several residential projects were featured in popular national magazines such as *House Beautiful* and *Better Homes and Gardens* and Schrickel became a regular guest columnist for *The New York Times*, where he discussed residential landscape architecture.

As word of Schrickel's talents spread, commercial work began to appear. Early commercial projects included Western Hills Inn in Fort Worth in 1957, the American Airlines Stewardess College in 1958, Bell Helicopter in 1961 and Dallas' famous Stoneleigh Hotel in 1962. By 1963, his reputation had spread to the point that the firm was hired to design projects throughout the DFW Metroplex and around the state.

Albert W. Rollins, P.E., former city manager and public works director for the City of Arlington, and later a director of the Texas Turnpike Authority and chair of the Texas Mass Transportation Commission, partnered with Schrickel in 1967. He served as principal-in-charge on more than fifty roadway projects and was project engineer on more than 600 projects at the company. He was an early pioneer in the use of lime in sub-grade and base course construction, a method commonly used today.

A few of the firm's major Tarrant County engineering projects include the east side of the new IH30/IH35 interchange that replaced the old Mixmaster, the IH35/Basswood interchange, the TRA Arlington Diversion Sewer, and the Rush Creek Sewer Interceptor.

Housing developments provided many of the early engineering and planning projects. In addition, the firm's planning division secured millions of dollars in Texas Park & Wildlife funding for local municipalities for park development. The firm's university master plans included Texas A&M and Southwest Texas State (now Texas State University).

The firm's philosophy is to remain a mid-sized corporation in Arlington to enhance close collaboration among employees, to ensure quality control of projects and to maintain a more personal relationship with clients.

✧

Above: This is an early example of Gene Schrickel's landscape architecture at a Fort Worth residence in the 1950s.

Below: SRA designed the fourteen-thousand-seat UTA Maverick Stadium, track, and artificial turf field.

THOMAS S. BYRNE, LTD.

Thomas S. Byrne, Ltd., now in its third generation of management, got its start in Fort Worth in 1923 when a native Texan and graduate of the Massachusetts Institute of Technology decided to start a company and name it after himself.

Throughout the next eight decades, Thomas S. Byrne has shaped the Fort Worth skyline and contributed greatly to the city's character by providing top-notch general contracting services to a wide range of construction projects. Projects include the original Firestone station on the West side to the award-winning world-class Amon Carter and Kimbell Art Museums in the city's cultural district.

Byrne, the state's largest minority owned general contractor, offers clients construction services of unparalleled quality and value through a high-performing team of construction professionals committed to excellence and client satisfaction.

This team is lead by John Avila, Jr., president and chief executive officer, who has encouraged the company to use new technologies in construction to build projects that exemplify the highest standards the industry has to offer.

The company specializes in constructing products within a negotiated guaranteed maximum price requiring a high degree of personalized management. These products also require both pre-construction and construction skills requiring one or more of the following:

- Establishing, controlling and meeting an owner's budget, starting with partially complete design documents through completion of construction;
- Unique architectural design and/or high quality finish;
- Scheduling complexity to meet tight time-frames and/or maintain owner's operations when in, or connecting to, existing facilities; and
- Highly technical, complex facilities such as healthcare, laboratory, computer-related, and aviation.

Byrne maintains the ability to perform those portions of work historically accomplished by the traditional general contractor. It does this by maintaining a core group of carpenters, laborers, ironworkers and equipment operators. The rest of the work is subcontracted on an open-shop basis using both union and non-union workers.

An important factor in the growth and continuity of the company is the volume of work it has performed on a negotiated basis for several repeat clients. Throughout the past eighty years, Byrne has delivered more than 200 projects to more than 60 clients.

Byrne has been a leader in construction organizations and associations throughout its history and has received more than seventy awards for excellence and innovation in construction.

Its reputation for quality is backed by its integrity, stability, competency and the desire to serve clients in the best possible manner and provide them with structures that meet or exceed their expectations.

The company plans to continue to expand its role as a leader in the construction industry while building relationships with clients and employees based on pride, trust, and confidence. Thomas S. Byrne, Ltd., has been dedicated to excellence since 1923 and looks forward to continued challenges in the future.

Thomas S. Byrne, Ltd. is located at 900 Summit Avenue in Fort Worth, Texas and on the Internet at www.tsbyrne.com.

Sponsors

A. E. Petsche....254
Acme Brick....256
AMSCO Steel....260
The Ashton Hotel and The Ashton Depot....206
Baylor All Saints Medical Centers....216
Bistro Louise....179
The Bombay Company....205
Brants Realtors....207
Classic Chevrolet....186
Coca-Cola Enterprises, Incorporated....250
Courtyard by Marriott....190
Crescent Real Estate Equities Company....201
DFW Movers & Erectors, Inc....252
DFW Urology Consultants....231
Eberle Engineering Company, Ltd....262
EECU....182
Family 1st of Texas Federal Credit Union....179
Fort Worth Convention & Visitors Bureau....200
Fort Worth Police Department....228
Fort Worth Stockyards Business Association....179
General Electrodynamics Corporation....265
General Motors Arlington Assembly....248
Grapevine Convention & Visitors Bureau....179
Harbison-Fischer Manufacturing Company....266
Harris Methodist Fort Worth Hospital....179, 222
Hilton Hotel Fort Worth....198
Justin Brands....264
Kenneth Copeland Ministries
Eagle Mountain International Church, Incorporated....220
Kenneth William Davis....240
LandAmerica Commonwealth Title of Fort Worth, Inc....179
Lena Pope Home....229
Marshal Utley Carpets....192
Medical Center of Arlington
North Hills Hospital
Plaza Medical Center of Fort Worth....212
Metro Golf Cars....204
Moncrief Cancer Center....226
The Murrin Family....237
National Farm Life Insurance Company....194
Onis Stone, Inc....258
Pier 1 Imports....196
Radiology Associates of Tarrant County....233
Reeder Distributors, Inc....247
River Legacy Foundation....235
Sam Pack's Five Star Ford....202
Sand Trap Service Co., Inc....267
Schrickel, Rollins and Associates, Inc....268
SkiHi Enterprises Incorporated....269
Southside Trim & Glass....208
Tarrant County Historical Society....236
Tarrant Regional Water District....224
Texas Christian University....230
Texas Land and Country, LLC....203'
Thomas S. Byrne, Ltd....270
The University of Texas at Arlington....234
Williamson-Dickie Manufacturing Company....244
YMCA of Metropolitan Fort Worth....232

For more information about the following publications or about publishing your own book, please call Historical Publishing Network at 800-749-9790 or visit www.lammertinc.com.

Black Gold: The Story of Texas Oil & Gas
Historic Abilene: An Illustrated History
Historic Amarillo: An Illustrated History
Historic Anchorage: An Illustrated History
Historic Austin: An Illustrated History
Historic Beaufort County: An Illustrated History
Historic Beaumont: An Illustrated History
Historic Bexar County: An Illustrated History
Historic Brazoria County: An Illustrated History
Historic Charlotte: An Illustrated History of Charlotte and Mecklenburg County
Historic Comal County: The Story of New Braunfels & Comal County
Historic Corpus Christi: An Illustrated History
Historic Denton County: An Illustrated History
Historic Edmond: An Illustrated History
Historic El Paso: An Illustrated History
Historic Erie County: An Illustrated History
Historic Fairbanks: An Illustrated History
Historic Gainesville & Hall County: An Illustrated History
Historic Henry County: An Illustrated History
Historic Houston: An Illustrated History
Historic Illinois: An Illustrated History
Historic Kern County: An Illustrated History of Bakersfield and Kern County
Historic Laredo: An Illustrated History of Laredo & Webb County
Historic Louisiana: An Illustrated History
Historic Midland: An Illustrated History
Historic Montgomery County: An Illustrated History of Montgomery County, Texas
Historic Oklahoma: An Illustrated History
Historic Oklahoma County: An Illustrated History
Historic Omaha: An Illustrated History of Omaha and Douglas County
Historic Overland Park: An Illustrated History
Historic Pasadena: An Illustrated History
Historic Passaic County: An Illustrated History
Historic Philadelphia: An Illustrated History
Historic Prescott: An Illustrated History of Prescott & Yavapai County
Historic Richardson: An Illustrated History
Historic Rio Grande Valley: An Illustrated History
Historic Scottsdale: A Life from the Land
Historic Shreveport-Bossier: An Illustrated History of Shreveport & Bossier City
Historic Texas: An Illustrated History
Historic Victoria: An Illustrated History
Historic Williamson County: An Illustrated History
Iron, Wood & Water: An Illustrated History of Lake Oswego
Miami's Historic Neighborhoods: A History of Community
Old Orange County Courthouse: A Centennial History
Plano: An Illustrated Chronicle